Cornubia's Son

Cornubia's Son

A Life of Mark Guy Pearse

Derek R. Williams

Francis
Boutle
Publishers

First published by Francis Boutle Publishers
272 Alexandra Park Road
London N22 7BG
Tel/Fax: (020) 8889 7744
Email: info@francisboutle.co.uk
www.francisboutle.co.uk

ISBN 978 1 903427 35 4

Contents

List of illustrations

MARK GUY! Cornubia's son, who, through long years
Bore the rich chalice of a radiant heart,
Though thou art gone there is no need for tears,
For thou hast said thy say, and played thy part.

This book is dedicated to the Cornish– in the homeland, beyond the Tamar and across the diaspora

Acknowledgements

This book has been some time in the making. I am grateful to the following individuals (some of them descendants of Mark Guy Pearse) and organisations for sharing with me over the past decade their knowledge of and enthusiasm for its subject: Rev. Fred Baker, Joyce Banks (Wesley Historical Society Library, Oxford), J. Bennett (Walker Art Gallery, Liverpool), Miss C. M. Blight (Cory Library for Historical Research, Rhodes University Library, Grahamstown), Colin Bourne, Claire Bowden-Dan, Ms N. Brangwyn (Ipswich Record Office), Angela Broome (Courtney Library, Royal Institution of Cornwall), Margaret Burton, Rev. Alf Cartwright, Mrs D. M. Cowley (Bainbridge, Newcastle upon Tyne), Des Cowley (State Library of Victoria), W. Glen Curnoe (London Public Library, Ontario), Tom Davies, Colin Dews (Wesley Historical Society, Yorkshire Branch), A. Fanarof (South African Library), John Farrell (Wesley College, Bristol), Imogen Gibbon (National Maritime Museum), Sally Gilbert and Andrew Griffin (St Bartholomew's Hospital Archives and Museum), Ronald Paul Grubb, Melissa Hardie (West Cornwall Art Archive), Sheila M. Hardy, Mrs C. E. Hay (Birmingham Central Library), J. T. Henderson (Lambeth Archives), Katie Herbert (Penlee House Gallery and Museum), Mrs C. V. Hingston, Mrs P. M. Hingston, William Mark Hingston, Lesley Holt (State Library of New South Wales), Donald Hosking, Arnold D. Hunt, Inverness Library, Elizabeth Jeffery (Bristol Central Library), John Lewis Partnership Archives Dept., J. Brynmor Jones (Cardiff Central Library), Elizabeth King (Royal Academy of Arts), Ann Landers (Devon Library and Information Service), Rev. William Leary, Gilbert Lefebvre (Montreal Central Library), Rob Linn, Suzanne Mallon (State Library of New South Wales), Tony Marshall (State Library of Tasmania), Rev. J. M. Mather, Barbara Mayfield (State Library of South Australia), Sheila McCabe (City of Westminster Archives), Richard McLelland (The Chicago Public Library), Elizabeth Meek (The Society of Women

Artists), Mrs A. Milne, Christine Mosser (Metropolitan Toronto Reference Library), E. Ruth Mutton, The New York Public Library, Jon Newman (Lambeth Archives), Joan Nicolls, Peter Nockles (The John Rylands University Library, Manchester), Jane Nowak (Los Angeles Public Library), Christopher Oldstone-Moore, Daniel Olivier (Montreal Central Library), Walter Osborn (Moody Bible Institute Library), Corinne E. Phillips (Nottinghamshire County Library), Chris Pickford (Bedfordshire Record Office), J.A. Pretorius (Transvaal Archives), John C. C. Probert, John L. Rapson, Donald R. Rawe, Margaret Rawling, Annabelle Read (The Morrab Library), Joan Rendell, Andrea Roberts (Manx National Archive), Miss M. Sanders (Worcester City Library), Patricia Sheldon (Newcastle Central Library), Sarah Skinner (City Art Gallery, Manchester), Diana M. Smith, Joanna Soden (The Royal Scottish Academy), C. J. Spittal (John Wesley's Chapel, Bristol), Jill Springall (Heinz Archive and Library, National Portrait Gallery), Barry Stephenson (Bedford Central Library), Brian Stevens (St Ives Museum), Suffolk Record Office (Ipswich Branch), Glenn Taitoko (National Library of New Zealand), Moira Tangye (Murdoch House Adult Education Centre, Redruth), B. Tate (The Society of Women Artists), Alison Taylor (Wesley's Chapel and Leysian Centre, London), David Taylor (Manchester Central Library), Wendy Thirkettle (Manx National Heritage), Charles Thomas, David H. Thomas (Cornwall Record Office), Barbara Thompson (Courtauld Institute of Art), Ms Alex Thomson (Victoria University Archives/United Church of Canada Archives), M. C. Tupper (Islington Central Library), Maria Twist (Birmingham Central Library), Margaret A. Walton, Elizabeth M. Watthews (Circuit Archivist, Ipswich), C. D. Webster (Isle of Wight Archives), Marion Whybrow, Gillian Winter (State Library of Tasmania). Last, but not least, a special thank you to my sons Trystan and Jethan for technical support.

Introduction

'Yew got the vam'ly vailin', I see, sur!'

At a country tea-meeting in the east of Cornwall some time during the latter part of the nineteenth century, an old man looked out from the row of people amongst whom he sat and, nodding familiarly at the visiting preacher, initiated the following conversation:

> 'Yew got the vam'ly vailin', I see, sur! You'm bald!'
>
> 'Yes, that is the head and front of my offending. But were my ancestors bald?'
>
> 'O' coorse they was. There was your feyther, Maister Mark Guy, as bald as a postie [post] just like you be, and there was his feyther, Maister Robert, your grand-feyther – you can mind 'en – bald as a postie too!'
>
> 'Well, you can't go back any further?'
>
> 'Ess, I can; there was Maister Thomas, that put up the first Sunday School to Camelford, was bald as a postie just like you be. I can mind 'en.'
>
> 'Well, you surely must stop there?'
>
> No, there was Maister Robert, his feyther. He was bald too.'
>
> 'I am very much interested. How do you know he was bald?'
>
> 'Well, you zee, he 'ad to take the chair at the tenants' dinner, because he was steward to the Duke of Bedford's estate, and when these chaps got too much drink, they began to take liberties with 'en. He was a very sober man, his own self, without a laugh in his insides, nohow. 'How be so bald, Mas' Pearse?' said they. He looketh round the table, and seed there wasn't a bald-headed man in the place, 'ceps hiz awn self. 'Gen'lmen,' says he, I do congratulate you, every waun of you.' 'What for?' says they, 'Mas Pearse?' '*You* ain't in the least mawsel of danger. You will *never* go bald,' said he. 'Why not, then, Mas' Pearse?' 'Gen'lmen,'

Self portrait of Mark Guy Pearse
(Courtesy of Margaret Burton)

> says he, 'there's two craturs upon the face of God's earth that never went bald nohow. Gen'lmen, *them's apes and idjets!*'[1]

This story – told by one of Cornwall's most famous sons, the celebrated Methodist minister, West London missioner, best-selling author and crowd-pulling lecturer, the Rev. Mark Guy Pearse – contains a number of ingredients that featured prominently in his long and interesting life, namely Cornwall, wit, Methodism, individuality and temperance.

The Pearses were an old Cornish family who hailed from Launceston[2] where the Rev. M. G. Pearse's great-great grandfather Robert established himself as a successful woollen manufacturer in the mid-eighteenth century. Though initially members of the established church, he and his wife Grace later joined a dissenting church in the town. Highly moral in their general conduct and rigidly exact in everything relating to religious observance, they kept up family prayer, carefully instructing their children by means of daily readings of the Scriptures. So strict were they in observing the Sabbath that neither the children nor the servants were allowed to go out on that day except to attend divine worship. Indeed, strong discipline was such a feature of the household that even the children's 'free' time before and after school was always filled up by some useful employment. For all that, '[w]hen a child,' wrote Thomas Pearse, 'my mother used to take three or four of us by the fire, on Sunday evenings, and sing Dr Watt's hymns with us so sweetly, that we loved the hymns, and loved our mother with greater affection for singing them to us.'[13]

Settling at Camelford after his marriage in the mid-1770s, Thomas regularly attended the parish church for a number of years. But, he observed, 'I frequently felt disgust at our conversation, while walking to and from the church, which is a mile from the town. I thought our worship is hypocrisy; we talk of wool, of farming, or any thing but God, even to the church door. While in the service, we pray that God may incline our hearts to keep his law; and sum up all by beseeching him to write all his laws there; and yet no sooner is the service over, than the same vain foolish conversation is resumed. This worship is vain; it is sinful: this is drawing nigh to God with the mouth, when the heart is far from him'. Convictions such as these led him to join the small Methodist society in Camelford, which at that time met in a private room. 'In the Spring of 1786,' he continued, 'on hearing a sermon from Mr Townsend, on the Power of Prayer, I determined to try what prayer would do for me; and began to pray more fervently and frequently, laying open my whole heart to God. Before the week expired, while meditating on this faithful saying, '*Christ Jesus came into the world to save sinners*,' the Lord was pleased to impart such light and comfort to my soul, that I could believe Christ Jesus came into the world *to save me*: and being then on a journey, like the Ethiopian eunuch, I went on my way rejoicing'. Thereafter, the love of Christ became the governing principle of Thomas's life and his domestic regime became as strict as his father's had been. On cold winter mornings he would leave his bed long before it was light and retire to a little room set aside for prayer. In the summer he would get up at four o'clock and pray and read the Bible until six. Two other periods of his day were similarly set aside for prayer and meditation. It was said, too, that he read two chapters or Psalms every day on his knees and that he 'carefully treasured up some passages of Scripture every morning, as a subject of profitable meditation, kept always in readiness to occupy his mind, when not necessarily engaged by his secular concerns'. With five sons and five daughters, Thomas and Susanna found by experience that daily family acts of worship needed to be carefully organised and that praying and reading the Scriptures were best done in the morning before breakfast and early in the evening before the younger children were put to bed. When ill health prevented him from

Roscarrock Farm, Port Isaac (Courtesy of Margaret Walton)

carrying out his duties as class-leader and local preacher, Thomas devoted himself and the money he earned as under-steward to the Duke of Bedford to distributing religious tracts. In several places he established, at his own expense, what he called 'Village Libraries', so that those who wished to read might be supplied with useful books. Indeed, he became so well known in this work that he was sometimes written to by strangers who did not know his address, as 'The Dispenser of Tracts at Camelford'. He was, too, a great promoter of Charity and Sunday schools and assiduous in visiting the sick and in healing both them and the needy with both his time and his money.[4]

'It is reasonable to suppose,' wrote the Rev. William Burgess, 'that the influence of that father's holy life and fervent prayers would be felt by his children; and this really was the case.'[5] When newly-weds Mary Pearse and William Ivey moved to Holsworthy in the opening years of the nineteenth century, they did so largely because her father wanted them to introduce Methodism there, if possible. Inviting the preachers of the Launceston Circuit to the town, they provided bed and board for them and paid for the rent of a room in which services could be held.[6] And the Pearses' eldest son – the Rev. Mark Guy Pearse's grandfather – was to prove himself as faithful a friend and as liberal a supporter of Methodism in the Camelford circuit as his father had been. Born on 21

March 1785, Robert Pearse joined the Methodist Society when he was about thirteen or fourteen, showing early on 'a sobriety of demeanour and a maturity of judgment far beyond his years'. While still young he became a local preacher and in fifty years never missed an appointment through carelessness or negligence. A great believer in both private and public prayer, he established fixed periods for the former, refusing, like his father and grandfather before him, to allow secular matters to interfere with it. He was widely read, being especially familiar with the standard works of Wesleyanism, to which he remained loyal when dissension shook the church to its foundations in the 1830s. A circuit steward for nearly thirty-nine years and a class-leader for even longer, he served, too, as a trustee for several chapels in the Camelford circuit.[7] Through Robert's marriage to Grace Guy at St Endellion Parish Church on 23 May 1805, the patronym Guy came into the family. The presence of Guys, who were yeoman landowners, in St Endellion and the neighbouring north Cornish coastal parish of St Minver can be traced back to the mid-sixteenth century, with the first Mark Guy dating from 1662. The family held Roscarrock Manor near Port Isaac, the former home of Cornish historian and hagiographer Nicholas Roscarrock, for three generations before it was sold in 1867.[8] Robert and Grace Pearse had at least six children, of whom Mark Guy was born on 24 June 1811. Such, then, were the impeccable Methodist credentials of the Pearses, whom the Rev. Matthew Male would later describe as 'one of the most honourable and excellent families that it has ever been my privilege to have any acquaintance with'.[9]

Chapter 1

'I am always thankful that I was brought up in a little town...'[1]

Camborne 1842–1857

When Mark Guy Pearse senior moved from Camelford to Camborne in the 1830s, he was doing what many Cornishmen were doing in an age of invention and expansion – moving to those parishes and towns which were central to the regeneration of mining which Cornwall was experiencing. In 1800 James Watt's patent rights to steam pumping-engine design lapsed and within twelve years Richard Trevithick had successfully introduced his high-pressure engine at Wheal Prosper in Gwithian parish. Not only much more powerful than the old engine but also considerably smaller and cheaper, it was instrumental in launching the rapid development of mining that characterised the first forty years of the nineteenth century in Cornwall. In 1800 there were seventy-five working mines employing some 16,000 people and producing 2,500 tons of tin. By 1837 there were more than two hundred employing 30,000 men, women and children who produced 4,100 tons of tin. With the new engines able to drain mines down to a depth of three hundred fathoms and the deposits on Anglesey virtually exhausted, copper production experienced an even more spectacular increase from 5,000 to 12,000 tons. The enormous increase in the demand for engines and machinery led to the establishment of iron foundries near the mining centres.[2] In 1839, for instance, John Holman established a boiler works and foundry at Camborne which, as a direct result of the mining boom, saw its population almost double in the years between 1820 and 1830. 'From being a very insignificant place,' wrote the compiler of *Pigot's Directory* in 1830, 'this town is fast riding into opulence and consequently importance, from the valuable mines of tin and copper surrounding it... Several new streets have been added within these few years and there are others projected in the vicinity of the church...'[3] Similarly, ten years later, local registrar and doctor Richard Lanyon drew attention in a report on the town to what he saw as the much-improved living and working conditions enjoyed by its 4,377 residents. 'It is delightful to observe,' he wrote, 'that all classes of the community, and particularly the labouring, are blessed with a much greater amount of the necessaries and luxuries of life... everyone residing in mining districts is aware that their cottages have undergone such improvements in conveniences and comfort, that they are palaces when compared with the hovels which at that time [1800] existed...'[4]

This, though, as Janet Thomas points out in her history of the town, is far from being a true picture. Cushioned, perhaps, by middle-class comfort, Lanyon chose to ignore the huge gulf that existed in mid-Victorian Britain between rich and poor, between the emerging middle-classes and the gentry on the one hand and the working classes on the other. At the end of the 1840s, the *West Briton* drew its readers' attention to the 'small, low, irregular and badly built' houses of Camborne and 'the uncleanly and indecent sanitary precautions on the part of all'. 'There is no proper sewerage in the place,' continued its reporter; 'all the filthy water from the stables etc. being conveyed away in open drains and all the contents of the privies etc. are carried through the street in open day, in defiance of the common rules of prudency and decency, a practice which in most places would be punished by penalty...'[5]

It was, then, to a town of contrasts that Mr Mark Guy Pearse brought his Devon-born wife Jane to start up in business as, possibly, Camborne's first chemist or 'druggist', which, as was the custom then, involved doubling as a grocer and tea-dealer. Wanting a qualified assistant, in about 1840 he employed Robert Hall from Stamford, Lincolnshire, in his shop at 36, Commercial Street,[6] which remained a chemist's until the late 1960s when Tom Kelynack retired. Here it was that the couple's second child and only son Mark Guy Pearse was born on 3 January 1842. Nearly three months later, on 31 March, he was baptised into the Wesleyan Methodist Church at Camborne Wesley by the Rev. John Boyd, the Superintendent minister of the circuit.[7]

*Dolcoath mine (J.C. Burrow/*Cornish Magazine*, 1898)*

Throughout his long life, Mark Guy acknowledged the important place in his heart reserved for the 'little town, where everybody had a chance of knowing everybody else, and all the comedies and tragedies and sweet commonplaces of life'.[8] He emphasised, too, that the influences that went furthest to shape his character were those of 'the old Wesleyan chapel… where one worshipped as a lad, the fervent singing of the hymns, and the earnest piety of the people, exemplified in such sturdy goodness as that of Dr George Smith of Trevu, and Captain Charles Thomas of the Dolcoath mine, and my own father, who, in regard to their principles, were made of Cornish granite, but whose faces were lit with a hopefulness and gladness as of sunshine upon granite'.[9] It is important, therefore, to examine in some detail the position that his father occupied in the commercial and religious life of the town to which Mark Guy returned again and again.

As we have seen, mining was central to Camborne's prosperity and was to remain so until the end of the nineteenth century and, indirectly, well into the twentieth. Occupying a prime site in the middle of Cornwall's mining heartland between Camborne and Redruth was the greatest of all the Cornish mines, the legendary Dolcoath which, though described at the close of the 1790s as 'a progressive new tin mine',[10] was in fact a very old one, unequalled in depth by any other tin-mine in the world. It was, though, as a copper producer that Dolcoath had re-established itself since re-opening in 1799, becoming in due course Cornwall's richest mine. After paying huge dividends at the beginning of the nineteenth century, it began to falter as the vast copper lodes gave way to a not-very-valuable mixture of copper and tin in the mid 1830s. The last dividend on copper was paid in 1836 when the mine was 210 fathoms deep and the tin which had so far been found, had been virtually ignored. The adventurers were all for abandoning the bottom of the mine entirely, but Capt. Charles Thomas, its chief agent, felt that it could be kept open for tin, and managed to convince them that some pumping should continue.

Many of those who were strongly opposed to any attempt to convert Dolcoath into a tin-mine sold their shares. One of those who supported Capt. Thomas's efforts was his friend Mark Guy Pearse who bought a large number of shares when the mine was at its lowest point and became in due course chairman of the adventurers' meetings. The two men were very similar in character, both, according to one commentator, presenting 'a fine combination of strength and gentleness, of shrewd common-sense and sane spirituality'.[11] As one of the mine's principal adventurers, Mr Pearse often took the interests of its employees to heart. At a meeting which took place in April 1880, for instance, he expressed his concern at the low wages paid to the bal maidens, the older women and girls who were employed on the surface of Cornish mines to break up the larger rocks and to dress the tin and copper ores. Indeed, he tried to get his colleagues to consider raising their wages and, as a token of his personal appreciation of the work that they were doing, gave each 1/- out of his own pocket.[12]

Gradually the results from tin became promising enough to encourage a resumption, in stages, of re-draining the abandoned lower levels of the mine. Capt. Thomas was appointed to the position of manager in 1844 and within five years Dolcoath was re-drained and sinking had resumed under the 210 fathom level. In 1853 he had the satisfaction of seeing the first dividend paid on tin. The transition of Dolcoath from a copper to a tin mine was a gradual process and initially the dividends from tin were small. By 1859, however, it was said that it had 'more tin in reserve than any three mines in the county',[13] paying a dividend of £17,542. Henceforth, riches once again poured out of the mine and the adventurers received handsome rewards every quarter. Indeed, thanks to Capt. Thomas, the value of the mine, calculated on the market price of shares, rose from £4,000 in 1846 to £90,000 in 1868, the year of his death. During the intervening period a staggering £147,854 was paid in dividends to the shareholders![14] Commenting on the report submitted to the April meeting of the adventurers that year, Mr Pearse described it as being 'one of a cheering and satisfactory character'.[15] It will come as no great surprise, perhaps, that he was amongst those who were instrumental in establishing a Savings Bank in Camborne in 1860.[16]

John Wesley made the first of his thirty or so visits to Cornwall in 1743. Although there were several false starts, the appeal to the independent mining population of his message of personal salvation grew as the years passed and, in due course, Methodism came to exert an enormous influence on the Cornish mining community. Dr H. Miles described thus the close relationship between the two:

> Methodism's appeal to one's own spiritual experience as an ultimate authority in matters of religion – the inward persuasion ('assurance') of forgiveness and acceptance with God – fitted in well with the independence of the miner and the Class Meeting (the central feature of the Organisation) appealed to his clannishness. Miners outside the bounds of organised society, neglected by the County Authorities, discovered that Methodism cared for them. The local Methodist Chapel invited the miner to a warm and vividly real fellowship providing an outlet for his emotions, feeding his imagination, and giving him opportunity to develop his gifts of speech and of organisation, however humble.[17]

And in his preface to *Daniel Quorm and his religious notions*, the Rev. Mark Guy Pearse himself paid tribute to the power of the Methodist system to 'develop the gifts of her lowliest members; finding some sphere in which to turn to advantage the various abilities of her people'. Working men of every kind – 'the thoughtful miner, the prayerful ploughman, the godly labourer' – were, and to some extent, still are amongst her most successful leaders and local preachers. John Probert has written that in every Methodist church fewer than half a dozen families stood head and shoulders above the rest in prominence.[18] Pre-eminent at Camborne Wesley, as in mining and commerce, were the Thomases, the Smiths and the Pearses. Dr George Smith was admitted into the Wesleyan Society at Camborne Wesley in April, 1821, appearing in due course on the 'Preachers' Plan' and assuming the leadership of an early

Sunday morning Society Class. His close friend Capt. Charles Thomas was, between 1817 and 1822, successively appointed a Prayer Leader, Class Leader and Local Preacher. He was, too, one of the first trustees of the new chapel that was built at Camborne in 1828, the year that the town separated from neighbouring Redruth and became head of a circuit. By 1848 the membership of Camborne Wesley had grown to approximately 800 full members. In 1829 the Sunday school moved from the site in Commercial Square which, under Mr Pearse, later became the town dispensary, to a new building adjoining the chapel capable of accommodating 400 scholars. A great religious revival in the Spring of 1839 resulted in an even larger number of children seeking admission to the school which, because of the very low standards of the time, provided them with a secular as well as a religious education. Prayer-meetings were held everywhere – in private homes, at the mines, both on the surface and underground, and in shops – and daytime meetings were conducted by local ministers in the chapels and public halls. Writing to the *Wesleyan Magazine*, Samuel Dunn who, as Superintendent Minister at Camborne Wesley, added more members and built more chapels in the circuit during his three-year ministry than any minister before or since, described how the chapel was filled to overflowing and how miners two hundred fathoms underground were found 'on their knees calling on the God of Heaven to bring them up out of the horrible pit and miry clay of sin'.[19] It has been estimated that out of a population of three thousand residing in the town, over one thousand met in class while, within a radius of two miles of the circuit chapel, two thousand four hundred were in church fellowship.[20] Dunn's assistant Thomas Withington likewise recorded in his *Reminiscences* the impact of the revival and returning to Camborne Wesley as Superintendent eighteen years later, stressed how much the circuit was 'indebted to such leading men as Dr Smith, Capt. Charles Thomas and Mr M. G. Pearse.[21]

With, as he put it in 1879, the strongest reasons for his attachment to the Church of his fathers,[22] Mark Guy Pearse senior would presumably have established contact with fellow-Methodists soon after his arrival in Camborne. The first mention of him in surviving records is as Society Steward, with James Lanyon, in the entry for 14 January 1841.[23] The following year he partnered George Smith, who had been poor steward in 1841, with James Lanyon becoming poor steward. There is no further record of him as Society Steward after 1843, though he served as poor steward – with James Rowe – in 1852 and again, with George Bailey, the

*Camborne Wesley Chapel (W.J. Bennets/*Mate's ... Camborne, *c. 1904*

following year. In 1842 Mr Pearse was appointed Class Leader at Camborne Wesley, appearing in the Register for the first time on 21 April. He continued to serve in this capacity until the end of 1855 and almost certainly beyond that date. In 1857 he was voted onto the committee of the Camborne Wesleyan Institute,[24] which had been established seven years earlier 'with the object of promoting the attainment of biblical, religious and general knowledge in direct accordance with the established theology, principles and policy of the Wesleyan Methodist Connexion…'[25] This was to be achieved by means of a Library, a programme of general and religious lectures and addresses, scientific lectures illustrated, when practicable, by experiments, and a weekly mutual improvement class. He returned to the committee in the mid 1860s and was still involved in the work of the Institute, though not as a committee member, as late as August 1869. When a renewal of the Trust of Camborne Wesley Chapel took place in 1863, he was one of the new members added by assignment.[26] At about the same period he served, too, on the Sunday school management committee alongside Dr George Smith, Capt. Charles Thomas, Capt. James Lanyon, Capt. James Rowe and other chapel stalwarts.

As we shall see, for much of his boyhood Mark Guy was away at school. However, memories of his early years in the town of his birth were 'treasured and sacred' and, together with glimpses of old Camborne in the 1840s and 1850s, were in later life often used to illustrate some point he was making in a lecture or in his published sermons and sketches. In 'King's Gardens', for instance, in order to illustrate the need to watch for enemies when tending the garden of the heart, he recalled how, as a boy, he used to set little heaps of 'grains' to attract slugs and snails, and then creep out at night with a lantern to catch them.[27] His daughter 'Mab' wrote of him drinking in the traditions of Methodism from childhood, and one of his earliest experiences would no doubt have been attending Camborne Wesley for the baptism of his sister Margaret Jane by James Mowatt on 29 February 1844.[28] One of those who in his earliest days made the young boy 'feel how good it was to be good', as he put it many years later, was Dr George Smith, 'that prince of men, so great and yet so genial'.[29] Another was the Rev. Mowatt's successor as Superintendent Minister, William Burgess whose gentleness won the boy's affection. Between 1848 and 1849, at a time of great turmoil for Methodism, the Rev. Thomas Collins was at the helm of the Camborne Circuit. Welcoming him to the town, a colleague wrote:

> Of the two chapels here, one is very spacious and handsome. The circuit ranks with the very first in the county; nor are there many in the connexion more compact. In ticket you will find fellowships of saints not scarce. The numbers are so numerous that you will both have to work yourself and take care that we do also...Cornish Methodists, with many excellencies, join some peculiarities. Preachers labouring in this region, Superintendents above all, must make straight paths for their feet. Uppish men are an abomination here; and, not seldom, get awkward thumps, and communications more frank than welcome.[30]

Collins took a great interest in the young, visiting schools, conducting a Bible Class for young men and meeting younger children at midday each Saturday. 'I see myself again as a little lad in the vestry of Wesley Chapel,' wrote Mark Guy in 1928, 'with a group of children that gathered for Thomas Collins' Saturday Bible Class. We used to write down, or suggest, the name of a subject for which we would search the Bible during the week. One child had written 'dogs'. I innocently wrote in large round hand the word 'cats'. I see again that face [Collins'] that shone with goodness, and have again his gentle hand laid on my head. 'You little rogue,' said he, 'there is no such word in the Bible.' I said nothing but when I got home I found poor pussy and told her how sorry I was for her.'[31]

One particular chapel memory highlights an approach to preaching that Mark Guy noted early on among some, at least, of his fellow-Methodists and went on to exploit throughout his life – that a good sermon should be an enjoyment, an entertainment. He and his father were walking along the street one Sunday morning when they met 'a grand old saint' returning from his place of worship. 'Well, Anthony,' said his father, 'I hope you have had a good service.' 'Sarvice! Bless 'ee, maister, there wadn't feelin' enough in the sarmon for to touch the heart of a grammar-sow.'[32]

As an eight or nine year old, Mark Guy accompanied his father to the Class Meeting, of which he was the leader. Such sessions later inspired the story of Daniel Quorm,[33] the pseudonym he used to present to the world Dick Rowe, an otherwise-unknown Camborne class leader whose pithy sayings were often repeated at local breakfast tables. Daniel is a shoemaker who lives at 'Penwinnin', a 'cluster of miners' cottages situated some three miles from 'Redburn' [Camborne-Redruth] and loosely based on the hamlets of Bolenowe, Carwynnen and Treslothan. Much of *Daniel Quorm and his religious notions* is pure autobiography and rich in local colour. A correspondent writing to the *Methodist Recorder* some ten years after the book first appeared, pointed out that although the names of individuals and of some of the places were fictitious, many of the characters were easily detectable and known to those residing in and around Camborne. 'A friend has informed me,' he continued, 'that he was well acquainted with "Frankey Vivian" [the former miner in the last stages of asthmatic consumption] and heard from his own lips some of the beautiful incidents mentioned in *Daniel Quorm*.'[34]

Of Dan'el's two classes, the larger and more popular met at 8 o'clock on Sunday mornings 'in what was called by courtesy, "the PARLOUR" – really the sanded front-kitchen – at Thomas Toms'[35] chiefly for the benefit of Sally Toms or 'Granny' Sally, a near-centenarian who had her bed in that room and who didn't like to miss the 'class'. Sally Toms was, in fact, based on Mary Ivey of Troon, the mother of Capt. Charles Thomas and grandmother of Capt. Josiah Thomas, a close friend of Mark Guy who supplied him with much of his material.[36] '...An eminently pious woman of more than ordinary mental energy and capacity

SUNDAY at Penwinnin was a fair specimen of "the Lord's Day" in the mining districts of Cornwall. A sacred stillness rested upon everything, strangely impressive after

*'Sunday at Penwinnin...' by Charles Tresidder (*Daniel Quorm*)*

for study',[37] 'Granny' is ever-ready with a fund of memories which Dan'el draws on 'to clench his argument and point his moral'. And how cosy and snug her cottage is as a venue in comparison with the chapel vestry:

> You feel that folks don't live there, and you can't readily make yourself quite "at home" in it. There, at Thomas Toms', was the canary hanging in the window, that always began to sing when the hymn was given out, just as if he had been a regular member of the Class... And at the week-day Class were homelier touches that made men talk about religion in a simple, every-day tone, the like of which it is hard to get in a vestry... Much of that strong social union to which Methodism has been so greatly indebted, and which in old time she so carefully fostered, came from the fact that people went from "house to house"; the Class-meetings and the prayer-meetings were in the houses of the people, and the Church itself was not unfrequently a "Church in the house".[38]

Another memory from the author's own childhood, which found its way into *Daniel Quorm* as an illustration of trust was the occasion when, as a little lad, old Dan'el had gone to spend the day with his grandmother. At dusk, just when he should have been starting home, a tremendous thunderstorm, with torrential rain, came on and they found themselves in something of a quandary. Just at that moment, though, the lad's father arrived in 'a great long blue cloak, like they used to wear in those times', and taking Dan'el under it, they set out for home. 'It was pitch dark in there, o' course,' the lad recalled, 'and outside I could hear the thunder crashin' about among the hills, and every now and then I took hold of his hand tighter, for somehow I could see the blaze o' the lightnin' right in under the cloak. I went splashin' on through the puddles and the mud, all right because I'd got hold of his hand.' Although he couldn't see where he was going, or tell where he was, Dan'el had complete trust in his father, who, despite the storm, managed somehow to see the road. 'And at last we stopped at our door; and they flung back the cloak, and there I was in front o' the blazin' fire, with mother getting' us all sorts o' things, and the supper waitin', and all lookin' such a welcome – like only a lad's mother can give him.'[39]

It goes without saying that religion played a crucial role in Mark Guy's upbringing and was sometimes the cause of some bewilderment. 'When we were children,' he wrote in the introductory remarks to 'My

Old Friend John', 'we had a very queer notion about men and their religion. We heard very much talk of being religious, and the world to us was divided into Church-people, Methodists, and Baptists.' Told that such a man 'went to Wesley', that 'old aunt belonged to Salem' and that 'grandfather' attended the parish church, the children eyed each with curiosity to try to detect the differences between them. At first they thought the answer lay with their dress; 'the large cap and the straight hair was Methodism, the solemn face was Salem, and all without these was "Church"'. This early notion, though, was soon outgrown and they came to see that different religions meant different characters, affecting the way in which people spoke to them, and looked at them, and generally impressed them. A happy man, even if, like former miner Frankey Vivian in *Daniel Quorm*, he was in the last stages of asthmatic consumption, meant a happy religion.[40] By way of contrast, Widow Pascoe's gloomy approach to religion was simply the outward expression of 'a nature so ice-bound and narrow'. It was the former's religion that the young boy was determined to make his own, and thereafter – until his death – gloomy people who were convinced that the world was going to the dogs found no friend in the Rev. Mark Guy Pearse.

As 'Mark Guy', the Rev. M. G. Pearse's name was a household word throughout much of the nineteenth century and well into the twentieth, especially in his native Camborne. From the stories told to her by her father Charles Tyack, who was one of his close friends, Muriel Sara concluded that they must have been 'two live sparks in Camborne'.[41] Like many local boys before and since, they roamed far and wide, either out to the North Cliffs between Portreath and Gwithian, or further inland to Carn Brea. Richly stocked with bracken and heather, the whole area was the natural and infinitely more satisfying equivalent of today's adventure playground or theme park. Often he and a school friend would make their way out of Camborne, through fields and lanes, over marshy ground and past 'a muddy red river flowing from the mines' until, climbing a steep hill, they stepped out onto moorland 'golden with the scented furze, purple with heather, and green and brown with the hardy bracken'. From there a little path by a shining stream led them into a valley which stood at the head of a deep gulf shut in on three sides by the cliff and where the stream ended its journey by spilling over the cliffs into the sea below. Hearing, as a lad, the text from Joel III, 14, 'The day of the Lord is near in the valley of decision', Mark Guy came to associate it with this valley and with the gulf at the end of it known as Ralph's

Cupboard,[42] which were both the scene of many adventures. On one particular occasion he and a friend were down under the cliffs, clambering over the rocks and exploring the caves, when they came to a little bay of white sand, shut in on either side by steep rocks that stood out to the sea at mid-tide and quite closed the bay. Although they knew that the tide had turned, they were convinced that they had plenty of time and continued to play until, before they knew it, the waves were breaking fierce and high and they found themselves cut off. They knew that where they were standing would soon be under water and that there was nothing for it but to climb the cliff above them. Though it was steep with black overhanging rocks, at one spot a mass of rocks had fallen away leaving a rough path up which they scrambled. Mark Guy recalled that he 'shuddered more than once as the loosened stones slipped from under my feet and went rolling down to the sea below, knowing what I must expect if I happened to slip'. Once again, the experience was used to effect years later when, in a sermon on 'The Valley of Decision', he remarked how foolish it was of them not to have got out when they could have done so easily and comfortably, and applied the lesson to those who, with the phrase 'plenty of time', put off the day of decision for Christ and His Kingdom.[43]

The memory of an earlier walk when he was a small boy reminds us that his was a privileged background though one, too, where, early on, a concern for others was encouraged. Dressed in fine clothes – a sort of plaid suit – he was sent for a walk and somehow got separated from his companions. Though probably frightened to begin with, he came upon 'a ragged lad who looked so hungry and wretched' that he quickly forgot all about his own predicament. When asked why he had no nice clothes to wear, the boy told Mark Guy that his father was dead, his mother ill, and that he had come out to gather a few sticks to make a fire. 'My heart was full enough before,' wrote Mark Guy, 'now it ran over. I took hold of the ragged sleeve of his brown smock frock, and cried, "You must come home with me; you shall. And my father shall be your father, and my home shall be your home, and we will send and make your mother better, and you shall have my clothes to wear".' With the older boy's help, he found his way home. Back at the pharmacy, he led the boy from room to room until he found his mother who duly kitted the stranger out with some of her son's clothes and 'a great basket of good things and promises of ever so much more' to take home with him.[44]

Mark Guy's early teacher was the Rev. William Wright Butlin, who in

1846 became the first incumbent of the newly formed parish of Penponds, near Camborne. Born in Nottingham in 1814, he ran a small private school in Camborne in order to supplement his stipend. In a meditation entitled 'The Gentleness of God: and our greatness'[45] Mark Guy recalled an occasion when, as a 'little lad, blundering at my first [drawing] lesson' he was trying very hard, but without much success, to reproduce what had been set before him. Trying to rectify what was already smudged and messed up by numerous rubbings-out only made things worse. Then his drawing master – probably William Butlin – took the pencil and in the twinkling of an eye, the sketch was done, every stroke firm, straight, exact. Disheartened at the ease with which the result had been achieved, the pupil laid down the pencil with a sigh and said, 'I shall never draw'. 'Nonsense,' said the master cheerily, patting him on the shoulder. 'You can draw as well as well as I could when I was your age.' This act of kindness – of gentleness – with the master putting himself in the place of the awkward beginner was a revelation to the young boy, making him, in turn, great. 'I was an artist then – if never since,' he wrote with characteristic modesty, for his talent in that direction found expression, as we shall see, on numerous occasions.

Later he was sent to a Moravian school[46] at Zeist, near Utrecht, in Holland. Although railway developments in Cornwall were making considerable headway in the 1840s, it was not until 1859 that Brunel's bridge over the Tamar at Saltash linked the land with Plymouth and established a direct line between Paddington and Penzance. When Mark Guy was away at school, the railway ran no further west from London than Bristol and it was therefore necessary for him to catch a small steamer which plied between Hayle and Bristol in order to join a vessel for Holland. A picture of those days supplies the closing illustration in his *Sermons for Children* which was first published in the mid 1870s. Wanting to show that Christ never forgot the very young, he took as his text, 'Our Father, which art in heaven' and recounted how once he was coming home from school in mid-winter on board the steamer. 'The tossing sea made me very ill and very wretched,' he wrote, 'and I lay down in the cabin as miserable as I could be. I felt all so lonely there in the steamer by myself, and so far away from everybody that cared for me, and was altogether as miserable as ever a little lad was in the world. But how foolish it was of me. For by-and-by the steamer got to the pier, and before I stirred there was a hand on my shoulder, and looking up I saw my father. And he told me how he had been watching for a long

Rev. William Wright Butlin, Vicar of Penponds, 1846–1896
(Courtesy of Rev J.M. Mather)

time. How he had climbed up a high hill and had watched the first far-off streak of steam. How he had kept his eye on it as it came nearer. How he pictured me on board, and then as soon as it drew near to land, hurried down himself to welcome me. Foolish little fellow, thinking myself so lonely and forgotten. Let us trust our Father, dear children.'[47]

On another occasion he was going home for the holidays and had boarded the steamer at Bristol with just enough money to cover his fare. Thinking, in his innocence, that he had paid for everything he needed in the way of meals, he helped himself while they were in calm waters. When they reached the open sea he retired to his berth and had been lying there for hours, very seasick and past caring for anything, when the steward presented him with a bill for the meal. He had no option but to confess that he had no money, whereupon the steward informed him that he would have to keep his luggage, and asked for his name and address. On being told, however, he instantly took off the cap he was wearing, with the gold band around its brim, and with a smile insisted on shaking the boy's hand. It transpired that some years earlier, Mark Guy's father had shown kindness to the steward's widowed mother, and he welcomed the chance to repay it by seeing the boy safely to the small boat used for landing passengers, paying his bill and giving him five shillings. 'As soon as I got ashore I told my father what had happened,' Mark Guy wrote. '"Ah," said he, "see how a bit of kindness lives! Now he has passed it on to you. Remember, if ever you meet anybody that needs a friendly hand, you must pass it on to them."' Many years later, when Mark Guy had become a celebrated preacher, he was standing by a station ticket office when he saw a little boy crying. Having asked him what the problem was, he discovered that the boy did not have enough money to pay for his fare. 'Instantly back upon me flashed the forgotten story of long ago. Here, then, was my chance of passing it on. I gave him the sum he needed, and got into the carriage with him. Then I told the little fellow the story of long ago, and of the steward's kindness to me. "Now, today," I said, "I pass it on to you; and remember, if you meet any one that needs a kindly hand, you must pass it on to them."'[48] It seems that the story was told by the boy's friends to a visiting minister who was so impressed that he wrote the hymn 'Pass it on', which begins 'Have you had a kindness shown, pass it on/'Twas not meant for you alone, pass it on'. The minister was, in fact, one of Methodism's greatest hymn writers, Dr Henry Burton, who was married to Mark Guy's elder sister, Ellen.[49] The most popular of all his hymns, 'Pass it on' was sung by evangelist-singers such as Gipsy Smith, W. H. Jude and Charles Alexander and in innumerable Methodist Sunday schools.

The young Mark Guy Pearse's education began in earnest in about 1853 when he was sent to Wesley College, Sheffield, which one journalist described as 'the alma mater of so many of the leading ministers and laymen of Methodism'.[50] Founded in 1838 as the Wesleyan Proprietary Grammar School by a number of gentlemen, both ministers and laymen, in order that the sons of Wesleyan families might receive a thorough education and be trained in the doctrines and precepts of Methodism, it was affiliated to London University six years later. During his years there, its governor and chaplain was Dr Samuel Waddy, whom Mark Guy described as 'brilliant, stately and statesmanlike – a noble man of God indeed'.[51] His fellow students included T. B. Stephenson, T. G. Osborn, W. Eastman and James Wood whom Hugh Price Hughes described as 'one of the most prominent and influ-

Wesley College, Sheffield

ential of all the lay members of the denomination' and 'the first leading official Methodist of our time who had identified himself enthusiastically with the social side of Christian work'. In one of his letters home, Wood, who started at Wesley College in 1856, referred to the earnest prayer meetings which the boys held among themselves on Sunday afternoons – prayer meetings which were often led by one of 'the bigger lads', T. B. Stephenson.[52] Mark Guy himself remained at Wesley College for some years, until circumstances outside his control led to his sudden withdrawal.

Chapter 2

'...there it was that I obtained much of my knowledge of the Cornish character.'

Liskeard 1857–1861

On 23 March, 1857 Pierre Emile L'Angelier, a Jersey-born clerk, died of arsenic poisoning. A week later his former lover, Madelaine Smith, the daughter of a Glaswegian architect, was arrested and accused of his murder. The ensuing trial, during which her uninhibited love letters to him were published, was held in Edinburgh between 30 June and 9 July.[1] Although the verdict was 'Not proven', the trial, which was one of the most celebrated and baffling of more recent times, stirred up a great deal of Victorian resentment against the accused and, indirectly, was the cause of some anxiety to Mr and Mrs Mark Guy Pearse down in Camborne, Cornwall.

Seventy years later when their only son and his family were gathered together to celebrate his eighty-sixth birthday, the news of Madelaine Smith's death in America awakened memories... 'When that trial happened,' he recalled, 'I was just returning from school at Sheffield...'[2] Although the main construction work on Brunel's Royal Albert Bridge had begun in 1853, six more years were to pass before the rail link over the Tamar was completed, and Mark Guy's train journey as yet ended at Exeter. From there he took a coach which, because of heavy snow,[3] got only as far as Camelford where he was forced to seek refuge with his uncle Warwick.[4] Ten days passed before he reached Camborne, where his parents, looking terribly grave and worried, greeted him. The young man was ushered into his father's study and presented with an opened letter postmarked Sheffield – an ardent love-letter addressed to him and signed with a woman's name. Initial puzzlement gave way to laughter as Mark Guy realised that two of his school friends were playing a trick on him! With evident relief, his father explained that he and Mrs Pearse had been very anxious indeed, seeing similarities between this letter and the one they had been reading about in the Madelaine Smith trial, and fearing that somehow or other he had become embroiled in the affair! The upshot of all this was that they had decided that their son should not return to Wesley College, but remain nearer to home. Consequently, they had already articled him to Dr Hingston of Liskeard to begin his training as a medical student. Although Mark Guy protested at the decision, his objection was probably, as his daughter and biographer later suggested, only half-hearted, for the whole saga must have been just a little flattering to a young man who was not yet sixteen, whatever the consequences!

When the young apprentice arrived at 'Rosedean' – probably in the autumn of 1857 – Dr Andrew Hingston's two young daughters Charlotte and Ann would have been little more than 18 and 6 months old respectively, but later they recalled with evident pleasure the four years he had spent with them. It seems that at first Mary Hingston had received him into her home with some misgivings, occupied as she was with a young family and reluctant to take charge of a young man and only son. However, pleading distant relationship,[5] Mark Guy Pearse senior was able to persuade her to accept his son, a decision she never regretted. One daughter recalled hearing her mother describe the young apprentice as 'a bit of a dandy' when he arrived. 'But my remembrance of him,' she continued, 'is how he used to amuse us by the hour; how, if we were poorly, he would have my sister and me in his room, put us on two little stools before a chair, give us pencils and paper, and set us to draw pictures... He would tell us wonderful stories. If we went for a drive with him, as sure as we got to St Cleerdowns [*sic*], he would get out and look amongst the rocks, and always came back with slices of cake or plum-pudding that he had found there – which, of course, we believed, but we never found any after he had left! On Sunday mornings, on mother's return from the seven o'clock prayer-meeting, he would be at the door with one of us on each of his shoulders, and would pop us out to give her a welcome.'[6] Her sister, too, had fond memories of his stay and of the love that he felt for them both, a love that continued down through the years. 'His last letter, in 1928, began 'My dear little maid'. I remember hearing my father say that he was more for drawing than for anatomy, and when supposed to be studying this subject he would be drawing the large bones, with grotesque heads, fighting one another. No wonder if Dr Hingston sometimes despaired of his pupil.'[7]

All the time, though, his mind was turning more and more towards religious matters, no doubt partly through the influence of the staunch Wesleyan household in which he found himself. Although only in his mid-thirties, Andrew Hingston was already a pillar of the local chapel, having some ten years earlier been instrumental in rescuing it in its hour of need. During the night of Friday 6 June 1845, the town's second Wesleyan Chapel, in Dean Street, was totally destroyed in an arson attack. So intense was the heat that glass in windows on the opposite side of the street was broken. After an hour the roof fell in and only the bare, black walls remained.[8] As can be imagined, there was considerable consternation when the congregation met for worship in the Town Hall on the following Sunday morning and it was discovered that the relatively new building had not been insured. Moreover, the debts incurred in its construction had not all been paid off, and now a further £1,450 was needed to rebuild. Yet less than four months after the fire, the foundation stone was laid, thanks largely to the efforts of two young men, Henry Lucas and Andrew Hingston. Having formed themselves into a committee, the pair moved, seconded and carried unanimously the resolution 'That we give all we can, and beg all we can, to build a chapel, and that we begin at once'. Placing their total savings – which in Henry's case amounted to £20 and in Andrew's to £18 – at the top of their subscription lists, the two young men sallied forth to raise funds for the enterprise. Their example moved the town, and Anglicans, Free Churchmen and even non-believers gave liberally, with the result that on 14 July 1846 Liskeard Wesley chapel was reopened. Both men continued their sterling work for the church, serving as class-leaders and circuit stewards, and became leading citizens of the town. As well as being elected a town councillor in 1860 and mayor the following year, Andrew Hingston was a firm supporter of the temperance cause, serving from 1845 on the committee of the local Temperance Society and subsequently becoming its president. No doubt his position on this and in Liskeard's Band of Hope, of which he was a founder member, was not lost on the young medical apprentice who would some ten years later take his first tentative steps along the path to total abstinence. In later life

Dr Hingston remarked, 'I have never known what it is to need money since the day I gave all my savings to the Lord.'[9]

An additional factor in Mark Guy's interest in religion was Mrs Hingston whose own faith he later described as 'a radiant gaiety' and who 'had not only herself drunk deep of the rivers of the pleasures of God, but who was herself a stream of goodness, always in the sunshine, and always brimming into song'.[10] Indeed, he said himself that he would never have become a Methodist minister but for her. In 'How I Preached my First Sermon' he recounted the events that led him to take his first tentative steps along that road. His first sermon was, in fact, thrust upon him. With the superintendent minister ill, Mark Guy offered to ride down to Couch's Mill, near Lerryn – a distance of some ten miles – with a message. Concerned at the news that there would be no service and rejecting the suggestion that the villagers hold a prayer meeting instead, the steward, an elderly shoemaker named William Olver, 'volunteered' the young messenger to take the service. Brushing aside his protests, he handed him a Bible and suggested he went out into the orchard and looked for a text. 'Now strangely enough,' continued Mark Guy, 'that morning in my reading I had come on a passage of which I had said, "I think I could make a sermon from these words if I were a preacher" – "Be strong, all ye people of the land, and work, for I am with you, saith the Lord of Hosts."' As I prayed and meditated my sermon came, and I went and preached it. And as I rode home in the summer evening I felt the die was cast, the Rubicon was crossed. Some day I knew I must be a preacher.'[11] This chance happening – probably in 1858 or 1859 – led him to spend more time, perhaps, writing sermons than studying medicine, invariably calling Mary Hingston from her household duties to hear another one that he had written. Often he and two friends, the Rev. R. P. Davey and the Rev. A. D. Cope, would meet together in the summer-house at 'Rosedean' on Saturday afternoons for prayer and discussion.

The young man for whom, many years earlier, 'Old Rosie' had prayed, exhorting God to 'make him a preacher', quickly made a name for himself in south-east Cornwall. One of his earliest converts was a Polperro fisherman whom he met on a return visit in 1873 amid stirring scenes:

> Such a service I never had before. It was wonderful. The place filled chiefly with sturdy fishermen. And the responses, and the

> attention, and the depths of spiritual feeling were extraordinary... Such voices and such vehemence, the tears of holy joy running down their cheeks... As I was walking up the hill a fine-looking fisherman came out and grasped my hand. He looked at me and said, 'Mester Pearse – iss, the same man as preached fourteen years agone in Polperro chapel, 'pon them words, 'In my Father's House are many mansions.' Ah, that night settled me. I was converted that night.[12]

Over the years Liskeard Wesley Chapel was enlarged and modernised. John Allen, whose history of the town was published in 1856, put the average attendance then at about 500, with seating for 700. Mark Guy took a keen interest in the chapel scheme that was set in motion during his stay, and when a public meeting was called to receive promises of help, sent up from the audience notes signed 'A minor, £1' and 'A working man, £1' in order to help matters along and encourage the others.[13] The 1860s were the high-water mark of Methodism in the Liskeard area, the new surge in interest and chapel membership coinciding with a mining boom which resulted in an increase in both the population and chapel attendance. In June 1860, the Wesleyan circuit alone reported 1,406 members, with a further 185 on trial. Liskeard Wesley itself had 344 members plus 52 on trial. There was a spate of chapel-building.[14] In September 1860, for instance, Mark Guy and fellow local preacher, R. P. Davey, walked over five miles to attend the opening of Minard Cross Chapel, near St Germans, having the previous year witnessed the stone-laying ceremony with Dr Hingston.[15]

Although *The Story of Billy Bray* is listed as having been published in America as early as 1860[16] and may have appeared simultaneously in this country, some years would pass before Mark Guy's career as a writer began to burgeon. All the time, though, if not actually writing, he was observing, and storing away images and ideas. '...There it was [Liskeard] that I obtained much of my knowledge of the Cornish character,' he revealed years later. 'On the one side we had the Cornish miners, who were from the west-country, and had all the characteristics of the Celt, and on the other hand I came into contact with the eastern agriculturalist, a type differing from the other not only in dialect and language, but also in temperament.'[17]

Except, of course, for his childhood in Camborne, the four-year spell that Mark Guy Pearse spent in Liskeard as a surgeon's apprentice was the longest period he stayed in any one place in Cornwall. By the time he left Dean Street in the summer of 1861, the Hingstons had four children and employed a housemaid, child's maid and nurse at 'Rosedean'.[18] These were formative years for the young medical student who would have fitted in well with both the growing family and with the community at large, preaching and probably attending meetings of the Liskeard Institution, of which Andrew Hingston was vice-president.[19] Addressing a packed congregation at Liskeard Wesley years later on the occasion of Dr Hingston's funeral, he highlighted his former master's equableness as the most prominent feature of his character, describing him as being 'like a lake amongst the hills, quiet, calm, deep, from which flowed hundreds of streams of beneficence, quiet and hidden, almost unseen, always unheard'. Mrs Hingston had died barely seven weeks earlier and Mark Guy's address was a deeply moving eulogy for two dear friends. 'I cannot stand amongst so many old friends,' he continued, 'and join with you in showing our deep love to Dr Hingston, without a thousand recollections coming back to my own heart, and without being compelled to express my own indebtedness to him… Back to my mind comes today the recollections of how, forty years ago, I came fresh from school to the house of our dear friend in Liskeard – though a distant relative, yet a perfect stranger – and how, without any suspicion or hesitation, they took me into the innermost heart of their home. I, perhaps, as all boys of that age, was particularly susceptible to kindness, and yet, with a boy's critical nature, quick to detect the little failings that are apt to betray themselves in the unguarded freedom of the family. The failings I never saw; the love I have never forgotten… I thank God that ever I knew him and her. I should not be here today – certainly not as a Methodist minister – had it not been for them. In connection with the beginnings of my life, how lovingly she conversed with me, and with what fatherly interest and counsel he prompted or restrained, cheered and encouraged.'[20]

Chapter 3

'O Lord, bless the little lad! Bless him, and make him a preacher.'

St Bartholomew's Hospital & Didsbury College 1861–1863

Some time before the beginning of October 1861, Mark Guy Pearse left Cornwall for London where he was to enroll at St Bartholomew's Hospital as a medical student. At that time students were required by the hospital authorities to sign a book as their undertaking to conform to the rules of the medical school, and in signing for the 1861/2 session, Mark Guy gave his address in London as 5, Stonefield Terrace, Liverpool Road, Islington.[1] He was enrolled in the Register of Students to study physiology, chemistry and medical practice[2] and would presumably have been present at the introductory address of the winter session which was delivered by Dr Edward Frankland on Tuesday 1 October at 5 o'clock in the afternoon.[3] Eight days later, through Holmes Coote, an assistant surgeon at the time, he paid 30 guineas (£31.50) as the first installment of his fees and £2 for the Library and Reading Room,[4] the latter amount being the subscription for four years. In the event, though, his stay at Bart's was considerably shorter for, not long after his arrival in the capital, the conflict between the dictates of head and heart which many people experience at some stage in their lives came to a head for the young medical student.

When he was a little lad of six or seven, Mark Guy, his father, his

'St Bartholomew's Hospital: The Square, looking south' by Thomas Godart, 1870 (courtesy of St Bartholomew's Hospital Archives and Museum)

mother and three sisters would pay regular visits to Old Rosie, a bed-ridden, one-hundred-and-five-year-old who lived in a tiny thatched cottage in a rather remote spot in West Cornwall. Every Sunday, after morning service at Camborne Wesley, the family would walk 'down three fields and across awkward stiles, great granite posts let into a ditch that little legs had to struggle across, round by the hawthorn tree, and past the duck-pond… past the farmyard… to three little houses. The one in the middle was smaller than the other two, and stood a little further back, and seemed to say, "Please, may I come in here? I won't be in anyone's way." It wasn't big enough to have a garden, but it made up for it. The roses and jessamine grew about the porch, then from behind somewhere the ivy came and twined about the chimney, and on the thatched roof grew great splats of house leek. It wasn't big enough to have a window on either side of the door, but it had one little window just above the door – a single pane of glass, which looked down on you like a kindly little eye and said, "Come in! Come in! It is no good knocking, because, first of all, there's no knocker, and if you do knock there's nobody to open the door, so you had better walk in." You put your finger through a round hole and lifted up a wooden latch; or, if you liked, you might take hold of a knot of string above and pull up the latch – but then you must be one of the grown-up people to do that, we little folks could only stand on tip-toe and put the finger in. You couldn't go wrong; there was nowhere to go but right up over the stairs, so up the stairs we went.' Outnumbered, it seemed to him, by his sisters, Mark Guy invariably ended up on a little stool at the old lady's side where she could hold his hand, turn and nod at him and smile. The little service always took the same form: a chapter from the Bible read by Mr Pearse, a hymn – usually 'Rock of Ages' sung to the tune 'Rousseau's Dream' so that the children could join in – and finally a prayer. Before Mr Pearse pronounced the benediction, Old Rosie would have her 'Bit of prayer':

> I see the hand uplifted still, the light shining between the old, withered fingers, her face upturned, and then the hand was laid lightly on my head, and the lips were parted to breathe this prayer: 'God bless the little lad! Bless him, Lord! *and make him a preacher* for Jesus Christ's sake, Amen.'[5]

Writing to his sister Margaret in April 1863, Mark Guy acknowledged that Old Rosie's 'smiling face and heavenly look' had gone down deeper in his memories than any sermon.[6] Indeed, he came to see the centenarian's action as 'a sort of prophetic intimation that I should be a preacher'[7] and felt 'as if it laid a spell on me that I was almost powerless to break. It was almost an ordination service.'[8] He wished at the time that she would not pray as she did; indeed, he fought against it:

> *I didn't want to be a preacher*. The preachers of those times were all so glum. I wanted to be a doctor. It seemed such a splendid thing to gallop about the world on a horse, and cut off people's arms and legs. I waited till everybody was out of sight, and then I put my foot down and said, 'I *won't*!'[9]

In a sense he continued to deny the call until he reached London, though by then, of course, he had already begun to preach and the struggle was essentially an inner one, with Old Rosie's words no doubt still exerting their influence.

Another early source of inspiration was the eccentric Bible Christian local preacher Billy Bray, who was the subject of one of his earliest pieces of writing and whom he mentioned in the same breath as Thomas Champness and Hugh Price Hughes as 'men audacious for their Heavenly King in enterprise and achievement'.[10] In his classic memoir, *The King's Son*, F. W. Bourne recalled how, shortly before his death in 1868, Billy enquired of the doctor bending over him, 'When I get up there [heaven], shall I give them your compliments... and tell them you

*'Old Rosie' by Charles Tresidder (*Short Stories*)*

will be coming, too?' – a question which made a wonderful impression on the listener. Cyril Davey is surely wrong, though, in asserting that 'That question related by the doctor [Dr Hingston] to his young assistant [Mark Guy Pearse] took another great Cornishman into the Wesleyan ministry', for it was by then seven years since he had left Liskeard and he was already in the fourth year of his ministry.[11]

Plagued by doubts about whether or not to end his medical career in favour of the ministry, Mark Guy joined a London circuit, only to find that no work could be found for him as either a Sunday school teacher or local preacher. In the loneliness of his first few days in the great city 'almost anyone might have had his soul for the bidding'. However, a kind Wesleyan minister saved him for Methodism by giving him work to do which opened his way to the ministry.[12] It was at the house of businessman James Duncan of Hackney that Mark Guy Pearse was introduced to the Rev. Thomas Vasey, 'a man of large heart, generous sympathies, and evangelistic zeal, to whose wise counsel and encouragement he is chiefly indebted for his position of conspicuous usefulness in the church'.[13] The Rev. T. Vasey, who was at that time superintendent of the Hackney circuit, not only encouraged the lonely medical student to get involved in activities at the nearest Wesleyan chapel, but, more importantly at this juncture, befriended him. A few evenings after they were introduced, Mark Guy found himself sitting in his new friend's study telling him all about himself and about his irrepressible sense of having been called to the ministry. 'This conversation,' he said himself, 'was the beginning of a kindness and interest that it is impossible to describe.'[14] In June 1862, the Rev. T. Vasey wrote to Mark Guy's father explaining his son's state of mind and urging him not to stand in his way. 'I can well understand your anxiety,' he wrote. 'It appears to me that your son has for some time past been much unsettled in his mind as to the path of duty, *his predilections always running in one direction*, viz. for the ministry, but his temporal interests and the wishes of his friends seeming to counsel a contrary course. This internal conflict seems to have reached its crisis on his coming to town to study for the medical profession, when he felt himself destitute of the professional ardour necessary to ensure success... His uncle conversed with him on the subject, and ascertained from him the deep undercurrent of his desires.' He went on to say that the young man had now definitely made up his mind to try for the ministry, and that he himself was satisfied that the call was genuine and that he was cut out for the work, being 'very acceptable wherever he preaches'. He finished his letter by assuring Mr Pearse that he had so much interest and faith in his son that he would do his utmost to prepare him for theological college. 'We want such men most urgently,' he concluded.[15] Needless to say, his parents raised no objection, and Mark Guy Pearse was proposed by the Rev. T. Vasey as a candidate for the ministry.

The Wesleyan Conference that opened in Camborne on 31 July 1862 was, in fact, the first to be held in Cornwall. A general committee had been appointed a year earlier to carry out the preparatory arrangements, Camborne's members being Capt. Charles Thomas and Mark Guy Pearse senior, together with the Rev. George Blanchflower (Superintendent Minister), Dr George Smith (Treasurer) and W. Bickford-Smith (Lay Secretary). As it did every year, *The Methodist Recorder* provided its readers with a portrait of the host town:

> Camborne cannot boast miles of streets, lined with beautiful shops, towering factories or palatial warehouses. It is simply an ordinary and unpretentious country town, containing a population of from ten to twelve thousand inhabitants, and situated in the midst of a rich and highly-productive mining district… Its society, both in numbers and influence, stands at the head of Cornish Methodism. Its well-built and spacious Wesley Chapel, with its commodious suite of vestries and other rooms, will furnish the best accommodation for the transaction of Conference business.[16]

The West Cornwall Railway Company, which Dr Smith was chiefly responsible for bringing into being, agreed to run special trains from Truro and Penzance to Camborne and back to tie in with the opening and closing of each day's sessions, and also to carry all the ministers during the whole of the conference by any of the timetabled trains, on production of their Conference tickets, for the sum of £110.[17] The 144 candidates who had been recommended for the ministry by their various district meetings had, in the meantime, undergone 'a more comprehensive examination which inquired into their health and their knowledge of literature as well as of theology'. After careful consideration, 31 were rejected, 103 were accepted, and the decision in the case of the remaining 10 was deferred for a few days, pending the results of further enquiry. There was, in fact, some debate about who should be received on trial, the Conference President, the Rev. Charles Prest, speaking strongly on the necessity of not accepting 'ignorant and unfinished men'. 'We live in an earnest age,' he continued. 'We have to do with men. You meet with vigour in the commercial, in the political, and in the literary world, and it will not do to attempt to grapple with an age of men with an agency that has only the feebleness of children.'[18] Strengthened, no doubt, by the crisis he had experienced some months earlier, Mark Guy would have acquitted himself with honour and, one imagines, with considerable pride, in the building in which he had been baptised twenty years earlier. Although he turned his back on a medical career, Mark Guy Pearse was to devote the rest of his life to healing people, substituting souls for bodies and dispensing 'the Lord's blessed cure-all', as Daniel Quorm puts it. Indeed, on at least two occasions he has his most famous character compare the class leader and the doctor:

> Now that be just what a leader ought to be – a kind o' doctor

> that can give each one the prescription he needs... that can deal out the Lord's medicines, and can make up a strengthenin' plaster for them as is weak in the back and can't stand very well, and can clap up a stiff blister to them as have caught the fever o' worldliness, and can make a pill for sluggish livers... That's what a leader ought to be...[19]

In October 1862, Mark Guy Pearse entered Didsbury College, Manchester, one of the two Wesleyan Methodist theological colleges that had been founded in the early 1840s with money raised at country-wide meetings held to celebrate the centenary of the movement. Almost as soon as he arrived, he wrote to little Annie Hingston who was to leave Liskeard for Sherborne in order to attend school and to 'take care of dear Grandpapa'.[20] Lamenting that he had no one to look after him, he continued:

> I have nobody at all coming in to see me excepting an old man who brings the coals and sticks for me to light my fire with, and the old woman who comes once a week to clean up my room. Nobody at all who loves me comes in now and then to see me, and the only people who do come are sometimes one of the other students, or some old preacher comes pushing in to ask me to go and preach for him... Then there is old Dr Hannah, who sits and lectures to us every morning. He sometimes comes in. And sometimes the 'Guv', as he is called, though his wife calls him Mr Bowers. He sits at table when we have breakfast or dinner, and sees that we don't eat too much.[21]

The letter, in which he affected sadness at being neglected, contained seven excellent though, in part, rather disrespectful likenesses of his pastors and masters. One of these was of Dr John Hannah[22] his theological tutor who, at the beginning of the autumn term, told his students that he had decided to part company with his pipe for ever. In the past he had always smoked one pipe of tobacco before retiring to bed, his wife always filling it and bringing it to him. However, having stayed in a home at Conference where his hosts strongly objected to tobacco smoking, he was deprived for three weeks of his nightly pipe and decided, on his return, that he could henceforth do without. 'Does that apply all round, sir?' asked a young student. 'Why do you ask that question, Mr Pearse?' 'Well, sir, did you say to Mrs Hannah, "My dear, I have been separated from you for three weeks without discomfort, let us part company for ever"?'[23] Impeccable logic from one who became generally recognised as one of the most accomplished humorists among the preachers of the age!

Mark Guy used to write fortnightly to his sister Margaret who was then at boarding school, under the title 'The Didsbury College Times', using a combination of 'sermon, intelligence and sketches'.[24] Though consisting mainly of fraternal advice interspersed with comic drawings, the letters sometimes mentioned day-to-day occurrences. Early in 1863, for instance, the editor of *The Methodist Recorder* visited the college and put on record his impressions of the establishment he had left some years earlier. One thing that met his approval was the sight of a hearty game of football in progress in the little close under the college walls. 'We envied them in their exhilarating sport,' he continued, 'and yet were thankful their lot was cast in better times than ours. It seemed to fall in with the dictum of the great master of the academy, "Gymnastics for the body, and dialectics for the mind"; and few will credit, who have not yet proved, how essential these are to each other. We were sorry to learn there was a disposition on the part of some to put it down...'[25]

If there were mutterings about such activities before the article, these could have been nothing compared with the furore which greeted its publication. Particularly vitriolic was a letter from a correspondent signing himself 'an admirer of Old Wesleyanism'. A member of the Society for upwards of forty years and an office-bearer for thirty-seven, he had witnessed 'many painful scenes, in the maintenance of "Methodism as it is"'. Few things, though, had pained him more than the article on Didsbury revealing that the ministerial students amused themselves by playing at 'the very *low* and *vulgar* game of foot-ball'. Cricket is bad for such a purpose,' he continued, 'but football much worse. What would the early Methodists and what would Mr Wesley have thought of such a worldly amusement, and such a mode of spending precious time? If it has come to this, that a Minister of our Body can approve of and advocate foot-ball for the students, I don't see why a *skittle-alley*, a *tennis court* and a *bowling green* should not form essential appendages to Didsbury and Richmond. Health, I know is pleaded as an excuse, but surely health could be promoted in a much less objectionable way. A good smart walk, to admire some beautiful production of nature or art, by which the mind might be enlarged and the taste refined; or a walk to see some sick and suffering saint, might supply ample recreation and activity for all the purposes of health. And if nothing else can be devised, let them run so many times round the Institution, as Mr Wesley used to run round the Charter-house yard. To un-"sensible" people like me, who have not had the advantage of training at Didsbury, it seems marvellous that Dr Hannah and the Rev. J.Bowers can sanction a game which has always been popular where cock-fighting and such like demoralizing games or practices have been most prevalent. The uniformity of type in our young men trained in the Institutions has often been urged in my hearing as an objection to them, but this disclosure of football-playing will be the most damaging of all. More than once I have heard it said, since the article on Didsbury appeared, "I shall never subscribe to an institution which patronises football-playing by our students." And I am persuaded, from what I hear, that the funds of the Institution will suffer, while the piety of the students will not be improved. I do hope, Sir, that some steps will be immediately taken to put a stop to a game so *ungentlemanly* and *unministerial* and which must eventually prove so damaging financially and morally...'[26] The same issue of the *Recorder* printed a similar letter from 'Another of the Unsensible people', cancelling his subscription! Our young, Cornish theological student referred to the affair in a letter to his sister Margaret, mentioning 'two slashing letters' which he and his friends had sent in by way of reply, although, unfortunately, the editor seems to have put an end to the correspondence before these could be published. 'Of course,' wrote Mark Guy, 'we still play vigorously enough, and could you see us you wouldn't think it "low or vulgar" – nor, if you came into one of our study prayer-meetings, would you consider us unministerial. I can just picture the old gentleman who wrote the letter "Old Wesleyanism".'[27] A lively illustration followed.

On Thursday 26 March that same year, the students of the Didsbury Branch of the Wesleyan Theological Institution celebrated their second Missionary Anniversary. After tea in the dining hall, they adjourned at six o'clock to the College Chapel, where the chairman, Mr Bamford Burrows, referred to the political changes that had taken place since they had last met, and the effect of the American Civil War on the country. Mark Guy Pearse moved the second resolution, 'That, acknowledging the great power of Christianity for good, this meeting pledges itself to increased efforts on its behalf.' He spoke of 'nations bound down in tyranny… stirring – their hearts… beating great with hope and strong with home love, and with conquering will… rising to hurl off the iron yoke and to take their place in the freed world – the new creation. To man belonged the direct work of proclaiming liberty, and bringing souls

'The Ministering Angel', original sketch by Mark Guy Pearse (courtesy of Margaret Walton)

to the light.'[28] The following week – over Easter – Mark Guy went on a walking tour with the Rev. T. B. Stephenson, a fellow student.

His official training ended that summer and at the Sheffield Conference he was appointed to the Leeds (St Peter's etc.) Circuit of the Leeds District, along with Joseph Heaton, Thomas Albrighton and Robert Coe.[29]

Chapter 4

'What with sermonizing, lectures and examinations, I really am quite full.'

Leeds and London 1863–1867

At the time that the twenty-one-year-old former medical student began what one source described as 'a rousing ministry among the intelligent artisans of Leeds',[1] the district was divided into four circuits. Although he was appointed to the one headed by St Peter's Chapel, it is unlikely that Mark Guy Pearse was a minister at St Peter's itself. His base may have been one of the other town chapels, such as Beckett Street, which was built about this time or, more probably, one of the country causes such as Halton.[2] On the evening of 6 October 1863, 3,000 people attended St Peter's Chapel for a love feast, one of a number of services being held in Leeds to mark the jubilee of the first Methodist Missionary meeting in the town. Mark Guy, who donated £5 5s 0d (£5.25) to the Jubilee Fund,[3] was almost certainly present. Ten weeks later, signing himself 'Your own loving Ould nuncle Jan Trenoweth', he wrote to his sisters Margaret and Fanny from 14, Springfield Terrace, Burmantoft, a suburb to the north east of St Peter's:

> ...I am so busy I can scarcely find time to reply. It is now nearly eleven o'clock, and I am sitting in my snug little drawing-room, taking a mouthful of bread and cheese and then writing another line. I have an especial amount of work just now – making my home mission plan to-day, and writing a sermon for Richmond

> Hill Chapel for Sunday evening and a mission sermon in the morning.[4]

It seems that with the opening of Brunswick, the more well-to-do members of the congregation at St Peter's left and it began to take on characteristics of a 'down-town' chapel.[5] At a great temperance meeting in the Manchester Free Trade Hall in 1883, Mark Guy described how he was thrown among working men in Leeds, where he found drunkenness a great hindrance to his work.[6] And there is certainly more than a hint of this in his letter to Margaret and Fanny, in which he describes how he found visiting 'in this wretched neighbourhood' a sickening and wearying experience.[7]

After a year in Leeds he moved to north London, having been appointed by Conference to the fledgling Brixton Hill Circuit. The Wesleyan cause there had its beginnings in a cottage in Coldharbour Lane in 1820. Four years or so later a chapel was erected on the site of the present church on the west side of Brixton Hill. A new chapel built on the same site in 1856 was, in turn, enlarged seven years later and in 1861 Brixton Hill Circuit was formed by division from Lambeth, and included what later became the Mostyn Road and Sydenham circuits.[8] Some months after moving in, Mark Guy wrote to his parents asking that one of his sisters might come up to look after him for a while:

> It would help me in my studies, as I should be less downhearted at times... and my part is the healthiest in London according to returns. Dalston stands first on the list.

The request was granted, for on Friday 3 February 1865 he wrote to Margaret from 2, Sinfield Terrace, Richmond Road, Dalston, telling her that things were being got ready for her visit and that in three weeks or at most a month, he would welcome her as his housekeeper:

> I am beginning to anticipate already. You don't know what a snug little place I have, and as the evenings get longer you'll have to take long walks with me. We are not far from Victoria Park – not far from the City. So Tuesdays and Thursdays, my walking evenings, you'll have long tramps of about three or four miles. We shall get along splendidly together. I'm reading Bickersteth's Life[9] at meal-times... You will enjoy yourself wonderfully... The friends are so very kind, the apartments so clean and com-

> fortable, and people so attentive, and everything so happy, I often think I have more reason to sing that old Pearse-psalm than anybody *in the whole world*. It is so delightful preaching when the heart's in tune, and visiting the poor dark people at our new mission, Homerton. You'll have to get some work when you come, but that I know will be all in your way.[10]

On the previous day he had been to hear Morley Punshon,[11] the celebrated Wesleyan preacher and lecturer, and was clearly impressed. 'He preached a *grand* sermon,' he wrote, 'but to me 'twas like a man going along a road fill'd with costliest apples of gold, or anything you like that comes tumbling down by him, and he stoops to pick up one, when another drops: he runs to it, and then comes another; he leaves the former for that one, and is drawn off by another, till he hasn't got one of the prizes, and only remembers their beauty. I couldn't send you now a *single* idea of his sermon perfectly, yet I listen'd most attentively, and can usually carry away the greater part of a sermon that interests me.' In the same letter he expresses his delight at the delicious mince-pies his mother had sent up from Cornwall as a treat.[12]

That he was happy in the Brixton Hill circuit is attested to by his daughter Frances; further proof comes in the form of another letter to Margaret Pearse dated 27 October 1865, which provides us with a lively picture of his busy life there:

> If you could peep in on me at any hour of the day you would not think me at all long in not writing to you, for I am engaged all day. This week a couple of sermons for our grand congregation at Brixton; then on Monday off to the missionary meeting at Dunstable; on Tuesday back to our missionary meeting here; then hard at work at a lecture on Chatterton for Tuesday week. There is every moment taken up till then, in addition to my other work – my ordinary work.[13]

The lecture on Chatterton was, in fact, the inaugural one for a sort of Young Men's Class that he had started, where the programme consisted of essays one week, readings another, lectures a third and essays a fourth. A typical day for Mark Guy and his close friend Alfred Vine, who was obviously preparing for the ministry, might involve '[a]n hour before breakfast at Greek Testament, then from 9 till 3.30 or 4 at hard work; then a walk till dinner time half an hour after, or if not walk a boxing match or other row… Then off to preaching, or a settling down to fag-

*Mrs Mark Guy Pearse (*Cornish Magazine*, 1899)*

ging again for the evening.'[14]

There was, of course, an added reason for the young Mark Guy Pearse to travel up to Dunstable whenever he could – namely, Miss Jeanie Cooper. It is probable that he first met his future wife while he was at St Bart's. Indeed, his daughter Frances writes that during the early 1860s his friends noted that wherever he was going, it appeared to be necessary to go via Dunstable! The first allusion to Miss Cooper comes in a letter to his sister Margaret dated 10 February 1863:

> I had a long letter from Mrs Cooper a few days since – full of kindness as usual. 'Twas rather strange; last time I preach'd I took for my text 'God is Love', and preach'd all about *Love*. Miss Cooper could not come out, nor any of the family, as all were poorly. 'Twas fortunate. I saw some of them smiling as I divided my subject. I have been ask'd several times if I am engaged, but there is really *nothing* – nor have I given cause for suspicion. What may happen in a couple of years nobody knows...[15]

A little over two years later he wrote again to Margaret who was, he believed, about to make a rather hasty decision concerning someone she had only just met:

> Marriage is an awfully solemn thing. For *two years* I went and came at Dunstable and watched dear Jeanie in every phase and shade of character, and let her see me in all possible moods. I daren't have proposed to her knowing less of her, or having given her less opportunity of seeing me. Jeanie had many suitors about her and many offers that I know of, but I simply pray'd about it and was assured, if it were the right thing, God would make my way unmistakably plain... I owe her to God's good providence. I watch'd her, and learnt to love more as I watch'd more, until I thought I had seen the whole inner Jeanie, and then proposed. Less than that I could not have done; less than that had been unworthy [of] Jeanie, and unworthy of any true-hearted girl who feels aright the awful importance of married life.[16]

The young couple was married at the Priory Church, Dunstable on 31 August 1866. The day before the wedding, Mary Hingston, who had been like a second mother to him, wrote, 'Now, my dear boy, you will have your Jeanie, to comfort you when depressed, and to *guide your impetuosity*.'[17] Frances Pearse's assessment of her mother's role was much the same:

> Her unerring sense of justice often corrected and modified his [Mark Guy's] impulsive and sometimes prejudiced judgements. Her invincible patience soothed his nervous irritability.

She was very much 'the controlling spirit of the household' and although, as we shall see, in due course she became an active worker alongside her husband in the West London Mission, it was as a wife and mother, as the stay and support of the whole family, that she would essentially have seen herself. Her deep interest in each of her children helped bind the family together, and her insight and tact soothed away the difficulties and misunderstandings that inevitably arose as she and Mark Guy grew to manhood and womanhood.[18]

Mary Jane was the eldest daughter of John Cooper and his wife Mary Sarson Wingfield of the Manor House, Dunstable. Born at Cheddleton, Staffordshire, John, together with James and George Cooper, had come

Dunstable Wesleyan Chapel (Courtesy of Colin Bourne)

to Dunstable from Manchester in the early 1840s and established Cooper's Hat Factory there on the site of Burr's Brewery. They built a row of cottages at the rear of Manchester Place for some of the workforce which, according to the 1851 census, numbered 'about 300 males and females'.[19] As a country market town, with its many and varied shops, its hat factories and its cottage industries, Dunstable leant itself to non-conformism and was recognised as a stronghold of Methodism. Although the first recorded mention of a Society is found in 1798, it was not until 1831 that a purpose-built Methodist Church was opened. When this was destroyed by fire in September 1844, another one was built and opened the following year when little Mary Jane Cooper, her parents and family were present at the laying of the foundation stone. The fact that this second chapel was enlarged on two subsequent occasions in the 1850s underlines the extent to which Dunstable was a boom-town during this period.[20] According to Frances Pearse, her grandmother was 'rather a remarkable character, well-known in Wesleyan circles through her "memorials"', which were written by the Rev. Henry Fish. Acquainted with her as a child, he described her as 'a gay, guileless, sportive, lovely little thing, in spirit and temper a miniature type of what she was all her short life'. Prone to exhibiting 'an earnest and heart-searching piety', she filled her diary with 'self-examination and self-reproach'.[21] It was into this deeply religious and rarefied atmosphere that Jeanie was born in April 1841, before the couple moved to Dunstable. From babyhood she was idolised by her mother, who lived long enough to leave an indelible impression on the mind of her sensitive daughter. In spite of her very delicate health and the loss of three children at an early age, Mrs Cooper ran a large Bible Class for young women, hundreds of whom were employed in her husband's straw-bonnet factory. Such was the depth of feeling for her that the class increased in size and had to be divided three times, each time into groups of fifty or sixty members. Towards the end of her life – she died when Jeanie was ten – she wrote in her diary:

> My eldest daughter is almost always in my thoughts. I fear much lest I should make an idol of her. She is so affectionate and thoughtful in my present state of weakness and suffering.[22]

In due course John Cooper remarried, but for many years the family continued to live at the old Manor House where they kept open house for Wesleyan activities such as anniversaries, missionary meetings and the like. It was on one such occasion that the young Mark Guy Pearse first made the acquaintance of Miss Cooper. The wedding itself took place under what the *Dunstable Gazette* called 'very auspicious circumstances'. Contrary to expectations, the weather was good and the sun shone as the bride and groom, with their many friends, made their way to and from the Priory Church. It seems that the town's inhabitants – particularly the young people – had long been looking forward to what was clearly a splendid spectacle:

> The beautiful attire of the charming bride excited universal admiration. Four bridesmaids and an equal number of groomsmen were present at the altar, full of bloom and beauty.[23]

Employees of J. J. & G. Cooper were given the day off and most of them crowded into the church to witness the ceremony before being treated to tea and other refreshments. After honeymooning in north Devon, the young couple set up home in furnished lodgings in Lower Norwood, Mark Guy having been re-appointed to this part of the Brixton Hill circuit by Conference a couple of weeks earlier.

The following June, Mark Guy wrote to Luke Tyerman, one of the circuit's supernumeraries, expressing the hope of the Chapel Building

Committee at Lower Norwood that he would be able to help out with re-opening services on Sunday 7 July. A postscript reads as follows:

> Mrs Tyreman [*sic*] will be pleased to learn that my wife got over her trouble on Wednesday last: a fine little girl.[24]

It was almost certainly the birth of this, their first child, Jean Drummond that was referred to in the letter quoted by his daughter Frances in her biography. In it he announced, with characteristic humour, the arrival of 'a fine edition of a little girl, quite new, very neatly got up, and not too highly coloured. Its orthodoxy is unquestionable, as it gives no uncertain sound; it is already making itself heard in some circles. I would not part with my copy for the world. Jeanie sends her love. P.S. – Get a copy as soon as you can.'[25] Like many others before and since, the Rev. M. G. Pearse found the itinerancy of Methodism a burden, though one with which for over twenty years he was forced to live. At least after 1866 he had Jeanie to support him as they moved from London to Ipswich, Bedford, London again, Bude, Launceston and Bristol before the opening of the West London Mission brought a greater degree of stability to their lives and, in the words of one writer, 'possibly saved Mr Pearse to Methodism'.[26]

As the years went by, the family grew; two or three letters to his sister Margaret, abundantly decorated with chubby babies tumbling about and screaming lustily, seemed to suggest a lively household. His daughter Frances remembered a devoted father, fond of romping with his young family; Mark Guy himself recalled 'a huge wooden idol worshipped in former times by my own dear ones at home, than which father and mother were scarcely more dear, whose name was Joan'.[27] After what he described as a 'battle royal' in Conference, his ordination was put back two years on account of his having married earlier than the rules of the Methodist Church allowed. Thereafter he took great delight in describing his two eldest children as his 'little illegitimates', for these two, having been born before his ordination, were not recognised by the Connexion, and received no educational allowance.[28] Whether in the pulpit, on the lecture circuit or at home, Mark Guy was a natural entertainer. His children never forgot the stories he told them, stories such as the romance of John Dory and Ann-Chovy and that of Johnny and 'Please for a pennorth of plum-pudden', or the queer old Cornish nonsense rhyme to a snail:

Jan Jake, Jan Jake, put out your long horns;
Your father and mother is dead,
Your brother and sister is to the back door,
A-beggin' for barley bread.[29]

In 1876, not long before the breakdown that, paradoxically, would result in such a happy year in Bude for the family, he composed the following letter to boost the spirits of his little six-year-old and seven-year-old daughters who had been sent away to boarding-school at Hawkesbury Hall, four miles north of Coventry:

> My Darlings Maud and Mab – How long it is since I sent you a letter. Here is one at last. We are always thinking of you and talking of you. And when your letters come we all jump for joy. Hawkesbury Hall now must begin to look very beautiful. The snowdrops and crocuses are out, and the violets are coming, I expect, and you roam about in the woods under the young green buds [picture of them doing so]. Then soon the birds will be building their nests, and be singing their songs and laying their eggs... *Be quite sure that God loves you as His children*, and now be His children every day... Bless you, my sweetest children. Mamma joins in much love to you. Your loving Father must now say 'Good night'.[30]

The letter ended with a picture of himself in a nightcap blowing out a candle. Although his preaching engagements often took him away and he was a welcome guest wherever he went, he was devoted to his home, and was always glad to get back. 'I do thank God for you,' he wrote to his wife in 1884 on the occasion of their eighteenth wedding anniversary. 'You have made me the happiest man alive!'[31] The keynote of Mark Guy's life was simplicity. Described in *The Times* as 'essentially an individualist, who hated ecclesiastical harness',[32] he disliked formalities of any sort, never dined out or went to entertainments of any kind whatsoever. 'This place is rather stiff and grand,' he once wrote from Edinburgh. 'Very kind – *after their kind*! Dress for dinner, and all that, and as they dine late, and I cannot do well with dinner before preaching, I make up for it at luncheon. Fancy, not a pipe or cigar since last Monday night – and now Thursday!'[33]

When, in 1886, the Pearses moved to London, to a house of their own at 11, Bedford Place, Mark Guy took a delight in planning it, choosing the furniture and curtains, and hanging pictures which, because he liked to encourage promising young artists by purchasing their works, were constantly increasing in number. 'I never see any house anywhere that I like so much as ours,' he used to say of the pleasant and roomy house in Bedford Place which, while the Pearses were attached to the mission, was heavily used for entertaining visitors from South Africa, Australia and even further afield. 'It was the rule, not the exception,' wrote Sister Lily in 1914, 'for Mrs Pearse to welcome them to her home, and to give them all the interest and help she could, and not to do this as if she were bored, but with a graciousness that will never be forgotten. We heard it said, over and over again, "I do not know what we should have done, here in London, without Mrs Pearse; oh! how good and kind she was!"'[34] And Emmeline Pethick-Lawrence who, as a young girl, stayed with the family in Bristol, described her as 'the sweetest and gentlest woman in the world' possessed of 'great wisdom and much strength of character'.[35] She took a keen interest in the varied work of the West London Mission where the Rescue Committee and the Sisterhood Council in particular had good cause to be grateful for her involvement. Though naturally retiring and rather reluctant to involve herself in anything which would mean publicity, she would, nevertheless, come forward when she felt that to do so would benefit others. She would take the chair at some Mission gatherings or say a few words of sympathy and encouragement when necessary, though it was not, it must be stressed, the sort of thing that came naturally to her.[36] She devoted considerable time and energy to the Mothers' and Class Meetings, choosing to prepare her lessons for the latter in the quiet of the early morning, before her busy household was awake.

Frances Pearse remembered that, initially at least, her father did not cope too well when his children began to mature and develop personalities of their own. Disliking discussion of any kind, especially in domestic matters, he would make rapid decisions when his wife wanted a chance to talk things over. The numerous strands to his work at the Mission made continuous demands on his time and energy, and 'Don't let us have any argument' was his usual response to anything that threatened to disrupt that work. While this attitude may have been acceptable to his wife, who was often able to work on him and get him to reconsider, it was not always too popular with his children. 'Young people growing up were hardly prepared to have their own points of view and firmly held opinions so swept aside, and the silence that followed by no means gave consent,' wrote Frances. All the same, they were left remarkably free to find their own way in the world. As they came of age, they were given latchkeys, together with an annual allowance of £50 each. Before this, whenever any of them were away, whether at school in England or Germany, at Cambridge University, or a Paris studio, or at Edinburgh Infirmary, their mother wrote each week. For Frances, she was 'the controlling spirit of the household. Her spontaneous and unfeigned interest, even more than her justice and understanding in every difficulty, made it *home*.' Realising gradually how diverse his six children were, Mark Guy always had a word of praise for their achievements. 'There were no overmastering successes,' wrote Frances, 'but the main object of all the family was to *do* good and to *be* good and he was unworldly enough to think that that mattered more than anything else. That there were no conspicuous failures was due perhaps mainly to the *belief* in them – the *implicit trust* of their parents, of which each child was aware. That trust was like an invisible hand that held one back from doing anything that would sully it.'[37]

Although there may not have been any 'overmastering successes', with the exception of their first-born Jean Drummond who, tragically, died at the age of fourteen, the Pearses' children realised their potential in a variety of ways. Frances Margaret (Mab) inherited her father's artistic talent and became a portrait, figure and flower watercolourist and pastelliste of considerable ability. While still living at home, she exhibited 'Chrysanthemums' at the Society of British Artists in Suffolk Street and, in 1890, at the Royal Academy. Six years later her painting 'The Lost Fairy' appeared in the Academy's list.[38] After the death of her husband, Professor George Unwin of Manchester University, at the beginning of 1925, Frances became a member of the Cornish artist colony, setting up studios at St Ives and Newlyn.[39] It was at her little cottage 'Up-Along' in this fishing port just outside Penzance that Mark Guy spent a few months with her each summer. As well as providing illustrations for volumes such as *Gold and Incense: a West Country Story* (1895) and *West Country Songs* (1902), she was, of course, with John Telford, her father's biographer. Isabel (Belle) studied for a medical degree and later married the Rev. W. Dick, an Eastbourne clergyman. The Pearses' eldest son, Mark Guy, lived for many years in Canning Town where he ran a community for boys. In later years he and his wife lived close by Mark Guy's flat at 29, Buckingham Mansions, West Hampstead, and were therefore able to visit him daily. Frances recorded that her father treasured a letter from his son's headmaster, in which he wrote, 'That son of yours is one of the best men ever placed on the staff of St Olave's, and I think the best loved, and the most potent influence for good.'[40] John Warwick Guy Pearse, the younger son, worked in the slums of West London for some considerable time before taking Holy Orders in 1901. The previous year he had edited a series of twenty-six illustrated saints' stories for children, which in the early 1920s were reissued as *The Children's Book of Saints*. His first appointment was as curate of a church near Fitzroy Square in the West End and in due course he joined the Mirfield Community. Having had a miraculous escape during the First World War when a shell burst over him, he became warden of Quarry House, St Leonard's, a holiday home for boys and young men.[41] The Pearses' youngest, Jean Marian, studied at Girton College, Cambridge before joining a High Church Sisterhood and taking a vow of poverty and celibacy. Their eldest surviving daughter, Maud, spent some years as a Sister in the West London Mission and, later, as a district nurse, before going out to India as a missionary. 'I had the great help and comfort of his [Mark Guy's] eldest daughter as nursery superintendent of my nurses in the Victoria Hospital in Benares in the years 1909 and 1910,' recalled Janet Gray, 'and she was wonderful in her great skill, especially with difficult and troublesome patients.'[42] When her mother's health began to fail in 1913, Maud gave up her work in India and came home to nurse her with the same devotion that she had given to her mission work. On Mrs Pearse's death the following year, she stayed on with her father, giving up her own interests in order to watch over him and to try to ensure that, for the rest of his life, he continued to enjoy the home comforts to which he had grown accustomed.

Chapter 5

'You know he's a wonder, is Mister Horn…'

Ipswich and Bedford 1867–1872

On 27 March 1861, six years prior to the appointment of the Rev. Mark Guy Pearse to the Ipswich Circuit, the town's Museum Street Wesleyan Church was opened. Among those who were instrumental in raising the necessary cash was a certain James Fulcher of Tattingstone who, like many other men and women living in the Suffolk villages where Mark Guy lived and worked in the late 1860s, served as a model for the aspiring writer, and subsequently appeared – in Fulcher's case, as James Horn – *in Mister Horn and His Friends*; *or givers and giving*, which was first published in book form in 1872.

The duty of giving was Mister Horn's hobby; there was nothing that he thought about, talked about, prayed about or preached about as much. And his greatest achievement in the way of giving was the result of a proposal to build a new chapel at Gippington [Ipswich], the Circuit town. Leader of the Sunday morning class in his home village of Tattingham [Tattingstone], Superintendent of the afternoon Sunday school, local preacher in the evening and sick visitor all the week round, Mister Horn refused to make any promise when asked for a contribution, but said he would do what he could. Wanting to feel that he himself was somehow giving, he resolved, after much heart-searching, to live on the few hard-earned pounds that he had saved and to give to the Lord all that he could earn during one year. And at the end of that hard year, his secret sacrifice was revealed when, at a meeting to launch the scheme for building the new chapel, he placed his subscription in the minister's hand, together with a slip of paper which read: 'One year's work, £100. He loved me and gave Himself for me. J. H.'[1] Some twenty-seven years later, the church again benefited from James Fulcher's generosity when his name headed the list of donations to the restoration fund. It was entirely appropriate, then, that Mister Horn's creator was present for the first of the re-opening services on 21 August 1888 and that in his sermon he underlined the need for thorough honesty and personal rectitude, describing his ideal as being a man whose Christian principles were seen in his life and in his conduct.[2] Mark Guy's reunion with those whom his daughter described as 'the honest yeomanry about Ipswich',[3] must have been a joyous occasion for all concerned.

One of the Pearses' first public appearances in Ipswich must have been at the baptism of their four-month-old daughter, Jean Drummond, on 15 October 1867.[4] Two more children, Maud and Frances, were born during their time in the town. The young minister and his growing family settled in well in the local community and Mark Guy was, by his own admission, very happy there. His 'cheerful temper, joined to an intelligent and refined taste, a good heart, and enthusiasm in his vocation'[5] endeared him not only to the people of Ipswich itself, but to the country folk from the outlying villages such as Tattingstone, Chattisham, Woodbridge and Framlingham. He was then, of course, a comparatively unknown minister, but later, when he had become one of the leaders of Methodism, many of those same folk had stories to tell of his time amongst them. It appears that on one occasion he was waiting in an anteroom for the moment to go on to the lecture platform when a worried steward bustled in and asked if he knew the whereabouts of Mr Jones. Five minutes later the same man re-appeared and asked if he had seen a man with one arm called Jones. A twinkle came into Mark Guy's eyes as he replied, 'I can't remember having done so, but it might help me if you could recollect the name of his other arm.'[6]

Organisations which benefited from his enthusiasm included the Working Men's College and the Mechanics' Institute to whose members he lectured on Sir Walter Raleigh and Hugh Latimer. Representatives of these institutions, together with those from the ragged schools and Sunday schools and chapels in and around the circuit town, were present at a breakfast held to mark his imminent departure in the summer of 1869. On that occasion John Glyde junior singled out the young minister's 'unsectarian efforts to elevate the masses' and his

'Mister Horn entertaining a group of youngsters'
*by Charles Tresidder (*Mister Horn...*)*

'willingness to work in any pulpit, and thus aid in breaking down the exclusive system of our churches' as the features of his work that had met with the particular approval of his friends and parishioners.[7] As can be imagined from the above, Mark Guy was generally fully employed during his two years in Ipswich. When not working, though, he found 'healthful recreation'[8] as he put it, both day and night, on the River Orwell, indulging his passion for fishing.

It was here, too, that he first began seriously to think of writing, and it is to the book which first brought him to the notice of the general public that we must turn for an inside and highly entertaining view of those two years, for the characters from *Mister Horn and His Friends* were real men and women who lived in the Suffolk villages where Mark Guy lived and worked. One such, as we have seen, was builder James Fulcher. Born at Peasenhall in the early 1800s, he enjoyed a fairly affluent life-style in the large house that he built for himself and his family at Tattingstone, surrounded by several acres of land and with a tennis court just across the main road.[9] A few years after the opening of a second chapel in the village in 1842, Thomas and William Keeble, both staunch Nonconformists, took farms in the neighbourhood and joined the Wesleyans.[10] It was with one of the brothers that Mark Guy used to stay when he preached in Tattingstone, sometimes marching around the room with one of his host's little boys on his shoulder and singing as he went![11] Fulcher's fictional counterpart, Mister Horn – the Mister to be written in full – began life as a farm labourer and had turned his hand to a succession of jobs – woodman, gardening, bricklaying and building – before reaching a good position as steward.

The particular charm of *Mister Horn and His Friends* lies in the author's portrayal of a whole host of characters. Mister Horn, himself, he describes as 'a little sharp wiry man, with a quick kindly eye, a mouth well shut, short legs walking so fast that they seemed always afraid of being left behind; carelessly dressed, yet everything about him looking like a part of the man himself, from his short-bowed neckcloth, to the strong unpolished walking-stick. A sort of compressed man. You felt that there might have been a good deal more of him fairly enough, but nature had dried him and packed him up small that he might not be in the way… It is your terrier that does most good – amongst men as amongst dogs – sharp-eyed, sharp-eared, sharp-tongued, and if needful, sharp-toothed; quick to smell a rat. Mister Horn was precisely that. Never in the way and good for a hundred things, if you took him right. If you didn't, he was a terrier still – he bristled and showed his teeth.'[12] James Fulcher's brother, Henry, lived in the little village of Holbrook, south of Ipswich, though Mark Guy does not mention him in his book. James frequently visited his brother and in the early years of the twentieth century, the villagers recounted how, as children, they used to gather on the village green and listen spellbound to the stories that he would tell them. One lady in particular remembered how his coming to

Holbrook was always a red-letter day, how he often took her on one knee and another little girl on his other knee while half the children in the village gathered round him. Then he would produce a packet of sweets and pass them round, and while the children munched away, he would tell one of his wonderful stories and make them cry and laugh in turn.[13] The Rev. M. G. Pearse obviously witnessed such a scene, either in Holbrook or in another village, for in *Mister Horn…* he described how the children of Tattingham 'trotted along by his side, looking up for a smile and a nod; the boys stopped him for a moment to fling their peg-top, or to have a turn at marbles; and on a summer's evening one might come upon a group under a shady tree, and there amidst a lot of delighted youngsters would find Mister Horn entertaining them with a story'.[14] As we have seen, giving was the cornerstone of Mister Horn's Christianity and the theme of Mark Guy's book. Indeed, 'A Homily of Mr Horn's', in which he preaches a sermon on the subject in Tattingham chapel, was published as a tract a couple of years before *Mister Horn and His Friends*. James Fulcher was instrumental, too, in the effort to build a third Wesleyan chapel in Tattingstone, one that would be an ornament and a credit to the village. He was supported in this by Thomas and William Keeble and others, with the new chapel being opened in April 1877.[15]

Chief among Mister Horn's friends was 'Old Friend Chaffer' of Hillingsham, whose portrait by Charles Tresidder appears on the cover of the illustrated edition of Mark Guy's book and who, in real life, was a Mr Chaplin of Chattisham. The admiration that Mister Horn and Chaffer had for each other usually expressed itself in the same terms, each being a 'wonder' to the other. Once again, Mark Guy has left us with an unforgettable picture of the farm labourer who, on ten shillings a week, had brought up a family of eleven children before he retired, at the age of seventy, on the princely parish allowance of five shillings a week:

> A little bent old man, with flat feet that shuffled along uneasily was what one saw at the first glance… As he shuffled nearer there was disclosed a figure quaint in feature, expression and dress. The hat, that once held the skull of an eminent divine, accommodated itself to this smaller head by lying back until it almost rested upon his shoulders and projected in front immediately above the eyes, just a fringe of flat hair marking the line of separation. Underneath was a pair of as pleasant eyes as ever

*'Old Friend Chaffer' by Charles Tresidder (*Mister Horn...*)*

> merry wrinkles played around; the cheeks and dumpy nose were scorched into a permanent glossy redness; the mouth, large and sunken, was fixed into an unchangeable smile that seemed to give a twist to all he said, making the husky sentences end in a sort of little laugh. A velveteen coat with sporting buttons hung in folds around the little old man. The trousers might have laid claim to all the privileges of apostolical succession, and like the doctrine itself, had to be much patched from many sources.[16]

Foreign Missions were Chaffer's passion, and although he had but five shillings a week to live on, for rent, food, heating, clothing and, of course, class money, he still managed to collect £1. 12s. for his chosen cause. As Mark Guy points out, it is hard for us to envisage just what this sum meant. It was the result of a year's hard and often painful work; miles of walking and many hours of waiting for a shilling or less; garden produce lovingly tended and eagerly sold for a few pence. One of Chaffer's most celebrated converts was the parson of the parish who was so impressed by his devotion and determination, that he promised him five shillings a year, a sum to which his wife added another half-crown. On his death in September 1876, Father Chaplin, who lived in a little cottage adjoining the Wesleyan chapel, was described in glowing terms by *The Suffolk Chronicle* as one whose presence was 'a power itself', whose life was 'a fine example of poverty sanctified by Christian graces' and who was 'for many a long year recognised as a real ornament of the little flock at Chattisham'.[17] Mark Guy's affection for this 'little flock' shines through in his short but compelling description of the strange band that led the singing in the little white-washed chapel:

> There was a clarinet which tried to make up in zeal what it lacked in skill; and the fiddle – the fickle fiddle! – that had its periodical fits of goodness, and then was periodically reported 'to have given up religion and gone to church'.[18]

Although, according to Morley Adams, the musicians' playing did not survive into the twentieth century, the meal which was enjoyed in the vestry after the morning service, did, and around 1908 was partaken of in much the same manner as it had been forty years earlier. In writing *Mister Horn and His Friends* Mark Guy did not bring the characters into being from the regions of his imagination. They are too real to be simply creations of the mind – real men and women whom he knew and loved, and whose hospitality he experienced at first hand.

When it was learned that Mr Pearse was leaving the circuit, it was felt by several prominent figures in Ipswich that a public farewell should be arranged. Indeed, his popularity was so great that it was realised that something on a grand scale was needed. Although, when approached, Mark Guy characteristically asked that the proposal be abandoned, eventually Mr Edward Grimwade offered to lay on a breakfast at his own house where representatives of the different institutions of the town could assemble to say their farewells. Among those present at Norton House was Mark Guy Pearse senior who saw his son receive a copy of *Lange's Commentary on the Acts*, elegantly bound in two volumes. Presenting him with the gift, John Glyde junior described him as a valued friend who, during his two years with them, had striven to make religion rather than theology the foundation of Christian brotherhood, whose cultured mind had made dealings with him a privilege and who, in the pulpit, on the platform and in social circles had shown himself their helper, friend, counsellor and guide. In reply, Mark Guy admitted that when he started in the ministry, he resolved not so much to make Methodists as to proclaim the gospel of Jesus Christ. To make people happy was his great concern, and to help all who were struggling to overcome bad habits, and to live a new life, under a Divine power. He believed that the Christian minister was bound above all men to take an interest in whatever was calculated to be of use or benefit to his fellow-men.[19]

Shortly after leaving Ipswich, Mark Guy journeyed north to attend the Wesleyan Methodist Conference which met that year in Hull. The public examination of candidates for ordination was held on the evening of Monday 2 August at Kingston Chapel and Waltham St Chapel where he was one of forty young men in attendance. Having spent four – or, in Mark Guy's case, six – years on probation, the candidates had been recommended for ordination by district meetings in various parts of the country. Although they had already, during the Conference, undergone a searching private examination, they were subjected to a public one in theology and each had also to address the gathering. In his address, Mark Guy said that his heart was 'almost overwhelmed' when he thought of the way in which God's goodness had led him to that place. Among his earliest recollections was going with his father to see an old woman, 105 years of age, who had served God ever since she was eleven years old and had received her class ticket from John Wesley himself. The centenarian whom, as we have seen, he later immortalised in his lecture 'Some Old Folks at Home' and in the best-selling tract 'Old Rosie', laid her hand on his head and appealed to God to make him a preacher. He recalled, too, how the good advice that he had received from Thomas Collins and from some of the ministers present on the platform had seemed to bid him to be God's boy. He and a school friend had agreed that they would tell no one about their feelings, but would always judge what God would like them to do, and try to do it. While he was at school among the Moravians, his whole soul had tried itself by the test, 'What would God have me do'. On being sent to Wesley College, Sheffield he gave himself to Christ after only a few weeks and was filled 'not with joy, but with unutterable peace'. He now made a formal commitment – body, spirit, and soul – to God, and it was his only wish, 'to live to God, and to do his work as He would like it done'.[20] Three days later, on the morning of Thursday 5 August, two services for the ordination of the ministerial candidates took place, and again, it was Waltham Street that Mark Guy attended. *The Methodist Recorder* for 10 August provides us with a detailed account of the proceedings. With the central pews in the body of the chapel reserved for ministers and the candidates themselves, members of the congregation and their friends occupied the gallery and side pews. The candidates were divided into four groups, each of which was, in turn, directed to the communion rail, where they knelt and were 'solemnly ordained by the imposition of hands'. Each minister was presented with a neatly-bound copy of the Bible, which was placed in his hands by the Secretary of the Conference who said, as he did so, 'Take thou authority to preach the Word of God, and to administer the Holy Sacraments in the congregations.'

It was at the 1869 Hull Conference, too, that the Rev. M. G. Pearse – together with John Bonser, W. Fisher Clark, John Burgess and supernumeraries Peter Samuel and John Ralph – was appointed to the Bedford and Ampthill circuit of the Wesleyan Methodist Church. Accompanying the Pearses and their three young daughters when they moved to Bedford that autumn were their 22-year-old Suffolk-born cook from Wickam Market, Ann Cox and Jane Smith, a 19-year-old nursemaid from Wetheringsett. In April 1871 the family were living at 30, Ampthill Street[21] and there is no reason to suppose that this was not the property that Mark Guy was referring to when, before the move, he wrote to his wife:

> This morning Mr Grey took me over the house. They have really done well for us. The drawing-room is a large room, and they are furnishing it well. There is a Brussels carpet and new red drawing-room chairs. I am sure we shall be very happy. My only fear is about the people's great expectations.[22]

His reputation obviously preceded him and grew rapidly during the three years he spent in Bedford, then a relatively small town with a population of some 16,000 people. One writer called his appointment 'epoch-making both in his own history and that of the circuit' and went on:

> The town of Bedford... was the scene of a remarkable revival of religion. Scores and hundreds of people were manifestly brought under the influence of the truth, and professed conversion. The revival was prolonged and progressive, and singularly free from extravagant excitement. It was a religious movement which flowed along the ordinary channels of church organisation, but in such extraordinary volume as to overflow their

> banks. Mr Pearse's ministry was made an unspeakable blessing to large numbers, and his own religious life was deepened and intensified.[23]

An example of this is Mark Guy's own story of how, one winter's night, he was walking home from a preaching appointment in a Bedfordshire village:

> My companion was an old labourer, whose way lay for a mile along the road, and whose company was always a joy to me when I preached at that little place. I can see him now – the tall, thin figure, somewhat bent with years and toil; the dark smock-frock, and the tightly-buttoned leggings reaching down to the heavy boots. His face, always lit with a smile, was reddened with the sun and winds in which he spent his days. Working away in the stillness of the fields he mostly had none to talk to but his God, and that blessed opportunity he turned to such account that he grew rich indeed in wisdom and grace. We had walked in silence for a while, for thinking was more in his way than uttering his thoughts, when he stopped and turned to me: "I been turning over a thing, sir, that I should like to say to you."
>
> "What's that, friend?" I asked.
>
> "Well – I been thinking that if you and me only knew all about everybody else, there is nobody in the world that you and me would change with."

Because they reached the spot where their ways parted before Mark Guy had his answer ready, he promised his companion that he would turn the thought over in his mind and discuss it with him when they next met. He soon came to see that it was 'a master truth to which all things did homage' and which 'opened new avenues of beauty'. 'Day after day,' he continued, 'it lived in me and interpreted the mysteries of life. My heart found in it a strength and a new song.'[24]

He achieved a great success at the annual meting of the local Agricultural Society, where his response to the toast of 'The clergy and ministers of other denominations' was much talked about. Many of the farmers who heard his speech went to hear him preach, and when the Royal Agricultural Show was held in Bedford in 1874, 10,000 copies of his tract 'Can I be Saved?', sales of which had by the end of the decade reached nearly 100,000, were given away at the gates. The following day – during what was obviously a return visit to the town – he preached to a

C.H. Spurgeon

large gathering of the Bedfordshire Union of Christians, which included about thirty ministers, among them the Baptist preacher and evangelist Charles H. Spurgeon. 'I got on comfortably,' wrote Mark Guy a year or two later. 'Then came dinner with Mr Spurgeon. He and I seemed to become rather thick, for before the day was over he asked me to preach for him in the Tabernacle[25] on Sunday morning, June 2. The deacon attending him pressed me to do so, and added that Mr Spurgeon had never asked a Wesleyan minister to do so before. It was, I am quite sure, the flattering estimate that Mr Fred Howard had been pouring into his ear that so stirred him in my favour.'[26] In the event, Mark Guy was not able to oblige, but over the years a close friendship developed between the two men which resulted in an occasional exchange of pulpits. And it was Spurgeon who preached the first sermon in St James's

Hall on the opening of the West London Mission in October 1887. On his death five years later, Mark Guy held a memorial service at St James's for the man he described as 'the foremost preacher of the age'. Spurgeon obviously had a profound influence on both his fellow-preacher's thinking and on his methods. On a more personal level, Mark Guy related how he had never picked up one of Spurgeon's sermons without finding his soul 'quickly aglow with love and praise'.[27] Fortunately, Mark Guy took the opportunity to convey his admiration for and debt to his Baptist colleague when the occasion presented itself. 'Some years ago,' he wrote, 'I sat with him on the platform at the Tabernacle; and, in an interval during the meeting, I whispered to him, 'When I was a young fellow in London, I used to sit right over there, and hear you preach, and you will never know how much good you did me.' I cannot forget the bright light that came into his face as he turned to me, and said, 'You did?' 'Yes,' I replied, 'and I am so glad to have this chance of telling you of it. You used to wind me up like an eight-day clock; I was bound to go right for a week after hearing you.' He put out his hand, and took mine in it, and the tears brimmed to his eyes as he said, 'God bless you! I never knew that.''[28]

James and Frederick Howard were mainstays of the Cauldwell Street Methodist Church, Bedford. Indeed, it was whispered at their Britannia Ironworks that a regular attender there had a better chance of becoming a foreman than had a non-chapelgoer.[29] Knighted in 1895, Frederick Howard would probably have reminded Mark Guy of businessmen such as George Smith and Charles and Josiah Thomas whom he had known as a boy in Camborne. Their friendship appears to have been a close one, for *Mister Horn and His Friends*, which was published during 1872, was dedicated to 'Frederick Howard, Esq., J.P. of Bedford, who, amid pressing claims of business, ever affords to the Church of Christ, what is so much more than gifts of money, his constant interest, his time and himself'.

Published initially in installments in *The Methodist Messenger*, *Mister Horn...* was Mark Guy Pearse's first popular success and marked the beginning of a writing career that spanned more than half a century. The *Buffalo Christian Advocate* described it as 'a splendid medicine for stingy people' which would do everyone good, while, nearer home, *The Bedfordshire Times* deemed it 'a good story, given in a telling style, conveying practical instruction and healthy sentiment'.[30] *The Christian Miscellany* could not decide whether to admire most 'its combined humour and pathos, the perfect naturalness of the narrative, or its sound and wholesome moral'. 'For pungent, pithy plainness of speech,' the reviewer continued, 'it is quite equal to Mr Spurgeon's most popular work *John Plowman's Talk*.[31]

Although Mark Guy was at this time a moderate drinker whose conversion to total abstinence was still some years away, in the early stages of his thinking on the subject he came to see that teetotalism was a capital thing for the working classes. This viewpoint is reflected in one of his earliest pieces of writing, 'Harry's pint; or, Threepence a-day', which was first published in *The British Workman* in January 1872. It is the story of how Harry, the ostler at The Green Man Inn, signs the pledge after hearing the author preach, and thereafter uses the sum that he had previously spent on a pint every day 'for the good of the house' to ensure that his family are well provided for with flour and coal. The incident later became an integral part of Mark Guy's lecture 'How I became a Teetotaller'.

Something that endeared Mark Guy Pearse to scores of people was the homely side of his nature – his ability to make himself at home wherever he was. He himself loved to tell the tale of how once, when he was in Cornwall, he was sitting in 'a body's house' when there was suddenly a knock at the door. His host got up, went to the door and said, 'Yes, come in, Mrs Jenkins; there's nobody here but Mr Pearse, an' he's nobody.' He confessed to being gladdened by his host's response, feeling prouder than if he had been made a Doctor of Divinity. It made him feel, too, that there was no dividing-line between the preacher and the layman.[32] On another occasion he left Bedford one Tuesday afternoon to walk the six miles to Hollrock where he was due to preach in the evening. There he found the Methodist family who were to look after him, sitting down to their evening meal. Asked if he would like a cup of tea, he joined them and replied, 'I should like some of that dish'! He enjoyed the rabbit and pork stew with dumplings so much that afterwards, it seems, he wrote and asked for the recipe. Unfortunately, though, what his own cook, Ann, produced was nothing like the dish he had enjoyed so much at Hollrock![33]

We have already seen how Charlotte and Ann Hingston discovered with joy how thoroughly at home Mark Guy Pearse could be with children. Many years later, in a letter to Emmeline Pethick-Lawrence, he recalled another child who was, in her words, 'one of many in whom he awoke a passion of love and adoration'. 'Fifty years ago or so (!),' he wrote, 'I was at Bedford and in one of the country places I stayed at a farm-house where an old uncle had adopted a little niece of some ten years. He was a surly man who did not care for children. It seems that I won her heart by some bits of notice, told her stories and filled a little book with sketches, and sometimes when I went fishing on the farm I took her with me. We parted and I heard no more of her. By chance Guy and Elsie [his son and daughter-in-law] got to know her, found her engaged in some literary work and invited her for Christmas. 'How I worshipped your father,' she told them – *for it was my little maid of fifty years ago*!'[34]

It was with considerable regret that Mark Guy Pearse left Bedford to return to London.

Chapter 6

'From the dainty suburbs to the reeking slums'

Highbury and Westminster 1872–1876

In the second half of the nineteenth century, London's expansion was aggressively suburban, with the well-to-do the first to move out of the centre in order to build solid, comfortable mansions within easy walking distance of their local railway station. Next, thousands of clerks, shopkeepers and small wage earners began to seek villas a little way out of town. North of the river the railway reached Wood Green in 1859, Highgate in 1867 and Finsbury Park two years later, with the result that the countryside began to disappear and the villages were absorbed into a suburban sprawl, relieved here and there by open spaces.[1]

In 1870, two years before the Rev. Mark Guy Pearse was appointed by Conference to the Highbury Circuit, a young girl by the name of Molly Hughes, whose mother was a Vivian from Reskadinnick near his home town of Camborne, moved with her parents and brothers into a big house in Canonbury. Her memories help us to picture the area in which he lived and worked for three years. 'No London child to-day [c. 1934],' she wrote, 'can realise the quiet of the road on which my window looked. A tradesman's cart, a hawker or a hurdy-gurdy, were the sum total of the usual traffic. Sometimes everything had been so quiet for so long that the sound of a passer-by or of a butcher's pony would take on a distant, unreal tone, as if it were mocking me.'[2] Sometimes, when the weather was particularly bad, the family went to a church nearby instead of walking all the way to St Paul's Cathedral. Molly Hughes remembered one of the old vicar's sermons about Ahab who had built himself an ivory palace. Modern businessmen who were similarly extravagant, he argued, would themselves come to a bad end. The words, 'You successful merchants, who build unto yourselves your ivory palaces in Highbury New Park...' she found particularly puzzling because, knowing the road from end to end, she had never noticed a house in any way resembling an ivory palace! The Pearses and the Hugheses would have had a great deal in common, though one major source of disagreement, had they ever met, would have been religion. For Mr Hughes, who worked in the Stock Exchange, did not, it seems, care which of the many places of worship his young family attended as long as it was not a 'schism shop', by which he meant anything Noncomformist![3]

It was, then, in all probability to 45, Grosvenor Road, Highbury New Park[4] that Mark Guy Pearse moved in 1872 in order to minister to a wealthy and influential congregation at Mildmay Park, but a stone's throw from Richmond Road, where he had lived seven years earlier. His colleagues during that first year in what was then, perhaps, the foremost circuit in London, if not in the Connexion, were already men of some reputation, two of them – John Walton and Robert Young – later both occupying the chair of the Conference. And it was during his stay here that Mark Guy himself emerged from comparative obscurity into prominence and popularity. Highbury was already a large circuit with chapels in Caledonian Road, Wood Green and Seven Sisters' Road in addition to those at Highbury and Mildmay Park. It was in these, in neighbouring circuits such as Hackney and City Road and, more occasionally, in those across the river that Mark Guy worked, though in order to concentrate ministerial efforts and modify the itinerancy as much as possible, each minister occupied his own pulpit once every Sunday besides taking the mid-week service.[5] A handsome Gothic building capable of seating about 1,150 people, Mildmay Park Chapel had been consecrated in October 1862,[6] one of the first to benefit from the Metropolitan Wesleyan Chapel Building Fund which had been established the previous year by Sir Francis Lycett.

Some ten years later the fund was a potent force in London and services and public meetings were frequently held to raise money for the task that it had set itself, namely to build fifty chapels in areas where Wesleyanism was noticeably weak. To this end, on 12 January 1873 the Rev. M. G. Pearse preached at Finsbury Park at 11 o'clock and at Highbury at 6.30 pm. He also offered prayers at a public meeting the following Wednesday.[7] Ten months later he was present when his close friend James Howard MP laid the first memorial stone of a new chapel at Green Lanes, Highbury New Park, the latest of four that had been built in the circuit within the previous seventeen years. At a public meeting that same evening, the Rev. John Walton said that the circuit had reached its maximum development and become virtually unmanageable. He appealed to those present to complete the current scheme by building the chapel at Green Lanes and another at Finsbury Park, and then the circuit would be ripe for division into three. Mark Guy congratulated the friends on the success of the day's services and thanked Sir Francis Lycett for his generosity and for the trouble he had taken on behalf of the chapel-building scheme. The rest of his speech took the form of a rallying-cry that showed precisely where he stood on some of the doctrinal issues of the day. He 'rejoiced that there was life yet in their dear old mother Methodism; they wanted true devotion, faith in the good old ways, an earnest belief in the Gospel which she preached, greater faith in entire consecration to God, and then he believed they would see her most glorious days. They had in Methodism an uncorrupted Gospel truth that had not been polluted; it had come to this generation as simple and pure as when John Wesley went out to preach it; they just pointed to the cross and cried, 'Behold the Lamb of God, that taketh away the sin of the world'. He was blowing the 'Methodist trumpet' now, and might as well blow a good blast whilst he was about it. Methodism would meet Broad Churchism; the best thing to upset that was experience of the heart; and as for High Churchism, if the heart rested upon God, it wanted no priest to step in. He had no fear of High Churchism if there was in the heart an earnest love to [*sic*] Christ, an entire consecration of themselves and all they had to God's service'.[8] The dedication services at Green Lanes Wesleyan Chapel began on Friday 15 May 1874 and continued until the end of June, with the Rev. M. G. Pearse preaching on the evening of 17 May.[9]

During his time at Mildmay Park, Mark Guy threw much of his energy into the weeknight service and succeeded in attracting phenomenally large congregations as a result. He paid particular attention to the children and young people in his charge, once a month devoting the service to them. Their hymns were used, prayers were very brief and simple, and the lessons explained in a way that would interest and instruct them. The specially prepared sermons were later published in a volume that he dedicated to 'the boys and maidens of Mildmay Park

Chapel'. As he explained in the preface to *Sermons for Children*,[10] there was no difficulty in making the first service a success. An announcement from the pulpit on the previous Sunday secured the services of the best advertisers in the world, the children themselves. They told their schoolfellows and friends, and thereafter it became easy to get hundreds at the monthly service. An added bonus – for all concerned – was that it broke up the monotony of the week evening services. The adults, some of whom were not 'great scholars', enjoyed the format, finding it something of a novelty 'in these very learned times' to hear a sermon which could be easily understood. Parents often accompanied their children and, in many instances, came in due course to attend chapel regularly. Last, but by no means least, was the benefit that the preacher himself derived from such services:

> To try and come down to the level of the little ones, to be gladdened by the sight of so many bright and interested faces, to become a child again in sympathy and thought, and to have the children's love so generously given in return – not many things will check so effectually as this all tendencies to dry-rot in the pulpit.

Mark Guy hoped that publishing the sermons would do further good, and suggested that Sunday evenings at home with the children could scarcely be more profitably employed than in holding such a service, provided that there was plenty of singing, a simple prayer, a chapter read, verse by verse, all round, and then the children's sermon. Such sentiments were echoed by the press when *Sermons for Children* was published for the Wesleyan Methodist Sunday School Union by the Conference Office which, towards the end of 1875, advertised it as 'The Best Christmas Present or New Year's gift for boys and girls'.[11] 'Racy, tender, sparkling, full of good thoughts which a brisk brain conceives,' enthused the *Methodist Recorder*. 'We give this little volume no stinted praise. It has caused us to wish to be young again... Surely the author has a vocation to the little ones, which he will do well to cultivate. He will strike those of larger growth by the way.'[12] As far as the *Sword and Trowel* was concerned, there was no better book for mothers who were in the habit of reading to their children.[13] It is difficult for us today to understand the runaway success of a volume such as *Sermons for Children*, which went into many editions. However, it must be remembered that from the middle of the nineteenth century onwards there was a rapid expansion

AST summer I stood at a little spring that was the beginning of a great river. Away up amongst the heather hills and granite boulders, it came leaping up clear and beautiful, where the ferns hung over it, and the wild birds came to drink. So the river began. Then almost immediately it seemed to be lost in a quag-

Charles Tresidder's illustration for 'Happy Work for Everybody' (Sermons for Children)

in children's reading of both the middle-class, 'respectable' variety and the cheap and sensational 'blood and thunder' magazines and novelettes. Organisations such as the Religious Tract Society were intent on harnessing this huge market and on competing with the penny dreadfuls, which were thought to be a corrupting influence on young people from all walks of life. To this end they created the very successful *Boy's Own Paper*, to which Mark Guy contributed 'Bass fishing at Bude' and two other pieces in 1879.[14]

Most of Pearse's writing was characterised by a healthy moral tone and imbued with direct religious teaching. It was something he never tried to hide. 'All the sermons,' he wrote, 'are aimed at this [the salvation of the children], and without this they will be the worst of failures.'[15] Although anecdote and moral are perhaps not as cleverly interwoven as the *Sword and Trowel* would have us believe, sermons such as 'The Valley of Decision' and 'A Question to ask and answer' do have a charm of their own and can, as we have seen in the case of the former, throw some light on their author's life. Of particular interest is 'Happy work for everybody', in which Mark Guy uses as one illustration of the need to praise the Lord, the story of Michael Verran, who was born in the Cornish parish of Kea, between Quenchwell and Baldu, in 1808. Under his mother's influence, he became a Methodist, growing up in close association with the Bible Christian Society. In 1837 copper ore was discovered at Caradon, near Liskeard, and Verran, who had spent his early years in the tin mines of his native West Cornwall, moved there soon afterwards to help exploit the deposits. Early one August morning in 1842 he walked the ten miles to Caradon, probably in the company of his fellow workman Peter Roberts, who was eight years his junior and a member of the Wesleyan Society at Callington. Once down the mine, the two men made their way to the rock face by the light of the candle that each carried stuck in his hat. Mark Guy takes up the story:

> He and his companion had bored the hole for the powder. Then they laid the fuse which was to light it, and cut that with a stone. It lighted at once, and each ran to the bucket that was waiting, and called to the man above to pull them up. He could not turn the handle with the two men in it, and called to them that it must be one at a time. They heard the fuse slowly hissing. They knew that in a moment more the explosion would come. They looked at each other – which should go up? Then, stepping back, the one said, 'You have little ones, I have none. Go on; another second and I shall be in Heaven.' The man whom I knew stept in and was drawn up the shaft. Directly there came the thunder, and the great mass of rock was hurled in a hundred pieces – one little piece flew up the shaft and struck my friend upon the forehead; and when he told the story he would lift his hat and point to the place where it had struck him. Then, as the smoke cleared, they came down the shaft to look for the mangled remains of this man. 'You can't tell, Sir, what I felt when I came down again,' the miner would say with tears. 'Why he had laid down his life for me and my little ones! How could I love him enough? Well, we began to search with axe and crowbar, heaving back the stones, when, as we lifted one great mass of

> rock, there we found him covered by a piece that had been shot out against the wall of the shaft, and roofed him over, so that he was not hurt a bit. Do you think I could thank him enough and be glad enough to see that he was not hurt?[16]

Verran's actions that day won him the admiration of Thomas Carlyle who, with the assistance of Caroline Fox, John Sterling and John Stuart Mill, in December 1842 drew up a petition to help him financially.[17]

It is clear simply from scanning the pages of the *Methodist Recorder* that Mark Guy Pearse was a very busy man during these years. In addition to the ordinary demands of office, which were by no means light, his increasing popularity brought extra claims on his time and energies. He was a popular choice, of course, for Sunday school anniversaries, sometimes preaching both morning and evening, as well as addressing the scholars in between. The Rev. Samuel E. Keeble[18] heard him address the children of the famous Radnor Street Schools at their anniversary in City Road, when the old chapel was crammed to excess one afternoon. 'The original roof,' he recalled, '...was touched at the back of the far gallery by a line of youthful heads, with rapturous eyes gazing at Mark Guy Pearse as he delivered the children's address. I can see him crouching in the pulpit, watching a lion, majestic and stealthy, on the prowl round a missionary's caravan in the African desert. The wife, the children, and the missionary are terrified lest the lion should spring and break through the slight cover of the van. They kneel down and pray. A light breeze springs up and lifts the corner of the cover, and then falls, and the cover flaps resoundingly. The lion is arrested by it – regards it with a fixed gaze. It rises and falls again from the same cause. The old lion leaps back with startled steps. A third time the process is repeated, and the lion turns tail and flees in panic. I can see Mr Pearse now watching with terror the approaching lion, and now retreating to the back of the pulpit with the frightened monster, and finally turning his back as the lion tears off. The thousand children present held their breaths whilst this narration proceeded, and rejoiced at this answer to prayer. The play of feature, the charm of his smile, the light of his eye, and the felicity of his narrative-skill can never be forgotten by me.'[19]

At the beginning of 1874 he chaired the annual meeting of the Juvenile Missionary Association at Mildmay Park and distributed the prizes to those who had collected the most.[20] In May the *Methodist Recorder* reported that in Exeter Hall on the 11th, the reading of the report in which the work of the Metropolitan Ragged Schools came under review was 'marked by the usual absence of enthusiasm in the audience'. It was not it seems, until the Rev. M. G. Pearse began his brief address to the children that their attention was attracted. Taking up a position near the end of the platform, he declared that the worst thing anyone could be was double-faced, though he almost wished that he could be two-faced for a while, so that he might turn his back on no one. He proceeded to tell the story of a man who used to live in a place called Ill-content, where everything was wrong – his house, his wife, his children, the town, the country, the Queen, the government and the Church. One day, though, he heard someone preach who told him that what he wanted was a new heart. Having tried to mend it himself and succeeded only in making things worse, he at last acquired a new one. Overnight everything changed and the speaker recounted, to the great amusement of his audience, how the man afterwards met his children and remarked what very nice children they were, only to discover, to his surprise, that they were his own, who had hitherto seemed so bad. This and a similar experience with regard to his wife was used to show how great a change had come over everything and everybody since the man had moved to the land of Good-content.[21]

Exactly six months later, on the evening of Wednesday 11 November, he was one of several ministers who took part in the initial public meeting of the Wesleyan Methodist Sunday School Union at City Road Chapel.[22] On the anniversary of the Wesleyan Missionary Society he invariably preached, both morning and evening, at Caledonian Road, Richmond Road (Hackney Circuit) or Mildmay Park, in addition to taking a service for the young at 3 o'clock. The annual meeting of the Wesleyan Foreign Missions, a subsidiary of the Missionary Society, also laid claims to his services, at Caledonian Road in December 1873,[23] for instance, and Victoria Chapel, Barrow Hill Road, St John's Wood on the evening of Wednesday 13 January 1875. On the latter occasion he expressed his pleasure at seeing the children gain some recognition for raising nearly £1,000 towards the mission's income that year. They deserved a fair slice of the meeting. He hoped, too, that before long their branch would have its own Juvenile Missionary Association. To those present he posed a riddle. He proposed to take one word, and try to make a speech out of it. The word he had in mind was on every Bible, and yet if they looked from Genesis to Revelation, they would not find it. It was, of course, the word 'Bible' itself, where the B represented the

Book, the I, in the heart where the good seed was to be sown, the B, bringing forth, the L, Love and the E, everlasting. He went on to expand his explanation of each letter with a suitable story.[24]

Two months earlier, on Monday 23 November, he had attended the first anniversary of the Metropolitan Methodist Lay Mission and supported the resolution put forward by the President of the Conference, the Rev. Dr Punshon, 'That this meeting, in view of the appalling spiritual destitution of the metropolis, is of the opinion that the Methodist Churches in London should make a vigorous effort to take the Gospel to those who are not and cannot be reached by the ordinary agencies of the Church.' Agreeing that 'appalling spiritual destitution' was, indeed, rife in the city, Mark Guy told of how, at one public house not far from Green Lanes Chapel, a policeman had counted no less than 1,100 people entering one Sunday morning between 11 and 1 o'clock, while there was not a church or chapel in the neighbourhood that had 1,100 people in it. He stressed the need to increase the Mission's funds, before proceeding to tell the story of an old gentleman who, having been converted late in life, was asked to contribute to a certain cause. Saying that he would subscribe a guinea a year, he proceeded to count out 70 guineas, at which the collector looked surprised. 'But,' said the old man, 'I promised to give a guinea a year, and 70 years are already gone.' The mission, the speaker argued, ought to have started twenty years ago, and therefore he asked them to give liberally in order to make up for the past.[25]

In his *Private lives, public spirit: Britain, 1870–1914*, Jose Harris describes the Nonconformist Churches as 'an aggressive and dynamic cultural and political force whose concerns… determined much of the agenda of public life throughout the 1860s and 1870s'. Certainly the idea that churches should save bodies as well as souls was already a commonplace among parish priests, dissenting ministers and city missioners in London at the start of the '70s.[26] At the annual meeting of the senior members of the Band of Hope in Exeter Hall on 7 October 1874, for instance, Hugh Price Hughes, Mr Pearse's future colleague in the West London Mission, described the essence of Christ's work as 'doing real, practical good to the bodies, minds, and spirits of men'.[27] Among the groups and denominations that were diversifying their labours into a variety of social and welfare schemes, was Thomas Barnardo who studied at Trinity College, Dublin before joining his father's furrier business as a clerk. Converted as a result of the evangelical revival that reached his home city from the north of Ireland in the autumn of 1861, he became acutely aware of the human suffering around him and, though only 17, started to devote his leisure time to social work and to preaching and Bible classes. As well as studying and qualifying as a doctor in the 1860s, Barnardo held Sunday prayer meetings in the streets and taught at a Ragged School in Ernest Street, just off Mile End Road, where in due course he became Superintendent. Early in 1868 he rented two small houses in Hope Place, and opened the East End Juvenile Mission, the forerunner of the Barnardo Homes. By October, there were weekly services for children, Bible classes for all, mothers' meetings and girls' sewing classes.[28] On Tuesday 8 December 1874 a public meeting took place at the Metropolitan Tabernacle, Newington Butts to publicise the work of the East End Juvenile Mission. Joining the Rev. C. H. Spurgeon and others in supporting Barnardo, the Rev. Mark Guy Pearse thanked God for what the doctor was doing and prayed that He might bless him in his work. He recounted how he had heard a story about the English poet William Cowper who, hearing a man respond very heartily in church on one occasion, reached across when he had finished and, putting his hand on his shoulder, exclaimed, 'God bless you, my friend, for praising the Lord so heartily'. In much the same way, as he looked at the boys and girls before him and thought of the life from which they had been rescued, he would say, 'God bless, you, brother Barnardo, for the work you have done for these boys and girls, and prosper you a hundred fold'.[29]

Other benevolent organisations which Mark Guy either helped raise funds for or supported in person were the Alexandra Orphanage for Infants, near Highgate, the Young Men's Christian Association, and the Young Men's Mutual Improvement Association at Mildmay Park, of which he was President. On one occasion a large audience of young men listened for upwards of two hours, 'enthralled by the eloquence and dramatic power of the orator', as he lectured on 'Chatterton the Poet; the Story of a Soul Adrift'.[30] Other popular subjects for lectures were 'Christmas' and 'Hugh Latimer, Bishop and Martyr' which during his time in London Mark Guy is known to have delivered to audiences in Hackney, Walthamstow, Spitalfields, Hampstead, Guildford and Green Lanes, as well as in Liskeard Chapel in Cornwall which he revisited at the end of June 1874. One young man who, in his early teens at the end of the nineteenth century, went to Studley Road Chapel in order to hear both the Latimer lecture and 'The Old Folks at Home', later confessed to being 'thrilled and amazed that an old gentleman could get all that out of his head'. 'I remember particularly,' he continued, 'his vivid account of the martyrdom of the burning of 'Little Bilney'...Then in the porch afterwards he was busy selling his books.'[31]

While the YMCA annual winter programme of lectures took place in Exeter Hall, the great Agricultural Hall in Islington was the venue for the Sunday afternoon services that had been inaugurated in 1868 for non-churchgoers by Thain Davidson, a Presbyterian minister. It is recorded that about 1,500 people listened to the Rev. M. G. Pearse's address there on 23 August 1874.[32] Both halls were used by American evangelists Dwight Moody and Ira Sankey when they reached London at the end of an extensive tour in the mid 1870s.[33] Prior to the first meeting of their four-month London campaign at the Agricultural Hall on 9 March 1875, prayer meetings were held daily at noon in the Conference Hall, Mildmay Park, to which Christians of all denominations were 'earnestly invited to pray a great blessing might attend the visit to London of Messrs Moody and Sankey'.[34] The Rev. M. G. Pearse was among those who presided over these meetings. Molly Hughes remembered her mother going to the Agricultural Hall to see the duo out of curiosity, her report to the family being that everything was 'too exposed' for her tastes![35] It appears that ministers from various denominations were appointed to lend support to the crusade by preaching on Saturdays at selected venues in central London, the evangelists' one day off. Mark Guy, for example, was the Saturday night preacher at the Victoria Theatre, New Cut, on 22 May.[36] He was almost certainly one of the six hundred ministers from all the major religious bodies in England who were part of a 2,500-strong audience of friends and supporters present at the pair's closing service in the Conference Hall at Mildmay Park on 12 July. Twelve years later he would accept Dwight Moody's invitation to tour North America.

It was during this second period in London that Mark Guy Pearse began to establish himself, too, as an author. Ever since *The Story of Billy Bray*, he had written both serious and light-hearted articles that had but one object, namely 'to show forth the beauty of holiness and to lead men to the Saviour'.[37] In between his first popular successes, *Mister Horn and His Friends* (1872) and *Sermons for Children* (1875), he contributed a stream of stories, articles and sermons to *The Methodist Recorder*, *The Methodist*, *The Methodist Pulpit*, *The Methodist Family*, *The City Road Magazine* and *The Wesleyan Sunday School Magazine* whose editorial council he had joined. February 1873 saw the publication of the temperance story 'John Tregenoweth: his mark', which quickly became a best-seller, and two new tracts entitled 'My old Friend John' and 'A Good Old Prescription. A cure for care'. 'Getting Saved', a tract for those seeking Christ, was issued by the Wesleyan Conference Office four months later. Elizabeth Wesley, the daughter of the Rev. Samuel Wesley, spent much of her short life working among soldiers in Gravesend, visiting them in hospital, holding services for them and writing thousands of letters to them. Writing to the Rev. M. G. Pearse on May 31st 1875, she recounted how a sergeant was saved from suicide and for Christ by reading his tract. She continued:

> We very often thank God that you ever wrote the tract entitled 'Getting Saved', for its simple teaching has been a great blessing to many sad hearts. The last year it has been my constant companion, for I knew that it could help sinners in seeking Christ far better than any words of mine... We have had several cases of conversion through reading that tract among civilians. The most blessed perhaps was that of a gentleman to whom I gave it some few months ago. He and his wife are now both earnest workers and members of our Church.[38]

This and a whole host of tracts, or 'Penny Books' as their author called them, were still working their magic forty years later when, in 1915, the Rev. W. H. Sarchet, Chaplain to the Forces, BEF, overseas, wrote to say how much good they had done, and how the men in hospital asked again and again, 'Have you got any more of those little books, sir? They were just all right!'[39] He also turned his hand to hymns, most of which were written during 1875 and published later that year, together with contributions from the Rev. G. S. Rowe, J. P. Dunmas, H. J. Foster and others, in a little volume entitled *The Child Jesus*. Of these, four were included in *The Methodist Sunday School Hymn Book* of 1879.

In terms of popular appeal, though, the high point of his writing career was the publication, on 21 December 1874, of *Daniel Quorm and his Religious Notions*. Dedicated 'To my Father, whose life has most endeared all that is truest and brightest and best in these pages', the work had appeared in installments in *The City Road Magazine* during that year and was advertised by the Wesleyan Conference Office under 'gift books for the season'[40] in order to cash in on the Christmas market. It enjoyed extraordinary success over the years – a new edition was published as late as 1927 – selling in excess of 100,000 copies in this country and achieving an even greater sale in America. A second volume of stories featuring the village shoemaker and his friends – also entitled *Daniel Quorm and his Religious Notions* – proved equally popular, both being read alike by the man in the street and the monarch. Indeed, with the passing of its author in January 1930, Miss Agnes Slack remembered staying a few years previously at the London home of her brother, Sir John Bamford-Slack, who, as a young law student, was a member of Hugh Price Hughes's congregation at Barry Rd. Chapel, Dulwich, and later became a circuit steward of the West London Mission. '...He told me one evening,' she wrote, 'that the Rev. Mark Guy Pearse had been to see him at his office that afternoon; and during conversation he informed my brother he had just met the Dean of Westminster, and that, on his asking the Dean after Lady Augusta Stanley (who was very seriously ill), the Dean replied: 'I left her this afternoon with Queen Victoria who, on entering the bedroom, said to my wife she had brought a book to read which has become a very great spiritual help to her – a book written by a Wesleyan minister' – and the Dean added, 'The book was your 'Dan'l Quorm'. I left the Queen reading it aloud.' Mr Pearse added it was cheering news to him to know that little book was helping people.'[41] So taken was Queen Victoria with *Daniel Quorm* that it seems she requested that all the other writings of its author should be added to her library.[42] Other contemporary opinions are to be found in a notebook[43] into which Mr Mark Guy Pearse copied items of sentimental value, including letters that his son received following the book's publication. 'My dear Sir,' wrote Canon Thynne,[44] 'I feel constrained to write you a line of thanks for a book of yours which I have just read, "Daniel Quorm". It opens to me ground which I had looked at through the hedge before. You have given me a "Photo" taken of course on a sunny day. Thank you all the more for it because it shews us that the true life of good people brings them into rapport with each other far more than they who only look at the outside imagine. Your chapter on meditation might have been written by Mr Carter, while Daniel jumping the gate would have appealed to Charles Kingsley and lay brother Lawrence would find in many a chapter the echo of his heart and experience. I have heard you are a fisherman – no one but a fisherman could have written it at all. God bless you and shew us all daily more and more of His truth and Himself.' In yet another letter to the author, a Gloucester doctor revealed how he had sent a copy of *Daniel Quorm* to a dying patient who, like other 'men of education', had found it 'a real help and blessing'. By way of proof – if such were needed – he enclosed a letter that he had received from the patient's daughter. 'Some time before my dear Father was taken from us,' she wrote, 'he was anxious that I should write to you again and tell you how in every way he was delighted with 'Daniel Quorm' – the simplicity of the book pleased him… and he seemed to see Christianity free from Priests and Priestcraft, ever a stumbling block to him. He told my husband when he went to sea again, he was to take a dozen copies of Daniel from home for the crew.'[45]

As I stressed earlier, much of *Daniel Quorm* is pure autobiography and brimming with local colour. Writing nearly twenty years after the publication of the first volume, H. Hawken described the work as being 'the most truthful canvas of Cornish life, with any pretension to size, yet painted, inasmuch as more than any other it emphasises the religious spirit which prevails [in Cornwall]'.[46] The Rev. T. W. Slater wrote in much the same vein in a short assessment of the author's career that he contributed to the *Cornish Guardian* in 1927:

> As a story of Cornish life and character, a picture of Westcountry Methodism, and an illustration of a Cornishman's loyal love for everybody and everything Cornish it is not easy to match and impossible to beat.'[47]

He also predicted a permanent place for it in Cornish literature on account of 'its perfect dialect', its Westcountry portraiture and its wit and humour, native of the soil'.[48] Although Mark Guy's name was still recalled with affection at Camborne Wesley in the early 1960s, subsequent changes in cultural and literary fashions have meant that his work, like that of many other Cornish writers, has been sadly neglected. It is to be hoped, though, that the formation of the Cornish Literary Guild and the high profile currently being enjoyed by Cornwall and the Cornish people will together contribute to a re-evaluation of such gems as *Daniel Quorm*. In speaking of the book's great success, its author considered that a certain amount of its popularity could be attributed to the illustrations of Charles Tresidder, a fellow Cornishman whom he happened to meet as a young man in London in the mid 1870s.[49] A Wesleyan and total abstainer, Tresidder became a member of Mark Guy Pearse's congregation, presumably at Mildmay Park. Learning that not only was he a fellow Cornishman with first-hand experience of Cornish Methodism and village life, but also an artist who engraved his own work, Mark Guy

Charles Tresidder's cover for Daniel Quorm and his Religious Notions

naturally saw in him the ideal illustrator for his writing.[50] In this way began a lasting friendship and an unusually perfect collaboration between writer and illustrator for, after *Daniel Quorm*, Tresidder worked on several of Mark Guy's books, including *Sermons for Children*, *Good-will: a collection of Christmas Stories* and *Simon Jasper*.

The young minister, then, found himself with little spare time. He was, in fact, overtaxing himself and failing to give his body and mind adequate rest. The itinerancy, the system whereby Methodist ministers are not only appointed to a circuit in order to 'itinerate' among the churches within its confines, but are also periodically moved on to pastures new, was a particular burden. Mark Guy's time in this prosperous circuit was drawing to a close. At the quarterly meeting at Highbury on Monday 28 June 1875, he received 'a cordial and unanimous vote of thanks for his valuable and successful services' during the previous three years.[51] A month later he travelled north to attend the dinner for 'old boys' of Wesley College, Sheffield, which he had helped to organise.[52] On Tuesday 10 August – with the Sheffield Conference finalising his future – he was invited by the members and congregation of Mildmay Park Chapel to join them for what turned out to be one of the largest and happiest meetings ever held there. After a public tea, Mr Edward Brown, who had been voted chairman for the occasion, spoke of the good work that had been carried out during the three years of Mr Pearse's ministry, and Mr Gerrans read an address that had been reproduced and beautifully illustrated in a handsomely-bound volume. Underlining the prosperity of the various departments of the chapels and schools, it acknowledged the devotion and success with which the Rev. M. G. Pearse had carried out his duties. It was supplemented by the reading of extracts from several letters which had been received from the various subscribers, among them Sir Francis Lycett. The leaving gift consisted of 'a very recherché silver tea set, enclosed in an oak chest. The ornamentation and inscription, including monogram and crest of Mr Pearse, were choice specimens of the engraver's art'. Also presented were a handsome walnut inkstand and blotting-book, a gold-mounted penholder, a silver, pocket communion service from one of the friends, and a beautiful cup and saucer from the young people. Making the presentation, Mr Wild spoke of the great love everybody felt for Mr Pearse and their deep regret at the prospect of his departure. In acknowledging the gifts, Mark Guy said that words failed to express how he felt about the great kindness that everyone had shown him from the very beginning of his ministry there. When the meeting was thrown open, a number of people, amongst them Mr Bourne, Superintendent of the Sunday school, 'testified to the great good they individually, and the institutions of the church generally, had received from the labours of Mr Pearse'.[53]

With his appointment to the Westminster circuit, the daily routines of Mark Guy's pastorate would have altered little, but the same could not have been said of the environment in which they were carried out. One source described his situation rather graphically as 'a striking change from the dainty suburbs to the reeking slums' where 'stolid indifferentism' took the place of middle class interest in social and religious questions.[54] Westminster Chapel in Horseferry Road was a large building, with a small congregation, situated in a very poor neighbourhood. Undeterred, he threw himself into the challenging work, doing his utmost to help many who were involved in a fierce struggle against want and temptation, and 'to arouse such a struggle in others who never found any heart and hope to begin it, and in others still who had lost all the heart and hope with which they had once begun'.[55] Preaching at the opening services of new chapels, celebrating Sunday school anniversaries, addressing missionary meetings and lecturing were still the order of the day. On Sunday 19 September he preached in a new chapel at Finsbury Park, which was presumably the chapel referred to by John Walton two and a half years earlier, and which had been recently opened thanks to the efforts of the Metropolitan Chapel Building Fund. A month later an advert in the *Methodist Recorder*, describing him as 'Author of *Daniel Quorm and his Religious Notions* etc', underlined his new found literary status.[56] His subsequent sermon at the public tea held to celebrate the opening of a new chapel out at Basingstoke was described as 'excellent and highly appreciated'.[57] Fund-raising meetings he was advertised to conduct in 1876 included those at Woolwich (Plumstead Common) on 26 January, Southwark (Peckham) the following evening and Lambeth (Clapham) a month later.[58] At the end of the first week of November 1875, he was on home ground, fronting the Sunday school anniversary celebrations at Horseferry Road, where he and his colleague, the Rev. Henry J. Foster, conducted five services or meetings between them over three days.[59] Two months later he was at Claverton Street Chapel, Pimlico, for the Wesleyan Day Schools' Anniversary services on 27 February when he addressed the scholars and their friends at 3 o'clock, before conducting the evening service.[60]

Where missions were concerned, he continued the sterling work that he had begun in Highbury, addressing himself whenever possible directly to the young. At the annual meeting of the Auxiliary Wesleyan Missionary Society for the London districts, which was held in Exeter Hall on the evening of Monday 11 October 1875, a packed audience included a thousand scholars from the Metropolitan Wesleyan Sunday Schools who were engaged to sing missionary hymns. Mark Guy moved the resolution 'That, in the openings for missionary work which more than ever appear in heathen countries, and especially in the spirit of revival vouchsafed to many districts, this meeting recognises a direct encouragement to earnest prayer, as well as a clear call to renewed effort for the conversion of the world to Christ'. Addressing the scholars assembled on the platform, he expressed his pleasure at seeing them at the meeting. It was something that he had long wanted to see, for the Missionary Society belonged as much to them as to anyone else. He went on to relate 'several telling anecdotes having a thoroughly missionary moral'.[61] Missionary-related work once again took him to adjoining circuits and, early in 1876, back to Ipswich where, on 24 January, a large gathering welcomed their 'old and esteemed friend'.[62] Exactly six weeks later he gave his well-known lecture on Hugh Latimer at Approach Road Wesleyan Chapel, Bethnal Green.[63]

With larger and constantly growing congregations attending his services, success seemed assured, but that spring his heath suddenly failed. On a personal level he had been overstretching himself for some time and, since settling in London, had begun to suffer from intermittent sleeplessness – one of the drawbacks, perhaps, of possessing both an artistic and a Celtic temperament. The Rev. C. Ensor Walters, a junior colleague at the West London Mission at the end of the 1890s, described the man whom he called 'my beloved master' as 'nervous and highly strung'.[64] And his daughter Frances has left us with the following honest analysis of what she called his 'variability of temperament':

> When his cheerfulness deserted him he was apt to go to the other extreme. Sleeplessness was his great trouble, and the depression it caused was natural enough. His habitual good spirits gave an impression of an equability which he never possessed. He lived at high pressure, and threw himself with intensity into whatever he undertook, and when sleeplessness followed he had no reserve of nervous strength, and paid for his success in exhaustion and misery. This nervous temperament was part of his make-up, but as time went on he was able to

> order his life so as to avoid strain, and consequently he suffered less.[65]

In the early days, the best remedy for the insomnia proved to be a few days of quiet and solitude in the country, away from the noise and bustle of the capital. These periods of rest not only served as a safety valve, but also had an impact on his preaching. Some twenty years later he recalled how he was going into St James's Hall one Sunday morning when a girl came up to him and said, 'Please, sir, are you going to preach a *Country Sermon* this morning?' 'A Country Sermon!' he replied, 'Well, I didn't know I ever preached Country Sermons.' 'Oh yes,' she said, 'I do like to hear a Country Sermon.' The encounter suggested a new purpose in a sermon, that of making it sometimes a Sunday excursion. Mark Guy felt that a man almost needed to live in the city to appreciate the full luxury of the country, where there was room to breathe. 'For us,' he wrote in the preface to one of his numerous books of essays, 'shut in by streets, and dwelling amid the ceaseless rush and roar, there is a charm in the great stretch of heaven and quiet beauty of the fields that others cannot know.'[66] In another publication he described thus the claustrophobia he experienced in the city and the release that leaving it behind brought:

> When one lives where there is nothing to be seen but the chimney pots opposite, and, by a cruel straining of the neck, a glimpse of smoke-stained sky above, it is almost as when the pilgrim lost his burden that a man stands under the great stretch of heaven, about him the wide expanse of earth.[67]

From the early 1870s onwards, these brief holidays were invariably spent with his close friend, Edward Pethybridge of Launceston, of whom he wrote on his death in 1907, 'There is no man I have ever known that I have loved more; always the same, so simple, so unselfish, yet so lofty in his ideal. Such sunshine was in his smile, such kindliness in all his ways, such a pleasant humour, that to be with him was a perpetual summer.'[68] It was from Edward Pethybridge that he learned to fly-fish for trout in the Inney or the Tamar. Although he had been familiar with sea-fishing from boyhood, fly-fishing was new to him and became the perfect recreation, combined, as it often was when he stayed with his friend, with long, moorland walks where the quiet, the solitude and the beauty of nature proved beneficial to both body and soul. Another spot that drew him when overwork brought on sleeplessness was Morwenstow, some six miles north of Bude, where he would stay with William Gregory Harris, another close friend. The need for stillness, solitude and relaxation was paramount. 'I am here luxuriating in this delicious quiet,' he wrote on one occasion. '...Sunday I stayed at home with my book and read aloud for a little while, but I found dizziness and exhaustion soon followed that. I must just exist, an animal existence, and leave my brains at home.'[69] Mark Guy became an enthusiastic follower of Isaac Walton and would become extremely animated when discussing what he called 'the cure for half the evils in life'.[70] The following description of the virtues of angling is from an interview he gave in 1899:

> Going after trout is splendid exercise, and you go home tired from head to foot, so that sleep comes to you without any coaxing. One wanders far afield in searching for the ideal trout stream, and, besides catching trout, you have splendid opportunities for thinking out your next sermon, while all the time you are enjoying delightful scenery and inhaling pure oxygen, with the ultimate result that you get home hungrier than any hunter...[71]

A man with a great sense of humour, Mark Guy used to say that there were two 'bridges' that gave him good fishing, a Pethybridge and a Bainbridge![72]

He was, too, a devoted father. In 1874, when his wife was away for a few days, he wrote, 'I have dear little Isabel sitting up beside me here, the image of darling mother, chatting away to the pictures. The others are very good. Maud is a beautiful little nurse, and has baby on her knee half the day long.'[73] Margaret Isabelle (Belle) had been born in Bedford, while 'baby' must have been Mark Guy junior, who was born on 3 September 1873. A second son and sixth child, John Warwick Guy, completed the family in the spring of 1875.[74] The pressure of being the head of a large and growing family, though, probably contributed to the unhappy situation in which the Pearses found themselves a year later. The circuit minister's house was generally roomy and old-fashioned, and often damp, with the result that Mrs Pearse twice suffered from rheumatic fever, as did the two eldest children. Indeed, a year or two of constant family illness preceded his eventual breakdown. In the spring of 1876, overwork again resulted in sleeplessness and on 17 May he was granted leave of absence by the committee of the Second London District meeting at Centenary Street, Bishopsgate Street.[75] Following a two or three week fishing holiday in Cornwall, he returned feeling much better and ostensibly fit for work, but later in the year he suffered a severe nervous breakdown. Addressing a devotional meeting in Wardour Hall eleven years later, he recalled the illness, and expressed the anxiety he had felt on returning to the capital:

> My former breakdown was so complete and so hopeless that when I got back to this busy metropolis I feared lest my old tremulousness and wretched nervousness might unfit me for all kinds of work among all sorts of people.[76]

Although, in the first draft of the Stations of Ministers, he was reassigned, together with Henry J. Foster, to the Westminster circuit by the Nottingham Conference, a week later Mark Guy Pearse was one of three ministers who were announced as retiring for one year.[77] In effect, he was appointed supernumerary to Kilkhampton[78] in north Cornwall, which meant that he could assist with circuit duties whenever he felt able to do so.

Chapter 7

'...its grand seas and glorious sunsets have become memories almost imperishable.'

Bude 1876–77

The Pearses had six young children to support, the eldest only nine years old, the youngest a little baby. Mark Guy's father, who had left Cornwall some seven years previously on the death of his wife and moved to London, was, it seems, unable to help, much of his money being tied up in Cornish mines, notably Dolcoath.[1] For at least a few days, then, the immediate future must have looked rather black. Then a telegram arrived from Edward Pethybridge offering them the use of his cottage at Bude for a year. A little later, a wealthy member of Mark Guy's congregation sent a generous donation, and this, in turn, was followed by an unexpected and substantial cheque from the Wesleyan Methodist Bookroom – proof of the fact that the British public were buying his books and tracts in their thousands. 'Instead of my lying awake wondering what I should do *for* money,' wrote Mark Guy, 'I was lying awake wondering what I should do *with* it!'[2]

Bude was at that time a small trading port twenty miles from Launceston, the nearest railway station. Lake Cottage, the Pearses' retreat, was situated near Poughill Churchtown on the north side of the bay, in what is now a prime holiday area. The rail journey from London was a long and trying one, and by the time they arrived at Launceston, Mark Guy was 'tired and worn out, the baby very ill and fretfull, and Jean, the eldest little girl, feverish and miserable'.[3] Tea with the

'The Chapel Rock, Bude' by L. Raven-Hill
(J. Henry Harris, Cornish Saints and Sinners*)*

Pethybridges would have provided some respite before the long drive to Bude. Even when they reached Lake Cottage, however, their troubles were not over, for Jean's illness proved to be scarlet fever and, with the exception of Mrs Pearse, the whole family gradually went down with it. What is more, local tradesmen refused to bring any provisions to the house, preferring to leave them where money and orders were left – on a little bridge nearby. Such an arrangement would be unthinkable today, but over a hundred years ago in a remote country area it worked. Even so, it often proved difficult to get the basic foodstuffs when they were needed, and had it not been for a kind farmer's wife who was not afraid to bring milk, butter and eggs to the house, they would often have gone short. Within a couple of months, though, they were well on the mend and thus began – for the children – 'the most blissful period they had ever experienced'.[4]

For the time being, at least, hated boarding schools were a thing of the past; indeed, there was no school for them to go to and no lessons either, as the nursery governess was fully occupied helping Mrs Pearse. When not rambling the length and breadth of Summerleaze and Efford Downs with their father whose 'endless store of knowledge about birds, flowers, cliffs, stars, and all the wonders of the universe'[5] was an education in itself, they ran and danced on the beach day after day. Mark Guy's health was gradually improving and under the influence of Bude's grand seas and glorious sunsets, he, too, was laying down what, years later, he described as 'memories almost imperishable'.[6] On 1 December 1876, he wrote:

> Every day the children have been by the sea, digging; yesterday and the day before there was warm sunshine. I was in a cave, and had lit a fire just outside with the driftwood on the beach, and sat there with my Bible and note-book jotting down a few thoughts that I have called 'A Bundle of Bude Lights'. I was summoned from my retreat to attend the funeral of a dead sea-bird that they had found. The grave was dug, and to the funeral dirge, 'Who killed Cock Robin?' he was tenderly laid to rest, and the pretty little grave was crowned with a cross of white stone.[7]

Frances, or 'Mab' as she was known, was six at the time and remembered many years later how each child had to be 'dipped by one or other of the very horny-footed old bathing-woman who constituted themselves the guardians of the beach...'[8] Two little white tents were provided for adults to change in, but the children undressed on the rocks. On one occasion a friendly donkey, who had made his way to the beach from the downs, helped himself to an immense bag of farthing saffron buns which were kept in reserve. The children were not the only ones to be caught by the tide. Mark Guy, who bathed in the deep pool cut into the rocks on the south side of the breakwater by local landowner Sir Thomas Acland, was on one occasion himself caught by a monstrous wave and was lucky to recover his socks, boots and trousers!

At certain times of the year sea-fishing from a boat is often difficult because of the heavy ground-swell at Bude even on the calmest day, and

*Illustration for 'Bass-fishing at Bude' (*The Boy's Own Paper, *1879)*

Mark Guy turned to alternative means of sport. Day after day his curiosity had been aroused by seeing a local man clambering over the rocks carrying a stout pole and line, and then coming back again five or six hours later with two or three large silvery bass. Encouraged by the response to his enquiries, he joined the old fellow on one of his expeditions. Shouldering his heavy rod, with its six or eight feet of line, and its large hook stuck in the crack of the pole, so as not to be in the way, they set off '[a]cross the grassy downs, sweet with the scent of wild thyme, and broken here and there with a bank of furze, covered with golden bloom; and then down the steep winding cliff-path, where the pole came in as a real help, and on to sandy beach, that was shut in by a ledge of rocks running right out to the breakers'.[9] From that day onwards, he was well and truly hooked, and 'sitting in all sorts of places, perched on rocks, where one's heels just got hold enough to keep one from sliding right down into the boiling sea below'[10] became second nature, though having been born and bred by the sea did not prevent him from being cut off by the tide on at least two occasions!

The rhyme 'From Padstow Point to Lundy light/Is a sailor's grave by day or night' is indicative of the extent to which shelter from storms is lacking along the north Cornwall coast. As naval historian Clive Carter revealed in his excellent study of Cornish shipwrecks, St Ives, Hayle, Portreath and Newquay were all dangerous to enter during an onshore gale, and Padstow and Bude Haven suicidal. What's more, because of rocks, sand-bars and the ever present Atlantic swell, their approaches could be just as deadly in calm weather. Although an exact count is impossible, Carter estimated that some 800 small sailing vessels, 200 larger sailing ships, 100 fishing boats and 94 steamers, exclusive of war losses, were wrecked on the stormy north coast between 1800 and 1920.[11] One such casualty was the local schooner *Elizabeth Scown*, which was wrecked on Bude breakwater on 3 March 1877, as she was bringing in a cargo of stone for the enlargement of the parish church. The Rev. M. G. Pearse's eyewitness account of the events provides a sobering contrast to the beach scene he described three months earlier:

> I got home about 9 o'clock, and, as I had to talk to the folks next morning, I hurried over my supper and then sat down to a quiet cigar to meditate on a text. Boots off, in slippers and dressing-gown beside a snug fire, I was just getting into my subject when I heard the bang of a loud report, and in came Mrs Wonnacott to say that a ship was gone ashore on the breakwater, and that the rocket apparatus had just fired a rope to the men. Of course, away went the slippers and off went the dressing-gown, and I was over the downs, seeing the glare of Blue [*sic*] Lights in the distance. Away down a steep sandy road on to the sands, and then away outside the farthest rocks I could just make out the sail of a ship. The ship was wedged right in between the rocks… As the tide was going out at the time, the men managed to step ashore, all except one, who was drawn ashore by the rocket apparatus. Meanwhile, however, the lifeboat had put out, not knowing in the darkness the position of affairs. They got through the breakers at the mouth of the harbour, and then were caught by a heavy sea and upset. All got back into the boat except one; the coxswain was missing. It is supposed that he must have been struck in some way by the boat. He was never seen again.[12]

James Maynard, the only crew member not wearing the regulation cork jacket, left a widow, who was heavily pregnant, and ten children, the youngest aged two, and the eldest a lad of fourteen or fifteen who attended the village chapel where he sang in the choir. Moved by the tragedy and by the plight of the now-destitute family, Mark Guy launched an appeal in both the *Methodist* and the *Methodist Recorder*, drawing the attention of their readers to 'a case that has a claim to much more than local sympathy and help'.[13] Within a week he had received £80, each post since the appearance of his letter bringing lots of donations, and in due course, enough money was raised to set Mrs Maynard up in business.

Although rest and relaxation were the order of the day, early on the Rev. M. G. Pearse was tentatively feeling his way back into the mainstream. Hitherto, there had been no morning service at the little chapel, and he took it upon himself to be responsible for one.[14] Mr J.W. Banbury of Bude recalled how, soon after his arrival in the village, Mark Guy began attending the weeknight prayer meeting, describing himself as an old hunter who could not refrain from joining in the chase.[15] As his health improved, he recovered the ability to write again and it was in Bude – and later in Launceston – that he became familiar with the character and dialect of east Cornwall, both of which feature so prominently in *Simon Jasper*. 'I am very thankful that I can write again comfortably now, and will send you a little sketch or two soon,' he wrote to his mother-in-law, probably in March or April 1877.[16] A summer by the sea completed the healing process, bringing health and strength to both himself and the children, and in the autumn of 1877 he officially resumed his ministerial duties, at Launceston under the Rev. Samuel Hutton.

The year that he spent at Bude was of critical importance as far as his health and spiritual and mental well-being were concerned. Indeed, it is doubtful that a year spent anywhere other than in his beloved Cornwall could have had the same, healing effect. But to what extent was this a two-way process? For many years the port's Wesleyan Methodists had been dissatisfied with the accommodation and position of the second chapel that had been built near 'The Villa' in the mid-1830s, and felt that they ought to have a better building in which to worship – one more in keeping with the growing position and importance of Methodism in the area. However, they were few in number and comparatively poor, and such an undertaking would need commitment and financing. Mark Guy's stay came just at the right time, for recognising the need for a bigger and better chapel, 'he espoused their cause and led them in the great enterprise. He scoured the country over on a lecturing tour – here, there and almost everywhere, this zealous and popular Cornish Preacher travelled, and devoted the proceeds of his lectures to the Bude New Chapel enterprise.'[17] Although the celebrity status he enjoyed as an ambassador for the West London Mission was still some years away, he had very definitely already 'arrived' as a preacher and speaker as far as his fellow-Cornishmen were concerned. Thanks to his efforts and those of the Bude Methodists themselves, a site was obtained on the west side of the river, at the foot of Shaldon Hill, between the river and canal. And about a year after leaving the area, Mark Guy was back on 1 August 1878, for the laying of the foundation stone of what one writer called 'the permanent memorial of his residence in the place'.[18] He spoke briefly about the reasons for building a larger chapel, before recalling his twelve months' stay in Bude, the many kind friends he had made there, and the involvement he felt in everything that affected the interests of the town. At the opening of a fund-raising bazaar that followed, he 'revitted [*sic*] the attention of his hearers for some time by giving an interesting account of the beginning of Methodism in Devon and Cornwall, and of early Methodist worthies'.[19] Later that same day, he was one of a number of celebrated Methodists who addressed a public meeting. Almost two years later Mark Guy returned to Bude once again for a lunch, covenant service and tea on the occasion of the chapel's opening on Friday 18 June 1880.

Chapter 8

'Do you happen, good reader, to know the old town of Dunheved?'

Launceston 1877–1880

Although Launceston was the administrative town of Cornwall until 1838 when the assizes were moved to Bodmin, the Wesleyan Methodist circuit centred on it was essentially a quiet country one. The Dingleys and the Pethybridges, two local families linked by business, religion and marriage, were pillars of Methodism in Launceston at the time, and they, together with Mark Guy's many other friends, did their best to guard him against too many extra engagements. The ancient stannary town was ringed around with chapels at villages such as South Petherwin, Egloskerry, Tregada and Yeolmbridge and, either walking or being driven in a Cornish 'jingle', he visited them all in turn. 'The congregations that gathered [in the little outlying chapels] were wholly agricultural,' he wrote in one of his stories, 'bringing with them the smell of a field that the Lord had blessed; and greatly delighted me by their simplicity and heartiness.'[1] For health reasons, he did not – certainly to begin with – undertake a full round of duties; it seems that on Sundays he preached alternately in a town pulpit and a country one. In addition, he used to reckon on getting his Mondays off, and in the shooting season would 'tramp with the guns',[2] as his daughter put it, and in the fishing season he and his close friend Edward Pethybridge would fish.

The Pearses were no strangers to the town. Indeed, through family connections, Mark Guy could almost have laid claim to being a

Launcestonian. At a public lunch held in the Town Hall on Thursday 8 January 1891 to celebrate the opening of a new Wesleyan Institute, he said that he was glad to know that the ancient mace presented to the borough so many hundreds of years previously bore the name of Robert Pearse.[3] In fact, his great-great-grandfather Robert (1733/4–1797), a local woollen manufacturer, is buried in St Stephen's churchyard, and his great-great-uncle, William Pearse (1766–1842), was also prominent in the town. It was William who was instrumental in erecting the first chapel on the Castle Street site, which opened in the summer of 1810. Sixty years later a third chapel, together with adjoining schoolroom and meeting rooms, was built there with substantial help from Edward Pethybridge, who delayed the erection of his mansion at Manaton in Dunheved Road so that he could contribute more liberally to its funding.[4] One of Mark Guy's first public appearances in the town was in connection with the Harvest Thanksgiving celebrations on Tuesday 25 September 1877, when the Rev. Samuel Hutton presided over a public meeting at which the new minister 'interested the people with a very racy and lively address'.[5] As I have already indicated, it is probable that he took things relatively easy to start with, a case in point being the series of special services for spiritual addresses and prayer that were held in the Castle Street chapel in February 1878. On Monday 11th addresses were given by the pastor, the Rev. J. Bamford and the Rev. M. G. Pearse who '...had come to listen, but willingly gave a very able address when requested'.[6] Six weeks later, when the quarterly meeting of the ministers and officials of the circuit was held in the schoolroom, Hutton, Pearse and the supernumerary minister, the Rev. J. Gregory, were invited to stay another year,[7] the arrangement being ratified by the Stationing Committee of the Wesleyan Conference when it met in Bradford that July. The following year, Mark Guy and John Gregory were again reappointed to the Launceston circuit, while Samuel Hutton was succeeded as superintendent minister by Thomas Wenn.

At that same quarterly meeting on 21 March 1878, F. L. Wiseman was unanimously recommended for the ministry, and it is him we have to thank for a first-hand account of Mark Guy's prowess as a preacher in and around Launceston. Though not necessarily a great 'divine', he was, wrote Dr Wiseman many years later, 'a mighty preacher and a great evangelist. I count it among the greatest privileges of my teens that I was a member of the Launceston congregation – indeed I was organist, when not myself planned elsewhere – during the time he was minister there.

You could not but listen when he was preaching, and must be blind indeed if you failed to see Jesus who was so evidently set before your eyes. He followed the good old rule of making Christ central in every sermon, and he was specially powerful... in skilful and persuasive application... He had the wooing and the winning note. The cultured were charmed by his dramatic and artistic presentation – his art being of the high quality that conceals art – while the common people heard him gladly and flocked to his services... With him the evangelism began with the first hymn. I can see and hear him still as he stands in the pulpit on one side of the apsidal chancel of the large and handsome early-English chapel at Launceston – the organ was in a recess on the other side so that I had a good view of him; his comely dress, his handsome features lit up with kindly expression, as with clear and cheerful, though occasionally throaty voice he commenced 'Let us sing to the Lord, dear friends, hymn___' – always a hymn of praise or aspiration'.[8]

Before long, Mark Guy was actively involved in the full range of ministerial duties at Launceston Wesley where praise, celebration and enjoyment were prominent features of whatever he led or took part in. On Thursday 9 January 1879, for instance, he addressed the congregation at a service of praise, which included selections from Handel's *Messiah* and other works performed by members of the chapel and friends, under Luke Wiseman.[9] Almost exactly a year later, in what was an annual effort to clear the debt remaining on the suite of schoolrooms and classrooms, a bazaar was held in the Sunday school, followed by an organ recital and other musical items. One of Mark Guy's Cornish stories 'convulsed the audience, which insisted upon his fulfilling his "To be continued" there and then', and helped raise £25.[10] A family man himself, Mark Guy was, throughout his life, thoroughly at home with children and was much in demand in both Launceston and the surrounding villages at Sunday school anniversaries. In 1878 the Sunday school in the little village of Egloskerry, four miles to the west of Launceston, celebrated its anniversary on Sunday 19 May and again the following Wednesday when Mr Wiseman addressed the children in the afternoon. Following a public tea, he delivered an address to a public meeting, after which the Rev. M. G. Pearse, 'in his usual happy style, engaged the close attention of those present for some time'.[11] Two days later he helped South Petherwin Sunday school celebrate its anniversary which, in spite of the poor weather, was a great success. On that occasion he addressed the children in the afternoon, and in the evening joined

Messrs Peter, Rawling and Jenkins in speaking to the gathering. On the morning of Sunday 2 June, he preached 'a very able and appropriate sermon' on the occasion of Launceston's Sunday school anniversary, basing his talk on the story of Hagar and Ishmael.[12] Seven weeks later he travelled out to Tregada for their Sunday school anniversary, addressing the children at three o'clock and preaching at half-past-six.[13] On Christmas Day he rounded off what was evidently a busy year by addressing a large congregation at Launceston, his text being 'Let us go into Bethlehem…'[14] The following June he returned to South Petherwin to help the village's Wesleyan Sunday school celebrate its anniversary,[15] and on the afternoon of Tuesday 5 August he returned to Tregada, presiding at a service interspersed with singing and addresses, and preaching a short sermon. At a public meeting at 7 o'clock, 'one of his eloquent and impressive speeches' was thoroughly enjoyed by those present. 'The weather was not all that could be wished, though the proceedings were better than was expected,' commented the *Cornish and Devon Post* rather cryptically![16] In 1880 his Sunday school engagements included the anniversary celebrations at Launceston at the beginning of June when the children assembled in Castle Green at 2.30 pm on Thursday the 3rd before walking in procession through the town. Along with Thomas Wenn and others, Mark Guy addressed those who gathered in the chapel after the annual tea meeting in the schoolroom at 5 o'clock. Three days later he spoke to the scholars and their parents at 2.30 pm and preached a sermon in the evening, when 'the edifice was crowded to excess'.[17]

Throughout his three-year stay in Launceston, Mark Guy Pearse devoted a considerable amount of time and energy to Wesleyan Home Missions, foreshadowing by some years the great work of his life in the West End of London. During the week commencing 12 May 1878, for instance, the Devonport District Committee, of which he was secretary, held a series of meetings in Launceston, beginning on the Monday evening with the annual meeting in aid of the Home Mission Fund. The report in the *Cornish and Devon Post* makes interesting reading in that it shows us something of Mark Guy the committee man, not a role, I imagine, in which he felt totally at ease. Called upon to give some information about the finances of the mission, he argued that the amount raised for it altogether was shamefully little, especially when compared with the fund for foreign mission work. While £140,000 had been raised for the latter, the total collected for Home Missions was but £35,000 with the Launceston branch contributing £42. 3s. 5d. [£42.17] the previous year. 'Looking at that,' ran the report, 'they could not but feel that there must be some truth in the old saying, "Distance lends enchantment to the view", those living a thousand or more miles away being better looked after in this monetary sense than the people at home. But he was glad to see that the committee did not let debt hinder them… and that they had spent more than their income…' Having pointed to the importance of the work of evangelisation and to the debt currently borne by the committee, he said that, in order for the Mission to function properly, its income ought to be £100,000, and asked each branch to treble its contributions.[18] Just over eighteen months later, in January 1880, he joined the Rev. T. Wenn in preaching one of the annual sermons in aid of the funds of the local Home Mission. On Tuesday 24 February the schoolroom was the venue for the Launceston Wesleyan Juvenile Missionary Society anniversary when tea at 5 o'clock was followed by a public meeting at which Mark Guy, together with 'several Juvenile and other Friends', explained the basis of missionary work. 'The Revs Mark Guy Pearse and T. Wenn addressed the meeting as the "professionals",' reported the *Cornish and Devon Post*. 'Mr Pearse with his usual vivacity and eloquence describing the origins of the Home Missionary Fund, illustrated it by such stories, the way to tell which he knows so well.'[19]

Then, as now, it was customary for those who were thought of as pillars of the community to be asked to support local causes. Unlike now, though, it was common for the details of their donations or subscriptions to be published in the press, presumably 'pour encourager les autres'. It is recorded, for example, that in 1879 Mark Guy Pearse donated 5s. 0d. [25p] to Launceston Fire Brigade.[20] A much grander undertaking altogether was the Thanksgiving Fund, which was inaugurated nationally at the Bradford Conference of 1878 in gratitude for the recovery of Wesleyan Methodism from the secession of the 1850s and for the relatively smooth introduction of a number of far-reaching changes in its structure, such as the admission of the laity into its assembly. Substantial allocations were made to overseas mission work while, at home, efforts centred on the training and support of the ministry, education and buildings. Locally there were preparatory sermons for what the *Cornish and Devon Post* called 'this great effort of connexional Methodism'[21] on Sunday 13 July 1879; then on the Wednesday there was a tea meeting at 5 o'clock, followed two hours later by a 'meeting of a lovefeast character' when Mark Guy was among those giving addresses.[22] In a letter which he wrote to the editor of the *Post* after the meeting, he made it clear that the list of contributors would not be closed for several months to come and continued:

> I should not like this great connexional occasion to pass without my having a share in it. For this effort to raise a quarter of a million to be completed without my being permitted to help it in any way would be a life-long grief to me.

He felt, too, that the promises made to the fund would be of interest to those in the future looking back on a bygone era – as indeed they are![23] For the record, out of a total of £521. 11s. 8d. [£521.58], John Dingley and family promised £130, Edward Pethybridge and family, £130 and the Mark Guy Pearses, £21.[24] The fund proved to be a great success, both financially and spiritually, and by the time it closed in 1884, the sum of £297,518 had been raised countrywide.

In addition to encouraging and attending chapel bazaars, organ recitals and Sunday school anniversaries in the vicinity of Launceston, Mark Guy was much in demand as a guest preacher further afield, especially in connection with chapel anniversaries. On Thursday 14 November 1878, for instance, he accompanied the Rev. John Gregory to Altarnun for their anniversary and listened to him preach in the afternoon. That evening he himself spoke to a very appreciative audience about Latimer, the Protestant martyr.[25] 'Honest Hugh Latimer' seems to have been a subject that was very dear to him, for he gave the lecture on no less than three other occasions while he was stationed at Launceston – at Canworthy Water in the Week St Mary Circuit and at Yeolmbridge on 23 March and 28 October the following year, and at Tremail, Davidstow on Easter Monday 1880 on the occasion of the chapel anniversary.[26] On Whit Tuesday 1879 he travelled 17 miles west to the slate-quarrying village of Delabole where he delivered sermons at two services that were held to celebrate their chapel anniversary.[27]

The 1870s were clearly years of expansion and prosperity for the Launceston Circuit, thanks, in no small measure, to the munificence of families such as the Pethybridges and the Dingleys. A founder of the well-known firm of bankers, Messrs Dingley, Pethybridge, White and Dingley, Edward Pethybridge was 'ever in the van of Methodist progress in North and East Cornwall', holding every office that a layman could hold, from circuit steward to class leader, as well as being a fine local preacher. The son of the prominent banker and Wesleyan Methodist Richard Dingley, John Dingley was an eminent preacher and trustee of chapels such as Rilla Mill and Coad's Green.[28] As the historian of Cornish Methodism, Thomas Shaw, pointed out, '[t]he services of such laymen, in material terms, to both church and community cannot be over-estimated', and '...many who were first trained as committee men in leaders' and quarterly meetings, and as public speakers in schoolrooms and pulpits, later took their place in local and county administration.'[29] On Tuesday 28 May 1878, the two bankers joined the Revs. S. Hutton and M. G. Pearse and Mr F. L. Wiseman at Yeolmbridge, two miles north of the circuit town, for the laying of the memorial stone of a new chapel. Mark Guy read the 132nd psalm and at 5 o'clock tea was served in a large marquee provided by Messrs Dingley and Pethybridge. Unfortunately the recent rain had flooded it in places, 'threatening wet feet, colds, and other ills which flesh is heir to; but planks, stone slabs etc. were speedily requisitioned by the Rev. Mark Guy Pearse, Mr Dingley and others, and everything was soon made comfortable'.[30] Mark Guy was amongst those who addressed a public meeting in the marquee that same evening. The following March he was back for the opening on the 18th, offering prayers at the 3 o'clock service conducted by his colleague Samuel Hutton and in the evening preaching 'one of those novel, unique sermons' which he alone could preach.[31] On a more personal level, his daughter Mab recalled how once, at Yeolmbridge, he gave away his greatcoat to a shivering old man called Kerslake who came into Launceston market the following Saturday and whispered to the donor that something had been left in one of the coat's pockets. (This was in the days when Christianity and tobacco were deemed by many to be mutually exclusive). ''Twere a pipe, measter,' said the old man. 'Do you smoke?' asked Mark Guy. 'Ess, 'pon a time!' 'Then take it, and thank the Lord for it!'[32] Bowithick, a few miles to the west of Altarnun, was one of six chapels where Edward Pethybridge served as trustee, and here it was on Monday 15 July 1878, that Mark Guy gave 'a ringing and eloquent address' after the corner stones of a new Wesleyan chapel had been laid and later that same day preached 'a very eloquent and powerful sermon'.[33] Almost exactly a year later, having recovered from the illness that ten days earlier had kept him at home on the occasion of the laying of the memorial stones of a new minister's house at Holsworthy, he returned for the opening services.[34]

During his lifetime, John Wesley and his assistants retained a firm grip on the structure of Methodism, but with his death in 1791, the question of the way in which it should henceforth be governed came into the open and resulted in a number of divisions in Cornwall and across Britain. With the formation of the United Methodist Free Churches in 1857, when Wesleyan reformers joined forces with the Wesleyan Methodist Association, Methodism in Cornwall was composed of five major groups, the Wesleyans, the Primitives, the United Methodist Free Churches, the Methodist New Connexion and the Bible Christians. All five were involved in negotiations from time to time, but half a century passed before the next union was achieved with the coming together of the United Methodist Free Churches, the New Connexion and the Bible Christians in 1907 to form the United Methodist Church. Although union between the various connexions was slow in coming, protracted discussions at national level did not prevent considerable local cooperation.[35] The Rev. M. G. Pearse was a firm believer in such cooperation and some of his most enduring characters belong to denominations other than Wesleyanism. Simon Jasper, for example, is a Bryanite or Bible Christian, and John Tregenoweth, a Primitive Methodist. His ecumenical outlook is, perhaps, most successfully embodied in Miss Zelia Tremenheere, the 'prophet's raven' whose charitable acts are all performed so quietly and graciously that the kindness is almost doubled as a result. Never belonging properly to either church or chapel, she somehow belongs to both, going 'to the Brianites in the morning, and to church in the afternoon, and in the evening… to our place [Wesleyan?] – except there was something special doin' over to the Primitives'.[36] Pearse often spoke out against 'sectarian division'. At the opening of Malvern Wesleyan Church, Adelaide in March 1891, he said that, as Wesleyan Methodists, they owed much to fellowships other than their own. Indeed, he believed 'that God knows no Methodists… that the churches are complementary…'[37]

He put such principles into practice on a number of occasions during his years in Launceston where, along with a minister from every nonconformist denomination in the town, he was present at a public meeting, which was held in the Western Rooms on Tuesday 8 July 1879, to celebrate the United Methodist Free Church Sunday School Anniversary. Before giving an address 'sparkling with humour and anecdote, and full of truth' on Sunday schools, he drew his audience's attention to the fact that when there was nothing to keep them away, they were willing to be present on the same platform in a display of brotherliness.[38] A little over three months earlier he had lectured on Hugh Latimer at the reopening of Canworthywater Free Methodist Chapel.[39] And the previous year he had shown what the *Cornish and Devon Post* called 'a liberality of spirit and brotherly feeling towards other denominations and people which many more would do well to imitate' when, at short notice, he travelled out to South Petherwin to address an audience in the Wesleyan Schoolroom on the occasion of the Baptist Chapel Anniversary. Notwithstanding appalling weather and the fact that he had spent a long day wrestling with reports, figures and other data at the Home Mission District Committee meeting in Launceston, Mark Guy came to the chapel's rescue when one of its speakers had to return early to Plymouth on account of illness in his family. He told his audience how, when he started out in the torrential rain, he thought, 'Now, there is a chance for them to come out strong at South Petherwin, and shew what stuff they are made of; for any man can praise God in fine weather, but it takes a good Christian to praise him under trial, and in weather like this'. He went on to express his pleasure at having the opportunity of showing his brotherly love to another denomination. He believed in the words that Charles Spurgeon had once addressed to him, when he said, 'We Baptists and you Methodists must stand together', a statement greeted with applause from the audience. He did not want to be known as a Methodist or a Baptist, or by any other name, so long as he was a preacher of the gospel of Christ.[40] On a lighter note, Frances Pearse recounted how her father had once exchanged pulpits with the United Methodist minister at Navarino, just outside North Petherwin. As he walked to meet the circuit conveyance after the service, he overheard a man ask his friend what he thought of the preacher. 'I did not think so much of him,' was the reply. 'I thought that he was a great man, but he has been so simple that I understood every word he said.' Mark Guy felt that no greater tribute could have been paid him.[41]

As well as 'Trevean' in Castle Street, for several years the Launceston Circuit of the Wesleyan Methodist Church rented houses in Dunheved Road for its ministers, and it was here that the Pearses lived. Contact between them and the Pethybridges, whose mansion was also in Dunheved Road, was extensive. Many years later Mr H. Pethybridge recalled dining with them when he was at school in Launceston, and still treasured 'the little cherubs he [Mark Guy] drew on the hymn-list when I was going to play the organ at one of his services'.[42] Edward Pethybridge served Launceston and Cornwall in a variety of ways during his lifetime. A member of the Town Council for twenty-two years, he was mayor in 1866 and again in 1881. He was, too, a member of the County Council from its formation in 1889 until 1904, a JP and chairman of the Launceston School Board. As chairman of the directors of Dunheved College, he took a keen interest in its welfare.[43] What is now Launceston College was the first of four secondary schools founded by the Wesleyans in Cornwall,[44] and was opened by the President of the Conference in 1873. In July 1878 and again the following year, Mark Guy joined his close friend and fellow-director on the platform for the college's Prize Day, leading the opening prayer on the former occasion and helping to present the awards on the latter.[45] Within a few years he would send his two sons there.[46] Towards the end of 1879 he attended the farewell supper for G. O. Turner, second master at the college, and with his colleague the Rev. John Gregory, 'responded to the toasts for the men of peace, 'The Ministers of Religion''.[47] Earlier that same year he was one of four ministers present at a banquet given by the mayor, T. P. Trood, for his fellow town councillors at the White Hart Hotel on Wednesday 15 October. Mark Guy used the occasion to express his delight that 'the old tendency to place a rigorous and intolerable barrier between people of different religious opinions was being done away with, that the old gap was, so to speak, dug out… [and] wished that they could meet oftener together in this way, so that they could not pick out as they sat there the Tory from the Liberal, the Churchman from the Dissenter, and where they all had their better sides presented to each other'. He concluded one of his usual warm and racy speeches with a Cornish anecdote that was greeted with roars of laughter from his fellow-guests.[48] Although, like his friend Edward Pethybridge who was chairman of the local party, he had strong Liberal convictions, he rarely spoke of politics, and never took part in political discussions. This was not, as his daughter Frances pointed out, from lack of interest, for he had the warmest admiration for Mr Gladstone.[49] It was simply that the winning of souls for Christ took precedence, and precluded him from overtly taking political sides.

Another deep conviction – and one to which he made a firm commitment towards the end of his years in Launceston – was total abstinence. Although it is difficult to be precise as to the exact time of his 'conversion', he described himself at a big temperance meeting that he addressed at the Colston Hall, Bristol, in 1882 as being 'but three years old as an abstainer'.[50] And some ten years later, when he delivered his address on 'How I became a Teetotaller', in Launceston, Tasmania, he explained that he was only ten years old as a total abstainer, having previously 'gloried in being a moderate drinker' who considered that it required more self-discipline to be temperate than to abstain.[51] Further proof of Mark Guy's involvement in the temperance movement is provided by a public notice that appeared in the *Cornish and Devon Post* concerning two resolutions passed at the joint meeting of the Ladies' Temperance Society and the Launceston Temperance Society in March 1878. The first, 'That in view of the evils arising from the custom of serving, at Audit Dinners, Tickets entitling the holder to obtain Intoxicating Drink', those merchants, traders and others allowing this form of discount off their bills should 'be respectfully requested to discontinue the custom of giving Grog Tickets on these occasions, and to give instead, if needs be, an Extra Discount in Money'. The second resolved that various local people should take charge of copies of the resolutions in order to obtain the signatures of all those who approved of the first and that the signed resolution itself should then appear as an advertisement in the local press. The Rev. Mark Guy Pearse was one of the signatories, though Edward Pethybridge and John Dingley were not.[52] We can, therefore, safely date what was undoubtedly a pivotal event in his life to the late 1870s, although it took him nearly twenty years to find his way to out-and-out total abstinence. In due course, though, it became so important to him that he lectured on it wherever he went and enshrined it in tale after tale. In the introductory chapter to his stories of Cornish Methodism entitled *The Ship where Christ was Captain*, he wrote that one of his earliest recollections was of one day hurrying to the door at the sound of the bell and the 'Oyez, oyez, oyez' of the local town crier, 'the angel in cocked hat and gay apparel who stirred the somewhat sluggish pool of our existence'. His announcement on this occasion concerned a Teetotal meeting at the Teetotal chapel that very evening, when 'four young chaps is going for to speak who never spoke afore'. 'I fancy,' wrote Mark Guy, who never missed a chance to crack a joke, 'my first impression of teetotalism was a mysterious process by which the dumb were enabled to speak.'[53]

The total abstinence movement had spread unevenly from its origins in America and Preston, reaching Cornwall in about 1837. In the early days, to be a teetotaler was to be something of a radical or revolutionary. Wesleyan Methodism was by no means opposed to the habit of drinking alcohol; indeed, to start with, temperance meetings were not allowed on

Former Teetotal Methodist Chapel, North Parade, Camborne, c. 2000 (author's photograph)

Methodist premises by an order of Conference. Acceptance of the movement, then, was slow and, even in 1875, the Wesleyan Methodist Temperance Committee allowed for moderate drinkers as well as total abstainers.[54] There was strong feeling on the subject, especially in and around St Ives where, in 1841, some 858 members left the old circuit and formed what became the Teetotal Wesleyan Methodist Connexion, with a number of chapels, mostly around St Ives and Penzance. The small, squat building which, until 1979, was the schoolroom of North Parade chapel in Mark Guy's home town, Camborne, was built by the Teetotal Methodists in 1842 and may well have been the venue referred to in the anecdote recounted above, although St Ives is another contender. The denomination eventually broke up after twenty years or more, and its people amalgamated for the most part with the Methodist New Connexion and other reformed branches of Methodism.[55] As Thomas Shaw explained in his definitive study of Cornish Methodism, apart from this small denomination, the various sections of Methodism came gradually – the Wesleyans last of all – to give their blessing to the teetotal movement, though not to make abstinence a condition of membership.[56] Indeed, the Rev. Hugh Price Hughes, who was afterwards a stalwart in the cause, and from the mid-1880s onwards, the Rev. M. G. Pearse's colleague in the West London Mission, described the group of abstaining students at Richmond Theological College in 1865 as the 'insane society'.[57]

In the early days Mark Guy liked nothing better than to argue with strong teetotallers, always referring to the Scriptures in support of his contention that moderate drinking was more in keeping with the teachings of the Bible. 'I never took what is called too much,' he told a Bristol audience. 'I never took it because I had any special liking for it. I have, as a minister, mixed socially all through these years with those who have been professedly religious. If circumstances can hedge the moderate drinker about with safety, if the amount one takes, and the place and the company in which it is taken determine the rightness or wrongness of moderate drinking, then I claim that no conditions can be found more favourable to utter and complete harmlessness than those in which I have moved'. Gradually, though, he was forced 'by the sheer force of terrible and appalling facts' to adopt total abstinence as 'the *only* right and safe standpoint for any Christian man'.[58] His first discovery – that total abstinence was a capital thing for the working classes – he would illustrate in his lecture 'How I Became a Teetotaller' by telling the story of Bill who signs the pledge after hearing Mark Guy preach at an outdoor service in Gravel Lane, 'away down in the worst part of the town'. The money that Bill saves enables him to buy much-needed flour and coal for his wife. Later Mark Guy moved to a church in a different district where one day he discovered the terrible heartache caused by drink in a beautiful, well-to-do home. 'And I had sat at this man's table,' he told his audience, 'and I had drunk of this man's wine, and I had lent the sanction of my position as a minister of Christ.' The resulting conviction – that total abstinence could sometimes be a capital thing for others besides the working classes – meant that, henceforth, he would only drink wine at home. Whenever he was out of the house, he would always turn his glass upside down, preferring not to drink where he was uncertain as to what the result of his example might be. The final step in the process, which led him to the conviction that total abstinence was the only thing for him, he would subsequently describe in some detail. 'I was living at that time in a little country town. I had been for some time out of health, and was just slowly returning to my work. It happened that in the town there lived one of those troublesome teetotallers...' who attended church regularly and had just lost his six-year-old son. Seeing him in church one Sunday morning and feeling very sorry for him, Mark Guy determined to make use of the doctor in himself and wear the man out with arguments about teetotalism so that he would go to bed exhausted, have a good night's rest and forget – albeit temporarily – about his loss. At home, though, he could not sleep; his thoughts kept returning to the father in his grief. Asking, half-aloud, what he could do to comfort the man, back came the answer: 'Sign the pledge, that would comfort him.' Why, though, he argued should he give up so much for this man? Because, came the reply, if he wished to follow the example of his master the Lord Jesus Christ, who had laid down his life for him, then he would surely give up his wine for the bereaved father. His meanness in arguing against this action struck him forcibly as he saw his Saviour on the cross: 'The tears streamed down my cheeks...The contemptible, the hideous selfishness of the thing! One thing I resolved to do, for my whole soul was set in another direction...' The next morning – a cold, grey morning in November – he went down to the man's house and signed his pledge-book.[59] Some years later, on the occasion of the laying of a temperance memorial stone to the Rev. Charles Garrett at the new Wesleyan chapel in Coinagehall Street, Helston, he expressed the wish that he could go back twenty-four years and begin his ministry as a total abstainer.[60]

Mark Guy Pearse expressed his feelings about 'the curse of intemperance' in a number of novels, short stories and tracts such as *Harry's pint; or Threepence a day*, *Matt Stubb's Dream or Christmas-eve at the Blue Boar* and *A Bit of Shamrock*. Harrowing descriptions of the degradations suffered by families as a result of the breadwinner's drink-dependency appear, too, in *Dick Croggan's Redemption* where the length of the periods that Dick's father – a drunken sailor from London's East End – spends at home is determined by the time it takes him to turn his pay into liquor;[61] in *John Tregenoweth: his mark* where Uncle John Tregenoweth's descent into drunkenness shows 'how the cursed drink hardens a man against those that he would die for when he is sober';[62] in *Rob Rat. A Story of barge life* which is set in and around the dismal Pickard's Wharf; and in *Simon Jasper* where, every market-day, Miller Hockin's wife awaits the return of her husband, 'reeling in hideous, rollicking humour – the bloated face, the thick speech, the foul breath'.[63] Mark Guy would already have seen much of the seamier side of life in Cornwall in the 1840s and 1850s, and in London in the '60s and '70s, and such first-hand experi-

Charles Tresidder's cover for the tract Dick Croggan's Redemption

ence eventually precluded his attitude to strong drink being anything other than uncompromising. In his writing especially, the moral message was all-important; in private, though, he could be – and often was – more relaxed. Edward Pethybridge junior, for instance, recalled how, when he was at Launceston, Mark Guy drew on the first page of Mrs Pethybridge's visitors' book a portrait entitled 'Mine Hostess of the Inn', and at the top of the next page 'A list of the Sinners who stayed with the Publican'. When he arrived there from London on one occasion, his hostess hurried to meet him and enquired what he would take after his long journey. 'Well, Aunt Emma, nothing suits me *better* than a little brandy,' he replied. Concealing her surprise at such a request from a teetotaller, she was bustling away to comply when he continued 'Stay a minute; NOTHING suits me better than a little brandy!'[64]

The Rev. Gregory Harris who, as a boy, spent long holidays with his uncle William Gregory Harris at Cleave House, Morwenstow, recalled many years later that Mark Guy Pearse loved to visit them there when he was in the neighbourhood. Another farmer friend was local evangelist John Rawling of Oldwit, near South Petherwin, who appears in *Simon Jasper* as 'my good friend Oldwit'. It was to this noted lay preacher, JP and County councillor that the writer was indebted for three or four incidents in that book. Indeed, Mr Rawling's own copy of *Simon Jasper*, which is still in the family's possession, bears the inscription 'To my dear friend J. Rawling of Oldwit, with M. G. Pearse's thanks and heartiest good wishes. Christmas 1882.'[65] 'In such homes as these,' confirmed the Rev. G. Harris, 'Mr Pearse found plenty of raw material waiting to be put into literary form. His famous 'Old Folks at Home' lecture was largely made up of stories collected from his fishing, agricultural, and mining friends.'[66]

As well as picking up many a story during the course of visiting the circuit villages, Mark Guy was, during his three-year stay, well placed to observe and describe the market town at its hub. *Simon Jasper*, which the *Wesleyan Methodist Magazine* for February 1883 described as 'a wonderful blending of pathos and humour, of striking incident and wise and racy conversation...', first appeared in that magazine the previous year as *Sketches from Life: Simon Jasper*. It opens with a delightful vignette of Launceston, nestling 'close under the castle, so snug and safe that it is content to sleep, for the most part, in the shadow of its ancient protection'. That 'for the most part' is important, for on market day and at the monthly cattle fair, the town is transformed:

> It wakes early in the morning and shakes itself with a kind of radical defiance of its aristocratic associations. Shopfronts are protected with boards, for the streets and by-ways are blocked with cows and calves, and droves of bullocks and pens of sheep, and many more that come to sell, or be sold, as the case may be. Crowded carts come jogging in from the country, and, having discharged the passengers and cargoes, are locked into each other along the street in what seems hopeless confusion. The goods of the shops flow over at the doors; the hawkers of watch-chains and braces, of razor-paste and shoe-strings, shout their

SIMON JASPER.

Chapter the First.

IN WHICH WE HEAR OF A HERO.

DO you happen, good reader, to know the old town of Dunheved? 'The chief town of Cornwall,' as every worthy native of it contends, on the strength of many geographies. 'Of Cornwall *East*,' says the western man, thinking of the brand-new city that has come amongst them. 'Next to Bodmin,' says he of the mid-county. Happy Cornwall! Where else could one find these mild ambitions thus amiably met, or such pet prejudices provided for? But be all that as it may, the

Charles Tresidder's drawing of Launceston Castle for the first page of Simon Jasper

wares. Everybody gets into everybody else's way, and stays there. Farmers and dealers, double-chinned and big-waistcoated – splendid specimens of the decayed agricultural interests – laugh and bargain at the street corners. Buxom farm lasses, their rosy faces shining like quarrenden apples, indulge in gossip with awkward lads. The labourer in Sunday clothes, and therefore ill-fitting and uncomfortable-looking, and the wife with a big basket on her arm, stand at the draper's door, anxiously turning over some article of juvenile attire; whilst the chubby juveniles themselves hang at her skirts sucking big sweetmeats.

> Blundering folks, dazed by the confusion, come open-mouthed, looking one way and going another; for everybody within ten miles feels bound to go to market, and, being there, to go in search of everybody else.[67]

On one such day Mark Guy stumbles upon his friend Oldwit who wants him to meet seventy-year-old, former road-mender Simon Jasper. Simon's story – from parish apprentice at eight, conversion, marriage, joining the Bible Christians and being accused of theft, through to the illness 'up to Exeter' of his only son – is a living example for the author of 'how wonderful a thing a bit of real religion is, whenever you can find it beyond the green bud state, full-bloomed and fragrant and rich-hued'.[68] In conveying that message, though, Mark Guy paints a number of delightful pen-portraits of village characters and their humdrum, though ultimately fulfilling, lives. Particularly graphic is the description of Simon Jasper's birthplace, 'one of the poorest of the "cob" cottages in the straggling village of Canworthy Water – an out-of-the-world place, made up of a bridge, at which some half-dozen ways meet, a score or so of houses skirting the high-road, an inn, and a couple of chapels that look askance at each other, one from under its thatched brows eyeing suspiciously the more recent and ornate intruder'.[69]

Some of Pearse's readers found his sketches of both character and locale in his numerous books so graphic that it was not unheard of for them to make pilgrimages – to the home of Daniel Quorm, for example. Needless to say, having failed to find it, they would return disappointed! Indeed, the *Methodist Recorder* wished it to be known that Mr Pearse was 'dangerous by reason of his tricks of fancy'![70] The mixing of fact and fancy in *Simon Jasper* appears to have occasioned more than a little controversy. Towards the beginning of July 1885, Henry Martin Guest made an appeal through the editor of the *Recorder* 'on behalf of the subject of the book "Simon Jasper", whom he described as having been a local preacher for over fifty-five years and a member of the Society for over sixty. 'He receives 2s 9d per week from one source,' he continued, 'and 1lb of beef from a gentleman in the same village; out of the above 2s 9d he pays 1s per week house rent. He is a thoroughly good old Christian. When I called to see him he was out visiting people who were ill.' He concluded his letter by assuring the journal's readership that he would each week forward any donation, however small, to the old gentleman.[71] This letter caused something of a stir at the Wesleyan

John Rawling of Oldwit (Courtesy of Margaret Rawling)

Methodist Conference that opened in Newcastle four days later. And the Rev. M. G. Pearse's early departure from the Conference served only to intrigue still further those delegates who were posing questions such as 'Is Simon Jasper a real character?' 'No such person as the Simon Jasper of the tale exists,' proclaimed the *Recorder* in its Conferences Sketches. 'The book bearing that name is a sketch from life in which the writer has grouped together incidents and characters and sentiments from many sources'. Having heard the man who was to serve as his model preach at a Watchnight service, he thought at once that he could put him into a book. No sooner thought than done! From someone who knew the Watchnight speaker he gleaned four facts which he subsequently elaborated into four chapters. 'But Mr Pearse never saw the wife of the supposed original of Simon Jasper and never was in his house. The story of Simon Jasper as to his early life at Stowcombe, his conversion, his courtship, his 'old dear', and the conversations and sermons have nothing whatever to do with the man for whom the recent appeal has been made. They were gathered in other directions...We feel bound to make these statements in the interests of Mr Pearse, although they may destroy the glamour of his story in the eyes of readers who share the love of facts which characterised Mr Gradgrind.'[72] The *Recorder* went on to stress that no criticism was intended of Mr Pearse for whom it had the highest regard. The appeal itself produced subscriptions totalling £9 6s 6d with individual donations ranging from 6d to £2.[73] Subsequently, a correspondent signing himself 'Truth' wrote to correct what he described as 'some erroneous statements which appeared in the Recorder a week or two since from our Conference Correspondent in relation to Mark Guy Pearse's publications'. Insisting that these were not of such an imaginary type as the correspondent seemed to think, the correspondent briefly examined some of the characters and incidents from *Mister Horn and his friends* and *Daniel Quorm* before concluding:

> As to 'Simon Jasper', he, too, is well known in the neighbourhood of Launceston, although I imagine the name is fictitious. He still lives, and is not so badly off as was represented by one of your correspondents a few weeks ago; the 'Ould Dear' has passed away.[74]

In point of fact, Mark Guy's character was based on a Richard Prout of South Petherwin who, on Sunday 18 November 1883, preached to crowded congregations in the Gospel Ark, Devonport, in connection with the Christian Workers' Mission.[75] A close friend of the Rawlings, Mr Prout seems to have enjoyed minor celebrity status, for in reporting on the anniversary of the Bible Christian Chapel at Camelford nearly three years later, the *Cornish and Devon Post* described the man who preached to packed congregations simply as 'the hero of the Rev. Mark Guy Pearse's book entitled 'Simon Jasper'...'![76]

In 1877, though, the writing and eventual publication of *Simon Jasper* were still some years away and *Good-will*, containing a number of Christmas tales dedicated to Edward Pethybridge, was the Rev. M. G. Pearse's seasonal offering that year to his growing readership. His stories were obviously considered just the thing for the festive season, for the 1870s saw the publication of such gems as *Mr and Mrs Rogers* (1877), *How they got the chapel at St Piran* (1878) and *Dick Curnow's Conversion* (1879) in the Christmas numbers of the *Methodist Recorder*.[77] Another atmospheric sketch, *Christmas Eve in the 'Vivid'* featured the old coach that ran from Launceston to '"everywhere" in the Western Land'.

Bearing her name in large yellow letters on a black background covering the whole length of her sides, 'the old lumbering van' was said to be capable of four knots an hour, though she usually made no more than three and a half. At the time of writing, though, she lay 'wheel-less, shaftless, stripped, dishonoured' in the yard of Mr Scown, coachbuilder, of Western Road. Having first appeared in *The Holly Bush*, the tale was serialised for many of its author's congregation in the *Cornish and Devon Post* at Christmas 1878. 'Wrapt from teeth to toes in my stout "Ulster", began Mark Guy, 'I hurried along the steep, winding, irregular streets of the little market town. The rain was coming down with a thoroughness characteristic of the county – there was a Cornish 'one-and-all'-ness about it, that was unmistakable'. Once aboard the 'Vivid' in the company of Jan Trigg, the driver and general proprietor, and his fellow passengers, the latter-day Chaucer discovers that his journey affords him a fine opportunity of studying character. To pass the time that blustery Christmas Eve, they tell stories, culminating in Trigg's tale of the perils of constantly frequenting public houses. In *Christmas Eve in the 'Vivid'*, Mark Guy combines to great effect his powers of character-delineation, his wit and his knowledge of the Cornish dialect.[78]

Other magazines – notably the *Wesleyan Methodist Magazine*, *Our Boys and Girls*, the *Boys Own Paper*, and the *Sunday Magazine* – carried articles by him during the late 1870s. *Short Stories and other papers*, dedicated to 'my dear friends A. Hingston Esq JP and Mrs Hingston, of Rosedean, Liskeard', was published in 1877, as was *The Child Jesus* in which he joined forces with G. S. Rowe to produce readings and texts from the scriptures, together with songs and music. The following year, *Rob Rat: a story of barge life* was issued anonymously. Inspired by and dedicated to the philanthropist George Smith of Coalville, with whom he later became friends, the tale is set on a narrow boat called *The Water Rat*, home to Rob and his sister, little Lizer, who suffer at the hands of their drunken father before being rescued by Noah, owner of *The Ark*. The moral of the story is 'Pass it on', a philosophy that was, as we have already seen, very dear to Mark Guy Pearse. The year 1880 not only saw reprints of a large number of religious tracts and of chapters of *Daniel Quorm* and *Mister Horn and his friends* as publications in their own right, but also the appearance of one of his most successful stories for children, *Old Rosie*.

Never one to rest on his laurels, Mark Guy was making a name for himself, too, as a lecturer, developing a talent that he would put to such good use on behalf of the West London Mission a few years later.

Indeed, in an interview that he gave in 1899, he told Arthur Lawrence that as far as the 'spoken word' was concerned, he had learnt much and practiced a good deal 'at home in Cornwall at various lectures and debating societies'.[79] On 7 October 1878, a large audience heard him speak on 'Thomas Chatterton, the Poet' to the Launceston Mechanics' and General Institute, of which Edward Pethybridge was vice-president. 'The lecture,' commented the *Cornish and Devon Post*, 'was a most interesting one, being full of lessons drawn from the life of the boy poet, and was delivered with that dramatic power and excellent elocution for which Mr Pearse is so well known.'[80] Just over a year later he was back at the Institute, lecturing – this time on 'Sir Walter Raleigh' – to another large and appreciative audience.[81] It was, though, for talks such as *The Old Folks at Home* and *A Little Bit of Bread* that he became famous. On Monday 15 March 1880, the Central Rooms, Launceston were unable to cope with all those wanting to hear him lecture on *Some Characteristics of West Cornwall*. 'In his usual happy, racy style,' reported the *Post*, he gave a number of anecdotes 'illustrative of the character of our more westward brethren,' many of which 'fairly convulsed the audience with laughter'.[82] Indeed, his use of humour was the key to the huge popularity as a lecturer of the man whom H. M. Cresswell Payne described as 'an actor-lecturer' who 'could have been famous on the stage'. As proof of Pearse's immense power over an audience, Cresswell Payne recalled how 'they laughed and they cried unashamedly'.[83] He considered that Mark Guy's gifts as a storyteller were inimitable, while for William Gregory Harris, he was 'the best raconteur Cornwall has produced for a generation'.[84] Writing in the *West Briton* a few days after Mark Guy's death, John Kinsman summed up with some precision just what it was that made Cornish men and women the world over encore him again and again:

> Cold print cannot convey the magic of his voice, but one remembers clearly the impression made upon a big audience by the tone in which he recited simple happenings. Once he told us he had just returned from Cornwall, where people still took the trouble to minister to their neighbours' wants; and he noticed an acute difference between the casual manner of the newspaper seller at Paddington and the boy who entered the train at Chacewater, with a bundle of papers under his arm and enquired, 'Do arry waun of ee want a West Briton?' Mr Pearse realised that a copy of the paper would await him at his

> Camborne home, and the other passengers were Londoners who were not interested in local news; consequently, nobody responded to the question. A London boy would have turned on his heel without more ado; but the Cornish boy was accustomed to politeness, and so he waited, and then said: 'Ef narry waun av ee daun't want a West Briton, plaise say so, and I'll go next door.' The way in which such little things were told reproduced the native atmosphere and made an evening with Mark Guy Pearse one of the chief joys in a London-Cornishman's life.[85]

In view of his commitment to inter-denominational co-operation and the interest that he always took in the 'boys and maidens' of the town, it was appropriate that Mark Guy Pearse should have brought to a close his official stay in Launceston with an address and sermon on the occasion of the centenary of the town's Sunday schools. The celebrations organised by the United Nonconformist Schools began on the morning of Sunday 25 July 1880, when about 800 children representing the Independents, Wesleyans, Union, Free Methodists, Baptists and Bible Christians, together with accompanying adults, packed the aisles and galleries of Launceston Wesleyan Chapel. Taking as his subject the story of Robert Raikes and the Sunday school, Mark Guy gave 'one of those addresses full of interesting descriptions and anecdote, and interwoven with facts of history so suitable for children and for which he is so well known'. He spoke, too, about the centenary medals to be handed out the following Thursday in memory of Raikes. That same Sunday morning he selected Christ's words 'I am with you alway' as the text for a touching and appropriate farewell sermon. However, because he had scarcely an hour he could call his own up to the time he was to leave Launceston for Clifton, and would therefore find it impossible to conduct 'that personal leave-taking all round which he should like', he took the opportunity to address a few personal words to his congregation before commencing his sermon. Although it was not a pleasant task to take leave of kind and loving friends at any time, this was particularly so after three years' ministry like that which he had had among them. All his past congregations, with their varied characteristics, were remembered by him, 'but the good people of Launceston and their children would live in his memory as long as memory lasted'. He had received such kindness from all quarters, and they had been so indulgent to him in many ways, that he wished to thank them from the bottom of his heart. He had often felt all too keenly the fact that the demands on his time were so great that he had not been able to carry out his pastoral duties as he could have wished, and visit every member of the congregation. 'If, however, he could not speak to them his thoughts, he had put some of them in a more permanent form, which he hoped they would accept as some set-off against what he had referred to. But for this, the fact of his pastoral failings would not only oppress but depress him.'[86] What exactly did Mark Guy mean by having put some of his thoughts in a more permanent form? Did he arrange for his farewell sermon to be printed, or was he, perhaps, alluding to *Simon Jasper* which was published two years later and contains so much of his feelings for Launceston and the surrounding villages? About three years after he was converted, Simon began to preach, convinced of the need among country folk for a simple, basic form of worship:

> I don't want it all to be nothing else but up in the parlour with the Sunday clothes and the best cloam... I never had no firstlies nor secondlies, but I used to tell people about the love of the Lord Jesus to me.[87]

It is clear from the book's closing pages that Mark Guy was impressed by the local character who served as a model for Simon Jasper and took with him fond and positive memories of the area that had nourished him for three years:

> 'Goodbye,' I said sadly... 'You [Simon Jasper and his wife] have done me good, and I shall always feel thankful that I knew you.'[88]

Chapter 9

'...I recall the days at Clifton and Portland...when I have seen many sitting outside the schoolroom door, unable to get in...'

Bristol 1880–1886

By the end of the nineteenth century Bristol had lost its position as Britain's second city and port, being overtaken by Manchester, Liverpool and Birmingham. However, it continued to expand, with its population and trade more than doubling after 1850 and between 1830 and 1880 thirty-two churches were built and five enlarged to meet the needs of this growing population. Gradually it absorbed such places as Hotwells, Clifton and Westbury which once enjoyed a separate existence. The non-conformist churches, too, shared in the general prosperity and a number of large chapels sprang up all over the city.[1] The Wesleyan Methodist Conference which met in London in 1880 appointed the Rev. George Bowden chairman of a district centred on Bristol that stretched from Clevedon to Gloucester and encompassed Chepstow, Newport and Cardiff across the Severn. The same conference agreed that, due to the rapid expansion of Methodism in the city itself, the Bristol circuit would be subdivided into three smaller ones – Wesley, Clifton and Portland. Before considering the impact that Mark Guy Pearse's ministry had on the district in general and Clifton and Portland in particular, it would be useful to look briefly at two contemporary sources that provide us with a picture of Bristol Methodism at the very time that he moved to the area. On Monday 26 September 1881, the Rev. J. Robinson Gregory presented a paper entitled 'The History of Bristol Methodism' to an ecumenical convention at Milk Street Free Methodist Chapel. In it he revealed that Wesleyans in the city had 3,383 members whose needs were catered for by 22 ministers, closely followed by the United Methodist Free Churches with 2,806 members and 11 ministers.[2] A month later the *Western Daily Press* conducted a survey of all those who attended the two hundred or so places of worship in the city itself on 31 October. Its findings revealed that out of a total of some 116,000 who worshipped at both the morning and evening services – well over half the population – 9,000 or 8% were Wesleyan Methodists.[3] The same survey showed that Victoria, the circuit chapel to which Mark Guy Pearse moved that autumn, had a congregation of 320 in the morning and 312 in the evening. During the first sixty years of the nineteenth century, the population of Clifton increased nearly fivefold, most of the growth being in upper Clifton where the well-to-do and professional classes erected big houses for their large families. While the Anglicans built new churches and created new parishes to cater for the influx, the non-conformists were slower to respond. As if to make amends, though, the 1860s saw them erect four new chapels on Whiteladies Road which became popularly known as the Via Sacra because of the number of places of worship it eventually contained![4] Victoria, which opened at the southern end, opposite the Victoria Rooms, at the end of June 1863, was the result of a number of worshippers at nearby Portland Chapel coming together to plan a new church, their own in Kingsdown having become overcrowded.[5]

By the time that Mark Guy, Jeanie and their seven children left Launceston to set up house at 4, Wetherall Place[6] within a stone's throw of the circuit chapel, he was not only enjoying good health again, but was at the height of his powers. When, in October 1883, the *Methodist Recorder* devoted much of one editorial to Methodism in Bristol, it voiced the opinion that if the chairmen of the districts were chosen not only for their business skills, but also for their ability to stir up the spiritual life of the societies, and if they were freed from circuit work and used their time to visit their district, then their position might be made even more effective than it already was.[7] It held up the strong leadership of the Rev. George Bowden as a shining example and certainly, together with circuit teams that included such able men as William Tweddle, George Keeble, John Rhodes and, of course, Mark Guy Pearse, he achieved a great deal during his five years in charge of Bristol, adding 2,203 members to the district between 1881 and 1885.[8] He started as he meant to continue and at the district meeting in September 1880, it was agreed to hold an evangelistic mission in all the circuits during the coming winter. As a preparatory measure, it was arranged for day-long conventions of ministers, office-bearers and church members to be held in Bristol, Cardiff and Gloucester for the sections of the district centred on those towns. Mark Guy accompanied his chairman to Gloucester where at Northgate Chapel on 21 October he gave a Bible reading and addressed the convention on 'Our Duty Now' in the evening.

After a period of relative isolation in Bude and Launceston, he travelled widely during his six-year ministry in Bristol, within the city itself, throughout the district – district meetings were often held in Cardiff or Newport – and further afield. The area had a comprehensive rail network – in 1884, Bristol alone could boast ten stations – and although the Severn Tunnel was not completed until 1885, services on each side of the river were linked by ferry. In April 1881 he returned to Finsbury Park, which he had seen open six years earlier, for the first in a series of missionary anniversary services.[9] Cornwall, too, still beckoned and three months later, at midday on Thursday 21 July, a substantial luncheon was laid on in the Drill Hall of the local artillery unit at Polruan, across the estuary from Fowey, on the occasion of the dedication of the village's new Wesleyan chapel. Flags, an arch of flowers and evergreens, and bunting greeted those who arrived for his service at three o'clock. Having given 'an excellent and impressive address', he preached an equally impressive sermon after tea, on the subject of the Prodigal Son.[10] Nearer Bristol, he attended the laying of memorial stones for a new chapel, school and manse at Clevedon at the beginning of October 1882, offering prayer at the ceremony, joining the 700 who then took tea in the Public Hall, and addressing the public meeting that followed.[11] He continued, too, to support the Radnor Street Schools in the capital, preaching at City Road Chapel on their behalf earlier that same year.[12]

Six months after moving to Clifton, the Pearses suffered the loss of their eldest daughter Jean Drummond, whom her sister Mab described as the pride of her father's heart. A bright, dark-eyed girl who showed a remarkable talent for drawing, she had already been weakened by attacks of rheumatic fever and her heart was affected when she fell ill again. The following letter, which he wrote on 21 March, arrived only just before she died:

> My Dear Little Jean, – Here is a little bit of a letter for you; just a good morning, miss, with a tiny kiss. Here I am in old Worcester, once the home of Bishop Latimer. The people want a lecture to pay for the warming apparatus in their chapel. I think the good old Bishop would rub his hands with much glee at the thought of how things come about: that his being burned should help to warm the folks in the old town where he lived and laboured! Bless you, my darling, I do hope and earnestly pray the loving Lord to give you a good night's sleep. His gift.
> Ever, sweet Jean,
> Your loving Father.

Her death – within two months of her fourteenth birthday – he found hard to bear; it became one of the things in his life over which he felt obliged to draw a veil, and only by never mentioning her, could he cope with the loss.[13]

Someone who got to know the Pearses intimately around this time was 12-year-old Emmeline Pethick, the daughter of a prosperous family with Cornish connections whose home was at Weston-super-Mare. The three eldest Pearse girls, Maude, Frances and Isabelle, were about the same ages as Emmeline and her sisters Mary and Annie, with the result that the six became firm friends. In her autobiography, Emmeline described in some detail how the Rev. M. G. Pearse's attractive and gracious personality awakened within her the first emotion of love and how the connection between the two families was maintained throughout her childhood and youth:

> At first I loved him impersonally as one loves the sun, as a creator of joy and delight. An incident happened, however, which made the mutual relationship a more intimate one. It was a winter night and he was due to preach at Banwell, a place eight miles distant from our home. My parents were to take him there in the carriage. When the time drew near for them to start, he used all his powers of persuasion to induce my mother to allow me to go too. As it was a cold night with deep snow on the ground she tried to resist the suggestion. But at last she gave in, and I, who was present at the discussion, could hardly believe my ears when I was told to get ready. We drove in a barouche [a four-wheeled, horse-drawn carriage with a collapsible hood over the rear half]. Father was seated beside the coachman; Mother and the guest of honour took the front seat, and I was on the small seat with my back to the horses. But this did not

> suit him at all. What was I doing, all that long way from him? There was plenty of room for me at his side! 'Certainly not,' intervened Mother. 'We will promise not to take up more than one half the seat between us,' he pleaded humorously. Again Mother gave in with a laugh. And wonder of wonders! there I was, encircled with his arm. On both sides of the roadway great snow-drifts were piled, which lit up to whiteness as the carriage lamps threw their beams upon them. We arrived at the chapel where he was to preach to find the place overflowing as usual, chairs down the aisles, and people in the porch unable to get in. But a way was made for us to reserved seats in the front. I remember many of the details of that service. He took as his text: 'Like as a father pitieth his children, so the Lord pitieth them that fear him.'
>
> When the service was over and all the farewells had been said, there was the drive home still to come. As he gathered me into his arm he murmured: 'Like as a father…' There was not much talk; but now and again he would say: 'Asleep, little maid?' I was never more wide awake in my life. Never before had I known such happiness. It was my first taste of pure joy. Thus began a relationship that was to be a supreme influence in my life for the next twenty years.

Mark Guy became so popular in Weston-super-Mare, both as a preacher and a lecturer, that none of the public halls were large enough for the audiences that he attracted. Whenever his engagements brought him to the locality, he would stay with the Pethicks and Emmeline would witness the effect that his talent as a raconteur of Cornish stories often had on their well-trained servants who would many a time dash unexpectedly from the dinner table into the hall in order to gain control of themselves! She recalled how he was 'The Pied Piper' to all the children, able to do all manner of fascinating things. They only had to give him an ink-pot and a saucer of water and out would come from his waist-coat pocket a little paint brush and a pen, and he would draw – with all of them squeezed up against him as close as they could get in order to watch the process. From a blot of ink thrown onto an envelope he would produce mountains, forests or oceans, using the texture of the hand at the base of the thumb to get the general effect and then the pen to bring birds, animals or children to life. There would be a picture for each of them before he had finished, and sometimes an illustrated envelope would reach one of them through the post, much to the amazement of the

Original sketch by Mark Guy Pearse (Courtesy of Mrs A. Milne)

postman. For young Emmeline Pethick, staying with the Pearses in Bristol meant experiencing the happiest times of her childhood. 'I was supremely happy in the atmosphere of harmony that prevailed in the home,' she recalled in the late 1930s, 'and I found a new freedom of expression in that magnetic attraction that delivered me from shyness and made me just a happy child whenever I was with him. To his own children he was "Daddy", and he asked me to call him by the same name. I soon became one of the family.' He wrote fairy stories for her in verse, providing an old oak box for her to keep them in. 'Often to-day, she wrote, 'if some slight illness keeps me indoors with time on my hands, I open this box and re-read these rhymes and stories that delighted me so much when I received them so many years ago. They are so numerous that I never come to the end of them, and so delightful that they still possess the power of bringing me into a world of enchantment and joy. He had the same happy relationship with other children that he had with me. With some of them I was acquainted, and our love for him made a bond between us. He shone into our lives.'[14]

Another local family whose hospitality he enjoyed at this period were the Tilleys of New Road Farm, Huntspill near Bridgwater, whose youngest daughter Connie would often look after the visiting preacher and became another of his 'dear little maids'. 'I see you in the crowd at Highbridge,' he wrote to her many years later, 'when I told the Mayor of Bridgwater, "There sits the lady whose influence brought me here" and I pointed to the proud and blushing Connie.'[15]

Towards the end of September 1881, Methodist Oecumenical Conference meetings were held throughout the land. At Bristol's Milk Street Chapel, on the 26th, Mark Guy addressed the convention on the Rev. J. F. Barnard's paper 'Scriptural Holiness and the special fitness of Methodist means of grace to promote it'. In his opinion, what they wanted that morning on the matter of holiness was 'to have, after the good hearty Methodist fashion, a 'love-feast''! Furthermore, they should go back to what Bishop Peck described as the 'dynamic force of Methodism', namely entire sanctification or Christian perfection. John Wesley's much-debated teaching on the doctrine he summed up as 'perfectly healthy religious life'. The results of Methodism had, he thought, made entire sanctification a thousand times more necessary then than it was a century earlier. The world did not regard the religious man as a hypocrite or an enthusiast; but the world had its own ideas about religion, and it required entire sanctification. There must be no flaw; little failings in Christians made the world shake its head; they could not afford to be behind the world's standards.[16] This and other 'thoughts on holiness' he would, in due course, incorporate in a book bearing that very title.

Writing in 1926, Canon Hay Aitken, a personal friend of Mark Guy Pearse, recalled those 'who used to shout 'Amen' and 'Hallelujah' to the no small disconcerting of astonished mission preachers…'[17] And Jack Mitchell of North Roskear, Camborne remembered a revival taking place at nearby Treswithian in the early 1900s when one lady, in the midst of prayer, suddenly jumped to her feet, arms waving, staring fixedly at the other members of the congregation and shouting, 'I got 'n, I got 'n.'[18] This kind of wild excitement – 'senseless ejaculations' his friend and colleague C. Ensor Walters called it[19] – was anathema to Mark Guy, offending the quietistic side of his nature, just as it offended farmer Gribble in the second series of *Daniel Quorm*. A letter that he wrote from Camborne – possibly in mid-September 1886 when he preached at a harvest thanksgiving in the town – revealed his own reactions to a not-too-dissimilar occurrence:

> I had tea at Captain Josiah's [Thomas]. At night Champness preached a very solemn and searching sermon. One woman screeched out at the very top of her voice, and went on screeching. I never heard such a dreadful noise. And, whilst I fell in with Champness as far as I could, I felt how utterly unfitted I was to take part in Cornish revivals.[20]

Towards the end of the nineteenth century, though, this old type of revival, during which chapels in the populous districts stayed open day and night for weeks on end, was already giving way to what many regarded as 'new-fangled' special missions. These were sometimes conducted by local ministers, sometimes by special agents of the denomination and sometimes by local preachers from other circuits whose abilities in such campaigns were proven.[21] On 18 November 1881, the *Methodist Recorder* reported that the Revs. R.W. Allen[22] and Mark Guy Pearse had just finished 'the most successful home missionary deputation ever held in Cornwall. The Sabbath Congregations were crowded, the services were seasons of blessings, and souls were saved. The meetings were most enthusiastic, the speakers both instructed the minds and stirred the hearts of our people, and a noble impetus was given to the cause of home missions.'[23] Recalling, perhaps, the impact of Hugh Price Hughes's deputation to Cornwall five years earlier, Mark Guy, together with R. W. Allen who was chaplain of the Woolwich Garrison and greatly experienced in home mission work, conducted a series of services and public meetings in some of Cornwall's larger chapels during the last week of October and the first week of November. The *West Briton* reported at some length on the progress made, recording how Mark Guy often preached for up to two hours to huge congregations. At one Camborne meeting he 'thoroughly rivetted the attention of his audience throughout', whilst another was 'simply enthusiastic from beginning to end'. At Redruth, on Sunday 23 October, he preached 'in his usually interesting and effective style', while at Penzance two days later he 'held the audience in rapt attention'. The series of engagements at Helston included a public meeting where he spoke for an hour and a half on the different phases of home mission work before sitting down 'amidst a burst of applause'. At Falmouth, where a month earlier he had lectured on *Some Characteristics of West Cornwall* in the Polytechnic Hall, 'he held the rapt attention of his auditors' with 'an address marked by thrilling eloquence, racy stories, and touching incidents' depicting 'the anxieties, vicissitudes, and successes of home mission work'. Very large congregations – up to 2,500 on one occasion – attended the deputation's services at Truro's St Mary's Wesleyan Chapel, with crowds of people coming in from the country districts around the town. 'Mr Pearse is an extraordinary preacher,' commented the *West Briton*'s reporter, 'his sermons being quite out of the ordinary style of preaching, and rendered so interesting as to enchain the attention of his hearers from beginning to end. The great truths of the gospel are illustrated and rendered clear and impressive by anecdotes, narratives of various incidents, and direct and searching appeals to the understanding and the conscience.' Commenting on the success of the deputation, the Rev. R. W. Allen said that nothing had given him greater pleasure than the experience he had had since coming to Cornwall and that he had been struck by the enthusiasm and earnestness shown by the county's Methodists. In many cases the financial results matched the spiritual ones, with collections showing a 70%, 80% and 100% increase on previous years.[24]

Meanwhile, in Bristol, as in Highbury and Launceston, Mark Guy continued to take a special interest in the young. Following a proposal by several local businessmen to the Wesleyan Ministers' Meeting that all the denomination's young men in the city should be invited to some convenient chapel, a meeting took place at Victoria on the evening of Friday 2 February 1883. Nearly 600 sat down to tea in the schoolroom before joining a further 200 in the chapel itself where the Rev. M. G. Pearse was the first speaker. Having been assigned the subject 'Christian Work and its relation to young men', he told of his exasperation on going to London as a medical student a little over twenty-one years earlier when he realised that there was no work for him as either a Sunday school teacher or local preacher. But for the kindness of a Wesleyan minister, the loneliness he experienced might have had dire consequences for his soul.[25] 'I think of the young man or young woman who has come up from some quiet country home to the great city,' he wrote in one of his sermons. 'Here life is a thing so different that you tremble. A thousand new weapons are raised against you. There is the dreary loneliness that takes all the heart out of one sometimes, and always most dreary on Sundays.'[26] A city dweller as a result of his calling rather than by choice, Mark Guy often wrote of how, in the loneliness of London, 'the sight of a friendly face, the touch of a kindly hand, the sound of a cheery voice' was 'a very whetstone of the spirit'.[27] On the plus side, he acknowledged that the current ran stronger in the cities and recalled on one occasion how he 'never knew the brotherliness of Jesus Christ and the sweetness of intimacy with Him' until he came as a young man to London.[28]

Victoria Chapel premises were used to provide refreshment of a rather different nature when, one winter's day, he saw about thirty men at work laying drains or something of the sort in the road in front of the chapel. 'It was the dinner hour,' he wrote a few years later, ' and there in the pelting rain they sat eating their provision – about as dreary and cheerless a set as one could see… I at once got the school-room opened, and bade the men welcome; promised it should be at their service so long as they were anywhere near; and had a fire at which they could warm their coffee and themselves. I told them that they were at perfect liberty to smoke after dinner, but the whole time not a man touched a pipe within the walls. It was the instinct of a true gentleman, awakened by a little set of kindness… On the Sunday some of those men walked a long way and endured the infliction of a sermon, because, as one explained, 'You see, one good turn deserves another'.[29]

Although his Wednesday Bible readings at 7 o'clock became quite a popular attraction, it was the prayer meeting at 8 o'clock on Fridays that he regarded as the pivot of all his work. This deep and passionate belief in prayer he explored in a booklet entitled *The Big Wheel of the Church, and some hints on working it*, which was published in 1889. The *Wesleyan Methodist Magazine* for June that year recommended that all those who loved social prayer, especially those who themselves conducted prayer meetings, should try to carry out its excellent practical suggestions. These included companies of Christians getting together in one another's houses to pray – praying parties or at homes – and the choosing of special topics for prayer each week, so that every section of the Church's work could be prayed for in turn. Looking back forty years later over a long and eventful ministry, he attributed whatever success he might have achieved mostly to the fact that he could never get a room big enough to hold the prayer meeting. Initially, the key to what he called the 'Big Wheel of the Church' was the fact that he always took it himself, having worked out his own methods. Another prerequisite was preparation, which took the form of an hour of quiet communion when he generally got a little message for the prayer meeting – often a message that he later found exactly suited the situation or circumstances of one of the participants. He encouraged the principal men of the church to come and take part. Indeed, unlike in some towns where they were rarely to be found at weeknight services, in Bristol the leading men were 'constantly at the front of spiritual enterprises, and… the sources of abundant encouragement to the ministers who yearn[ed] to see the prosperity of Christ's cause'.[30] The most wonderful week was that in which he asked for slips of paper from those who wanted prayers to be offered for unconverted relatives or friends, all of whom, of course, remained anonymous. At the prayer meeting the following week slips were sent up for special answers to prayer. 'I do not think it ever happened without having sometimes wonderful – it ought not to be wonderful – cases of conversion,' he wrote. '…I recall the days at Clifton and Portland, and elsewhere, when I have seen many sitting outside the schoolroom door, unable to get in, and remember how people came sometimes a distance because they heard that folks got converted there.'[31] Mark Guy Pearse's earnestness and eloquence stirred the city in a big way and seekers after truth from a variety of backgrounds and denominations flocked to hear him. His engagements ranged from preaching on behalf of the Bristol Benevolent Institution and lecturing on topics as diverse as *Some Characteristics of West Cornwall*, *Hugh Latimer*, *Christmas* and *Billy Bray*,[32] to a Blue Ribbon meeting with the navvies at Port Skewet.

Amidst it all, though, he continued to find time to write. Indeed, his talent was seen by the Wesleyan Methodist Church as a powerful force for good when, in 1879, it carried out a review of its ministry. A chapter on the intellectual characteristics of its ministers described him as having 'attained a name beyond his own denomination for a species of literature which cultivates a new field. His talents are unique, and his books have enjoyed an extensive circulation, and one given to but few men. We look upon them as healthy works, and sainted men and women throughout the Connexion have read them without endangering the keenness of their own spirituality.'[33] Largely as a result of book sales, Mark Guy was already, at the beginning of the 1880s, a household name. In virtually every issue of the *Methodist Recorder*, the Wesleyan Methodist Book Room drew special attention to his publications and in the summer months, adverts such as the following were common:

> Visitors to the Seaside should send a P. O. O. for Twenty Shillings to the Wesleyan Book-Room, and receive (carriage free to any Railway Station) a Parcel of Little Books by Mark Guy Pearse, containing 100 'Can I Be Saved?' 100 'Getting Saved' and 300 of other kinds, assorted (500 in all).They are well printed on good paper, with an attractive illustration on the front page. Suitable for presentation to rich or poor.[34]

The perils of such widespread popularity and literary fame were brought home to him shortly after his arrival in Bristol when he wrote to the *Recorder* in order to warn its readers not to be taken in by a vagrant who was using his name:

> In one of my circuits I knew a very pleasant and respectable family, with whom I used to visit. The only son, a lad of 16 or so, was a special favourite of mine, whose heart seemed opening to the best things, well-educated, generous, with life opening fairly before him. I left the circuit with the expectation that I would find him growing into a respectable, useful and prosperous man. That is 14 years ago, and a few days since he called upon me with a pitiful tale – had suffered much at sea, walked from Liverpool, was now on his way to some friends whom I knew in the West, and wanted money to reach them. My heart was touched; I gave him clothes, a dinner, and money. I talked with him of the old times, and, in parting, I gave him a copy of one of my books, in which I wrote his name. I find now that he is utterly unworthy of any help. He is a regular tramp, refusing other ways of getting a living, and has practiced the art of lying to such perfection as it admits. It is a miserable thing to find one's charitable impulses imposed upon – sadder still to find a lad such as he was grown to such a scamp.

His customary optimism momentarily deserted him, and he finished the letter with the words, 'Alas for our poor world.'[35] The publication of *Thoughts on Holiness*, which he dedicated to his friends at Clifton as a memorial of his ministry among them, was announced towards the end of 1883.[36] Within ten years some 66,000 copies had been sold, finding their way into a variety of households. A friend of the Pearses recalled how once, while in Copenhagen, he was given a tour of the Royal Palace which included the monarch's private study. There, open on the table lay a copy of *Thoughts on Holiness* which had been sent to the king by his sister, the then Princess of Wales.[37] At the other end of the social spectrum, books such as this were treasured in thousands of humble cottages, whose occupants often felt compelled to write to the author to express the effect his words had had on their lives. Reviewing the book, the *Methodist Recorder* was of the opinion that 'there is much in Mr Pearse's way of putting the truth…which will help to encourage the timid who would know more of God and the holiness without which none can see Him'.[38]

In 1883, on Mark Guy's appointment to the Portland circuit where the Rev. John Rhodes was superintendent minister, the Pearses moved to 'Grosvenor Villa', Southfield Road, Cotham. Situated in Kingsdown, about a mile from Victoria, Portland Street Chapel itself was completed in 1792, the year after John Wesley's death, because the New Room, which he had founded as the first Methodist chapel in Bristol, was becoming overcrowded.[39] Since its establishment as a separate circuit in 1880, with chapels at Old Market Street, St Philip's Marsh and Redwick, Portland had enjoyed what the *Methodist Recorder* called 'that condition of vigorous life and healthy development which is the essential characteristic of the revival state'.[40] As we have already seen, much of the credit for the healthy spiritual state of the district as a whole could be attributed to the Rev. George Bowden under whose vigorous chairmanship it was 'moving upward to an exceptionally strong position', with the prospect of becoming 'at no distant day, conspicuous for its spiritual power'. In its editorial on Bristol Methodism, the *Recorder* cited the highly successful Sunday afternoon services as one example of the generally religious tone of the city. Started originally by the congregation at Broadmead Baptist Chapel, these services or lectures took place all the year round in the Colston Hall at three o'clock. Conducted on broad principles by both Anglican clergymen and ministers of other denominations, they attracted an audience of between three and four thousand people, though when E. G. Gange or Mark Guy Pearse was announced to preach, the hall would be filled to capacity. 'We do not think that the assertion that the most numerously-attended Sunday afternoon service in England is held in Bristol can be successfully disputed,' wrote the *Methodist Recorder*. The aim of the lecturers was to give their addresses attractive titles, so as to make them as popular as possible and easily understood by all-comers, thereby reaching those who did not as a rule attend a place of worship. In a move that foreshadowed the format used at St James's Hall and Wardour Hall, Mr Riseley, the organist at the Colston, accompanied the hymns and gave a sacred recital at each service.[41]

Before settling in to a new Methodist year at Portland Street, the Rev. M. G. Pearse lent the cause a hand further afield – at Oxford where, on 13 September, he was involved in the opening services for a new chapel at Walton Street, and at Torquay where, on the afternoon of Monday 1 October, he gave an impressive Bible reading in order to help the Union Street chapel reduce a crippling debt.[42] Returning to Bristol, he joined a number of his fellow ministers for the first of a series of conventions designed 'to realise the deepening of the spiritual life, to stimulate to renewed consecration, and to seek a baptism of power for better service'.[43] The inaugural addresses – on 'The Baptism of the Holy Ghost' – were delivered on Tuesday 9 October at King Street chapel. On the Wednesday, King Street was again the venue for an all-day meeting which saw Mark Guy and his colleagues lead the discussion on topics such as 'Seeking Holiness', 'Enjoying Holiness' and 'Holiness, a Preparation for Christian Service'. The evening service was, it seems, particularly memorable, with people occupying the chapel's aisles and pulpit in order to listen to the ministers and enjoy the singing of a carefully chosen choir.[44] The following January Pearse, together with George Bowden, conducted another successful convention at Swansea, laying the foundation for a five-day mission that Hugh Price Hughes, his future colleague at the West London Mission, began at Wesley Chapel on 23 March.[45] In much the same way, 1885 saw a series of special mission services at the various chapels and mission rooms in the Bristol Wesley circuit, preceded by a holiness convention. Again, Messrs. Bowden and Pearse were among those taking part.[46] At the beginning of 1886, Portland Street Chapel was itself the focus of great activity when the Rev. W. B. Doherty, vicar of St Matthews, Cotham, invited George Clarke, a well-known missioner, to conduct a series of revival services in the church schoolroom. The invitation was accepted by Mr Clarke, on condition that on one or two occasions he could preach in the Wesleyan schoolroom and that the services throughout should be of a united character. As it happened, so many people turned up on the first Wednesday of the mission that it was agreed that Mr Clarke and his congregation could, in the interim, take possession of Portland Street Chapel which would be the venue for all the remaining services. In what was a truly interdenominational mission, the Revs. John Rhodes, Mark Guy Pearse, and A. D. Cope joined the vicar of the parish, a Congregational minister, and a number of Christian workers from various churches in the neighbourhood in conducting the prayer meetings and assisting at the Bible readings and in the 'inquiry room'.[47] In the spring Mark Guy was in Greenwich for an all-day convention for the promotion of personal holiness that was advertised as taking place at the Wesleyan chapel on 9 June.[48]

The American Blue Ribbon Army, which was founded by Richard T. Booth in April 1878, had by the 1880s established itself as a powerful temperance movement. In Bristol it shared a very crowded stage with such organisations as the Band of Hope Union, the Black Ribbon Army, the Western Temperance League, the White Card Army, the Abstinence Society and the Church of England Temperance Association.[49] As we have already seen, Mark Guy's interest in the temperance movement culminated in his adoption of total abstinence as a lifestyle and creed towards the end of his ministry in Launceston. In all probability, the big temperance meeting at which he spoke in 1882 was part of the campaign which was organised by the Blue Ribbon Army early in the year and which was said to have materially affected the receipts of public houses and the sale of alcohol generally in the city.[50] As the following account shows, it may have been at this time, too, that he nailed his colours firmly to the mast and formally donned 'the blue':

> When I first put it on I felt more shy than at any time since I was married. I took it at the first of Mr Booth's meetings, and the next morning everything seemed blue. The sky was blue, and all Bristol seemed blue; look where I would I would see that 'bit of blue'. Everybody I met nudged somebody else and smiled. I got into a tramcar. It was the same in the car as in the street. There ran round a cold, shuddering whisper, 'He has the Blue Ribbon on.' Next came in a working man wearing it, and he looked sheepish too. We caught sight of each other, and up went our heads. We could now look the whole world in the face.[51]

As a Blue Ribbon man, Mark Guy campaigned strenuously for total abstinence for the rest of his life, believing, as he put it when lecturing on *Some Characteristics of West Cornwall* at the City Temple, that the best of narcotics for the weary was a good laugh, and the best of stimulants for hard work was a healthy bit of humour.[52] In October 1883, the Manchester District Temperance Committee secured the Free Trade Hall for a great public meeting to be held on 11 December in connection with Temperance Sunday. Among those joining the Rev. M. G. Pearse on this occasion were the Rev. Charles Garrett, ex-President of Conference, the Rev. Dr Pope and W. D. Stephens JP of Newcastle-on-Tyne. Before calling on the now-famous author, the chairman, Dr Pope, asked how many of the audience had read *Daniel Quorm*, whereupon probably a third held up their hands. For this, his first appearance on a Manchester platform, Mark Guy received a magnificent reception. The essential ingredients of *How I Became a Teetotaller* and the stages in its author's 'conversion' are explored elsewhere. It is worth recording, though, that when he recalled his previous position, he appealed to his audience not to judge moderate drinkers too harshly.[53]

The following year the friends and supporters of the temperance movement organised a meeting in the Colston Hall where George Bowden, Hugh Price Hughes and Charles Garrett joined Mark Guy Pearse on the platform. Bad weather did not prevent a large audience from hearing the latter express his great joy at the firm and leading stance on temperance being taken by the Methodist Church. In much the same way that he had not always been an abstainer, so the Methodist Church had not always taken a lead. Indeed, twenty years previously, leading men among them would shake their heads and predict that the next great connexional split would be on the subject of total abstinence. Mr Garrett was regarded as a sort of arch-conspirator, believed to carry metaphorical pistols, stilettos and daggers. That scare, though, was long dead and buried, while Mr Garrett lived on! As for the assertion that attention to the temperance movement diverted men from their proper work of saving souls, Mark Guy argued that, on the contrary, those who were the most earnest in saving souls were also the most earnest in advocating temperance. He maintained that John Wesley had made Methodism a total abstinence society. They had no more stringent pledge in any of their temperance societies than that which stipulated that no member should buy or sell intoxicating liquors. In concluding his address, he urged that they should realise their own responsibility in the matter and, as members of the Methodist Church, carry out the spirit and word of their great founder.[54] In 1885, a particular feature of the district meeting that took place in Cardiff that spring was the public services held in connection with it. One of them took the form of a temperance meeting which was attended by upwards of 3,000 people who, on Thursday 14 May, crowded into the New Park Hall to hear a number of speakers, including Mark Guy Pearse, and the Cardiff Blue Ribbon Choir. In addition to the usual morning and evening services, midday and open-air meetings for working men were organised, and that same Thursday Mark Guy had what the *Methodist Recorder* called a 'homely talk' with the workmen in the yard of the Taff Vale Railway, Bute Docks.[55]

A vivid account of one such temperance meeting – held on board a warship that had been turned into a floating chapel or 'Bethel ship' at Bristol – appears at the beginning of a story entitled 'Bob':

> I had previously been attending another meeting and had to come from a distant part of the city in a cab, winding in and out through the misty darkness until I found myself set down on a quay, where I could dimly make out chains and ropes and all the signs of shipping. A friendly hand piloted me across the gangway, and along the deck of a vessel, until I reached a narrow, winding staircase, down which I felt my way through the darkness. Then, as a door was flung open, a blaze of light fell on me suddenly, and I found myself in the midst of the meeting. It was a large place, in which nearly a thousand persons must have been gathered. The sides of the long, low rooms were decorated with the flags of all nations; and this, as well as the faces and dress of most of the audience, and the whole tone and freedom of the meeting, suggested the heartiness of the sailor. The songs were lustily applauded, and the chorus was rung out with that rollicking vigour which no one understands so well as Jack ashore. The very speeches seemed irresistibly to catch a kind of nautical flavour, and the illustrations came from the sea.[56]

By his Deed of Declaration of 1784, John Wesley assigned the legal conduct of Conference business to a select hundred preachers and their successors. At the 141st Conference of Wesleyan ministers which opened at Burslem a hundred years later, the Rev. Benjamin Gregory, the editor of the *Wesleyan Methodist Magazine*, announced that he 'wished to bring before them the name of one whom the Lord had greatly honoured, and whom the brethren would delight to honour – a man of brilliant and powerful genius, and one whose genius was entirely consecrated to the cause of God'. Known far beyond the bounds of their own church, Mark Guy Pearse had 'the heart of a Methodist preacher, was an ardent evangelist' and 'had served God by the press as well as by the pulpit', for which 'his name would never die out of Christian literature'. Cheers greeted Gregory's submission and that afternoon Mark Guy Pearse was duly elected to the Legal Hundred. Underlining the popularity of the election and the great satisfaction that 'the multitudes that honour and love his name' would derive from it, the *Methodist Recorder* described him as 'one of our most effective evangelists' who, in his own line, reigned supreme in the department of Methodist literature that he had created. Two days later, on 24 July, the Rev. George Bowden read a letter from the Rev. M. G. Pearse in which he acknowledged his election and, incidentally, threw some light on how he saw his role within the Methodist Church:

Dear Mr Bowden,

Will you please convey to the fathers and brethren at Conference my grateful appreciation of the honour so unexpectedly conferred upon me? I would come in person to tender my thanks, but must ask for a dispensation from personal attendance, as my Superintendent, the Rev. John Rhodes is necessarily at Burslem. I trust, therefore, that my letter will not be taken to imply any lack of courtesy. I think I may say I have been ambitious of the honour of trying to do my work with all my heart and strength, but there my ambition ended, and I certainly never thought of any recognition of this sort. But none the less do I find in this trust a token of the regard of my brethren which I do greatly appreciate and for which I thank God – Praying that all richest blessing may rest upon your assembly, believe me, dear Mr Bowden, Yours right heartily,

M. Guy Pearse.[57]

His involvement in a series of opening services at the new Wesley Chapel at Newport between June and September, together with other ministerial duties, prevented him from attending Conference in 1884, but the following year he travelled up to Newcastle for the one that opened there on 21 July. 'Right glad were we to see, seated between Mr Kelly[58] and Dr Stephenson, Mr Mark Guy Pearse, whose appearance in the Conference is a cause for special congratulations', commented the *Recorder* enthusiastically. 'As he subsequently received a vote for the Presidency, he ought to feel that he has not yet fulfilled his destiny as a Methodist preacher.' Although Mark Guy himself was re-appointed to the Portland Circuit, there were a number of changes that affected the Bristol District, notably John Rhodes' election as chairman – by 163 votes to Mark Guy's 17. George Bowden was appointed governor of Kingswood School, Bath.[59] Then, as now perhaps, there was as much, if not more, interest in what was happening behind the scenes at Conference as there was in the public proceedings. The main topic of conversation in one of the select groups who had adjourned to the lobby was, it seems, nothing less than 'the premature flight of Mr Pearse from the Conference'! Although officially appointed to write the reply to the Address of the South African Conference, Mark Guy had left, leading the editor of the *Recorder* to register in the paper's 'Conference Sketches' his bitter disappointment, and to ponder on what might have been:

How the "Minutes" would have sparkled if Mr Pearse had con-

> tributed 'A Talk with the South African Lambs' to the literary treasures! We will be patient, and assuage our feelings![60]

One of the high points of the Methodist year in Victorian times was the Harvest Festival or Thanksgiving. The custom of using the new wheat to make bread which was then offered at Mass and solemnly blessed, is generally said to have been revived at Morwenstow in Cornwall in 1843 by the Anglican cleric and poet Robert Stephen Hawker, although there is evidence of earlier harvest festivals. By the middle of the century, an annual festival was common in both the Church of England and in the Free Churches. The ear of wheat or grain of corn was a powerful symbol for the Victorians, most of whom were intimately familiar with the process whereby it became the flour that was turned into bread. In her autobiographical writings, Muriel Sara, who was born at Camborne in 1884 into a family closely associated with Wesley Chapel and whose father was a close friend of Mark Guy Pearse, described the long country walks that she and her family took, watching farmers ploughing the land, then sowing the grain. At harvest time she would stay with a farming relation who allowed her to carry 'crowst' or lunch out to the men working in the fields. Subsequently, seeing the grain turned into flour was a thrilling experience for her and her friends:

> So flour was a very real, alive and interesting thing to us. We were never allowed to waste any bread and, except in sickness, crusts were never cut off to be left... I may be old-fashioned, but I hate to see pieces of bread cut off and thrown away as useless. I remember the uses our Victorian mothers would have made of them – for puddings, stuffings and as dried crumbs for fish frying. Often the babies of poor parents had nothing to eat but "pap" made of dried and rolled crusts, with milk added.

She recalled, too, Mark Guy Pearse telling a story which reinforces this point – that of old Becky whom he had once visited when she was finishing her midday meal and found her smacking her lips over the last spoonful. Asked what she had eaten with such relish, she replied, 'A basin of kittle broth. 'Tis nourishing and 'tis easy to make and 'tis cheap...'Tis like this 'ere, when your teeth can't eat so well as they used to, crusties is things that's hard to manage; for all that, they're things a poor body can't afford to throw away. So you sets them in a basin and put in a sprinkle of salt and pepper and a lump of butter. Then you pour

Harvest Festival at Camborne Wesley Chapel, mid twentieth century (Author's collection)

boiling water over the lot and lev' it soak – and there you are, a dainty dish to set before a king. And that is kittle broth, so now thee knows.' Perhaps it was Becky's recipe for using up her old 'crusties', Muriel Sara mused, that led Mark Guy to preach his famous harvest thanksgiving sermon on 'Bread and the Living Bread'.[61] It was certainly a time of year that was invested with significance for him and one during which he was in demand as a preacher and lecturer. On the evening of Monday 7 September 1885, for instance, he preached the harvest thanksgiving sermon at Roath Road Chapel, Cardiff which, on the same occasion a year earlier, had seen one of the largest congregations ever assembled within its walls and where, in October 1879, his youngest sister Fanny had married J. C. Shepheard Lewis.[62] Two weeks later he was in London where on 22 September Helen McKenny, whose father was then Superintendent of the City Road circuit, heard him preach 'a very beautiful sermon on the "Miracle of the loaves"' to another large congregation.[63] The following day he was back in Bristol to take the harvest services at Portland Street,[64] after which he travelled down to Liskeard. The custom of decorating chapels and churches with farm produce gradually grew in popularity over the years with the results becoming ever more elaborate.

The decorators at Liskeard certainly pulled out all the stops for the Cornishman who had spent four formative years in their midst in his late teens, the result being described in the local paper as 'chaste, artistic, and beautiful'. Above the pulpit, the front panel of which bore the text 'The seed is the word', hung bunches of luscious grapes, while underneath were the best apples, plants and evergreens. The whole was encircled by festoons of greenery and grain. With a covering of large fleeces of snow-white wool, the stove served as a pedestal for a very large vegetable marrow, while around its base were spread the best specimens of the year's root crop. From the reading desk, which was covered with moss, greenery and flowers, a line of pot plants embedded in moss, interspersed with flowers, stretched the length of the chapel on the tops of the pews. Under the gallery at the other end were the words 'Give us this day our daily bread'. On the front of the organ, imitation harps were placed on the pipes themselves along with festoons of evergreens, while on the front panel of the loft was the word 'Alleluia' in silver letters on a red background enclosed in a fringe of fir. The front panels were covered with green baize, on which appeared the words 'We praise Thee O God' in daisies, tastefully surrounded with a border of grain and flowers. The panels around the gallery were alternately decorated with green trellis work, and festoons and evergreens intertwined with flowers, with plants on the cornice in front. The pillars supporting the gallery were also alternately covered with grapes, flowers and ivy. On the window sills were large marrows, cucumbers, pumpkins and apples embedded in moss. Imitation baskets of flowers and stars hung from the side walls, while continuous festoons of evergreens ran along the angles. Over the clock a neck of corn was placed, with a foreground of flowers and evergreens. It was in this splendid setting that on the evening of Monday 23 September, Mark Guy preached to over a thousand people on 'A handful of corn'. Holding sometimes an ear of wheat, sometimes a single grain of corn, he used it to illustrate a number of points, drawing a particular analogy between the various processes through which it passed on its development into golden corn and man's often arduous spiritual journey.[65]

In order to try to ensure that there would be no repeat of the breakdown that resulted from overwork in Highbury and Westminster, Mark Guy spent many holidays fishing in Cornwall while stationed in Bristol. As we have already seen, one spot that drew him like a magnet was Morwenstow on the north coast near Bude. At 'Cleave House' he found

William Gregory Harris

just the kind of rest and recreation that his mind craved, experiencing 'a spirit of peace, a spirit uplifting, expanding, hallowing'.[66] Its owner, his close friend William Gregory Harris, became one of the central figures of *Bridgetstow* which, as the Rev. Tom Shaw pointed out, is – in part, at least – Mark Guy's thinly veiled pseudonym for Bridgerule, nine miles south east of Morwenstow.[67] Before the boundary changes in the middle of the nineteenth century, Bridgerule was divided by the Tamar, part of the parish being in the hundred of Stratton. 'You might say 'tis Devonshire and you might say 'tis Cornwall and not be out of the way,' says the cab driver whom Adam Reddiford hires to show him around London. ''Tis most between the two.'[68] It seems that while he was on one occasion staying at Holsworthy some four miles to the east, Mark Guy went over to Bridgerule and was introduced to John Chapman, a gardener, postman and local preacher. The story of Chapman's conversion and subsequent attempts to better himself obviously made a great impression and, as James Cobbledick, he became one of the central characters of *Bridgetstow*. Wiliam Gregory Harris was described by his nephew as 'the largest farmer in the parish and... the very *beau ideal* of what an English yeoman should be' and Tom Shaw recalled being told by a member of his congregation that he had the kindest heart and wore the biggest waistcoat of any man he had ever known![69] Although a nonconformist, he was also people's warden at Morwenstow Church and he and Robert Stephen Hawker understood each other well, sharing a love of good literature. 'I was chosen, at his request, upwards of twenty years since to be churchwarden, though a Wesleyan and local preacher...,' wrote Harris himself in a letter to a local paper on Hawker's death. 'For forty years I have known him as one of my best and dearest friends. He never reproached me for being a Wesleyan, but I had every encouragement to virtue, and Wesleyan ministers in the early years of his incumbency were always welcome guests.'[70] If we compare this with Mark Guy's description of Farmer Gregory in *Bridgetstow*, then we can see to what extent his 'novel' is a composite picture of characters from both Morwenstow and Bridgerule:

> My friend Gregory was the class-leader, and more than that – the father – of the little Methodist church of Brigetstow; local preacher, too, and circuit steward for much more than the allotted time, by the law of survival of the fittest. By far the largest farmer in the parish, and, indeed, in the district, and also the people's churchwarden, he was one with Parson Montgomery in all that made for the welfare of the place.[71]

Generally speaking, Hawker, who died in 1875, never took any trouble to conceal his poor opinion of dissenters and said himself that he never spared 'heresy or schism ministerially'.[72] And it is just possible that Chapter V of *Bridgetstow* – 'Concerning Bedey Chugg, and Betsey, his wife' – contains a less than flattering portrait of the late vicar whose death is described as having 'given rise to very much general interest [with] both the literary and religious journals [giving] it prominence'.[73] It has to be said, though, that Hawker was neither vindictive nor uncharitable towards those who had forsaken the Mother Church, and Mark Guy's 'late vicar' may be a former incumbent of Bridgerule or simply a product of his imagination. Imagined conversations between *Bridgetstow*'s Parson Montgomery and Farmer Gregory are used both as a peg on which to hang a fund of stories about the remote north Cornish parish of Morwenstow and the border parish of Bridgerule, and as a novel means of exploring the beliefs of Methodists and Anglicans and of expressing his thoughts about the natural world. 'We need to come into contact with nature to put us into the true possession of ourselves,' muses the Parson one summer's day as he and Farmer Gregory sit together under the cliffs after bathing.[74] And years later William Gregory Harris's nephew explained how the sight of the huge Atlantic breakers 'churned to milky foam, hurling themselves against 'the thundering shores of Bude and Boss'' was a tonic in itself for Mark Guy. What is more, flowing through the Coombe meadows is a little trout-stream which empties itself into the sea at Duckpool. 'To watch 'Mester Pearse' whipping the stream, with an almost uncanny cleverness, was a sight I have never forgotten,' continued the Rev. Gregory Harris. 'The day's sport over and the evening meal finished, Mark Guy and Uncle William would forsake the dining-room for the big farm kitchen, with its open hearth and fragrant wood-fire, and then – their pipes drawing 'sweetly' – what tales were told, what glorious gossip there was!'[75]

On visits that he made to the Kilkhampton circuit in the spring of 1885 and, accompanied by the Rev. W. J. Dawson, again in 1886, Mark Guy and his colleague preached and lectured at Kilkhampton itself, Holsworthy and Bude. Outside the circuit, Bodmin Wesleyan Chapel benefited both spiritually and financially when he preached at its re-opening services towards the end of May 1886.[76] When he delivered his lecture on *Characteristics of West Cornwall* to a large audience at Kilkhampton on Easter Tuesday 1885, his friend William Gregory Harris, who was circuit steward, presided.[77] Many years later Mr Harris's nephew wrote that those who had heard his famous lecture on *Some Old Folks at Home* willingly gave him the palm as the best raconteur that Cornwall had produced for a generation.[78] The inspiration for his lectures and sermons – and for much of his outlook on life in general – came from his love of Cornwall and its people, a love and an understanding that deepened whenever he came 'home' on holiday and tapped into his roots. 'Now I am off for the day,' he wrote to his wife from Morwenstow in April 1886. 'I have my pipe, my rod, my manuscript of Psalm ciii – the next chapter – and I am going down in the glorious valley under Stowe, with Charles Kingsley's scenery and romance all about me. I shall eat my dinner under the cliffs, looking out across the Atlantic, and listening to the thunder of the breakers; the scene that *intoxicates* me. It is lovely from here; the long line of the coast right away to Tintagel and the bare heights of Row Tor [*sic*] or Brown Willy away in the distance, suggesting dear Father and a thousand family associations. If I don't pick up inspiration to-day, and some trout, and some fresh air, it won't be for want of expecting it all.'[79]

Although he travelled extensively between 1883 and 1886, Portland, of course, also benefited enormously from his knowledge and skills. From 592 in 1880 the circuit membership increased steadily until the quarterly meeting reported that in 1884 there were 857, with 88 on trial and 52 in junior classes.[80] The following year saw a further increase, with Portland Street chapel itself recording a membership of 323 with 18 on trial – the highest in its history. Indeed, the church became so crowded that it was found necessary to fix tip-up seats to the ends of the pews to make accommodation in the aisles for the worshippers.[81] In spite of these measures, the lobby, vestries and even the communion rail and pulpit stairs were sometimes filled. Over a thousand were once counted as they left the chapel. 'He lifted the whole spiritual life of the circuit, and of the vast crowds who came to hear him,' wrote his old circuit steward, Charles Gardner. 'In those days we had Sunday and week-day preaching, and a fine prayer-meeting. Dear Mr Pearse was the most faithful and regular in the attendance at all his appointments, and particularly punctual. I remember that once I came in a few minutes late, so he said, 'Brother Gardner was late, so we will begin that hymn again'.'[82] To his congregation at Portland Chapel he dedicated *Some Aspects of the Blessed Life* (1885), which was, in style and treatment, a companion volume to *Thoughts on Holiness*. 'Every page has some specimen of pleasant pictures, graphic illustrations, or simple, happy mode of presenting familiar truths which makes it fresh and refreshing,' enthused the *Methodist Recorder*. Those expecting definitions, formulae and elaborate systems would look in vain, but those wanting 'a sip in passing at a fresh, sparkling book, full of glancing lights' and 'simple but not trite comments to light up and make more precious the already precious words of Scripture' would not be disappointed.[83]

In 1885 the Rev. Hugh Price Hughes, who was then Superintendent of the Brixton Hill circuit in south London, argued that Methodism had reached the parting of the ways. It could either go back into 'the obscurity of a class religion, and the impotence of a moribund sect' or go forward into 'the blessed opportunities and far reaching beneficence of a national religion' which preached the Gospel to the poor.[84] The mid-1880s represented a parting of the ways, too, for the Rev. Mark Guy

Pearse. Although the Conference which met at Newcastle in July 1885 reappointed him to the Portland circuit, his role was changing at what was a time of great change across Britain. In many ways, the fourteen months from June 1885 to August 1886 were amongst the most momentous in recent British history. In addition to a political crisis, the country underwent an economic one, with food and land prices falling as a result of the deepening trouble that agriculture found itself in, and trade and industry following suit. An alarming rise in unemployment in the cities resulted in widespread rioting, and troops were sent in against Welsh quarrymen in January.[85] At the beginning of February, the Rev. M. G. Pearse addressed enormous audiences under the auspices of the YMCA in Exeter Hall on the 'Deepening of Spiritual Life'. On Tuesday the 2nd he gave his first address – described as being 'for those who were dissatisfied with themselves and were longing after the fullness of blessing stored up in Christ Jesus' – in the lower room. However, it proved impossible to find room for all those who wanted to attend and subsequent meetings were held in the large hall, the basement of which was packed. A few days later, a demonstration organised in Trafalgar Square by the Labourers' League in order to draw attention to the plight of the unemployed was hijacked by the Revolutionary Social Democratic League. Although recognising that 'distress presses just now heavily upon a large portion of the working classes,' the *Methodist Recorder* deplored the looting and vandalism that ensued in the West End streets. And the Rev. John Telford, the future co-author of Mark Guy's biography, called the riot which saw the richest district of London in the hands of criminal elements, one of the 'most disgraceful and painful chapters in Metropolitan history'.[86] Such extreme spiritual and material dissatisfaction had been brewing in the capital – and elsewhere – for some considerable time and would result in a sea-change for the Rev. Mark Guy Pearse who, instead of opting for the 'quiet and half-hidden ministry' away from the public gaze[87] that he had set his heart on, would leave the clamour of Bristol in order to minister to the spiritually destitute and degraded in London's West End.

Chapter 10

'You would edify the saints and I would pursue the sinners.'

The West London Mission 1886–1903

London in the 1880s had a greater proportion of its work-force jobless than did any other part of Britain.[1] What is more, the influx of hundreds of thousands of people into the capital greatly aggravated the existing housing shortage, causing rents to rise sharply. With no unemployment insurance available, the jobless were all too often either dependent on spasmodic charity or forced into the workhouse. The publication, in October 1883, of the Rev. Andrew Mearns' twenty-page pamphlet *The Bitter Cry of Outcast London* drew attention to the shocking conditions in which the city's poor were living. At the same time, Methodism – in common with other churches – were being stifled by a rigid conservatism. As we have already seen, the great secession of 1849 dealt it a body blow which arrested its progress for over a quarter of a century. All parts of the country were affected, but London bore the brunt and between 1846 and 1855 the membership fell from 26,183 to 17,055, even though the population was rapidly increasing all the time. The tide turned in 1855, but the level of 1846 was not reached again until 1869. For it was not until 1861, when the Metropolitan Chapel Building Fund was founded, that the Methodists really began to understand the problem and try to address it. Over the next twenty-five years no fewer than sixty-nine large chapels were built and the number of sittings increased from 36,000 to 119,000. During the same period the number of ministers in active work rose from 51 to 120.[2] Even so, many of the huge chapels in cities such as London, Manchester, Liverpool, Birmingham and Leeds were often nearly empty because the services and methods of work had not been adapted to the changing environment. For people outside them, there was little or no thought. Mearns, then Secretary of the London Congregational Union, issued a stark warning:

> While we have been building our churches, and solacing ourselves with our religion, and dreaming the Millennium was coming, the poor have been growing poorer, the wretched more miserable, and the immoral more corrupt; the gulf has been daily widening which separates the lowest classes of the community from our churches and chapels and from all decency and civilisation. We are simply living in a fool's paradise if we suppose that all the agencies now in operation when combined are doing a thousandth part of what needs to be done, a hundredth part of what could be done by the Church of Christ. We must face the facts, and these compel the conviction that this terrible flood of sin and misery is gaining upon us every day.[3]

The churches, especially Wesleyan Methodism, were stung into action by Mearns' exposure of the physical deprivation and spiritual destitution of the people living in the inner city. One of those who was greatly influenced by *The Bitter Cry* was the Rev. Hugh Price Hughes, a young Wesleyan minister who described the ceaseless toil for the people inside the Church at the expense of virtually any altruistic spirit as 'coddling the Saints'.[4]

Born at Carmarthen in 1847, Hughes was the son of a prominent surgeon who rose to high public office in the town. His grandfather, a distinguished Wesleyan minister, was the first Welshman ever to be elected a member of the Legal Hundred. When Hughes was thirteen, a fleet of Cornish fishing boats sailed into Swansea Bay. Among the fishermen on board were many Methodists who attended the meetings held in the little Wesleyan chapel at The Mumbles. The Welsh lad was greatly impressed by the enthusiasm of these fellow-Celts, especially the heartiness of their singing and the fervour of their prayers. Referring later to the episode, he said, 'I was convicted of sin about that time through general influences, but the visit of these godly fishermen brought matters to a crisis.'[5] After much soul-searching, he accepted Jesus Christ wholeheartedly and at fourteen was put on the plan of the

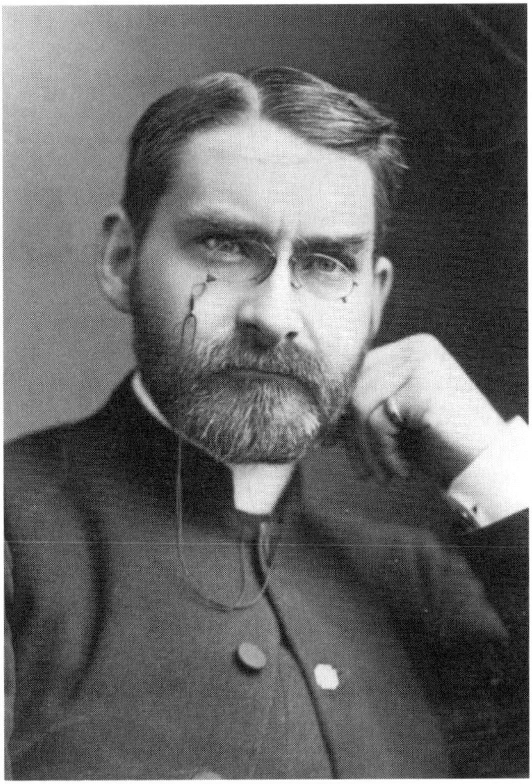

Rev. Hugh Price Hughes (Author's collection)

Swansea circuit. In 1865 he went to Richmond Theological College where his studies were so brilliant that the usual limit allowed for training – three years – was extended by a year. On graduating in 1869, he was appointed by Conference to Dover and over the next twelve years what he later described as 'the straight waistcoat of the three years system'[6] took him to Brighton, Tottenham, Dulwich and Oxford. As a result of an initiative called 'A Revival in Every Circuit', Hughes was, in the autumn of 1876, at the beginning of his second year in Tottenham, appointed to the Home Missionary Deputation to Cornwall. Such was the impact and success of the meetings held in the Truro circuit that, on his return to London, he was urged to return at once. Another week of crowded meetings followed and subsequently the revival spread throughout Cornwall and secured for Hughes the reputation of a powerful mission preacher. The impact he made would surely not have passed unnoticed by the Rev. Mark Guy Pearse who was convalescing in Bude at the time. In 1884, Hughes returned to the capital to take up the superintendency of the Brixton Hill circuit where he was, according to his wife Katherine, 'stirred to the depths of his being' by Mearns' *The Bitter Cry*.[7] The same Wesleyan Conference that was responsible for his appointment also instructed a committee to look at spiritual destitution in London, and to present a scheme for tackling it at the next conference. Simultaneously Hughes, who was convinced that Methodism had been 'too exclusively individualistic' in concentrating solely on personal salvation and that Christians should do their best to promote the social welfare of the people, established and edited a new weekly newspaper, *The Methodist Times*. The first number on 1 January 1885, stated his objectives clearly enough in its leader, 'Our Raison d'Etre'.[8] Echoing what Mearns had written sixteen months earlier, Hughes argued that the falling away of the working classes from Methodism was the result of its failure to adapt its methods of both worship and teaching to the circumstances and needs of the people. 'Many of our chapels have fallen into a deep rut,' he wrote, 'and we must pull very vigorously to get them out. Our arrangements must be much more elastic, and we must burn a great deal of the red tape which is strangling the work of God.'[9]

At City Road Chapel on Tuesday 10 March 1885, there took place the inaugural meeting of a new movement to evangelise the neglected parts of London – Wesleyan Methodism and Destitute London or 'The Forward Movement', as it was already popularly called. Ten days later Hughes spelled out precisely what the movement was up against when he wrote, 'It is impossible to deal effectually with the spiritual destitution of London unless you deal also with the physical and mental destitution.'[10] He urged that the enterprise should be carried out on a large and unprecedented scale. Large central buildings would be needed to attract workers, to stimulate enthusiasm and to generate the energy that would be needed to carry out such work. At a meeting in June, a sub-committee nominated the 'chief agents' of the Mission; Hughes was asked to take charge of the work in the East End, and Edward Smith of the work south of the Thames. Hughes considered his position for a week before informing the next meeting of the sub-committee that he would undertake the work only if the appointment was postponed for twelve months so as to give him time to complete the extensive schemes for which he was responsible at Brixton Hill. He also believed that those given the task of evangelising the great cities should be freed from the yoke of the itinerancy so that they could stay in one place long enough to have a real impact on the people. He reiterated that a grand scheme was needed, maintaining that 'although sometimes work on a small scale was best, the new movement in London would be much more likely to succeed on a large scale'.[11] When the Conference met in Newcastle-on-Tyne in July, the new London Mission occupied much of its time. Although the ideas put forward by Hughes and his friends for the East End were considered too radical, two appointments were made – the Rev. Peter Thompson to the east, and the Rev. Edward Smith to the south – and Conference formally committed itself to establishing the London Wesleyan Methodist Mission, with the object of carrying the gospel 'to such regions of London, and especially of Central London, as are most spiritually destitute and degraded'.[12]

While the two missioners already appointed set to work, the General Committee of the London Mission were persuaded to look at the West End. Here they found a vast district, three miles long by two wide, with a population of more than 400,000, in which Wesleyan Methodism was unrepresented except for the existence of two or three small mission rooms. When, therefore, they met in January 1886, the Committee were unanimous in recommending the opening of a West End centre and determined, when they met again in February, to ask the next Conference to designate Mark Guy Pearse and Hugh Price Hughes for the task, with effect from July 1887. The Committee thought it likely that Mr Pearse might be able to assist the Mission during the intervening year by helping to secure the funds necessary for such an important new development. In the opinion of the *Methodist Recorder*: 'Each of these has marked power in attracting and interesting the multitude, while each possesses the culture needful for addressing the educated, and especially young people of good social position. The gifts of the two are, however, in some respects quite diverse, and united they will admirably supplement each other's work...'[13] Once again Hughes' initial reaction was to take time out to pray and reflect before declining the call, but gradually he came to the conclusion that he would make his answer dependent on the response of his fellow minister. On 21 January, therefore, he wrote to his colleague in Bristol asking him if, on the days that he was in London for services at Exeter Hall in connection with the YMCA, he would conduct noon services in the Brixton Hill Circuit to tie in with similar meetings that he himself was planning. With the invitation came a sixteen-page letter which included the following:

> I want to have a long talk with you about a matter which may affect the whole of your future and mine. At a meeting of the London Mission Committee I was asked to undertake a mission in the West-End of London at the close of my ministry here in 1887. This is a new idea, but it is strongly urged on me, and it has so much in its favour that I'm already disposed to say 'yes' to the proposal on one condition – that you consent to be associated with me in the enterprise. I was told some time ago that you were still willing to go to Cornwall if I would go with you. The West-End of London is even more important than Cornwall. Why should we not undertake an analogous task in the West-End? I should be responsible for the work and for the organization; you would be free to write and to do anything to which the Spirit of God led you. Of course we should be relieved from the yoke of the itinerancy and the details of circuit work. You would have that liberty and that permanence of action which you crave. London is the place in which an author should live, and you could reserve ample time for using your pen in Christ's service. You are well-known outside Methodism, and your co-operation would be invaluable in the West-End. Besides the upper classes there are thousands of young men and young women in the West-End shops. In different ways you and I are better fitted for this work than any two of our contemporaries. A number of young men and young women have volunteered to give their lives to this work if I will undertake it. My wife could organise a sisterhood of ladies. My lay evangelist, Josiah Nix, would be simply invaluable among the working classes. It seems to be a unique combination of advantages. The responsibility of decision now rests with *you*, for if you say, 'Do all that is in thine heart; turn thee, behold, I am with thee according to thine heart,' I shall feel that the die is cast, and I am ready to give the rest of my life to this great work. Perhaps the Cornish catastrophe in your case and some unexpected events in my own are all a part of the Providential leading by which you and I are to be thrown together in the greatest work Methodism has ever attempted. If, after God and your friends, you approve of my suggestion, we could make all necessary arrangements during the year, and enter definitely upon the work after the Conference of 1887. You would edify the saints and I would pursue the sinners. With the blessing of God we should have such opportunities as no other arrangements would secure. I had a long talk with Clapham about this last night, and if you

> and I go into the work he is prepared to concentrate his remarkable powers and influence for the Mission, and to back us through thick and thin. I pray Christ with all my heart that in this crisis in your life and mine we may know and do the will of God. Amen. Yours affectionately, Hugh Price Hughes.[14]

Mark Guy, in turn, hesitated. He had planned to free himself from the itinerancy, which he found just as distasteful as did many of his colleagues, in the hope of settling in Cornwall with Dr Bowden and devoting the rest of his life to Cornish Methodism. Then had come Dr Bowden's appointment as governor of Kingswood School, Bath, and the subsequent collapse of his plans – 'the Cornish catastrophe' to which Hughes alludes, perhaps – and he was left uncertain as to his movements. He was still set, though, on going 'home'. The popularity of his books meant that money was not an issue. 'I knew nothing whatever of Mr Hughes,' he wrote later, 'had preached indeed for him once and shaken hands with him on that occasion only.[15] My own heart turned in quite another direction than London. I had dreams of the miners and fishermen of Cornwall, of its moors and cliffs. I had always a shrinking from prominence and publicity, and would have vastly preferred a quiet and half-hidden ministry with leisure for such literary pursuits as I loved. To accept Mr Hughes' proposal would mean that I must stand in the blare and glare of this great new movement in the West-End of London.'[16] Mark Guy did not know then about Hughes' seminal encounter with the Cornish fishermen some twenty-six years earlier. If he had known, then he would, he acknowledged, have read the letter with added interest and would quite possibly have been prompted to make a more immediate decision. As it was, he had very mixed feelings. On the one hand, perhaps it was divine providence that the proposition had come just at that juncture in his life. He and Hughes undoubtedly had much in common, including a firm belief in teetotalism and a Celtic background. On the other hand, they were utterly unlike in everything, except that they were both, in Pearse's own words, 'pig-headed men'.[17] Although he was sure that where Hughes was there would not be much room for anyone else, he agreed to come and discuss the proposal. In the meantime, he thought long and hard about it and consulted others, as the following extract from a letter to Sir William (?) , dated 30 January 1886, makes clear:

> I write at once as I am just leaving home for a week, [presumably in order to travel to London for the YMCA services at Exeter Hall]. My movements are so uncertain that I am quite unable to make any arrangements for after the Conference of this year. I should like to see you and talk over a proposal made to me by the Committee of the London Mission – that I should be set apart for the year to work either at home or abroad on behalf of the proposed Mission Hall. If I could see my way to raising £25,000 I would venture to Canada and the States and perhaps to Australia, but – well, it is a long way and I must have a good prospect of success before I commit myself to it.[18]

If this letter is anything to go by, then Mark Guy had already more or less made up his mind when, one afternoon during the first week of February, he left 29 Kensington Court and travelled out to the Superintendent's house in Clyde Place, Brixton Hill, which was familiar to him from his own time in the circuit twenty years earlier. Having greatly impressed Hughes' children by dashing off some of his famous pen and ink sketches for them, he disappeared upstairs to the study with their father.[19] His own version of that memorable meeting reads as follows:

> Almost before he had finished his greeting with his characteristic eagerness and force, there came a look of much solemnity, and he waited for me to speak. There was a minute's silence. 'Well,' I said presently, 'I am with you heart and soul.' At once he arose and opened the door. 'Katie,' he called, 'it is settled;' and Mrs Hughes came in to join us...[20]

According to Hughes himself, Mark Guy made his decision after listening to him for forty minutes.[21] Katherine Price Hughes, though, paints a rather different picture of the interview, having her husband talk for two hours without stopping as he set forth his ideas and plans! During all that time Mark Guy never uttered one word and, having agreed to join him, 'bolted... so rapidly that Mr Hughes had not time to ask him for his London address'![22] In due course, claimed the Rev. J. E. Clapham, he came to see the proposal as 'a Divine opening'.[23] On 18 February Hughes announced in *The Methodist Times* that the Rev. Mark Guy Pearse had agreed 'most heartily' to join him.[24]

At the Methodist Conference in London five months later, the final stage of the struggle to establish the West London Mission was reached.

Addressing the Conference on Thursday 29 July, the Rev. J. E. Clapham said that the Committee of the London Mission believed that if they could get Mr Pearse to serve the Mission's cause by giving lectures or preaching, or holding conventions at home or in Australia or other British colonies, he would be able to interest people far and wide in its work. They believed that he would be able to get at sources of revenue outside Methodism and that no burden at all would fall on the Connexion. The following afternoon he drew the Conference's attention to what he considered to be Mark Guy Pearse's strengths – 'his supreme power in the conduct of a prayer meet, in the exposition of Scripture, and in the teaching of the Scriptural holiness; also... his influence outside Methodism'.[25] There was still considerable opposition to the idea, especially from the Hinde Street and Great Queen Street circuits, and many were apprehensive about Hughes' radical approach. However, when it came to the vote, the resolution in favour of establishing the Mission was carried by a large majority and a famous partnership began work.

Between the Conference decision of August 1886 and the opening of the Mission in October 1887, Hughes and Pearse were very busy raising money for the new venture and explaining its purpose to Christians the length and breadth of the land. Conventions were held in a number of large towns with the purpose not only of stirring up and keeping alive the interest in the Mission of Methodists out in the provinces, but also as the means of reviving the religious life of the very centres in which they were held. One of the most important of these conventions took place in Newcastle during the first week of November, 1886 and embraced not merely Newcastle and Gateshead, but all the towns on the Tyne and Wear. Although the proposal for the convention had originated with several leading Newcastle laymen, there was considerable opposition to the idea at the District Meeting in September. After 'animated conversation', however, it had been resolved that Messrs Clapham, Pearse and Hughes should be received and the projected conference held, but on the express understanding that no appeal should be made for financial help in aid of the London Mission Fund.[26] Mark Guy had already paid two visits to the area that year and Hughes was well known to northern audiences. Clapham was less well known. The Newcastle Wesleyan Methodist District Convention began on the evening of Tuesday 2 November when the Rev. M. G. Pearse delivered a preparatory sermon in a crowded Town Hall. Taking as his text, Matthew 17, verse

LONDON
WEST CENTRAL MISSION.

OPENING SERVICES,
FRIDAY, OCT. 21.

ST. JAMES'S HALL, 11 a.m.,
SERMON BY
REV. C. H. SPURGEON.

WARDOUR HALL, 3.30 p.m.,
DEVOTIONAL MEETING.
ADDRESSES BY
Revs. M. G. Pearse, W. H. Tindall, and
H. P. Hughes.

WARDOUR HALL SCHOOLROOM, 5 p.m.,
PUBLIC TEA.
TICKETS NINEPENCE EACH.

ST. JAMES'S HALL, 7 p.m.
(Doors open at 6.30 p.m.),
PUBLIC MEETING.
ROBERT W. PERKS, Esq.,
In the Chair. Addresses by
Revs. the President of the Conference,
The Secretary of the Conference, Dr. Greeves,
E. E. Jenkins, M.A., J. Bush,
Dr. Watts, T. Guttery, F. Hastings,
Arthur Hall, J. Bond,
James Ernest Clapham, Mark Guy Pearse,
Hugh Price Hughes, M.A.,
Peter Thompson, W. J. Brown,
T. Morgan Harvey, Esq., and others.

SUNDAY, OCT. 23,
ST. JAMES'S HALL.

11 a.m.—Rev. Mark Guy Pearse.
3.30 p.m.—Rev. Hugh Price Hughes.
The Brass Band will begin at 3.
7 p.m.—Rev. Hugh Price Hughes.
The Orchestral Band will begin at 6.30.

MONDAY, OCT. 24,
WARDOUR HALL, 8 p.m.,
PRAYER MEETING,
Conducted by Rev. M. G. PEARSE.

SATURDAY, OCT. 22,
POPULAR CONCERT
At WARDOUR HALL,
At Eight.
Conducted by Mr. HEATH MILLS.

ALL SEATS FREE. COLLECTION AT EVERY SERVICE AND MEETING.

Announcement in the Methodist Recorder, *20 October 1887*

4 – 'Let us make three tabernacles here' – and Luke 9, verse 33 – 'Let us build three tabernacles here, so said Peter, not knowing what he said' – the preacher said that Peter had wanted to build in the wrong place, away from all the misery and unpleasantness of the world. The Church had got to come down from the mountain top, 'from its selfish raptures into the very midst of the people who needed Christ's presence, into the very midst of the heart of the pressure of our temptations and difficulties of everyday life'. It had also to refrain from exalting human arrangements, ritual, plans and methods at the expense of Christ, and to learn to take the sins and sorrows of the poor world upon its soul, carrying them as Christ carried the sins and sorrows of men when He was in their midst.[27] The Convention resumed in Brunswick Place Chapel the following morning when the business proper began. There was such a large attendance that benches were placed in the aisles to provide extra seating, and when these were full, several people were forced to stand. Once Hugh Price Hughes had delivered an address on 'The Doctrine of Holiness', Mark Guy introduced the subject of 'The Life of Holiness' in a speech that a Methodist correspondent on the *Newcastle Daily Chronicle* described as being 'of such magic force, that those who heard surely cannot soon forget it or lose its influence'. Pitching the tune himself, he got the audience on to their knees to sing the hymn beginning 'Thou knowest my feebleness…' The strongest men were seen to weep. When he proposed to bring his address to a close, there were cries for him to continue; this address was, in turn, followed by a discussion. At the afternoon session he spoke of the need for preparation by prayer before preaching, and his good friend Thomas Bainbridge, to whom he dedicated *The Gospel for the Day*, opened the discussion on 'The Work of the Class Leader', a subject close to Mark Guy's heart. Bainbridge spoke, too, at the evening meeting when two thousand people crowded into the chapel to hear about the London Mission. He announced that his father would give £1,000 and that he himself would donate £100 plus £50 a year for the next four years. At the end of the Convention, the following resolution was proposed and carried unanimously:

> That this meeting, having had the opportunity, for which it is devoutedly thankful to the Great Head of the Church, of hearing the statements of the Revs. Messrs Clapham, Pearse, and Hughes relative to the London Mission, would avow its conviction of the necessity and importance of that glorious enterprise,

> and its determination to further its interests to the utmost of its ability.[28]

This pattern was repeated elsewhere. At Carr's Lane Congregational Chapel, Birmingham, the following January, Pearse advocated 'healthy handshaking' in preference to preaching, oratory or intellectualism as a means of reaching the masses who were said to have slipped out of the hands of the Church.[29] Two months later, when he and his colleagues were in Manchester, he described how he came to be associated with the Mission before endeavouring to impress his audience with some idea of the utter vastness of London and, consequently, of the task they faced. Within sixteen miles of Charing Cross there was a population of 5,200,000 souls, of whom 2,600,000 were outside all religious provision.[30] Hugh Price Hughes denied that theirs was a mission to the aristocracy though, in his opinion, the aristocracy were in greater need of evangelistic effort than any other class in the land. The West End he described as the 'Vanity Fair' of the world, competing not unsuccessfully with Paris itself. It was the centre of vice and wickedness, and therefore the one place above all others that the Methodist Church should seek to enter and to save.[31] The style of the conventions was not always to everyone's taste. Reporting on the one that was held at Nottingham towards the end of March, the *Methodist Recorder* confessed that it was not always in agreement with Mr Hughes and Mr Pearse:

> No doubt their slashing paradoxes are popular, and, at the moment, help their purpose. But it is open to question whether, on the whole, and in the long run, they would not be more effective if they maintained a more rigid discipline among the sentinels who presumably guard the doors of their lips.

Leaving aside, though, what it called the 'wild free-lancism' of the meetings, the *Recorder* gave thanks for the 'world of truth and freshness, of zeal and genuine pathos' that it found in the sermons and speeches by which Messrs Hughes and Pearse and their colleagues were rousing the people. 'How thankful we ought to be,' it concluded, 'that they are finding a sphere in which their peculiar gifts and graces may be most usefully exercised.'[32]

Shortly after his return from North America towards the end of June 1887 – the first of many tours that he made to foreign parts on behalf of the Mission – Mark Guy Pearse, with Hugh Price Hughes, was formal-

Preachers in their pulpits: Mark Guy Pearse at St James's Hall, Temple Magazine, *1896–97*

ly appointed at the Manchester Conference to the West Central Branch of the London Mission, their brief being to act under the direction of the Committee of the London Wesleyan Methodist Mission. With his principal aim being to bring people to Christ, Hughes was not concerned with sponsoring a denominational crusade. Indeed, he stressed that the organisation of the Mission was to be 'on a catholic basis', enjoying the co-operation of members of all Christian churches.[33] This inter-denominational approach was something else he shared with his colleague who, as we have seen, sought from his early days in the ministry to break down barriers. It was entirely fitting, then, that it was the famous Baptist evangelist Charles H. Spurgeon who was invited to conduct the opening service of the Mission at 11am on Friday 21 October 1887 in St James's Hall, which had been acquired for Sundays and Fridays at a reasonable rent. There was some concern as to whether the hall, with a seating capacity of 2,500, would be filled on a weekday morning. In the event, these fears proved to be groundless and Spurgeon, whom one member of the packed congregation described as looking 'very ill and suffering', preached 'a beautiful sermon on "Ask for the old paths"'.[34] That same afternoon, the half-hour prior to the time announced for the start of the devotional meeting at Wardour Hall was spent in singing snatches of sacred song. Surrounded on the platform by a score of fellow-ministers, Hughes underlined how Methodists and other Christians might become more useful in the service of Christ. His prefatory remarks and the singing of the hymn 'Just as I am, without one plea' were followed by devotional exercises; these were followed, in turn, by two or three addresses, one of them Mark Guy Pearse's. 'I am sorry to have experienced already a little bit of discouragement,' he began in his customary forthright style. 'I found it hard to ascertain from policemen or cabmen the whereabouts of this hall, and although I took a hansom, I had to get out and walk part of the way before I could manage to reach Wardour St... I am not one of the half-timers, and I only hope there will be no half-timers among the people who shall gather here'. He went on to describe his relation to the mission as being so peculiar that he could hardly think of anything else. Had anyone told him two years previously that he would work in London again, he would have looked upon that person as being past arguing with, with his former breakdown militating so strongly against such a course of action. However, his way seemed so hedged about that he could not but respond to the call. 'I feel just thrust into this work by the Lord,' he continued. 'I am very anxious to give Mr Hughes the first place in connection with this work in which he and I are associated. I am his assistant. The firm has not got much room in it when Mr Hughes is there. I am glad he has full scope, and we are looking for grand things. We do bless God that our friend has so much "go" in him, that he is full of steam, and that his heart and soul are as big as this great London'. His own part in this new departure – 'so much smaller than his [Hughes]' – would consist of taking a Sunday morning service, preaching – when able – on Friday mornings and holding a Monday evening prayer-meeting in Wardour Hall.[35] The opening services continued in St James's Hall at 7 o'clock when Mark Guy was one of many who addressed a large public meeting presided over by Robert Perks MP, one of the first and most generous supporters of the Mission. He reiterated that his contribution to the mission had been, he might almost say, reluctantly given, in view of the fact that he had plans for 'quite another work, amongst the Cornish people, and not under the smoky skies of London'. Prolonged applause greeted the statement that 'his contribution to that work, now most gratefully, no longer reluctantly given, was himself'. At this point in the proceedings, the hall suffered a power cut whereupon he at once began to tell a story 'just to enlighten the darkness' until the gas, which was kept in reserve, was turned on.[36]

Two days later, at 11 o'clock, the regular programme of Sunday services began, with Mark Guy preaching for the first time in St James's Hall. The huge circulation and popularity of his devotional writings attracted a large crowd from the beginning and for the next fifteen years he drew one of the biggest and most cosmopolitan congregations in London. Simplicity was the hallmark of these Sunday morning services, which were made as informal as possible. There was no band or orchestra, although on that first Sunday Mr R. Heath Mills was at the hall's large organ leading a mixed choir. An American organ, which was more economical to run, was used for future services. Fresh flowers adorned the reading stand. Taking as his text Nehemiah 1, 4, 'And it came to pass, when I heard these words, that I sat down and wept, and mourned certain days, and fasted, and prayed before the God of heaven', Mark Guy dwelt at length on what he considered to be the deplorable condition of London, on the homeless and the outcast, and on how the Church had been put to shame by the activities of the Press in calling attention to the situation. 'The troops of little children flocking breakfastless to school,' he continued, 'the scenes of riot and debauchery every night close to that hall, the great sea of iniquity surging about the very place where they met, the thousands of dens where even decency was impossible – they could not be called homes – Christians must rouse themselves to look at these things.' For him, though, the saddest thing of all was that Christians could see such things and not fret about them. Throughout his sermon he continued to home in on what he called 'the curse of indifference' and the need for practical solutions. What was wanted in stages, among Christian people, was 'deep personal interest, passing into importunate prayer and earnest effort'. He stressed that he himself would not touch this work were he not satisfied that God would give him all the money he needed for His work. Those present were not invited to St James's to hear bright services, or pretty music, or interesting sermons, they were there to help forward God's work. He warned that if they looked to Mr Hughes and his co-workers for the success of the mission, they would achieve nothing.[37] In the preface to a published volume of sermons preached in St James's Hall entitled *Naaman the Syrian*, Mark Guy underlined the thinking behind the presentation and style of these Sunday morning services:

> Whilst Sunday Evening Services are very common in the Theatres and Halls of London, I do not know that there is another *Morning* service of this sort – held in a place which is used ordinarily for secular purposes. We commenced in connection with the West London Mission six years ago, the congregation numbering some four hundred persons. We have now a congregation of little less than two thousand. The service has been called one of Quaker-like simplicity.[38] We have no orchestra band, not even using the large organ of the Hall. Everything is done to make the service hearty, homely, bright, and simple. In this lonely London, homeliness and brotherliness are blessed ways to the Father's House, and the presence of our most gracious Lord, the Friend and Brother of us all. The preaching necessarily partakes of this freedom and homeliness. It is as natural to *talk* from a platform as it is to preach from a pulpit. And the character of the congregation encourages such a style. To those who have not been in the habit of attending any place of worship, a public Hall is much nearer than a Church. A Church is regarded as the private property of those who worship there; a Hall is everybody's. There are no pews, and there are no privileges. To go into a Church is to take upon one's self some degree of religious profession; but curiosity is enough to prompt a stroll into a Hall...[39]

There were those who claimed that the city's poor and desolate who were helped during the week by the social workers of the Mission were not the ones who filled the seats in St James's and Princes' Halls on Sundays.[40] And Hughes himself conceded that 'the morning congregation consisted largely of young men and young women from the great West End houses of business'. It was also frequented by 'earnest seekers after saintliness'.[41] Emmeline Pethick-Lawrence, though, remembered 'large congregations where rich and poor sat side by side, and visitors from the Dominions, or from the Provinces, mixed with the London crowd' and William Lax described how 'crowds came from the ends of the earth'.[42] Mark Guy received numerous letters from those who had been saved from despair by the warmth and humanity of his message. 'Last October,' wrote 'L. M.', enclosing a £20 donation for one of the Mission charities in which Mark Guy was most interested, 'I came to a Sunday morning service, heavy-hearted and sad – for my way laid through the desert, and my heart was failing me for fear. I cannot find words to express my gratitude to you for your message of help and cheer that day! I felt it to be a real message from God to my soul – the very words that were so sorely needed.'[43] Before the collection was taken at the second of his Sunday morning services, on 30 October, he protested against the idea that the Mission was a money-making concern and expressed the hope that no poor person would stay away because they were unable to give.[44] Nevertheless, money was needed to finance the numerous social welfare schemes which it sponsored from its foundation and, as well as taking his place at one of the main doors at the close of his services in order cordially to shake hands with people as they crowded out, Mark Guy often took the opportunity to sell his own books, donating the money to the Sisters of the People.

Aware that, in the 1880s, the music hall had eclipsed the theatre in terms of popularity, Hugh Price Hughes concluded that if the Church was to gain adherents, it must offer music, a hopeful gospel and warm and friendly surroundings.[45] At 3 o'clock, therefore, on Sunday 23 October the Mission brass band struck up in St James's Hall to attract an audience for the first of his 'Conferences' in which he proposed 'for… one brief hour… to deal with that public application of the Gospel which has been so long and so perilously neglected by those who are the followers of Jesus Christ'.[46] He maintained that the organised Churches had hitherto been so absorbed by the interests of the individual soul that the ills of society were neglected; so preoccupied were they with the delights of Heaven that they overlooked some of the most urgent duties of earth. This was the Christian Socialism that his colleague, the Rev. M. G. Pearse, came to advocate. It was no use preaching to the people merely about a life beyond the grave. It was necessary, too, to try to make their circumstances more comfortable and their lives more useful to themselves, their friends and the community at large.[47] 'It is but a one-handed gospel, and that an exceedingly awkward and left-handed gospel,' he stressed in *Short Talks for the Times*, 'that offers men a home in heaven when, for the present, it is of so much more importance that they should find a decent home in London.'[48] The audiences at these afternoon conferences varied in number between 1,500 and 2,000 and the questions that Hughes had to deal with were not merely political, but social – touching on 'morality, righteousness, truth, and the well-being of the people'.[49] Shortly after 6.30 pm that same day – prior to the start of the evening service – an orchestral band consisting of about fifty instrumentalists began playing in the already well-filled hall, their first piece being Mendelssohn's 'Cornelius' March. By 7 o'clock almost every seat on the floor and in both the end galleries was occupied, and very soon afterwards the seats at the back of the orchestra, too, were filled. Hundreds were unable to gain admission. After a highly individualistic and evangelistic service, there was what was variously described as an 'inquiry meeting', 'after-meeting' or 'at home' when a few of the Sisters and stewards moved quietly about the hall, welcoming those in attendance and targeting anyone who gave a sign that they needed spiritual advice.[50] On average, from forty to sixty people responded to the offer of a sympathetic ear, something that Mark Guy Pearse saw as an essential ingredient in the Mission's work. 'I believe,' he wrote, 'that the greatest blessing that you could give to tens of thousands of men and women in London is this – some one to whom they could fully and freely open their hearts. I think the workers in this Mission would tell you that the grace they need pray for most constantly is not the grace of courage, not the grace of hope, but the grace patiently to listen to the stories of those who come to them.'[51]

Mark Guy was a source of strength and support to the Mission on weekdays as well as on Sundays. For him, the measure of an individual's religion was 'not in feeling, but in doing; not in services on Sunday, but in service all through the week...The religion of Sunday is an empty sham and a rottenness, unless it helps us through the seven days of the week to be simple, self-forgetful, brave, true, brotherly, glad to help anybody anywhere.'[52] And his friend and colleague Hugh Price Hughes believed that the Friday evening devotional meetings that he himself led in the Princes' Hall were the pivot around which the whole Mission turned. The opening services continued on the Monday when at 8 o'clock Mark Guy conducted the first of his weekly prayer meetings at Wardour Hall, a Congregational chapel on the south side of Oxford Street that had been placed at the Mission's disposal by the Rev. Andrew Mearns. Four days later, on 28 October, he was back at St James's Hall for the first of his Friday morning services which his daughter and biographer described as 'a means of reaching many leisured people, of relieving much unspoken sorrow and loneliness, and putting new hope and new aims into harassed and empty lives'.[53] On the previous Sunday morning he had announced that the services would be divided into short sections of about twenty minutes duration, with a view to encouraging businessmen and others to devote at least that amount of time each day to prayer.[54] In *The Christianity of Jesus Christ: Is it Ours?*, which consists of addresses he delivered at these Friday midday services, he exhorted his listeners – and readers – to join him in encouraging 'men and women everywhere to try their genius at saving the waste of humanity round about us…[and] to find many new methods of successful service.'[55] Many of those who became involved in the battle to improve the lot of the materially and spiritually impoverished living in the slums of Oxford Street and Piccadilly came to those addresses and found themselves strengthened and refreshed.

This pattern of services and other activities was followed throughout the year, except that Hughes's afternoon conference was discontinued in July, August and September. October 1887, then, marked a memorable departure in the work of Methodism in London. The response from the public was tremendous and the initial momentum was maintained for years. Hugh Price Hughes grasped the nettle and a fortnight after the opening of the Mission, he devoted his Sunday afternoon conference in St James's Hall to the subject of 'Jesus Christ and Social Distress', declaring that the time had come for Christians to discharge their duty in public in addition to saying their prayers in private. His beliefs and those of his colleagues and backers gave rise to a programme of social schemes which was heralded by Josiah Nix's appeal for 'two sacks of split peas, one sack of rice, two sacks of onions, two sacks of turnips, two sacks of carrots [and] one sack of pea-flour' for the soup-kitchen which was to open on Monday 7 November.[56] 'Every earnest Methodist, and thousands of godly souls in other branches of the Church of God,' declared the *Wesleyan Methodist Magazine*, 'will watch with interest and uphold with continued prayer the efforts made at Hinde-street, St James' Hall and Wardour Hall for the recovery of the sinful souls who swarm in the fashionable streets or cower in the obscure places of this portion of the metropolis. To win such for Christ, to save new-comers to the great city from swelling their numbers, to strengthen the hands of those who are already the Lord's, is a task peculiarly in harmony with the genius of Methodism, and one to which we cannot grudge even such men as Hugh Price Hughes and Mark Guy Pearse.'[57]

The notion of a partnership between the two men was greeted with some degree of ridicule when it was announced in February 1887. People said that they would fight like cat and dog – an opinion based on the knowledge that they were indeed chalk and cheese. A greater contrast than Hugh Price Hughes and Mark Guy Pearse could not be imagined! Described by a minister of another Church as 'the embodiment of force',[58] Hughes, on the one hand, was 'well nigh peerless as a debater and a declaimer… at home in a fray and rarely at peace, except when at war'. He was, too, a skilful organiser, a natural leader of men and 'an ecclesiastic to the finger tips'.[59] Furthermore, Dorothea Price Hughes wrote that her father's ability and power in debate were such that, sweeping the way before him with a determination to carry his point, he appeared to give the impression that he would not be easy to work with.[60] Such descriptions are echoed by the Free Methodist minister Silas K. Hocking, for whom Hughes was '[a] cleric to his fingertips, and an emphatic believer in the ministerial order. Dogmatic and sometimes overbearing. A fine platform speaker, and a fearless advocate of what he believed to be right; lacking somewhat in sympathy, and in the saving grace of humour; his driving force was tremendous'.[61] Mark Guy, on the other hand, was more unconventional, more of an individualist. 'Gifted with genius, endowed with rare intellectual gifts, a writer of distinction, a lecturer of marvellous charm, a mighty preacher and an artist',[62] he had little time for Church problems, his supreme ambition being to preach the gospel. Writing much later, Arthur Lawrence recalled attending the Mission as an eighteen year old and seeing Mark Guy talking to his audience 'with… Cornish benevolence and understanding', in contrast to Hughes who 'denounced the Devil and all his works with stinging vehemence'.[63] Both men, though, had a deep concern for the welfare of others. 'One of the most thoughtful and affectionate of friends, and one of the most brotherly of ministers' was how J. Gregory Mantle described Hughes,[64] while, as far as the Rev. C. Ensor Walters was concerned, there was no one kinder or more generous than Mark Guy Pearse, a man in whom multitudes found a never-failing friend.[65] This shared sympathy with the social aspects of Christianity and aversion to red tape as a barrier to effective Christian work ensured that, against all the odds, the partnership – 'the firm', as Mark Guy called it – was not only famous, but successful. When asked how this wonderful harmony was achieved, Hughes would answer, with a twinkle in his eye, that it was as simple as Euclid: parallel lines never met, and therefore could not cross each other. Each had his own work, and did it in his own way.[66] Others were able to see just how this harmony of contrasts rather than of correspondence worked. For the Rev. C. Ensor Walters, who on Hughes' sudden death in 1902 succeeded him as Superintendent, he was the Mission's master-builder, whereas it was Mark Guy Pearse who 'welded it together by his wonderful preaching and exposition of Christian love'.[67] Whilst Hughes was the Superintendent, 'zealous in every department of the Mission, alert and mighty at committee, public meetings and Conference' Pearse was 'the beloved brother with a heart of gold'.[68] Another Mission worker, the Rev. William Lax, painted an endearing picture of the contrasting personalities and styles of its two leaders:

> In his moods of banter, which were frequent, Hughes would tell Pearse that his duty was to coddle the saints in the morning, whilst he himself caught the sinners in the evening. To which Pearse would reply that his congregation got sermons in the morning, and Hughes's crowd got 'a few remarks' in the evening! How they loved to chaff one another! Each was the perfect foil of the other. If there was a human explanation of the West London Mission's influence a generation ago, it was Hugh Price Hughes and Mark Guy Pearse.[69]

Time and again, in recounting how he came to be involved in the Mission, Mark Guy would describe how each of them had his own way, and let the other have his. Each would put his foot down firmly enough, but it was on his own quarterdeck, and so no harm was done. The two understood each other. Mark Guy was staunchly loyal to Hughes who, during his superintendency, was no stranger to controversy. What is more, his affection for the man who was technically his boss went very deep. On Hughes' s death he wrote:

> It was an acquaintance that became at once a friendship, and that soon ripened into love – to know him was to love him – none could help it, and those who knew him best loved him most... I loved him as perhaps it is given to few men to love a man.[70]

Hughes and Pearse had a very clear picture of their aims in establishing the West London Mission: to bring people of all classes to Christ through its meetings, to cheer the lives of the poor and to enlist the sympathies of the wealthy. The division of labour had already been agreed upon, with Hughes being responsible for the work and for the organisation, leaving his colleague free to write and to do anything to which the Spirit of God led him.[71] Before they could begin their work to 'edify the saints and... pursue the sinners',[72] however, there were some practicalities to be settled. They were apparently given free reign to fix their ministerial stipends, with Mark Guy's version of how the matter was resolved reading as follows:

> When we began our work, he said to me, 'We are our own stewards. We can appoint our own salary. What shall we take?' 'Well,' I said, 'it is for you to settle that. You must remember that it is your livelihood. You might be making your £10,000 a year,' I said, laughingly, 'if you had chosen to go to the Bar.' 'Well,' said he, 'let us take £200 a year all told,' and this, apart from the house and furniture, was the sum which this man fixed as his salary when he entered upon his work in the West London Mission.[73]

House and furniture in each case were provided by the Mission. Both knew that sales of Mark Guy's books – estimated at between four and six million copies – brought him a comfortable income.[74] In fact, during his sixteen years service at the Mission, he contributed some £500 annually to the Sisterhood, in whose work, as we shall see, he took a deep interest.[75] It was decided, too, that like most of the Mission's full-time workers who lived either 'over the shop' or within walking distance of it, Hughes and Pearse would live within the area they were serving. Accordingly, the superintendent and his family moved to 8, Taviton Street, WC1, while the Pearses installed themselves nearby at 11, Bedford Place.

New ideas were always taking shape and experiments were always being tried out in the early days of the Mission, so that by the turn of the century J. Gregory Mantle could justifiably describe its work as 'bewilderingly many-sided'.[76] Excluding Sunday schools, Bands of Hope and Mothers' Meetings, over three thousand services and meetings were held every year, many of them in parks, streets and alley-ways. Vigorous temperance work was done in a variety of venues and, once again, in the open-air. To ensure that visits to the poor and vulnerable were properly co-ordinated, there were Room-to-room Guilds, a Public-House Guild, a Lodging-House Guild, and a Workhouse Guild. There were Men's and Women's Slate Clubs, Penny Banks, Clothing, Provident and Boot Clubs and Goose and Christmas Clubs to encourage thrift. To give the unemployed a fresh start, the Mission opened up a men's Labour Exchange within a year of its foundation. Other initiatives in this field included a Servants' Registry which aimed to help the girls in the Mission classes find employment in Christian families, and a wood chopping 'factory'. The Mission had its own medical department, with two dispensaries and a staff of hospital-trained, duly certificated and qualified nursing sisters who visited hundreds of poor people in their own homes. A crèche catered for the infants and young children of working mothers, while St Luke's House was a home where, in the words of its Medical Superintendent, Dr Howard Barrett, 'respectable but well nigh destitute poor… can retire to die in decency and comfort'.[77] The Guild of the Brave Poor Things catered for the needs of the mentally and physically disabled, while teas were provided every month for the elderly in a number of workhouses. There was a Preventitive Home and a Rescue Home for women in moral danger, People's Drawing Rooms for the poor, and Cycle Clubs, Rambling Clubs and University Extension Lectures for young people in business. A Poor Man's Lawyer gave free legal advice on a weekly basis, while members of the Sheen Society made and collected garments for distribution among the poor who lived in those districts visited by the Sisters, thereby enhancing their prospects of getting jobs. With infant mortality in the slum area of Somers Town at 232 per 1,000 compared with a London average of 130, in 1907 a School of Mothers was established, providing a weighing machine for mothers and babies, demonstrations and lectures on all aspects of baby care and information about food, cooking and health care. The varied and numerous activities of the Mission, of which the foregoing is but a glimpse, can be divided into two categories, the first broadly pastoral and evangelical, the second, as Philip Bagwell points out, embracing social welfare work and thereby foreshadowing the creation of the Welfare State. Although, as we have already seen, Mark Guy Pearse took an active part in the Mission's pastoral and evangelical work, it was in its welfare schemes that he found work after his own heart. He firmly believed that the future of the world belonged to 'the common people' and that the religion of the future was that which had most room for them. 'To visit the poor,' he wrote, 'is a command to all of us – not only to relieve them when they visit us. We must study the conditions in which they live, and use every power to secure homes for decent people when decency is possible, and we must demand that somehow comfort shall be within reach of the thrifty.'[78]

It was, then, in those centres of activity which were more withdrawn from the limelight than the two halls in Piccadilly and where the social work received greater prominence that Mark Guy was often to be found, showing what he hoped was 'a Christlike brotherliness' towards others. In *The Christianity of Jesus Christ – Is It Ours?* he expressed the hope that one result of such a considerate attitude would be that every church and chapel would have some place open every night – warmed, cheerful, and attractive, as easily reached as the public house, as comfortable as the lounge bar, where men and women and young people could sit and read without being either lectured or patronised, but welcomed simply as brothers.[79] Of the numerous social welfare activities in which he was closely involved, perhaps none merits more attention than the Sisters of the People. Hugh Price Hughes described them as 'by far the most important departure of the Mission',[80] an opinion to which his colleague added a more personal touch when he said, 'When I get among the Sisters at their work, my heart bubbles up and runs over at my eyes... One Sister is worth ten parsons at this work [caring for the physical needs of the poor].'[81] The idea of a Sisterhood was conceived by Katherine Price Hughes who had observed what was being done by ladies in the Roman Catholic Church at one end of the religious spectrum and by the enthusiastic and self-denying officers of the Salvation Army at the other. Pearse himself acknowledged the great assistance they had received from the Salvationists and maintained that the Wesleyans would have been too frightened or too prejudiced to permit sisterhoods in their denomination had they not seen the religious work done by their women officers.[82] Early on the Hugheses indicated that they were looking to recruit 'ladies of leisure, culture, refinement and devotion';[83] and Mark Guy firmly believed that Christian fathers and mothers should be prepared to give up their daughters for life and work amongst the people and that the Church that would make the best use of its women was the Church that would come to have the most authority in the world. Further views on the same subject, which he expounded in *Jesus Christ and the People* – to the effect that the average young lady of the day was 'a waste product'[84] – did not always go down too well with some audiences at his lectures! Beyond wearing a uniform, living together in one of the Mission's buildings and reporting weekly to the Sister Superior, the Sisters were under no hard or fast rules, but were free to manage in their own way the work for which they felt they had a special aptitude. The result was that individual schemes were tried out and, if they proved useful and successful, were incorporated into the permanent features of the Mission. The Sisters were totally different from the ordinary lady visitors in that they not only visited the household, but helped with the work when required. Where there was sickness, they would lend a hand at nursing, or when the mother was laid up, would take charge of the household, sending her away to the country to recuperate. They were prepared to put their hand to anything, from bandaging an injury, to sweeping the floor or cooking a meal, as well as reading from the Bible. It was almost certainly the Sisters that Mark Guy was thinking of when he wrote, 'Do not think of them [God's angels] only as about the throne singing rapturous hymns and having golden harps. Look for them amongst the savoury smells of the soup kitchen... Search for them superintending penny dinners for hungry children at the Board Schools. God's angels are not sentimental creatures who can only sing; they can cook a digestible dinner and find their heaven in seeing a hungry man eat it.'[85]

For him, such practical religion established a bond between those involved that no amount of preaching and instruction could accomplish. Of the many stories with which he entertained audiences at home and abroad, some concerned his daughter Maud who was herself a Sister. And she was not the only one of his children who had links with the West London Mission. St Christopher's Boys' Club, which was situated in Fitzroy Square, began in 1894 when his younger son Warwick Guy gathered together some fifty working boys in part of a hall belonging to the Mission. He was assisted by some of the sisters, among them Emmeline Pethick and Mary Neal, and like some of them, took a flat in a particularly rough court. The club grew until its membership reached over two hundred and thrived for many years, with activities ranging from boxing to acting. Indeed, over five or six weeks each year, he would organise a summer camp for a hundred or so boys, many of whom came from the criminal classes. A former St Christopher's Club boy later wrote of its founder:

> I think he has done more than any man living to teach young men to treat and respect one another in the way of life – he is the loving Patron Saint of St Christopher's and you can find a tinge of it in any who have come into contact with him.[86]

Emmeline Pethick had written to Mrs Price Hughes in 1890 and was welcomed by her into the Sisterhood. From then on, her personal relationship with Mark Guy developed into one of 'comradeship and union in a common purpose'. She retained her position as one of the family and spent many happy hours at 11, Bedford Place telling him about the people with whom her work brought her into contact. At Cleveland Hall, according to Vera Brittain, 'she won the affection of the high-spirited but frustrated girls by teaching them the active games which amused her young brothers' and soon learned the difference between their values and hers.[87] In 1895 she and her friend Mary Neal founded the Esperance Girls' Club and Social Settlement, a move which did not immediately meet with 'Daddy's' approval. 'So entirely did he enter into the thoughts and aspirations of the young,' she wrote, 'and so closely was he in touch with his children, with whom I too was in touch, that when I made up my mind to unfold my plan for coming into closer contact with working girls by living amongst them, I expected understanding and response. In my ignorance of the normal reactions of human nature, I had not foreseen his displeasure that I should wish to leave the organization with which he was connected.' Shocked by a display of coldness from the one person who had never failed to give her anything but affection, she broke down in front of him. He, in turn, was mortified at the distress that his displeasure had caused and from then on there was no one more interested in the new enterprise and so eager to help make it a success. Faced with the problem of how to live on a joint income of £80 a year, the pair had hoped that Mary would get some work as a journalist, but this proved hard to come by. Mark Guy came to their rescue by proposing to take with him on his weekly travels some of the stories that Mary had had published in book form. These he would sell alongside his own books, keeping a separate account, and then nearly every Friday he would climb up to the girls' little apartment in order to 'bring his wages home'. He helped, too, in other ways, on one occasion providing a farm labourer's smock which was needed for a play that the children in their club were producing. 'It was these little things about which we could laugh that touched me most of all,' wrote Mrs Pethick-Lawrence. 'In this all-sufficing friendship, in which all my needs, great or small, were foreseen and provided for, I felt like 'a tree planted by rivers'.' Although he would later find himself totally at odds with the direction her life was taking, his endorsement of this enterprise was total. 'I have watched and followed you step by step,' he wrote at the beginning of 1897, 'sometimes hand in hand have gone with you. You have lived a life and done a work that have been a mighty inspiration. The best and finest is the example you have set as a pioneer. It is easier for everyone for what you have done, my own dear comrade.' Four years later he officiated at her marriage to the wealthy lawyer, Frederick Lawrence, whom she had converted to socialism.[88]

One of the early successes of the West London Mission was the 'Dinner for the Lonely' on Christmas Day. Although the meal was served at 1.30 pm, the guests – mostly young people in business who could not return home – were invariably entertained until 11 pm. Over 150 would come, only too delighted to pay 2/6 [12p] to have a merry, as opposed to a sad Christmas. Mr Pearse was, it seems, the life and soul of the party, regaling those present with his Cornish stories for hours on end and joining in their games.[89] The Drunkard's Dinner was a feature of the Mission's temperance work which, as the years went by, met with considerable success. Mark Guy recalled how when the first was held, they had no difficulty in finding a sufficient number of qualified persons in the immediate vicinity of the hall. Later, though, they had to go further and further afield for their drunkards, which is not surprising given that, in some months, as many as 800 signed the pledge and that the Mission's Band of Hope boasted 2,000 members.[90] Another feature of the Sisters' work that he always drew attention to in his lectures was the entertainment they provided for those who were ending their days in the workhouse. The inmates, it seems, were allowed outside the walls once a fortnight – the men one Wednesday, the women on the next. Before the Sisters took them in hand, the public house was the only place of entertainment for them and the majority frequently returned to the workhouse the worse for wear. The Sisters, therefore, waited for them outside and invited them either to Wardour Hall, Cleveland Hall, Craven Hall or Charlton Street Hall where they made them at home, playing all manner of games with them, talking with them, singing to them and then praying with them. Refreshments, too, were provided. Instead of going to parties among their own friends, the Sisters helped in this family party of Christ's.[91] Those who were too sick to leave the workhouse were visited once a week.

The loathing that the poor felt for the workhouse – a loathing that lasted well into the twentieth century – was well understood by the Sisters, and in 'deserving' cases, they tried to provide small allowances, particularly for the elderly, to enable them to remain independent.[92] As Dr Howard Barrett, Katherine Price Hughes's brother, knew only too well, if there was little room to live in the crowded houses of West London, there was even less room in which to die. 'I have no words nor heart,' he wrote in 1891, 'to speak of the misery in the dying faces that haunt me, the pathos of their inarticulate pleading, or the apathy of despair that is past complaint.'[93] Consequently, after a two-year search for suitable premises, the West London Mission opened St Luke's House on 14 July, 1893. This home for the dying poor was entirely free, though next of kin were expected to meet the cost of removal and burial. The disease from which the patient suffered was immaterial, provided it was not infectious. The first chaplain at St Luke's was, of course, the Rev. Mark Guy Pearse. His successor, the Rev. C. Ensor Walters, later described the first-hand experience he had of the 'joy, comfort and strength' that Mark Guy brought to the dying, personal qualities that Arthur Lawrence attributed to his Cornish upbringing:

> The piety of Cornwall, of the fisherman and the miner, is not of the armchair description, nor is it worked out in the minutiae of a mediaeval theology, but it is a Christian piety, which has been found to weather the storm and to enable a man to face catastrophe on the seas or in the depths of the mine without cowardice. It is the piety of those, indeed, who are facing death daily, and it is such a piety that Mr Mark Guy Pearse brings to his work among the dying in St Luke's House...[94]

During his years as chaplain, Mark Guy conducted a short and very simple service in the wards each week, using a brief 'Service for the Sick' that he had composed for this purpose, 'to serve,' he said, 'as a vehicle in which our lame and broken thoughts can be borne towards God'. To a short selection from the prayer-book, he added collects, readings and a 'Litany of Praise'. If the patients were too weak to say anything and too faint to hear any words, he had his own way of comforting them. On one occasion, when Dr Jowett asked him what he said to such individuals, he replied that sometimes he said nothing, drawing them a little sketch that they could look at day by day instead. In response to the question 'What sort of sketch?', he took a half-sheet of notepaper and drew on it with pencil and moistened finger a little seascape, representing two shores and a gull flying between. At the bottom of the card he wrote 'Homeward Bound'. 'Something of that sort,' he said, as he handed it to Dr Jowett.[95] It is clear, though, that he did not always find it easy to comfort the dying and was aware that his efforts seemed painfully inadequate when compared to God's understanding, made perfect through suffering. Howard Barrett did everything he could to ensure that St Luke's was an attractive last home for its residents. The wards were painted in bright colours and always adorned with flowers, while outside, each window had its box of marguerites and geraniums. The widespread use of flowers at St Luke's and elsewhere in the Mission made a deep impression on those who were fortunate enough to benefit from its services. In a little volume entitled *What the Flowers Did*, Mark Guy told fourteen stories illustrating the extent to which flowers had brought to some of the most hopeless cases 'nothing less than the beginning of a new life'. Many feature members of the Guild of Brave Poor Things which was founded in 1895 and run by Sister Grace for those with such disabilities as lameness, blindness and partial paralysis. Mark Guy was closely involved in the work of the Guild and saw for himself the new faith, the new peace and the new hope that flowers and birds – 'the ministry of the country' – could bring to the poor and distressed.[96]

Among those whom Mark Guy Pearse supported and encouraged at the Mission was Josiah Nix[97] who, in addition to being Hugh Price Hughes's organising secretary, was in charge of Wardour Hall where there were services or meetings of some description every day of the week. There were so many, in fact, that Mark Guy described it at the close of the nineteenth century as a place 'soiled by the many uses to which it was put in the service of the poorest of the people'.[98] In a memorial account which he wrote many years later, he cast his mind back to what he called 'those old and blessed times' and the debt that the Mission owed to Josiah Nix. 'He caught from Hugh Price Hughes,' he continued, 'the splendid audacity that ventured on all kinds of new and daring enterprise for the Lord Jesus.'[99] By means of features such as orchestral concerts on Saturday evenings and lantern lectures on

Cover for What the Flowers Did

Thursdays, more people from the immediate neighbourhood were drawn into the life of this community church. The projection or magic lantern – the precursor of the modern projector – consisted of a wooden or metal box containing a light which shone through a slide to produce a picture; when magnified by a projection lens, the picture appeared on a screen.[100] Acting on the principle that many of the people were unable to follow logical sequences in their minds, but needed to see an illustration, Nix began a series of magic-lantern services. A hymn was projected onto the screen so that each individual in the audience could see the words. Alternatively, a succession of scenes representing incidents in the Gospel might be used, or pictures of a young man or woman leaving a peaceful country home and 'gradually being polluted and befouled in the murky moral atmosphere of London until a miserable or shameful death comes in the river'. Mark Guy claimed that this form of service had a double advantage over the more conventional one. In the first place, it impressed the truth more vividly upon the minds of the audience; secondly, it quickened in each spectator a sense of his own responsibility which, in London, was often lost as he or she simply drifted along with the crowd. At a magic-lantern service, where his eyes were fixed upon the one bright object in a darkened room, his sense of individuality came back to him. Some of the scenes ran like 'a successful play', more especially when their title was taken from a popular melodrama. Audiences, it seems, demanded them Sunday after Sunday in order that their friends might have the opportunity of seeing them – something which, in the eyes of a reporter on the *Tasmanian Mail*, might lead an outsider to ask whether salvation by magic-lantern was really all-powerful.[101] On a more secular level, the programme of Thursday evening lectures included topics such as 'Niagara', 'Cromwell', 'Ireland', 'Our teeth: how they come' and 'Our teeth: how they go'![102]

In the letter that he wrote to Mark Guy Pearse inviting him to join the proposed Mission, Hugh Price Hughes stressed that, not only would he be released from the straitjacket of the itinerancy, but also would have 'that liberty and permanence of action' that he craved and would be free to write and to follow his religious inclinations.[103] And write he did! Virtually every year between 1886 and 1903 saw the publication of either new titles such as *Jesus Christ and the People* (1891), *The Gospel for the Day* (1893) and *Come, break your Fast* (1897) or reprints of best-sellers such as *The Christianity of Jesus Christ, Is it ours?*, *Daniel Quorm* and *Mister Horn and his Friends*. Almost all the new titles were either religious tracts or collections of sermons, parables or meditations. Notable exceptions were *Gold and Incense – a West Country story* (1895) which within four years sold nearly 40,000 copies, *His Mother's Portrait, and other stories* (1899) and *West Country Songs* (1902). In 1890 he began editing *The Preacher's Magazine* – formerly *The Local Preacher's Treasury* – with the Rev. A. E. Gregory. Intended primarily for preachers, teachers and Bible students, the magazine contained sermons and biographical and literary studies as well as features such as 'About Men & Books', 'Homiletics', and 'Reviews'. Mark Guy was himself a regular contributor. When not working in the metropolis itself, he was often preaching and lecturing the length and breadth of the land in order to raise funds for the Mission. Wherever he was, he took its interests with him and, as a result, became known in almost every circuit, his name a household word throughout the Methodist Church. Indeed, if all his years in the Mission's service were as busy as the last quarter of 1894, it is surprising that there was no recurrence of the breakdown that he suffered years earlier. 'I am quite ashamed to say that I have not an afternoon or evening free,' he wrote, presumably in reply to an invitation to lecture or preach. '... Ten services last week and nine this – with my weekly word [?] for the press makes [?] me always in a hurry – but thank God never in a worry. I have looked through my list of engagements and find my first free day is Xmas week'[104]

His native Cornwall was, of course, a life-long passion and there would have been few – if any – years during which he would have failed to return to 'God's own country'. Before attending the series of conventions planned for the winter of 1886–87, for instance, he preached at a harvest thanksgiving at Camborne Wesley on Tuesday 15 September, the service being reported as the first of its kind ever held in connection with Methodism in his home town.[105] Towards the end of 1888 he was in nearby Helston in connection with the laying of the foundation stones of the new Wesleyan chapel in Coinagehall Street. At the beginning of 1891 Launceston welcomed him back for the opening of its new Wesleyan Men's Institute, and during the summer of 1899 he lectured and preached at St Austell before travelling on down to Camborne to prove, as one local reporter put it, 'that a prophet is not always without honour in his native country'. On the morning of Sunday 3 September, Wesley Chapel was besieged by those anxious to attend the first of the services celebrating the Sunday school anniversary. There was not even standing room left anywhere inside the building before the preacher entered the pulpit. If anything, this was more so in the evening when crowds thronged to the chapel from all directions. The following day there was again a large congregation to hear him deliver the lecture 'Christian Socialism' in which he dealt with his work at the West London Mission. Although both his parents had died some years before, Mark Guy was very definitely amongst friends at Camborne Wesley and was welcomed by John Holman as one of whom they were proud as Cornishmen, and doubly proud as Cambornians.[106]

Another place which, during his early years at the Mission, laid claim to his affections was the Isle of Wight, where his father spent the last years of his life. Mr Pearse had remained in Camborne until the death of his wife in 1868 or 1869 and had then, with his daughter Ellen, moved to London where, chiefly through his generosity and exertions, a large Wesleyan church was erected in Prince of Wales Road, Kentish Town. On leaving London, he finally settled at Warwick House, Sandown, where he became a generous supporter of the Wesleyan Church and its work in the circuit and where everyone knew, respected and loved him.[107] He was, it seems, particularly at ease with the town's children, and his granddaughter Mab remembered how, in summer, he liked to have a great party of his grandchildren – at times, fifteen or more – to stay with him. The notebook kept by Mr Pearse contains not only letters which his son had received about *Daniel Quorm*, but also poems written for him by his grandchildren. In addition to three charming examples from 'Mab', [Mark] Guy and Warwick Guy thanking him for the hamper he'd sent them one Christmas, is the following account of an outing they'd enjoyed together to Alum Bay on the Isle of Wight:

Dear Grandpa took us out one day
In a coach and four to Alum Bay
With three black horses and one grey
And thus we went on our way O.

The whip was cracked with a ? sound
The horn was blown and the wheels went round
The horses trotted over the ground
And so along our way O.

In Brixton [Brighstone] they stayed for a drink and feed
The horses were very pleased indeed.

And then away rush black fiery steed
And so along our way O.

At Alum Bay we sat to eat
Pork pies and other delicious meat.
The boys tucked in, the girls ? sweet
All at the end of our way O.

It was late before we started at night
And we begged the moon to lend us her light
Or else we should be in a sorry plight
Before we reached our den O.

Good Mrs Graham she jumped out of bed
Why really, they've all come home she said
And of course they will all want to be fed
As soon as they reach their den O.

Now thanks to Grandpa for such a jolly day
A thousand times we all do say
And may he live for ever and a day
With us in our den O.[108]

'Unforgettable days,' wrote Mab many years later, 'when they [his grandchildren] lived amphibious lives on the sands and in the sea, in that paradise of childhood, with their dear old grandfather presiding over everything and revelling in their enjoyment as long as he was able. When he grew more feeble, one or two of the older ones would remain to be with him. One remembers how he used to sit for hours at a time, looking out over the silvery sea and reciting hymns, of which he had a great store in his memory.'[109] Mark Guy preached in Sandown on several occasions when visiting his father and laid a memorial stone for him when the schoolroom was built in 1888. On his death in August the following year, his funeral was attended by most of the ministers and principal tradesmen of the town, with many of the shops closing and drawing their blinds.[110] A Cornish cross still marks his resting-place in Christ Church graveyard.

During his fifteen years at the helm of the West London Mission, Hugh Price Hughes often found himself at loggerheads with the more

Sketch by 12-year-old Mab Pearse at Sandown in 1886
(Courtesy of Margaret Walton)

conservative elements within Wesleyanism who resisted the changes he was trying to bring about under the auspices of the Forward Movement. Throughout, Mark Guy Pearse's loyalty to Hughes remained steady, though he did concede on the latter's death that his colleague may have been mistaken sometimes.[111] The Missionary Controversy of 1889–1890 started when Hughes's *Methodist Times* published a series of articles by Henry Lunn alleging that Wesleyan missionaries in India, from where he had returned the previous year, were living in comparative luxury while failing to convert the native population. After months of acrimonious debate, both in and outside the pages of the *Methodist Times* and the *Methodist Recorder*, the Wesleyan Missionary Society successfully defended itself. And although there was considerable hostility to both Hughes and Pearse from certain sections of Conference and although the controversy impaired the former's influence in official Wesleyan circles for a while, a moral victory was achieved at the Conference of July 1890 when a motion expressing appreciation of the West London Mission was passed.[112] 'Of his [the Rev. M. G. Pearse's] personal friendship to me, and of his steadfastness in the dark days of the Missionary Controversy I cannot cherish too warm a memory,' wrote Lunn several years later.[113] A dominant theme of the Forward Movement in the early 1890s and one which was dear to the hearts of both Hugh Price Hughes and Mark Guy Pearse was the uniting of Nonconformity – and even of all

Protestantism – under the banner of national religious, moral and social regeneration.[114] Once again Henry Lunn, who in 1891 founded *The Review of the Churches*, a paper devoted to the cause, played a central role. He it was who organised and skillfully promoted the 1892 Grindelwald Conference of religious leaders which for four years was an annual event. Mark Guy Pearse, who believed wholeheartedly that the churches were complementary, would have backed such an initiative to the hilt and was certainly a speaker the following year at the Reunion Conference at Lucerne which was advertised as 'a unique Swiss holiday'.[115]

The outbreak of war with the Boers of South Africa in October 1899 and the way in which it was waged by the British, would surely have troubled the Rev. M. G. Pearse whom Emmeline Pethick-Lawrence described as 'a man who hated conflict in any shape or form'.[116] It would also, I believe, have put a strain on his loyalty to Hugh Price Hughes, who was himself a vociferous advocate of the military solution. As we shall see in a later chapter, in 1896 Mark Guy had experienced at first hand the growing tensions between Boer and British settler. Although he believed at the time that Englishmen in the Transvaal should use only constitutional methods to secure what they wanted, he nevertheless admitted that he had seen enough of the outrageous conduct of the police in their dealings with the natives 'to stir [his] blood to a fever of indignation'.[117] Almost the whole country was enthusiastically in favour of the war when it came and, initially at least, all but a fraction of Church dignitaries supported it. Nonconformists were more divided, with many of Hughes's closest associates opposing it. Hughes himself believed that the Boers were an obstacle to all the British Empire stood for – Christianity, liberty, democracy and the greater social good – and viewed the crisis, too, as a conflict over native rights which he saw the Empire as championing.[118] There was in Mark Guy's native Cornwall a vocal anti-war faction which feared that hostilities would dry up the flow of financial support to the Duchy. Indeed, in the General Election of 1900, the people of the Mining Division Constituency (what is now Falmouth-Camborne), voted against the national trend and elected the Liberal Radical and pro-Boer W. S. Caine in preference to the Liberal Unionist A. Strauss.[119] Given that he always maintained very close links with Cornwall, I believe that Mark Guy Pearse would have been only too aware of feelings and developments both here and elsewhere and fully in tune with the personalities who helped shape them. In January

1900, for instance, the former United Methodist Free Church minister, Silas K. Hocking, established the Stop the War Committee, the most vociferous of the pro-Boer agencies. A little later their fellow countryman, Leonard Courtney, was one of the moving spirits behind the more moderate South African Conciliation Committee. It was round about this time, too, that Courtney, the MP for Bodmin, appointed as his private secretary none other than George Unwin who, in the summer of 1902, married Frances (Mab) Pearse. Interestingly enough, the first work that he was called upon to do was to analyse the Parliamentary papers on the South African crisis! Other prominent members of the Cornish pro-Boer/anti-war faction were Leonard Courtney's niece, Emily Hobhouse, who visited the camps in which Boer and native families were 'concentrated' by the British, the philanthropist J. Passmore Edwards and Arthur Quiller-Couch who took the chair for the public meetings which Lloyd George, another impassioned pro-Boer, conducted in Cornwall. If we add to all this Emmeline Pethick-Lawrence's statement that 'All the leading spirits of our social circle were 'pro-Boers'', I can see no reason not to conclude that Mark Guy may well have been one of the 5,000 Nonconformist ministers – 500 of whom were Wesleyans – who in October 1901 signed a manifesto against the continuation of the war.[120]

That summer Mark Guy withdrew from active participation at St James's in order to give himself more freedom to answer the many calls on his gifts and energies. Up to 21 July he was preaching morning and evening, the doubling of his duties being called for by the ill-health of the Rev. H. P. Hughes who did not resume his work at St James's until September. When, however, during the second week in July, the London Mission held its Committee of Review preparatory to the approaching Wesleyan Conference, the West Branch reported an extremely difficult year owing to the illness of its superintendent minister and 'the lessening work of the Rev. Mark Guy Pearse'.[121] At the Conference itself, which opened at Newcastle upon Tyne on 23 July, Pearse stated that he had received a letter from Dr Howard Barrett who had been attending Hughes throughout his illness. Although his period of rest needed to be prolonged, his health appeared to be almost fully restored.[122] In the first draft of the Stations of the Ministers for 1901–1902, Mark Guy's name appears immediately below that of Hughes and before those of J. Gregory Mantle, Charles E. Walters and William Lax in the list of those responsible to the committee of the

London Wesleyan Methodist Mission.[123] By the time the final draft was published, though, he had been relegated to fifth place, outside the direction of the committee, indicating that his withdrawal had taken effect.[124] His decision, though, did not in any way mean a separation from the Mission, but more of a leave of absence. Everyone knew that he would plead its cause and beg money for it at the Antipodes, just as he did when he was at home.[125] Indeed, he had already hit the campaign trail, as it were, making several visits to various places on Tyneside during the second week in September before preaching and lecturing at locations as far apart as Torquay (13 October) and Edinburgh (3 and 4 November).[126] A year later, on Friday 14 November 1902, he was at Katherine House for the admission service of two probationers who were entering the Sisterhood, one of whom was known to him. Little did he realise that this was to be his last meeting with his friend and colleague Hugh Price Hughes. They greeted each other like brothers, so delighted was each to see the other. Shortly afterwards Mark Guy recalled how '[e]verything about him gave us abundant hope of his complete restoration to health'.[127] On the Sunday evening Hughes preached his first sermon in over a year at St James's Hall with his customary vigour. The following afternoon, though, he suffered a stroke as he was returning to central London from a meeting of the Christian Social Union and died at home that same evening in the presence of his family. His funeral service at Wesley's Chapel, City Road on Friday 21st was attended by a veritable cross-section of London society. In his sermon, Mark Guy spoke of the manner of his colleague's going. 'We cannot think of that warrior spirit, fretted by a growing feebleness, worn with age,' he said. 'It was a sublime and beautiful thing. Whilst we mourn our loss far greater than we yet can know, the heart must glow with gratitude to God that it was given to this prophet of fire to go away as in a chariot of fire – swift, triumphant, glorious.' He concluded:

> I have one word I have kept until now. Of all the splendid gifts of our dear friend, I covet most of all his gift of leading men and women to decision for the Lord Jesus Christ. I cannot wear his armour, but the silence of that voice may speak to us as the voice itself has never spoken. That swift and sudden removal has a message for every one of us.

He then asked for a minute or two of silent prayer and while heads were still bowed, he started singing the hymn 'Just as I am', which the congregation then took up unaccompanied.[128] The service was followed by interment at Highgate Cemetery where Mark Guy committed to the grave the coffin which bore on it a solitary wreath from Katherine Price Hughes and the children. At the memorial service in St James's Hall two days later, he described how, the previous day, he had visited St Paul's Cathedral in order to look at the monument to General Gordon. 'It had come to my mind,' he said, 'as a fitting memorial of our fearless and devoted friend. The left hand, the hand of love, rests on the Bible, the right hand had laid the sword aside. So fought Hugh Price Hughes, ever with the sword of the Spirit.'[129]

Hughes's sudden death, at the comparatively early age of fifty-five, had repercussions for all those involved with the Mission, not least his colleague who cancelled a return visit to North America[130] and resumed for a time his ministry at St James's without either stipend or other remuneration, in order to help Hughes's successor, the Rev. Charles Ensor Walters, through the difficult winter of 1902–03. And Walters, who had been appointed to work in the Mission in 1895, found in the man who was thirty years his elder a 'true father in God'.[131] By the following spring, however, the emergency seems to have been well and truly over and amongst the matters discussed on the first day of the Second London Methodist Synod on 12 May was 'the request of the Rev. Mark Guy Pearse to be released from pastoral work...'[132]

Without a doubt the West London Mission was the great work of Mark Guy Pearse's life and its debt to his seventeen years' ministry was incalculable. On a purely financial level, he managed over the years to raise more than £12,000 for the Sisterhood and its work. 'I can see him now,' wrote Muriel Sara, 'standing in the vestibule of the chapel [Camborne Wesley], presiding over a bookstall of his publications which he sold autographed for his West End Mission.'[133] All this was, of course, in addition to the standard collections made on its behalf at home and abroad. Money, though, as he emphasised in *Jesus Christ and the People*, was not going to save London and, as we have seen, the help and support he gave to the Sisters went way beyond the financial. Indeed, throughout his ministry he attached great importance to the concept of Christian service all through the week, and constantly spoke out against Sunday-only religion. More than most, perhaps, he translated those beliefs into actions. 'Great and honoured as he was elsewhere,' wrote Sister Lily, 'it was in the West London Mission that he was at his best. He was our unfailing friend; to rich and poor he gave unstintingly;

and often was it said, 'When you brought Mr Pearse to see me, I felt that Christ had come into the room.'[134] In similar vein, Katherine Price Hughes wrote in 1908:

> From the very beginning, twenty-one years ago, he has been the kindest, warmest, and most faithful friend. We cannot realise what we should have done without his never-failing sympathy and help. Sisters struggling with difficult cases knew that they had only to relate the piteous story to Mr Pearse to obtain prompt sympathy and generous help. Sisters who were ill and overwrought were cheered by his visits, so full of sunshine and humour... Humanly speaking, we could not have lived through all the unsettlement and difficulty of the last few years had it not been for Mr Pearse's splendid and generous services.[135]

This was not, though, a one-way process, and in giving to the Mission his highest powers, those powers seemed to become ever more potent and effective. Certainly, a change came over his attitude to the Christian life, and his time at the Mission had a profound effect on his mind. The quest for personal goodness and personal salvation, which he had formerly espoused came to look almost like selfishness as he embraced socialism as the only cure for the evils of slum life. When lecturing at Camborne Wesley in September 1899, he asked his audience not to be frightened by the word, as it belonged to Christianity. The greatest socialist who ever lived was Jesus Christ, and the Christianity that did not mean socialist was not, in his opinion, worth much. There were two forms of socialism. The first, which was of the devil, aimed at pulling down everything that was up. The second, which was inevitable, was 'the great, deep, true Socialism of Jesus Christ'[136] and would tend to set up everything that was down. The remedy of the former was not to denounce it, but to endeavour to bring in the second. He considered that the ugliest thing in the world was the religion which was concerned only with self, while a religion which only saved souls and forgot bodies made him afraid.[137] 'God save us from our selfishness,' he told another Camborne Wesley congregation twenty-five years later. 'When you knock at the door of Heaven you will not be admitted unless you have given of your love on earth...The only way to Heaven is to make a Heaven for others here...'[138] His feelings on the subject were, perhaps, encapsulated in his assertion that he was 'more afraid of unsocial Christians than of Christian Socialists'.[139] In a perceptive analysis of

Mark Guy's power both as a writer and preacher, W. J. Dawson underlined what he described as 'the gradual development of his democratic sympathies'. By nature autocratic, and even aristocratic, he had come, with the deepening of his religious life, to possess an ever-keener sense of the mission of the churches to the common people.[140] Although this change – from the Rev. Mark Guy Pearse to plain 'Mark Guy' – was already under way before he began work at St James's, the pace accelerated substantially during those momentous years. Towards the end of his life Mark Guy asked the Rev. Ira Goldhawk, who had recently been appointed Superintendent of the Mission, to come and see him. During the evening they spent together, he spoke at length of his own ministry there and when asked what he thought of the present state of the Mission and of its future, he jumped to his feet and replied:

> The West London Mission offers you the greatest ministry in the world. I wish I could put the clock back forty years and have your opportunity...[141]

Chapter 11

'[T]o... advocate the claims of the West London Mission to the prayerful and practical sympathy of our kinsmen beyond the seas.'

North America 1887 and 1903–1904

In addition to fifteen years of devoted work in the capital and throughout Britain, Mark Guy Pearse's decision in 1886 not to retire to Cornwall, but to accept Hugh Price Hughes's invitation to join him in the West London Mission resulted in extensive tours abroad to publicise its aims and achievements and to raise money – tours that brought him into contact with Cornish communities in North America, Australasia and South Africa. North America was the first destination of those who left these shores to seek greater freedom and independence abroad, although for many Cornish people the republican 'land of the free' was never a foreign land but, rather, 'the next parish to St Just and Sennen, just across the water which surged against the rocks of Cape Cornwall and Tol-pedn-penwith'.[1] Wherever they went, the Cornish emigrants carried with them their own rich and distinct culture and, as often as not, the first permanent buildings they erected were the Methodist Church and the Sunday school. Indeed, it was not exceptional for a Cousin Jack to be superintendent of both mine and Sunday school, nor for a tributer on the Monday morning shift to have preached the night before.[2]

Following on from twenty-three years of circuit work where, as we have seen, home and foreign missions both played a vital role, a roving commission to raise the profile of the West London Mission must have had its attractions for a consummate preacher who, at the age of forty-four, was at the peak of his powers. As the *Methodist Times* was careful to point out on the eve of his departure for Australasia four years later, the raising of money was not the prime motive behind the four tours that Mark Guy undertook between 1887 and 1904:

> Mr Pearse is going… not to make money, but to promote his health, enlarge his experience, and advocate the claims of the West London Mission to the prayerful and practical sympathy of our kinsmen beyond the seas. He says himself that his forte is not raising money, but he strongly hopes that the wealthy colonists, who have so many personal and religious ties with the mother country, will, notwithstanding, enable him to render substantial service to the West London Mission, even when he is so far from it… We believe that when our kinsmen and co-religionists on the other side of the world are weeping, and laughing, and rejoicing, and applauding under the influence of Mr Pearse, they will not forget the mission which owes so much to him, and which is struggling with gigantic evils at the very fountain-head of British influence.[3]

During the course of 1886 he had received a letter from the American evangelist Dwight L. Moody urging him to tour America. For the best part of three years Moody had undertaken an extended revival campaign, and from September 1882 to the following April he and Ira Sankey had wandered through the provincial towns and industrial centres of England and Wales. With Swansea, Cardiff, Plymouth, Bristol, Portsmouth, Brighton, Liverpool and Birmingham all included in their itinerary,[4] it is inconceivable that Moody and Pearse did not meet, most probably in Bristol where the latter was stationed that autumn. Four and a half years later, having spent several months touring England with colleagues from the London Missions, Mark Guy was in a position to accept Moody's invitation. He recorded his impressions of the time he spent preaching, lecturing and fishing in the north eastern United States and Quebec in long letters home.

Travelling north from New York in April 1887, he was welcomed at the first Canadian railroad station by Alfred Mason whose comfortable home he made his headquarters. From the train he had observed the landscape of what he called a 'curious country'. Everything was unfin-

Dwight Moody

ished with 'the stumps of the trees of the primeval forest left standing in the fields. Everything wooden and patched together. The engine carrying huge bells, which keep tolling as the people walk along the railways; the engines have long, fan-shaped projections in front to lift any cattle or other critters comfortably off the line.'[5] On a sunny day early in May he met the Rev. Egerton R. Young, a Canadian Methodist missionary, writer and lecturer who was stationed at Meaford, a town on the shores of Georgian Bay, Ontario, to which he had come to give a lecture. Passing the river, which was crowded with boys and men snatching with leaded hooks at the mullet that swarmed in shoals from Lake Huron, the two ministers sat on a pebble ridge at the water's edge and talked. Mr

Young and his wife had been pioneer missionaries for many years in northern Manitoba in the days before the railroad, when the dog-train was the normal means of transport in winter, and the canoe in summer. Needless to say, he had a fund of stories which captivated his colleague. 'I had but to ask a question here and there and sat entranced,' wrote Mark Guy; 'the people, the country, the cold, the dogs, the bears, the whole surroundings of the life began to live before me, and with many a wild scene of adventure, and many a wonderful story of conversion, that afternoon sped away, – for me, much too quickly, – and ever since it has hung up in "the chambers of my imagery," amongst its most vivid and most treasured pictures.'[6] The stories continued when Mark Guy went home with Mr Young to meet his wife and children. Standing on a mat made of some interesting-looking fur, the Cornishman asked his host about its origins; the reply and Mark Guy's reaction to it were recorded many years later by E. Ryerson Young, jnr.:

> 'It is the skin of a wolf that nearly made a meal of my boy,' came the reply, and Mr Pearse looked at me, a boy in my teens. Of course the story had to be told… Mr Pearse could hardly eat his meals, or let my father and mother eat theirs, either. He must hear and they were glad to tell. He almost forgot what he came to Meaford for.[7]

At last, though, he had to leave for his service and then cross the lake in a rowing boat for home. Before they parted, however, he got his host to promise that he would cross the Atlantic and tell people 'at home' the story of his Mission. It was some years before circumstances were favourable, but in due course the Rev. E. Ryerson Young gave up the pastorate and went to England.

Contact between the two families was obviously maintained for, on his second 'official' visit to Canada in 1903, Mark Guy asked Egerton Ryerson Young jnr., who was then stationed at Port Carling in the centre of the Muskoka Lakes district, to arrange his programme for him. Though discouraged from doing so, notably by his mother – 'You do not know Mr Pearse,' she argued. 'He is one of the most loveable of men, but he is very hard to please.'[8] – Young remembered what Mark Guy had done for his father, and agreed. He planned the itinerary from Montreal to Vancouver and enjoyed the great man's company immensely – especially his wicked sense of humour. Considerable upheaval ensued in the Young household, though, when it was learned that Mr Pearse was bringing his wife with him. In order to be in a position to entertain her distinguished guests properly, Mrs Young felt that she had to install a maid. So a neighbour's daughter was duly engaged and carefully drilled in the tasks that she was to perform, most of which were decidedly foreign to her free and easy manner of living. Having heeded and followed all the instructions, on the morning of the guests' arrival she refused to stay and went back home. 'Consternation reigned in the little parsonage that nestled so cosily on the winding Indian River,' wrote the Rev. Ryerson Young years later. 'It was November, and a snow storm blew up. But the Navigation boat came in safely and, with faces shining with happiness in spite of the gusts of snow that whirled around them, there appeared Mr and Mrs Pearse, and behind them, to our great relief, Mrs Allen, Mrs Young's mother! She was never more welcomed in any place on earth than she was in Port Carling on that day. The guests were made acquainted with one another, and all were quickly taken to the little parsonage. Of course, at the supper table, the joke of installing a maid and of her flunking, had to come out. It appealed greatly to Mr Pearse. He sprang to his feet, and tucked his serviette under his vest. 'I'll show you how an English butler does things,' he said; and, to the end of his stay with us, he played the English butler, to the amusement of us all, unless Mrs Pearse objected. He, himself, declared it was one of the happiest experiences of his life. He certainly had the 'run' of the house. I told him that he was welcome as my father, to do whatever he liked; and he took me at my word."[9]

When not preaching at his host's Home Mission Church or lecturing, Mark Guy insisted on being taken out fishing, although it was often so cold that the line would freeze as soon as it was removed from the water. Bundled up in Mr Young's fur coat, though, he was as happy as a sandboy. Later he recalled being driven, on one of his Canadian visits, to a lonely lake and being left there for a day's fishing. When, having missed a fish, he swore in broad Cornish, a gruff voice behind him remonstrated with him. Realising, though, that he was Cornish, his hearer – an elderly man – changed his tone and persuaded him to come back home with him and visit his Cornish wife who hadn't heard a Cornish voice for twenty years. In the couple's shack Mark Guy sat beside the wife, who was very hard of hearing, and spoke into her ear-trumpet in broad dialect while the tears streamed down her cheeks.[10] If ever there was one, this was a living example of what Mark Guy considered to be true Christianity as practiced by men and women for whom religion was not 'a respectable orthodoxy, not a selfish salvation, but a living Christ-likeness of pity and love'. Only in this way, he felt, could the deep gulf, which divided mankind, be bridged. On a visit to Niagara Falls, he saw the suspension bridge which spanned the gorge and stretched high above the whirling rapids, and was told how initially a slender thread of silk had been carried from one side to the other by means of a kite. The thread brought the stouter rope, the rope, a cable and the cable, chains until, little by little, the massive bridge was completed. 'Surely,' he argued, 'it is the figure of the Christian, whose very rising to Heaven is an influence upon earth like that silken thread, by which the great gulfs that sever men are bridged over, and those afar off are brought near to one another and linked in love.'[11]

In 1887 Mark Guy attracted large congregations and audiences wherever he went, his lecture on *Some Old Folks at Home* in particular seeming to link the young Canada with the old country. As the weeks went by, so the interest grew. On 18 May he arrived in Toronto where a public reception was given to him on the Saturday evening in the parlours of the Metropolitan Church.[12] Having been officially welcomed, he addressed the large congregation at considerable length, concentrating on Methodist City Mission work in London. On the following day he preached, morning and evening, at the same venue which he described as 'the finest Methodist chapel in the world'. At Coburg he stayed with his father's eldest sister, Aunt Margaret, 'a very handsome old lady' who had married and gone out to Canada some fifty years earlier.[13] Though Coburg would have changed appreciably in fifty years, it was still very much a quaint, rural backwater for someone who had spent most of his adult life in centres of population in England. 'The roads are mere tracks,' wrote Mark Guy, 'and the pavements are all planks of wood, with planks running up to the front doors of the houses. The horses and carts have a curious look of wildness; the absence of much harness, the high wheels of the carriages, and then, too, the long tails and long manes of the horses flying in the breeze, are very curious to me.'[14] Generally speaking, he found travel in the Canada of a hundred or so years ago rather haphazard and uncomfortable; steamers missed trains and trains missed steamers, and on long journeys the food was impossible. Sometimes lack of organization meant that he had to take a 'mixed train' consisting of cattle trucks, lumber-wagons, and a couple of passenger coaches where the travellers fared as best they could. If the steamer missed the train by just five minutes, they were forced to stay the night in some unknown spot and miss a service that had been publicised. From Rivière du Loup in Quebec province, where French was widely spoken, he wrote:

> I sat down to dinner a rough affair my companions the guards and brakesmen of the train, but that is always the case in this democratic country... It is a first-class country for third-class people. It is a third-class country for first-class people. It would suit those who are willing to help themselves and who want the chance. It is a poor country for those who like to be helped and are willing to pay for it. There are no porters, and society is equal.[15]

There is a hint of peevishness here. Much has been made of Mark Guy's love of the common people. Undoubtedly, back in Cornwall he was very much at home among humble folk and could speak their dialect. However, he was, too, a man of fastidious tastes and artistic refinement, and it would seem that, as one percipient colleague put it, Mark Guy's 'democratic sympathies' were not always strong, but increased as his religious life and sense of mission deepened.[16] Although he liked the country and its people, he did not enjoy the discomfort of long rail journeys and having to travel for many hours without food. 'Sleeping in the railway sleeping-cars,' he wrote, 'is very much like sleeping under a Coercion Bill – you are pushed here and jolted there, and jostled and wrenched and shoved about all the time, and are half conscious of it.'[17] Towards the end of May he travelled east through New Brunswick to Nova Scotia, visiting Halifax – which he found 'very cold and foggy' – Annapolis and St John where, on 2 June, he preached in the Centenary Church on 'Holiness: perfection in Christ'. Shortly afterwards he crossed the border again to Northfield, Massachusetts, in order to honour his promise to Dwight Moody.

Although, as we have seen, the American evangelist toured the British Isles a second time, he placed less emphasis on his career as a professional revivalist in the 1880s, choosing to devote much of his time and energy to Christian education. Having, in 1879, opened the Northfield Seminary, a preparatory school for girls, some eighteen months later he founded Mount Hermon School for boys. What is now Northfield Mount Hermon was established in order to provide a first-rate, non-sectarian secondary education for young people, regardless of race, religion and economic circumstances. Mark Guy estimated that there were some 250 'very fine-looking, smart lads' and about 200 young women being trained as evangelists and for all kinds of religious work in the numerous buildings scattered about amongst the trees and on the hilltops. The trustees of the buildings, some of the wealthiest men in America, were much in evidence, among them James Talcott of New York whose gift to Northfield, the Talcott Library, Mark Guy helped to open with an address.[18] 'He met me at the station,' wrote Mark Guy of Moody, 'with a pair called here a "team" and a "rig", which is what we call a trap, and two huge dogs... [He] was up this morning *at five o'clock* driving round the hills, knocking at the people's doors and rattling them up to come and hear a 'celebrated preacher from England'.'[19] Church-wagons were used to ferry people in from the isolated farm houses to what Mark Guy described as 'a hive of religious industry, swarming with bees and full of honey'. One particular 'free and easy' afternoon service before a vast crowd consisted of a heady blend of choral pieces, solos from Ira Sankey and others, communal singing, and religious expositions and Cornish anecdotes – Old Rosie, Anthony Cock's wife's conversion et al – from their Cornish guest. Altogether it was 'a glorious time, dear old Moody at my side laughing and crying together, as happy as he could live... I can give you no idea of the beauty of the place, such as one has read of or dreamed of but never seen before...'[20]

Two weeks later he was in Montreal where, towards the middle of June, the heat was tropical. In a short story set among the lumber-camps of New Brunswick, Mark Guy describes how '[n]ature, as if in pity for the long and bitter weather, comes with such a glorious summer in this country, and such sunshine, that I think of Canada rather as the 'Lady of the Blue Skies' than as the 'Lady of the Snows'.'[21] Indeed, the glare of the afternoon sun was so fierce on Saturday 11 June that, on the occasion of the laying of the cornerstone of a new Methodist church on St Catherine Street, an awning was erected over the platform on which a number of the congregation and some distinguished visitors had assembled. As the representative of the mother country, the Rev. M. G. Pearse spoke briefly before Senator Ferrier placed in position a tin box containing an historical synopsis of the history of Methodism in Montreal, a number of coins and assorted periodicals. The following evening he preached in Dominion Square Methodist Church which was crowded to overflowing, the aisles being filled with chairs and the doors blocked with people standing. The church was consequently very warm, and chairs and fans were at a premium. The reporter covering the service for *The Gazette* seems to have been as distracted as anyone by 'the shuffling of people tired of standing, the heat and the flutter of fans inside, and the chirping of the sparrows and the rustling of the leaves outside', with the result that he found Mark Guy's sermon 'unconventional enough' though 'by no means as startlingly interesting as [his] Bible readings. His gestures, attitudes and mannerisms were the same, and once in a while he made a hit at some of the denominational absurdities that caused a titter to run through the audience.'[22]

It was in Montreal that the Pearses first made the acquaintance of the Finleys, at whose city home and summer residence in the Thousand Islands on the St Lawrence they were to spend many long and happy days on later visits. As his daughter 'Mab' points out, Mark Guy was with them in sorrow as well as in joy, for it was during one of these visits, many years later, that Mr Finley was taken ill and very suddenly passed away. In 1920 he described to one of the Finleys' daughters how she had reminded him of 'memories treasured and sacred, amongst the dearest of the past... I sit often by the Half Moon Bay [Vancouver] and hear the whip-poor-will. All else hushed, as if it would break the spell of its charm to say a word.'[23] Towards the end of the month he was back in Toronto for farewell services on Sunday 26 June, when he preached to large congregations in the new Sherborne Street Church in the morning and in the Metropolitan Church again in the evening.[24]

Mark Guy Pearse's official retirement from the West London Mission in the spring of 1903 facilitated a second visit to North America in order to raise both the Mission's profile and money for its work, especially that of the Sisters of the People. Lasting some nine months, this extended tour, which enabled him to spend more time in the United States than he had done sixteen years earlier, is well-nigh impossible to follow in any great detail. It began with a three-day visit to London, Ontario, where his coming had been looked forward to for several weeks. Under the banner headline 'Famous English Divine Occupies London Pulpits' the local *Advertizer* reported at some length on the services he conducted in the city's two leading Methodist churches. At the Dundas Street Church on the morning of Sunday 11 October he pointed out the folly of worrying, taking as his text the latter part of the sixth chapter of Matthew's Gospel containing Jesus's instruction 'to take no thought for your life, what ye shall eat, or what ye shall drink; nor yet for your body, what ye shall put on... for your Heavenly Father knoweth

Rev. Mark Guy Pearse Addresses Immense Audiences.

Hundreds Unable to Gain Admission at Each Service.

“Don't Worry,” the Theme of an Interesting Sermon—His Address to Young Men.

REV. Mark Guy Pearse, the eminent London, England, divine, whose coming has been looked forward to by Londoners for several weeks past, occupied the pulpits of the two leading Methodist churches of the city yes-

‘Famous Divine Occupies London Pulpits’, report from the London Advertizer, *Ontario, 12 October 1903*

that ye have need of all these things’. Nothing was to be gained by worrying, he argued; on the contrary, the moment we began to fret, we began to sin, becoming the servant of the problem instead of the master. Mammon was not money, but whatever a man fretted about. The *London Free Press* devoted a whole column to what it called ‘Pearseisms’, one of which was ‘Don’t worry. It’s the sulphuric acid that eats into the vitals of human-kind and destroys them’. He laid stress on the idea that

God meant us to be interested in the world, and severely criticised those 'lackadaisical souls' who were continually sighing about 'the world'. 'I have no sympathy with those miserable, lean, long-faced people...' he continued. 'There are a few of them over here, and we have a few of them over the sea... They are sometimes at prayer meetings when they should be at home paying their debts... He will never be right with heaven who is not right with earth. He will never be right with God who is not right with man. Don't let us talk such miserable rubbish about earth. Some people speak as if the world were nothing to them, and then they go home and get their dinner off it'. What was needed, in theology, creeds and everyday life alike, was more common sense:

> I am sick of your intellectual disquisitions and sublime orations. What is wanted is common sense at the desk, behind the counter, in the home, seven days in the week. I am sick of mere creeds, and theories, and notions, and orations, when the poor world wants a bit of homely, common sense that can keep its temper and make it master of things.

In the afternoon the Auditorium, like the Dundas Street Church a few hours earlier, was filled to overflowing when he gave a practical address to an exclusively male audience on the business of religion, making it plain that by this he did not mean the religion of business. Amongst the maxims that he suggested they take down as being worth living up to were 'A day at a time' and 'Be sure that you are in the right road'. On a more practical level, the 'Pearseism' 'Make Christ the head of your firm and don't forget to give Him a share of the profits when the stock-taking comes along' certainly pulled no punches! Shortly after 6 o'clock in the evening, the doors of the First Methodist Church on the corner of Dufferin Avenue and Wellington Street were thrown open and within half an hour the immense building was full. People were still thronging to the church, though, and before 7 o'clock it was found necessary to close the doors. By the time the service began, hundreds stood in the side and rear passageways, both upstairs and downstairs. Having for his lesson read the fourth chapter of Mark, and commented in passing on the mixing of religion with everyday life, Mark Guy took his sermon from the same chapter, using as his text verse 38, 'And he was in the hinder part of the ship, asleep on a pillow: and they awake him, and say unto him, Master, carest thou not that we perish?' In putting across the message that Jesus was a personal, sympathetic friend who had himself experienced all our problems and who heard the smallest of prayers, he told a number of entertaining and pertinent stories. Throughout his life Mark Guy stressed the need for a working, everyday religion, not one confined to Sundays and to particular buildings. This is enshrined in such 'Pearseisms' as 'I want Christ more on Monday than on Sunday, because the devil is more busy on the week day', 'We have our religion too much in spots and lumps – too much on Sunday and not enough on Monday' and 'Who cares for Hallelujah raptures on the Sunday night if you can't keep your temper on Monday'. He often attacked churches which closed their doors six days out of seven, one American newspaper reporting him as saying, 'A church so closed is the greatest waste I know. The higher in the scale of life, the more capacity for rottenness. A stick may be rotten, but not to the offensive extent that an egg may become rotten, and so on up the scale, and religion may be the rottenest of all.'[25] In the words of the *London Free Press*, he preached 'the personal Saviour... the Christ of a workaday world, a world that needs a Comforter and Guide, not a "pretty little something to sing hymns to" as he himself expressed it...'

Although his message and the words he used in his sermons and talks to put it across were deceptively simple, his style of delivery was not, and on this tour, as on every previous one, it was his originality as a character that enchanted the crowds. While flowery language, high-sounding words and carefully constructed phrases were not for him, his style is described again and again as 'out of the ordinary', 'most unusual' or 'striking'. For one London reporter he was as different in his pulpit mannerisms as it was possible to be, with unconventionality breathing from every accent and gesture. 'The years are white upon his head,' he wrote, 'but the man has all the fire and energy of his earlier days, and speaks with every whit of the eloquence and the burning conviction that has made his name famous from one end to the other of the United Kingdom'. Another expressed the view that, though well advanced in years, being, possibly, considerably over 60 [he was in fact just 61] he possessed greater vigour than the average preacher half his age. He had no difficulty whatever in making his voice distinctly heard in every part of both Dundas Street and First Church. It appears, too, that he used no notes at all, but discussed his chosen text piece by piece, illustrating and clarifying every point wherever possible, by relating incidents which, as a rule, came from his own experience, or, as the *London Free Press* put it, by using 'homely simile and commonplace parable'. It was this personal, homely touch which endeared him to so many and which was at the heart of his success. His concern that the congregations were not getting the most from his services expressed itself in a number of ways during that weekend in London. At Dundas Street in the morning, for instance, seeing that a number of worshippers who were grouped around the communion rails had no hymn books, he reached up to the choir gallery, obtained three or four from the singers and handed them to those below. And it was the same throughout the day. Often he was so intent on getting his message across that he could not bear the slightest incident to distract the attention of those he was addressing. In the morning, for instance, he stopped in the middle of a crucial point to allow the slight commotion caused by someone coming in late to cease. 'We will now give our thoughts to the Word once more,' he said in resuming, and every eye was fixed upon his face as he continued. Again, when a baby cried in the evening, he turned with a smile to the distressed mother and assured her that as long as it did not disturb the congregation, he himself was not at all worried. And during the same service at First Methodist Church he went so far as to remark, with a thump on the offending item of furniture, that he wished the pulpit was not so high, 'for I can't see some of you down there'! On the Monday he preached again at First on 'Our Daily Bread' and the following day he returned to Dundas Street to deliver his ever-popular *Some Old Folks at Home* lecture.[26]

As we have already seen, in November he stayed with the Youngs at Port Carling in the Muskoka Lakes District. His friend and tour organiser E. Ryerson Young recalled how much fun they had in Toronto where, after a big engagement, with crowds of people wanting to meet him and shake hands, he would say, 'Let's go away from the world, the flesh, and the devil' and, carrying their coats and hats, they would slip out of a side door and away to the hotel. When comfortably seated in the lounge, with his cigar alight, Mark Guy would say, 'Now, Egerton, tell me a Muskoka fish story.'[27]

The welcome that Mark Guy enjoyed in Canada that autumn was repeated in the United States where he travelled widely for six months. The newspapers advertised him as 'the greatest living English divine' and 'the Apostle of Good Cheer' and used sayings of his such as 'Don't fish with an empty hook' as headlines. He was spoken of too as 'one of the greatest Socialists of the day'.[28] At the First Methodist Church, Oakland, San Francisco, on the morning of 17 January 1904 he told his congregation that Jesus hated three things: long faces, long robes and long prayers. He went on to explain that He did not mark Himself off from other people by a sanctimonious air, or by lifting His voice in long, loud prayers for the amazement of His hearers. He was not, he believed, one of those who went around with sour religious faces, turning the water of life into vinegar. Those who made a parade of their religion, who came around with a glum, holy light in their eyes and could not address you except as 'Brother this' or 'Sister that' Mark Guy had no time for:

> They are the kind of people who think religion is just a plan for getting people to heaven when they die. I don't see any long faces there. They do not come out on wet days.

He had no objection to ministerial clothes, but did not believe in wearing any garment that would make a man think himself holier than his neighbour. 'I often wonder,' he said, 'how our good old Methodists ever got to heaven, they were so proud of their plain clothes. Any man who makes an exhibit of his religion is to be watched.' He could measure a person's religion by asking them how much they cared for the children on the streets. People generally, he felt, were too eager to buttonhole their neighbours about their spiritual welfare to find out if they were suffering physically. What a lopsided Gospel it was that was always asking, 'Brother, are you ready to die?' and never 'Brother, are you able to live?' The following Friday evening he lectured at Oakland's YMCA building on *Some Old Folks at Home in Cornwall*.[29]

Mark Guy spent March in Chicago where his sermons and lectures in a number of Methodist Episcopal churches helped give an impetus to the mission work already being undertaken in the city. From the 18th to the 24th he and his wife stayed at the Bible Institute which Moody had founded in 1886 and which was renamed the Moody Bible Institute after his death thirteen years later. Combining Bible study with evangelistic fervour, Moody aimed to turn his Chicago students into successful missionaries who, unlike their colleagues at Northfield, could be thrust immediately into evangelistic work and thus learn by doing. Mark Guy addressed them one morning on the 23rd psalm, recalling how, when he was a little lad, he used to visit the homes of some of the country folk. Their old cottages had large fireplaces, on the mantelpiece of which was often to be found an ornament – a young gentleman with golden hair, tied up with blue ribbons, with a floral waistcoat and silk breeches and stockings. He leaned against a green tree which had a brown trunk; three white sheep stood nearby. Beneath this figure was the title, *The Shepherd*. '... I said to myself, "What a funny shepherd." The first great mistake about that shepherd is his dress, and his conduct. Most of us are apt to make an ornament of Christ, the great Shepherd, and to hold Him up only for Sunday use. He is a Man of life, a Man who can go after lost sheep. Make Him real, make Him real, dear friends. The next mistake was the three white sheep. I knew that sheep were dirty, greasy things, that had no poetry in them. We think that the blessed Lord Jesus has come into this world to save sinners, but some think He has come to save beautiful sinners, sinners that come to church. I often hear folks talk about the Lord's dear people. Did you ever see them? I have, just once, and never want to see them again. Where are they? On a church window, with their hands clasped, faces upturned and sweet smiles on their faces, and dressed beautifully. They have no flesh or blood in them. I saw through them! Christ is a Saviour of real men and women, and came to save sinners.' Another memory which he used to illustrate his text was of preaching in the Scottish Highlands. After the service, one of the shepherds in the congregation came to him and told him the moving story of a little shepherd lad to whom the local minister spoke one day about the 23rd psalm:

> 'Well,' he said, 'there are just five words in it, 'The Lord is my Shepherd,' one word for the thumb and four fingers of your hand. There is one of those words which, if you can say it, you can say all – that word is my. I want you to put your finger on this one so [the first finger of the right hand upon the third finger of the left hand]... Now put both on your heart and say, "The Lord is my Shepherd."

The little lad did as he was instructed and the minister prayed with him and went on his way. A few days later he again climbed up into the hills and knocked at the door of the hut where the lad had lived, only to learn that he was dead. When his mother drew back the sheet for him to see the body, the minister saw that the boy's fingers were rigid in death, so that they could not be separated, the first finger of his right hand upon the 'my' finger of his left hand, and both hands over his heart. '"My" is beauty,' concluded Mark Guy; 'it is strength! Thank God for a Saviour who is mine, who understands me, who corresponds to me. "The Lord is MY Shepherd."'[30]

He urged his American congregations not to sell the old down-town churches in their great cities and move away from the people, but to initiate new types of work which would bring them in touch with the people. 'You cannot reach them in the old orthodox style,' he argued. 'You must use up-to-date methods. No Church can live on her old traditions'.[31] The American press seems to have been preoccupied with Pearse's physical appearance, personal descriptions often being accompanied by sketches provided by press artists. 'What little hair remains on his head is snowy white,' ran one account. 'His deep-set blue eyes look kindly down at you as he grasps your hand, and you can realise on the instant that quality that makes him the wonderful power that he is among the poor of London's great west side.'[32] Inexplicably, the *New York Times* chose to end its report of the services he conducted at the Hanson Place Methodist Episcopal Church, Brooklyn, on 17 April with the following:

> Mr Pearse is over 6 feet tall, with broad shoulders. His face is of ruddy hue, smooth shaven, the only hair about his head being a light fringe of curly white covering the back part. His voice is deep and resonant.

In one of his Brooklyn sermons Mark Guy turned his attention to what he considered to be the mark of true love – something he felt was in short supply in the world. He recounted how, nineteen years previously, during a big London meeting, he had shaken the hand of 'a poor unfortunate' and had thereby given him such hope that he had reformed and become one of the best-known English businessmen. He contrasted, too, asylums where inmates had been treated sympathetically but without any positive results, with those where a little love had been shown, to great effect.[33] According to the *New York Times* for 18 April 1904, the Rev. M. G. Pearse was en route to the Methodist Episcopal Church Conference which was held in Los Angeles during May. As such, he was, presumably, one of a number of representatives who attended from the British Isles, for Dr R. Waddy Moss was reported as addressing the conference as 'our Fraternal Delegate'.[34] This was probably his last port of call before embarking for England where he was expected home in August.[35]

Chapter 12

'An' all the time there's that great Australia over there…'[1]

Australia and New Zealand 1891

On 15 January 1891, *The Royal Cornwall Gazette* carried a short item to the effect that the Rev. Mark Guy Pearse was about to start on a visit to Australia, Tasmania and New Zealand in order to 'enlist the sympathies of the Colonies in the West London Mission'. Just the previous week he had been in Launceston, preaching and attending meetings held to celebrate the opening of a new Men's Institute in the town.[2] And on the following day, 9 January, 'in view of his approaching departure for Australia', he was presented with an illuminated address at the quarterly social tea at Princes' Hall.[3] 'It is likely to strike some Colonial men as somewhat odd,' continued the *Gazette*, 'that a mission in the richest city of the world should be under any necessity to beg money at the Antipodes.' Given, though, that Australia was second only to North America in terms of the number of Cornish emigrants who left for its shores between 1840 and 1880, there was nothing odd about the Mission's decision to send its roving Cornish ambassador there in order to raise money to fund its extensive outreach programme. At the same time that Mark Guy was making last minute arrangements for his tour, his colleague Hugh Price Hughes and other representatives from the West London Mission were in the West Country. They spoke at Weston-super-Mare, Exeter, and Plymouth before crossing the Tamar for a series of meetings with Cornish Wesleyans at Launceston, Penzance and Truro which culminated in a convention at Camborne Wesley Chapel on Thursday 22 January.[4] Although a sudden, last minute illness almost resulted in the cancellation of Mark Guy's second overseas tour, his doctors strongly recommended the sea voyage and on Friday 30 January he and his wife and daughter (Maud?) left England on the 6,000 ton, four-masted barque *Ormuz*.[5] The combination of sunshine, sea air and a complete rest meant that he was soon fit and well again. On 14 February he wrote home from the Suez Canal as he sat 'under the loveliest skies on a June day of perfect beauty'. The Ceylonese capital Colombo he found 'a dream of loveliness' and at the port's Mission House he and his family received a warm welcome. Having touched Albany on the south coast of Western Australia, the *Ormuz* proceeded to Adelaide, the capital of South Australia.

Although Burra, some ninety miles from Adelaide, seems to have marked the northern limit of Pearse's travels in South Australia, he nevertheless enjoyed a real Cornish welcome wherever he went. Indeed, many communities would, like Gawler, have been making early preparations for his visit.[6] On Wednesday 4 March about thirty Cornishmen met at the Institute to discuss the formation of a local branch of the South Australian Cornish Association. With 'Cousin Jack' enthusiasm much in evidence, the Rev. G. E. Rowe,[7] who had been instrumental in the formation of the Cornish Association in Adelaide Town Hall in February 1890, outlined the success it was enjoying, with branches also being formed at Wallaroo and Kadina. Whether in town or country, the objects of the Association were 'to assist towards the establishment and maintenance of friendly intimacy amongst those hailing from the county of Cornwall; to revive and strengthen the interest in the customs of the country; to disseminate as far as they could such information as they thought would be helpful to their friends at home concerning their adopted land... [and] [t]o afford such help as might be needed to aid their country people in distress.' James Short seconded the proposal of T. O. Jones JP 'that a branch of the Cornish Association of Adelaide be formed in Gawler', recalling how about twenty Cornishmen had gone down to Adelaide to attend the opening banquet of the Association there. When it came to the vote, the motion was carried unanimously and James Martin was elected President. At a committee meeting held afterwards, it was decided to inaugurate the branch with a Cornish tea on the evening of the Rev. Mark Guy Pearse's lecture in the town.[8]

That evening, though, was still ten days away when the visiting speaker arrived in Adelaide where the South Australian Wesleyan Methodist Conference was in session. A group of ministers had stayed the night at the port in order to greet him on board ship at daybreak, 'clothed from head to foot in white duck', as he later put it.[9] Mark Guy's arrival generated great enthusiasm and excitement in Adelaide and people thronged to hear him.[10] Pirie Street Wesleyan Church, for instance, was packed when he preached there at noon on Friday 13 March, the tenth day of the Methodist Conference. Before preaching his sermon, he thanked the church authorities for arranging that the collection should be in aid of the West London Mission, the success of which he briefly described. What touched London, he felt, touched Australia; the Mission itself concerned Australia, for it would largely depend on such ventures whether the surplus population which found its natural outlet in the colonies would be intelligent and respectable, or otherwise.[11] Two days later the same church was 'filled to its utmost capacity' half an hour before the beginning of the service;[12] his sermon that Sunday morning took account of the fact that it was the Sunday school anniversary. Deploring the use of the name 'school', he preferred the term 'children's service', which had been adopted some years previously by the Bolton Wesley Circuit Sunday School Union and which he considered more aptly represented the work then being done in Sunday schools. In the ordinary weekday schools, children were taught to read and write and to do other things, and the best way to achieve good results in the Sunday services would be to avoid any association with the weekday tasks as far as the content of the teaching was concerned. He had no desire, he stressed, to destroy the Sunday school, which was an admirable institution, but simply to improve it. The schools should be adapted to the children's needs. In board schools, for example, scholars were not allowed to sit for more than about half an hour without some form of physical exercise, and some good lessons could be learned by Sunday school teachers from principles followed in the day schools.[13] That evening, at Archer Street Wesleyan Church, hundreds of would-be worshippers could not find even standing room and an overflow service was conducted in the Lecture Hall by the Rev. W. H. Tindall, with whom Mark Guy had worked in Bristol some years earlier. Taking as his subject the changes that had occurred in the style of preaching, he maintained that a growing consciousness that the old form repelled rather than attracted attention and was both unnatural and ineffective had resulted in reform and in a widespread and healthy revolt against conventionalism. He regarded C. H. Spurgeon as the leader in the cause of unconventional preaching and mentioned Henry Ward Beecher[14] as another preacher who was not bound by ecclesiastical traditions. The improvement that had taken place was not to be attributed solely to reform in the style of preaching. Another factor was the change that had come about in the spirit of Christian ministration, a change that had exhibited itself in recognising the claims of the social, and even paying some attention to the more specifically material sides of life. While observing that he scarcely appeared to have been in his happiest vein, *The South Australian Register* was of the opinion that Mr Pearse was himself a striking example of the preacher who had broken away from the old grave and gloomy traditions of pulpit ministration, and proceeded to give a detailed analysis of his ideas.[15] Mark Guy also found time that day to visit Archer Street Sunday School and on the Monday Adelaide Town Hall was the venue for a lecture to a capacity audience on *Some Old Folks at Home*.[16]

Earlier that year – four days after the Pearses left England, to be precise – John Colton,[17] a prominent figure in South Australian Wesleyan Methodism, had suggested to the Malvern Trust that the foundation stone for the new church at the corner of Cambridge Terrace and Marlborough Street, to which he had contributed £100, should be laid on 17 March. Although his own name was proposed, he felt that Mark Guy Pearse would be a more suitable person to do the honours. Subsequently, on the Wednesday afternoon in question, the ceremony culminated in Colton presenting the Rev. M. G. Pearse with an Australian silver trowel and a mallet crafted from mallen [eucalyptus wood] and inviting him to lay the stone. Having spoken of how the church at Malvern had been formed without sectarian exclusiveness, Mark Guy expressed the view that, as Wesleyan Methodists, they owed much to fellowships other than their own, particularly the Church of England 'with her rich learning and forms observed through many ages' and the Congregationalists 'whose sturdy resoluteness gained for them the precious boon of religious freedom'. Without these – and others – Methodism could not have existed. 'I respect highly other denominations,' he continued, 'and I utterly reprobate a bitter sectarian spirit. I believe that God knows no Methodists. I believe, however, that the Churches are complementary the one of the other, and wherein they beget a spirit of large-hearted, healthy emulation they are helpful. An ecclesiastical monopoly is not desirable.' As Rob Linn points out, his comments came at a time when Christian unity was much in vogue, when 'the thought of Methodist union was working as strongly in the community as was the political movement of the Australian colonies towards federalism'.[18] On a lighter note, he said that one thing that had given him particular pleasure during the time he had so far spent in the colony was the sunshine. In contrast, parts of 'the old country' were lying twenty feet under the snow that had commenced shortly before noon on Monday 9 March. The Great Blizzard dominated the news in Cornwall during subsequent weeks and was covered by the Australian press. Ten days after the onset of the severe weather, the *Royal Cornwall Gazette* was still carrying headlines such as 'A tramp frozen to death', 'Sleeping in the snow all night', 'The story of a snowed up guard' and 'The Helston Train buried'[19] – headlines highlighting events that Mark Guy and his hosts must have talked about at length. On the evening of the 17th, when the local St Patrick's Day Celebration Committee had marched in procession through Adelaide, he addressed a public meeting at Parkside Wesleyan Church. The following day he lectured at Archer Street Church, north Adelaide on Hugh Latimer, the sixteenth century English Protestant martyr.[20]

Mark Guy's next port of call was Glenelg, where on the afternoon of Thursday 19 March, he assisted the Rev. W. H. Tindall of Manchester with a Bible Reading in the Wesleyan Methodist Church. Later he preached in the Congregational Church which was lent for the occasion. On the Friday he was back in Adelaide itself to give a lecture entitled *How I Became A Teetotaller*. Tickets for the evening, which was arranged by a number of local temperance and total abstinence organisations and presided over by John Colton, were available from the Wesleyan Methodist Book Depot in King William Street where many of the speaker's books could be bought.[21]

As I have already indicated, his visit to Gawler which, in the 1850s had been one of the state's most important settlements, was eagerly anticipated with the town's weekly newspaper, *The Bunyip*, carrying adverts to remind its readers. His hosts, the local branch of the South Australian Cornish Association, provided a 'Cornish knife and fork tea' in the Institute Hall in order to celebrate their recent formation. The mouth-watering spread, provided free of charge by the town's Cornish ladies, included 'Cornish pasties, squab pie, licky pie, pigeon pie, trifles (two dishes), tatie cake, seedy cake, saffron cake, currant hobbon [*sic*], junkets, heavy cake, fowls, ducks, geese, hams, tongues, figgy hobbon, Cornish cream, dish of "this and that", tipsy cakes and "other sweets too

Amusements.

"ONE AND ALL"

SOUTH AUSTRALIAN CORNISH ASSOCIATION.

GAWLER BRANCH.

The Inauguration of the above will be held in the

INSTITUTE HALL, GAWLER,

ON

TUESDAY, MARCH 24th,

When a

CORNISH KNIFE AND FORK TEA

Will be provided at 5.30 sharp.

Hon. Jas. Martin, M.L.C., in the chair

The celebrated Cornish Wesleyan Preachers

REV. MARK GUY PEARSE,

REV. G. E. ROWE,

And others will speak. Tickets, 1s. 6d. each, can be obtained of the Committee and Secretary.

COME "ONE AND ALL!" THE PUBLIC ARE CORDIALLY INVITED.

Don't Forget ! !

THE REV. MARK GUY

PEARSE

LECTURES

IN THE

WESLEYAN CHURCH,

GAWLER, ON

TUESDAY, MARCH 24,

ON

"SOME OLD FOLKS AT HOME."

The Hon. J. Martin, M.L.C., will preside.

Doors open at 7.15; to commence at 8

Notice in The Bunyip, *Gawler, 20 March 1891*

numerous to mention"'. Amongst those present were James Martin, Gawler branch president, Mr J. Provis, secretary, Edwin Wedlock, secretary of the South Australian Cornish Association, Mr G. E. Harvey, secretary of the Cornish Musical Association, the Rev. G. E.Rowe and Mr and Mrs W. H. Cox, mayor and mayoress of Gawler. Seconding Mr Martin's resolution that the meeting welcome the Rev. Mark Guy Pearse and congratulate the members of the Association upon having the distinguished Cornishman as their guest, the Rev. G. E. Rowe reminded those present of his background, his sympathies, his achievements, particularly with the West London Mission, and his purpose in visiting them, namely that of 'recruiting his health and enlisting sympathy in that work'. On rising, Mark Guy conveyed the meeting's gratitude to the ladies for the feast they had provided. 'Next to being back in dear old Cornwall,' he continued, 'was to have a squab pie... He was reminded when he came in and saw the tables all laden as they were, of a similar occasion in Cornwall. There was a great talk of depression, but the tables were well provided, and a Cornishman observed, 'Well, we fellows do live well, however we do die'... With regard to Cornish ladies – well he had given in in a good many things. He had given in that Cornwall did not have half as much sunshine as Australia, but then it had more shade... They had more dust in Australia, but then in Cornwall they had more mud... so that they could balance matters... But when it came to ladies – he had met men who were as good as Cornishmen, but he never yet met any one – except his wife – who could come up to a Cornish lady – (laughter and applause).' He continued to entertain the meeting with a number of 'racy anecdotes'. The South Australian Cornish Association secretary, Edwin Wedlock, revealed that during the previous year a good number of cheques had been drawn to help Cornishmen who had been hard up or in trouble, whether or not they were members of the Association. It was also intended that, by and by, there should be a room in Adelaide for the use of Cornish people and a library providing Cornish newspapers.[22]

Later that same day Mark Guy delivered his lecture *Some Old Folks at Home* to a large and enthusiastic audience at Gawler Wesleyan Chapel. The church authorities had made every provision possible, even turning the roof of the entrance porch into a sort of temporary gallery, thereby ensuring seating for eight hundred, nearly double the ordinary capacity of the Institute Hall. In the event, their efforts were rewarded by the attendance of between 600 and 700 people, many of whom flocked to the church an hour early. On the platform with the chairman, James Martin, were no less than eight clergymen. At forty-nine, Mark Guy was at the height of his powers, both physically and intellectually, and the reporter who covered the evening for *The Bunyip* was obviously impressed, describing him as 'a man of splendid physique, and winning expression, with a voice of remarkable resonance and power' who 'soon gave evidence of the possession of exceptional platform abilities and... won the full sympathy of the audience from the outset'. Before touching on the sketches of Cornish religious character which comprised his lectures, he outlined what he thought were some of the more general characteristics of his fellow-countrymen. 'Who are these conceited people?' he asked his audience, 'for we are awfully conceited people... No body thinks so much of his country as a Cornishman. People are born elsewhere... but they don't seem to make half so much fuss about it as Cornishmen.' Much of this attitude he attributed to what he called their 'far-awayness'. The old ways and old customs tended to linger on long after they had died out elsewhere. Things had changed, though, and he contrasted the Cornwall of old where 'a sort of wholesome leisureliness' existed, with 'its present Londonised state'. The comings and goings of the single coach that linked them with the outside world when he was a boy, he contrasted with the railways currently crashing through, making it seem as if London was next door. In the days when there was more leisure, people had their own way of expressing things – there was 'a certain roundaboutableness about them'. They thought for themselves, or went without, whereas 'nowadays we pay other people to think for us and we buy it for a penny in the next morning's paper'. He contrasted what he saw as the individuality of people in times gone by with the lack of it in the present, and expressed his regret that parish pride had all but died out. Before moving on to his three sketches, he made an earnest appeal to any present who had left 'old folks at home' to remember them and to write to them. *The Bunyip* reporter provided his paper with the following critique of *Old Rosie*, *The Cornish Miner* and *The Cornish Fisherman*:

> Each of the characters was the concentration of simple, fervent piety, the recital of which, embracing as it did the whole range of Cornish character from its irresistible native humour to its touching pathos, could not fail to have its due effect on the hearers. At times as the lecturer dealt out in inimitable fashion some

> quaint specimen of Cornish humour, in the county vernacular, the audience were beside themselves with laughter. At other times when some pathetic incident was being related with dramatic ability of a rare order, the audience were roused to a pitch of intense sympathy. The recital of these sketches was also made the medium of many weighty words of wisdom, and also of racy comments on a variety of subjects.

As he had done on similar occasions elsewhere, Mark Guy made a point of mentioning humour, which he considered to be one of God's best gifts to man, 'for work a stimulant, for worry a narcotic'. For all that, there was prominent throughout a spirit of devotion on the part of the lecturer, and his magnetic power over the audience was plainly felt as he led them in the soul-stirring hymn *Rock of Ages*.[23] Not everyone seems to have been as well briefed as the folks of Gawler about the celebrated preacher and the reason for his visit. At a prayer-meeting that was held in Burra, for instance, one local Methodist is reported to have said, 'A stranger has come amongst us, today. He is with us now – Guy Fawkes, But I am not sure about his name, O Lord, but Thou knowest it, Bless him.'[24]

Pearse's last public appearance in South Australia was on the occasion of the Cornish Association's annual banquet at Adelaide on Thursday 2 April when he occupied the place of honour on the right of the then premier of the colony, Mr Justice Boucaut[25] who presided over the proceedings. The Hon. J. L. Parsons,[26] who described himself as 'born not far from where old Dunheved's Castle lifts its time-worn keep', made a brilliant speech praising Cornwall and its people before proposing the toast of the evening, 'The Old Home'. By way of reply, Mark Guy opted not to try and outdo his fellow-Cornishman's eloquence, instead setting before his audience 'in very simple words and homely fashion [his] thoughts of the old home':

> As I sit here I can recall the old county. The picture rises before me. It is early spring time. The young leaves are just out on the trees. The music of the lark is rising in the woods. One hears the note of the thrush and the blackbird. In the lanes the primroses and the violets are blooming. I am quite willing to admit that Devon is the queen of English counties. A stately and fair queen in her beautiful hills and silver brooks winding through her meadows and vales down to the seas. But if she is the queen Cornwall is the king. His throne is crowned with the granite

> tors rising up against the deep blue sky. Never have I seen the skies of Australia a deeper blue... It is its nearness to the sea and the constant vapor that makes it seem so clear... As I walk along the high road with no hedges... I see the workings of an old mine, then suddenly come on top of a hill and look down over the red valley, red everywhere, and hear the crash of the stampers... Down the lane with its little groves of Cornish elms, the leaves clinging to the tree all the way up, to the river which works the mill... I still climb up the hill, with the granite cropping up in the road until I stand over the sea... Oh! You young people, save your money, go home, and when you get there make your way to Cornwall, and look down from that rocky coast. See the glory of that sky against which the white gulls come with scarcely a beat of their wings, and when you come back you will say, 'Yes, I saw a good many things in England I liked, but I saw nothing to compare with that grand old Cornish coast.[27]

On occasions such as these Mark Guy had his audience eating out of the palm of his hand and invariably pressed home his advantage by adding either a general Christian message or, as on this occasion, an unashamedly sentimental appeal not only to the Cornishmen before him but to those scattered throughout the colony 'to bring to their minds the old home and the tender memories associated with it. I think I see again,' he continued, 'the poor old house with the little orchard about it... Do not let us forget the old folks. Life with them is growing very short. Your opportunities of showing kindnesses to them are rapidly passing away. How often when I have gone into the little cottage the old woman's face was brightened. How often I have seen tears of joy gather in her eyes as she talked about her boy in Australia. I want her boy in Australia to once a month at least see that a letter goes home to gladden the old home.'[28] A few years later many of the sentiments expressed in this and in other addresses and lectures found their way into *West Country Songs*, which were written to 'revive in Cornishmen the wide world over... sweet memories and treasured associations of the dear old home'. One poem in particular, 'The Miner in Foreign Parts – Australia' which begins 'Zacky, my boy, come here and sit down,/Lev us touch a pipe for a bit;/The heat is enough to kill a chap/Down there in the stifflin' pit'[29] sums up much of what he had to say on that April day in Adelaide. If his visit should have any influence, he concluded, if his words should reach any heart anywhere, then he wanted them to carry

F Mabelle Pearse's illustration for 'The Miner in Foreign Parts: Australia' (West Country Songs)

the following message: if there had been in the past any neglect, they should make haste and ensure that the few days remaining [to loved ones back home] were filled with happiness.[30]

The first stage of Pearse's Australian tour was undoubtedly a great success; indeed, his visit to Adelaide was described by the *Christian Weekly* as being 'a source of joy and spiritual profit to thousands of persons'.[31] Not only Methodists but ministers and laypersons belonging to all the churches flocked to hear him, and the largest buildings were filled to overflowing – and would have been filled had they been double their size. 'He has moved his audiences alike to tears and laughter,' continued the *Christian Weekly*, 'and very many persons have been stirred to seek for the "fullness of the blessings of the Gospel"'.[32]

On Saturday 4 April, two days after he was guest of honour at the Cornish Association of South Australia's banquet in Adelaide, Mark Guy arrived in Melbourne and was driven to the residence of his host,

John McCutcheon, at Hawthorn, a suburb some six miles east of the city centre.[33] He thought it one of the finest cities he had ever seen, an opinion he was more than qualified to give after spending the best part of three weeks lecturing and preaching in its vicinity. The programme of his services and lectures was described as 'something astounding', a view all the more apposite when one remembers that it was partly to promote his health that he undertook the tour in the first place. Having preached to overflowing congregations at Brunswick Street on the Sunday morning and in Wesley Church in the evening, he attended his first major function on Monday 6 April. At the invitation of local businessman John Coates, a large number of ministers and laymen, together with their wives and families, assembled in the upper dining hall of the Federal Coffee Palace to welcome him to Victoria. After the multi-course breakfast, John Coates spoke briefly of the reasons for such an occasion, although their visitor needed no introduction – he was known by his books, his work and his life. Furthermore, their work in the West London Mission had raised both him and Hugh Price Hughes 'to the pinnacle of their fame'. Welcoming Mr Pearse on behalf of the Baptists, the Rev. S. Chapman recounted how once, when he was ill, instead of sending for the doctor he had sent for 'Daniel Quorm', and a fine time he had with him! On behalf of the laymen, James Campbell welcomed Mr Pearse 'as a minister, as a Cornishman, also as an Englishman – observe the fine distinction…' and expressed the wish that he would settle in Australia. Mark Guy touched on Mr Campbell's invitation at the beginning of his talk about the West London Mission and his work for it. So great was the contrast between the poverty and misery of London and the comfort and ease of Australia that he felt himself driven back home by it, unable to desert the thousands who found themselves in abject poverty and wretchedness in the West End of London. Although God had called Hugh Price Hughes and himself to work together, they were utterly unlike in everything, except that they were both 'pigheaded men'. Each went his own way, used his own methods, and did not attempt to dictate to the other. He acknowledged their debt to the Congregationalists and to the Salvation Army for preparing the ground – the former by the publication of *The Bitter Cry of Outcast London* and the latter by their employment of women, something which paved the way for the Sisters of the People. Much of the Mission's work among the poor was done by these 'gifted and cultured young ladies' who 'shrank from nothing, however repulsive, in their work'. As an example he told of a five-roomed house, built for a family of eight, which had forty people living in it and of the Sister who went to live there to experience for herself what conditions were like. Mark Guy brought his address to a conclusion with 'a beautiful and most graphic account of a Sister's ministration to a sick man whom she found in a cellar'.[34]

During the remainder of his first week, he spoke to audiences at South Melbourne, Hawthorn, Brunswick Street and Prahran before travelling seventy miles west to Ballarat which, together with Bendigo, became a leader in gold-mining technical development at the turn of the nineteenth century. While in Victoria Mark Guy himself donned 'the rough dress of the miner', lit his candle and 'splashed along through the pools that filled the tramways' to see for himself what so many of his fellow-countrymen experienced underground. Later he used the experience to some effect, likening the expert who detects the precious metal in a line of white quartz to God, who can detect what is precious in humanity, itself 'so commonplace, so dull; sometimes so ragged and hungry sometimes so stupid and mean; sometimes so cruel and bad'.[35] Of Ballarat, where he spent four days preaching, and lecturing on 'Temperance', 'Some Old Folks at Home' and 'Hugh Latimer', he wrote in a letter home:

> What a joy it was, so far away, to be perfectly at home; to grasp by the hand one and another – and Cornish people do know how to shake hands – until mine fairly ached. How many dear old faces lit up as we talked together in broad Cornish about the old places and the old folks at home, a joy that was nonetheless because it laughed and cried out at the same time. I long to write of the names that might be familiar to many at home, but were I to begin could I ever finish? I see their faces, I hear their voices, I clasp their hands again, and my heart goes over the thousands of miles, and is in Ballarat once more as I write.[36]

Back in Melbourne, he preached and lectured in and around the city before heading south-west to Geelong, about thirty-seven miles along the coast. Three days later he returned to Melbourne yet again for another important engagement at which he and his wife and daughter were guests of honour – the Cornish Association of Victoria's luncheon on Tuesday 21 April when about 250 guests sat down to table in the Masonic Hall. With the meal and toasts to 'Her Majesty the Queen', 'The Duke of Cornwall', 'Copper, Tin and Fish', 'Our Adopted Home' and 'Our Home' out of the way, Mark Guy, who was received 'with long continued acclamation', delivered an address which was 'full of wisdom, full of beauty, enlivened every now and then by a Cornish story, told as none but Mr Pearse can tell it, and saturated with the pleasant conviction that '"there's no place like home," when that home is in Cornwall...' In seconding Mark Guy's vote of thanks to the Association's president, the Rev. S. Knight said that, though not a Cornishman, he had been mixed with so many that he had acquired 'strong Cornish proclivities'. Moreover, he would like to die in Cornwall, and thereafter, if possible, go to a Cornish heaven. In his concluding remarks Mark Guy said that he had known the President's uncle, Jimmy Mayne, and proceeded to tell a story about him which served as a fitting climax to all his stories and duly brought the house down. Compelled by business elsewhere to leave at this juncture rather than stay on and listen to songs and recitations by Association members, the reporter for the *Spectator and Methodist Chronicle* confessed to feeling 'some what oppressed by a sense of inferiority, arising from the lamentable fact that we do not share in the stupendous advantage of belonging to the great Cornish nation'. The thought of being shut out from Mr Knight's 'Cornish heaven' weighed heavily upon him, too. 'But, after a while,' he continued, 'we comforted ourselves with the reflection that there are possibilities even in men who had the misfortune of being born in other parts of England, or in Australia itself, if they be caught young, and removed to more profitable surroundings'![37]

At the turn of the century, the Scottish MP for Maldon, Sir John McIntyre, asserted that 'Bendigo is the Cornwall of Victoria' and it was here, in what was generally considered to be one of the most beautiful mining centres in the world, that Pearse lectured on 23 and 24 April. Newspaper accounts reveal that, from the earliest days, the Cornish made a considerable impact on Bendigo. The first known religious service, for instance, was conducted by a colourful Wesleyan lay preacher from Illogan named James Jeffrey. It was the Wesleyans, too, who built the first primitive church and conducted the first school on the Bendigo goldfield, both in Golden Square. In 1853 the first Tea Meeting was recorded at nearby White Hills as being 'attended chiefly by Cornish folk and got up in the best style of Cornwall'. The Bendigo resident who, on a trip to England in the 1890s, swore that he had heard more broad Cornish spoken in one day at St Just (or Pasty) Point, Long Gully than in a whole week in St Just, Cornwall, would surely have enjoyed

Mark Guy's *Some Old Folks at Home*, had he been present.[38] A few days later, an immense crowd gathered in Wesley Church, Melbourne, to hear his account of the West London Mission. Long before 7.45 pm, when the proceedings began, every available inch of seating and standing room was occupied. 'You could not have got another decent-sized mortal into the church without the aid of a hydraulic ram,' wrote one reporter rather vividly![39] Contrasting what he had seen in Australia with what he had left behind him in the West End of London where 'wealth, and luxury, and gilded vice' existed alongside 'grimy vice, crushing poverty and hopeless lives', the speaker presented his audience with a very detailed account of how he had been led into his work with the Mission. All too late in the evening for most people, it seems, he came to the Sisters of the People, giving many examples of both their work and of the esteem in which they were held by the people they served. Leaning forward over the pulpit desk, he concluded his account with the following words of advice: 'Young ladies! Try this work. You'll find it better than afternoon tea'. To Dr Watkin's whispered enquiry as to what they should do with Wesley Church, Mark Guy turned to the audience and cried:

> What shall you do with Wesley Church? Burn it down! Build a magnificent hall in its place, and go in for the Forward Movement. Hitch up with the Primitives, and the Bible Christians, and the rest of the Methodists, and go at the devil all together![40]

There was always the danger that such extravagant language would be misinterpreted, and this was the case a couple of weeks later when, at one of his meetings in Sydney, he was reported to have stated that the result of modern female education was to turn out young girls who were a sort of 'waste product' fit only to pour out afternoon tea! What the *Spectator* called 'a prolonged howl of rage' sounded from the correspondence columns of the daily papers, the contents of which would undoubtedly have unsettled the preacher had he been in the habit of reading them. Springing to his defence, the *Spectator* pointed out that he had been misinterpreted and that he had been speaking of the 'sort of girl whose only ambition is to dress in the height of fashion, how hideous soever it may be, to "do the block" for the purpose of exhibition, and eventually to secure a husband rich enough to enable her to continue as a wife and mother the same frivolous and useless sort of existence'.

Whether or not Mark Guy would have favoured any more that other 'Girl of the Period' praised by the *Spectator* for being 'the beauty and the grace of her home, her father's joy, her mother's loving daughter and companion… a ministering angel in the house, and an angel, too, who knows how to make home beautiful as well as comfortable' is debatable.[41]

Mark Guy went on to spend four weeks in New South Wales where, at that date, thirty-three members of the Legislature were Cornishmen. He and Mrs Pearse broke their journey at Goulburn where their daughter suffered a very severe attack of typhoid fever and lay dangerously ill for six weeks in the house of the people who had offered to entertain them for the night. Leaving her in her mother's care, he travelled on alone to Sydney and eventually to Tasmania, meeting up with them nearly three months later in New Zealand.[42] In order, no doubt, to capitalise on the interest that the Rev. M. G. Pearse's visit was generating and to whet its readers' appetites for his farewell service, the *Spectator and Methodist Chronicle* announced at the beginning of May that it had arranged with him for a series of original tales to be published in its columns. The first, *Dick Croggan's Redemption*, appeared on 15 May and was followed in subsequent weeks by *Old Rosie*, *The Cornish Fisherman* and *How I get my stories*. On the evening of Wednesday 27 May a meeting was held in the Town Hall to enable the celebrated writer and preacher to bid farewell to his numerous friends in Melbourne before leaving for Tasmania. Among those present on the platform that evening was Thomas Vasey who had helped him considerably when he was a medical student in London and had subsequently proposed him as a candidate for the ministry.[43] Mark Guy took with him many pleasant memories of his stay and left an equal number behind him in Victoria where thousands were 'blessed and quickened by his addresses' and where his lectures as well as his sermons were 'means of grace'. The only regret – one that was voiced wherever he travelled – was that his stay could not have been longer. 'If he could have given us another week, and devoted it solely to talks about the London Mission,' commented the *Spectator*, 'the desire of our hearts would have been fulfilled, and we could then have asked for a fortnight more.'[44]

He was very taken with Tasmania which he described in letters home as 'as large as Ireland' although its geography he found 'very confusing: the North and South Esk fall into the Tamar, and Ben Lomond is in the heart of Cornwall! The railway is very up and down, and with many

Portrait of Mark Guy Pearse from the Spectator and Methodist Chronicle, *Melbourne, 3 April 1891*

curves, and in the compartment on either side of where I was, people were sea-sick! The climate is the ideal climate of the world – Italy without the Italians'.[45] He spent some nine or ten days in the island state, dividing much of his time between Launceston and Devonport in the north and Hobart in the south. The Tamar River estuary was discovered in 1798 by Matthew Flinders and George Bass, who were attempting to circumnavigate Van Diemen's Land in order to show that it was not joined to the rest of Australia. Launceston itself was the third attempt at a settlement on the river and was originally called Patersonia after its founder. Just over a century later, though, in 1907, the city was renamed in honour of Governor King of Launceston, Cornwall.[46] It was in the

Mechanics' Hall on Saturday 30 May that the visiting speaker addressed a large and appreciative audience on *How I became a Teetotaller*. He prefaced his address by stating that the show of open hands and hearts that he had already witnessed contradicted what he had been led to believe, namely that Tasmanians had no enthusiasm. 'Mr Pearse,' wrote one local reporter, 'is an easy fluent speaker who from the moment of his appearance on the platform inspires his listeners with confidence, which weaves a sympathetic cord between them. As his tale unfolds itself, the binding strengthens until when the discourse is ended all appear to have made one friend the more, and to have added an acquaintance worth knowing on their list. It is this charm which added to a good address, an excellent delivery, and a fund of illustrative chatty narrative which ensures his success as a public orator. The lecture is in itself a work of art, and the stories which are brought in as it progresses are all aptly told and well-applied.' Noticing the scores of people who were that very night walking the streets, he felt that the temperance movement was not as assiduous as it might be in both trying to save men from becoming drunkards and in encouraging others to do likewise; there was a need for it to have 'more steam'. He wished, though, that the people of England had a clause in their Licensing Act making Sunday closing compulsory and a measure enforcing a local option, as Tasmania had.[47]

Over the next four days he continued to reveal to the Launceston public his unique skills as a speaker, preaching to packed congregations at Patterson Street Wesleyan Church on Sunday morning and evening and addressing the pulpits of Margaret Street Wesleyan Sunday School in the afternoon. The following day he lectured to an audience of a thousand at the Albert Hall on *Some Old Folks at Home* and on the Wednesday he was back at Patterson Street, addressing a large gathering on *The West London Mission* in the afternoon and preaching on 'Peter's mistakes and our mistakes' in the evening.[48] It is rare to come across adverse comments about the content or style of Mark Guy's lectures, but at the close of that afternoon's address, which was attended mainly by women and children, there was according to the *Launceston Examiner* 'a feeling of disappointment predominating'. It seems that so much time was taken up with 'opening services' – what we would now call 'preliminaries' – that when he started on his subject, 'its continuity was so often broken by the speaker's recollections carrying him away, that a good many were compelled to leave before he had fairly introduced his subject'.[49] On the previous day, Tuesday 2 June, he had travelled fifty miles east to West Devonport where his evening lecture on *Some Old Folks at Home* in the Giglin Memorial Hall was attended by the largest assembly of people in its history. All the adjoining districts were well represented and some people were present from Launceston, although special trains laid on from Latrobe and Ulverstone were poorly patronised. Having explained the reasons for undertaking a lecture tour, Mark Guy drew his audience's attention to the name of their town and to his familiarity with another Devonport thousands of miles away in England. He then treated them to some Cornish dialect, giving its English equivalent, and dwelt at some length on the characteristics of the Cornish people. Mark Guy based his 'old folks at home' on characteristics he had known in Cornwall as a young man. Foremost amongst these were, of course, tin and coppers miners, and in relating some tragic incidents which revealed the precarious life led by those working in the bowels of the earth, he invariably showed his considerable dramatic powers. On this occasion he described the scene between miners Peter Roberts and Martin Dell, when a fuse connecting some explosives accidentally ignited and only one of them could be hauled up the shaft away from the danger.[50] 'From a shoulder of sadness,' wrote one reporter, 'he took his audience into roars of laughter, as he reiterated a conversation between himself and an Irishman on the Home elections.'[51] The Cornish fisherman was another essential player in his stories, especially Moses Dunn 'than whom there is none living that I am prouder to call my friend'.[52] Having regaled his audience with several anecdotes about Moses, he went on to Cornish local preachers, in particular Joe Smitham of Hayle, whom he considered had preached the finest sermon he had ever heard in his life. Showing what the *North West Post* called 'wonderful powers of mimicry', he recounted at length Joe's sermon,[53] all the while keeping his audience 'in a ripple of laughter which ever and anon would burst into loud applause, as some quaint passages… were repeated'. In recounting passage after passage of the impromptu sermon, he retained throughout 'the mimicry and curious twang of the Cornish tongue…'[54]

By the end of the week he had made the 100 mile journey south to Hobart, Australia's second-oldest capital city whose residents welcomed him with 'a monster tea meeting' in the Temperance Hall on the evening of Friday 5 June. After justice had been done to the ample tea, Mark Guy addressed a public meeting on *The West End Mission of London*. Amongst the many dignatories and church and religious leaders present was the Rev. Dr R. W. Thompson, the foreign secretary of the

London Mission Society. 'Possessed of rare oratorical gifts, and being thoroughly in earnest, 'reported the *Tasmanian Mail*, 'the speaker soon enlisted the sympathy of the audience... The reception which the Rev. gentleman received was prolonged to the vociferous by the juvenile portion of the audience.' He revealed that when he began working for the Mission, the first thing he learned to do was to make himself 'of no reputation'. Whereas formerly he had been careful of his reputation and preached sermons in the ordinary, orthodox style, in the new environment he felt he could no longer do that. He did not preach opinions, creed or theory, but a great burning conviction which thoroughly possessed him, and went right into the hearts of the people. He asked a direct message from the Lord, and waited until it came. Amongst the other subjects he covered in his address were the good accomplished by Mr Nix with his magic lantern views and the work of the Sisterhood. On the Sunday he preached, morning and evening, to large congregations at three more services at the same venue where, on the following day, he delivered his lecture on *Some Old Folks at Home*. 'Rich rollicking humour largely pervaded the address,' reported the *Mail*, 'and on many occasions the recital was interrupted by the convulsions of laughter by which those present found themselves affected.'[55]

Hobart obviously impressed the visiting preacher enormously. 'Of all the places he had ever been in,' wrote his daughter forty years later, 'he thought he would say "Give me Hobart".' Generally speaking, he seems to have appreciated the unassuming, no-nonsense approach to life of his Tasmanian host and hostess, writing of them:

> They are very pleasant, homely people; he is reputed to be worth three millions, and there they are, living in the simplest way, without a picture on their walls or anything half as good as we have![56]

Although Mark Guy never returned to Australia, the memory of his visit lived on. Eight years later he recalled it with obvious pleasure:

> I found Cornish societies at every town of importance... I was nearly always invited to spend a Cornish evening with them, and have a drawer full of illuminated addresses presented to me, remaining as pleasant memorials of those delightful occasions.[57]

For the duration of his tour, his books were extensively advertised in the press and copies of *Daniel Quorm*, *John Tregenoweth*, *Sermons for Children*, *Cornish Stories* and many other titles found their way into thousands of homes. Indeed, the foremost scholar on South Australian Methodism, the late Dr Arnold Hunt, recalled that his father, a blacksmith by trade, was still using some of the Cornish preacher's works as the basis for the sermons he preached in rural South Australian chapels in the late 1920s or early 1930s.[58] However, back in 1891, New Zealand – and his wife and daughter – were eagerly awaiting the preacher's arrival…

When the Rev. Mark Guy Pearse arrived at Bluff, the port for Invercargill, on Monday 22 June a 'plan' of proposed services drawn up by the Rev. William Morley at the request of the Conference President was awaiting his approval. This gave him exactly one month to tour as much of both the North and South Islands as possible for both pleasure and 'business'.[59] It seems that he very much wished to visit both the Southern Lakes and the Rotorua district of central North Island which is famous for its thermal springs, geysers and boiling mud pools. In the event, the latter may have proved impracticable, owing to the limited time at his disposal. By dint of working early and late, though, he was able to conduct a series of services in the four principal cities – Auckland, Christchurch, Wellington and Dunedin – and to give one evening to a number of the more important towns. With characteristic enthusiasm, he added to the list that had been prepared for him by holding afternoon Bible readings wherever possible. Such was his reputation that the Railway Commissioners accorded him the courtesy usually extended to illustrious visitors – that of providing a free pass on the government lines.[60]

If he kept to the schedule that was published in the *New Zealand Methodist*, he would have preached or lectured at Invercargill on the day of his arrival, before spending some time visiting the beautiful Lake Wakatipu, the second largest lake in the South Island and the third in the whole country. By Friday 26 June, the Pearses had arrived in the bustling city of Dunedin, where Mark Guy spent three days preaching and lecturing before beginning the 228 mile journey to Christchurch. Breaking their journey at Timaru – where eight years previously Helston-born Bob Fitzsimmons, the future world champion boxer had made his first appearance in the ring – and at Ashburton, he and his wife and daughter arrived on Thursday 2 July in what is now New Zealand's third largest city and the hub of both the Canterbury region and of the South Island.[61]

That very evening the large Durham Street Church was filled by those who knew the illustrious visitor through his writings and were curious to see what he looked and sounded like. Having apparently done his homework and researched the background to the visit, the chairman for the evening, the city's mayor, proceeded to reveal – much to the surprise of both Mark Guy himself and his audience – that the lecturer was not a Cornishman at all! 'Cornishman or not,' commented the *New Zealand Methodist*, 'as soon as Mr Pearse rose to his feet to tell something of the "Old Folks at Home", it was not hard to see where his heart was, and that the old Celtic Fire was that which burned within him.' Having already given a Bible reading that morning and travelled over fifty miles from Ashburton, he kept his lecture short, confining himself to sketches of *Old Rosie* and *Anthony Cock*. The correspondent for the *New Zealand Methodist* found it impossible to give an adequate idea of either the content or style, simply likening him to 'a skilled musician' who 'played upon his audience as he pleased'. When, after *Old Rosie*, they were asked to sing softly two verses of 'Rock of Ages', they felt as though they could hardly keep the music down, wanting to give vent in loud tones to the enthusiasm which had been kindled. The highlight of a second installment the following Monday was Joe Smitham's sermon.[62] On the Friday, following lunch at the Morleys with the ministers of the district, he met a deputation of the Cambrian Society in the vestry of Durham Street Church. The President, Mr E. W. Humphreys, presented him with an address illuminated in green and gold, the Welsh colours. Enclosed in a handsome morocco case and signed on behalf of the Society by its president, vice-presidents and secretary, the address read as follows:

> To the Rev. Mark Guy Pearse. Dear Sir, – On behalf of the Cambrian Society of New Zealand, we tender you a hearty and sincere welcome to Christchurch. We feel proud of you as being a representative of that noble branch of the Ancient Britons, the Cornish, who, together with the Welsh, are noted for their devotion to the teachings of our Divine Master; their ardent love for race and country; also for their loyalty to the British Crown and Constitution. Your combined talents, which are always ably and successfully exerted on behalf of the highest interests of mankind, and your able contributions to religious literature, are of world-wild reputation, showing the Celtic influence on the civilised world to be both extensive and fruitful

> of much good. The fact of your being a colleague of our illustrious countryman, the Rev. Hugh Price Hughes, in the mission work in the West End of London, is gratifying to us, and we hope that you will be spared to fill many years of loving labour, and may Heaven's blessings attend you in all your efforts. The Cymri of this colony will always be interested to hear of your welfare, and earnestly wish you and your family continued health, long life, and happiness.

Mark Guy was obviously moved by the presentation and in his reply said that he would treasure the address not only as a token of the regard in which they held him, but also because it was to him 'a very singular and beautiful proof of the oneness of races that the Welsh people should be good enough to meet him as a Cornishman and brother of a race whose name they loved'. Although the Cornish language had died out, what he called 'the old feeling' persisted.[63] At four o'clock he made himself available in one of the vestries to the many people who were anxious to have a word with him, and an hour later sat down to 'a most sumptuous repast' in the Durham Street schoolroom. Speeches from representatives of the various churches, including the Anglican, followed, with the guest speaker thanking God for 'the bond which bound him to the colonies through the circulation of his books'. He rejoiced, too, in what he saw as the unfettered condition of the churches in New Zealand and the other colonies and hoped they would lead the Church at home out of the ruts it had got into. A few hours later he addressed a packed audience in the church itself on *The London West-End Mission.*[64]

His schedule over the three remaining working days of his stay in Christchurch was just as full. On the Sunday he preached to packed congregations at Durham Street where many failed to get inside after walking miles to attend. At the morning service there was a 'wonderfully representative crowd', with Englishmen, Irishmen, Welshmen, Scandinavians, Germans, Frenchmen and Cornishmen all present, the latter 'trying hard to look humble but failing gloriously with a smile that did everything but crow'. There were daytime Bible readings on Monday 6 July and again the following day when he went on to conduct a farewell service at 6.30 pm before leaving, by train, two and a half hours later in order to catch the steamer for Wellington at Picton over 300 miles away. A striking feature of the congregations at the Christchurch services – and something that was undoubtedly the case wherever he went – was their very mixed character, with Wesleyan

Methodists from town and country rubbing shoulders with representatives of other churches – other Methodists, Presbyterians, and Anglicans – and with those who were strangers to churches altogether – 'people likely and unlikely', as the *New Zealand Methodist* correspondent put it. Scores came directly from work to the evening meetings, crowding around the doors for hours before the church was opened. The interest generated by the gifted preacher's visit was such that there was a huge demand in New Zealand – as elsewhere – for photographs of him. He agreed to sit for the well-known firm of Messrs Eden George & Company, and enamelled cabinet photographs – the only ones taken in New Zealand – were duly available, price 1/6 each, with all the proceeds going, at Mark Guy's insistence, to the Wesleyan Jubilee Thanksgiving Fund.[65]

The Pearses arrived in Wellington, the country's capital, on Wednesday 8 July and that very evening Mark Guy lectured on *The Old Folks at Home* in Wesley Church, Taranaki Street. This was to be but a taster for local people, because the following morning he left for Auckland, via the coastal town of Wanganui.[66] The former capital which is, even now, home to just over a quarter of the country's entire population, played host to the celebrated preacher over a period of four days. On the evening of Friday 17 July he returned to Wellington via the train from Taranaki and the following day delivered his lecture on the West London Mission at Taranaki Street Wesleyan Church. His brief stopover ten days earlier had obviously whetted the public's appetite, and although it was a time when many people had business commitments, there was a large audience. Having described the size of London's population and the lack of religious facilities, particularly in the West End, he acknowledged the Mission's indebtedness to the other churches and gave a detailed account of the means and methods it adopted in its work, emphasising, as he always did, the crucial role played by the Sisterhood. For him, the Church that would make the best use of its women was the Church of the future. While not advocating celibacy or vows of any kind, he drew attention to the fact that, in the Catholic Church, men of position were expected to give one of their daughters to the service of Christ, with a dowry just as if they were going to be married. Similarly, he argued, Protestant girls should live together so as to be free from the claims of social life and be able at all times to serve the sick and poor. 'Why should not some of you well-to-do ladies and gentlemen,' he said, 'say to your daughters, here is the dowry I gave to your sister, go, if you will, and be trained as a nurse, and then give yourself for Christ's sake to administer to the needs of the sick and poor'.[67] On the Sunday he preached twice at Taranaki Street which, in the evening, was filled to capacity with seats, aisles, the rostrum and vestries all occupied and still people being turned away.

Of the morning service, there exists an impartial, eyewitness account in the form of a letter[68] written to the *Auckland Star* by Robert Stout in response to criticism of the preacher from their contributor 'Uncle George'. Sir Robert Stout (1844–1930) was an important figure in New Zealand's history. A barrister by profession, he was also an MP who served in several ministries, being at various times Attorney-General, Minister of Education, Minister of Lands and Immigration and, from 1884 to 1887, Prime Minister. Impelled by 'criticism of a kindly stranger' to put pen to paper on a subject he would not normally have discussed, Sir Robert made it clear that it had been some time since he had entered a Methodist church. Hearing, though, that Mr Pearse was 'a type of the new preacher', he decided to attend Taranaki Street on 19 July. 'The church,' he wrote, 'is a pretty large wooden building with an organ facing you as you enter. A small gallery runs around three sides... and a small one is alongside the organ; there the choir sits. There is a small platform fronting the organ gallery, in front of it a reading-desk, and on it two cane-bottomed chairs. I went early, as I expected the church to be filled, and soon there was no sitting room. In the gallery, on the left-hand side fronting the pulpit, there was a space set apart for the boys attending the Sunday School, and on the right a similar place for the girls.' At five minutes past eleven a young clergyman entered and announced that the Rev. Mark Guy Pearse had been detained, but would be with them shortly. 'The hymns to be sung had been printed, and were distributed in every seat. Looking over them, I noticed only one had been written by the Wesleys, and one other had been translated by John Wesley from Gerhardt. The rest were by Massie, Toplady, and others. I can remember when only the old Wesleyan collection was used, and when nothing but hymns composed by Charles or John Wesley were sung. Was this, I asked myself, a witness to the change that was coming over Methodism? Mr Pearse came in about twenty minutes past eleven, and read a chapter, making a few remarks as he went along. It rather jarred on me to hear him read about casting out devils out of a poor epileptic. Do the Wesleyans really treat such passages literally? Mr Pearse did not say. His sermon was founded on the Transfiguration and on

Peter offering to build three tabernacles, or, as Mr Pearse said, "little houses", to Moses, Elias, and Christ.' Moving on to the preacher's style, Sir Robert used words and phrases that others before him had used, describing how Mark Guy had passed 'from tears to laughter – from the pathetic to the comic' and the wonderful hold he had over his audience. 'About six times there was a distinct ripple of laughter passing over all parts of his congregation… At other times the audience was moved to tears, and I saw and heard many sobbing. Truly a master speaker,' he concluded. As far as content was concerned, he detected a tinge of Calvinism in what the preacher said. He stressed the need for practical, helpful work below rather than 'resting in cloudland', the need for doing good rather than rushing to erect churches for saints or people. He denounced sacerdotalism and the idea of any place, or any man, or any elements (sacrament) being consecrated. The building, after prayers or hymns by an archbishop or the president of a Wesleyan Conference, would remain as it was – wood, iron, bricks; no change would come over the materials. The true Church did not exist in any one building, but where 'two or three were gathered together to do good' or to worship. He also said that the time for relying on preaching had passed. Men and women should do good, should try and elevate humanity. That was the mission of the day. In fact, Sir Robert detected a strong current of humanitarianism running all through the sermon. Conspicuous by its absence was any mention of heaven or hell, of atonement or of being saved from a future wrath. There was little concerning the philosophy or dogma of Christianity which, for the preacher, was more a case of 'living… the life that Jesus lived, and following his maxim so far as life in this 19th century can be lived, differing as it does from the life in Syria nineteen hundred years ago. Our problems are different, but if we strive to do good and to work for – not merely love – our neighbour, we may raise humanity'. Sir Robert Stout concluded his letter by saying that he had no doubt that men like Mark Guy Pearse were indeed a force for good in the cities and criticised what he called 'the carping criticism of those who do not seem to understand either him or his mission'.

On the following day, Monday 20 July, Mark Guy thrilled an audience in which the Cornish were well represented, with a second installment of stories featuring Frankey Vivian, Moses Dunn and others. Prior to the lecture, a number of the Protestant ministers and officials of the circuit, together with their wives, assembled to meet the speaker and wish him well in his work. Nearly all Wellington's Protestant ministers were present 'with the exception of the Anglican clergy, who characteristically declined'. In formally welcoming the guest of the evening, the Rev. J. J. Lewis mentioned the fact that New Zealand was one of the four Annual Conferences that had extended the actual invitation to Mr Pearse to come out. He referred, too, to a resolution carried at the recent quarterly meeting of the circuit, deprecating the visits of so many travellers from Britain who expected the aid of the Churches and of the ministers, but whose motives seemed decidedly mercenary, the filling of their pockets occupying first place in their consideration. A refreshing contrast to this was the self-denying labour of Mr Pearse, who received and expected nothing for his work, which was indeed a labour of love. In his reply Mark Guy referred to 'the delicious freedom from poverty and care experienced in the colonies, and contrasted the suffering, destitution and drunkenness, so difficult to cope with in London, with the prosperity of New Zealand'. He spoke, too, of the large number of letters he had received from those who had read his work. It was these letters which had induced him to pay the visit – a visit not to see New Zealand and Australia, but their people.[69]

The following morning the Pearses travelled north-east to Napier, viewing the spectacular Manawatu Gorge, north of Palmerston North, on the way and the Rimutaka Gorge on the return journey. Arriving back in Wellington at midday on the Thursday, Mark Guy held a Bible reading that same afternoon. In the evening he took what was scheduled as his farewell service in New Zealand. Preaching to a very large congregation on 'The Master Sleeping', he ensured that 'his message was practical and sympathetic, exactly suited to the needs of working men and women, and distinguished for its home-thrusts and ripe personal experience'.[70] Mark Guy Pearse was no orator in the conventional sense of the word, but a brilliant exponent of practical preaching who used the broadness and homeliness of his views to reach people's hearts. On the very day of his departure from Lyttelton Harbour on board the *SS Arawa*, the *New Zealand Methodist* looked back on his long Australasian tour and summed up thus its outstanding success:

> Mr Pearse is not the first prominent English minister to come out to these Southern lands, but not one of his predecessors has made such a deep impression... No man has got at the hearts of the great masses of the people, in the various places he has visited, like Mr Pearse; of no man's brotherly talk and genial

> Christian spirit will such kindly recollections be cherished...

Financially, the towns and cities he visited profited considerably and the West London Mission was the richer by a very substantial sum. The most gratifying outcome of the tour, though, and the one to which he would himself have attached the greatest importance was 'the mental and spiritual quickening' which resulted from it. Its influence, 'like the stone thrown into the pool', would go on expanding and enlarging, and 'only the last Great Day' would 'unfold all its good, its inspiration to labour and to deeper holiness'.[71]

Chapter 13

'Have I got hold of you yet? If I have, we'll make the collection.'

The Isle of Man 1893

Returning to London from the Isle of Man on the morning of Wednesday 3 May 1893, the Rev. Mark Guy Pearse may well have missed the *Ramsey Weekly News*' criticism of the lecture that he'd delivered the previous Friday, although some idea of its contents would, I imagine, have eventually found its way back to him. A kind, generous and essentially humble man, Mark Guy was sensitive to criticism and could be – and often was – hurt by it. He was, too, as the Rev. C. Ensor Walters acknowledged, 'often misunderstood',[1] and this, perhaps, is the key to the Manx reporter's estimation that he seemed to be a man of considerable powers who had somewhat run to seed by becoming accustomed to addressing audiences easily pleased and exited.[2]

Mark Guy's first contact with the island was on the evening of Thursday 27 April when he arrived at Douglas on the *Ben-my-Chree* and was met at Victoria Pier by the Revs. T. Rippon and H. Jutsum, the circuit ministers, and other well-known Wesleyans. As usual, his itinerary was a full one and that same evening he lectured in Rose Mount Chapel on *Some Old Folks at Home*.[3] In his introduction the chairman described the lecturer's home county of Cornwall as 'the hotbed of Methodism and of all kinds of fervent religious life'.[4] In his own opening remarks Mark Guy said that, having often heard and read about the Isle of Man and once even caught sight of it from afar, he was at long last delighted actually to be on what he called 'this advanced Island where Home Rule had been established ever so long and where Women's Suffrage was the law'. What an enfranchised and glorified county [*sic*] the Isle of Man was! Laughter greeted his assertion that he felt himself almost unworthy to breathe their air![5] He went on to say that he was not responsible for the choice of the lecture that night. He was no lecturer – for which he thanked God with all his heart – but a preacher of the Gospel. Perhaps, he argued, the reason that he was advertised as a lecturer had something to do with the fact that a sermon had to be finished in twenty-five minutes, whereas in lecturing he was allowed to go on for an hour and ten minutes! As for the subject, he wondered what possible interest his fellow countrymen in far away Cornwall could hold for Manx men and women. Further laughter greeted his assertion that he himself was the meekest and humblest man under the sun; it was the Rev. Rippon who had arranged for him to be there and he must take the responsibility! It was banter such as this that was to get him into trouble twenty-four hours later. Declaring that Cornishmen, like Manxmen, were proud of the land of their birth, he launched into the first part of a lecture which the *Manx Sun* described as 'homely, simple, kindly, full of racy anecdote, and clothed with beautiful illustration…'; it was, too, 'rich in humour, brimming with satire, and bristling with sarcasm, keeping the congregation in the highest spirits from exordium to peroration…'[6] Comparing the easy-going old times with the matter-of-fact present, he singled out *Old Rosie* for special attention. After an interval for the collection and the singing of the old lady's favourite hymn, *Rock of Ages*, he turned his attention to an honoured name in his native Camborne. Following his conversion at a Sunday evening service conducted at Camborne Wesley by the Rev. James Nance, Anthony Cock, a miner, took charge of two classes at the chapel. His spiritual insight made him an usually capable Leader and he was eventually appointed Assistant Town Missionary at Gustavus Mission Room in Tehidy Road, an opportunity which, it seems, he used to great effect. Unfortunately, his wife did her utmost to torment him, although in due course his forbearance, love and kindness won through and eventually resulted in her being led to seek and find salvation, too.[7] An interesting letter which Mark Guy Pearse wrote to the Rev. Albert Brockbank shortly after the latter's appointment as Superintendent minister at Camborne Wesley throws further light on Anthony Cock. In it he repeats the story, told to him by Selina Budge[8] some years previously in India, of how her father James Budge the draper had given her half a sovereign as a seventeenth birthday present. When, at the end of a very happy day, she knelt to pray, she became convinced of the need to go and see Anthony Cock, a fellow member of Edward Burgess'[9] class at Camborne Wesley. 'It was late,' wrote Mark Guy, 'and Anthony lived down in College Row, but the impression was so strong that she put on her things and called to the servant-maid to go with her to Anthony's house. She found him, late as it was, pacing the little garden in front of his home. 'Aw Miss Selina, to think of you comin' down here this time o' night. Whatever have 'ee come for?' 'Well, Anthony, I had to – somehow I thought you were in trouble. What is it?' 'Aw my dear sister, I am in trouble. My little maid is dead and we been havin' poor speed [luck] up to the bal [mine] – livin' pon 'sist [subsistence] pay. And there's no money in the house to pay for her funeral.' 'Now I know why God sent me,' said she, as she put the half-sovereign in Anthony's hand, and hurried home happier than ever.'[10] Having dispensed with the usual votes of thanks – a move which the *Manx Wesleyan Methodist Church Record* described as a good example which it hoped other lecturers and speakers would follow – Mark Guy brought the meeting at Rose Mount to a close with a brief prayer and the benediction.[11]

Many of those who attended Waterloo Road Wesleyan Church, Ramsey the next day to hear the celebrated preacher were from country areas such as Kirk Michael, Lonan and Tholt-e-will. Despite the fact that the chapel was by no means full, his visit was, according to the *Ramsey Weekly News*, anticipated with pleasure and 'an intellectual treat' was expected. 'But,' continued their reporter, 'blessed are they that expect little, for they shall not be disappointed… Of the lecturer and the lecture we are obliged to say that they were both disappointing. The lecturer at once gave the observant hearer the impression that he suffered from an over-estimate of his powers; that he had come to patronise his audience; and that he considered his presence ought to be sufficient to arouse the greatest enthusiasm.' Mark Guy's subject was, once again, *Some Old Folks at Home* and he began, as he had done twenty-four hours earlier, by thanking God that he was no lecturer – an oratorical device which, as far as the reporter from the *Weekly News* was concerned, backfired. 'If Mr Pearse describes his efforts of Friday night as a lecture,' he wrote, 'those who listened to him will say 'Amen' to that sentiment.' Mark Guy had himself gone on to say that he liked to move his audience himself, but not with 'gas'. 'Such being the case,' continued the journalist, 'it is to be regretted that he brought so small a supply of any other motive power with him.' Many of Pearse's remarks tended to provoke resentment rather than arouse sympathy. After the singing of two hymns, for instance, he declared that he hadn't heard the audience sing yet. He understood they were going to sing a closing hymn, at which time he would judge whether they could sing. 'Such remarks, under the circumstances,' wrote the reporter, 'can only be described by one word, not often used in polite society. The Manx people are noted for their musical talent, and if they could not sing as well as the great Mark Guy Pearse can lecture (to judge by Friday night's attempt), they would deserve either commiseration or contempt.' He considered it in poor taste, too, for the lecturer to have stopped in order to ask the audience, 'Have I got hold of you yet? If I have, we'll make the collection.' 'For any public speaker to reveal himself by telling his audience that he is only endeavouring to "work them up" in order to get something from them,' he continued, 'is great folly. If we had the opportunity, we should like to tell Mr Pearse that Manx birds are not to be caught with chaff; we are not quite the people he thought us to be.' Conceding that Mr Pearse was doing capital work with the West London Mission, he closed his report with a rather dismissive statement to the effect that the *Old Folks at Home* was about the Cornish people, concerning whom Mr Pearse told two or three stories.[12] Of course, Mark Guy may simply have been off form – he had, after all, been giving the same lectures for years. But this in itself would not explain the bitterness of the attack. In what is unquestionably the best analysis I have come across of his abilities, the Rev. W. J. Dawson refers to his 'overflowing vitality' and to his directness. 'He fears no man,' he wrote, 'and hits out right and left in the most daring fashion. Possibly he is sometimes a little unjust; but if so, it is always unintentionally. The first article of his preaching creed is, Thou shalt not be dull. And the second is like unto it: Thou shalt be thyself.'[13] It would seem, then, that on occasions Mark Guy tried too hard not to be dull, sometimes overstepping the mark! At Ramsey he was, as modern parlance has it, too psyched up! His outspokenness had got him into deep water before, notably two years previously in Sydney where his description of educated young girls as a sort of 'waste product' provoked outrage. In Ramsey, though, it was more the tone of the lecture – the badinage with his audience in which he liked to indulge – that misfired and served only to alienate the local reporter, rather than the content of his lecture or any perceived lack of it! A hallmark of Mark Guy's treatment of his subject

Illustrated title for The Manx Wesleyan Methodist Church Record

matter was his ability to move from tears to laughter, from the pathetic to the comic. Again, such an approach obviously proved a non-starter with this particular member of the press although, to be fair, it is clear that he was not alone in his judgement. Indeed, the *Manx Wesleyan Methodist Church Record* felt the need to refer, in a roundabout way, to the criticism, concluding that 'Mr Pearse disappointed some while delighting others. The truth is that the secret of his popularity lies more particularly in his style, and his style is his own. He must be heard frequently to be appreciated: the first hearing is usually disappointing. But the disappointment is due, not to the fact that he fails to come up to the expectations of his hearers, but rather to the fact that those expectations formed beforehand a false picture of the man.'[14]

On Sunday 30 April the Sunday School at Victoria Street Chapel, Douglas celebrated its anniversary, having secured the services of the Rev. M. G. Pearse for the occasion. The school was obviously thriving and could boast 42 teachers, 517 scholars, a library containing 1,000 volumes, a branch of the Juvenile Home & Foreign Missionary Society and a membership of 130 in its junior Society classes. In the morning the church was packed to overflowing a quarter of an hour before the start of the service, a pattern of events that was repeated in the evening when the rush was so great that people began to assemble at five o'clock, with the result that at six – half an hour before the service was due to commence – there was not a vacant seat anywhere. The service was therefore begun at once, twenty-five minutes before the advertised time. At both services Mark Guy addressed the children especially, complimenting both them and the choir on their singing in the evening.[15] On the Monday he was at Castletown where, making use of a specially chartered train, a large number of 'country' people attended the circuit church to hear him lecture on *Some Old Folks at Home*. The following day he was back in Douglas to give a Bible reading in the afternoon at Rose Mount Church and to lecture in aid of the Sunday School at Victoria Street Church in the evening. In the light of his comment that he had heard a good deal of the Isle of Man, the worst thing being that it was a 'tight little Island' – an ambiguous description, if ever there was one – it was probably just as well that the venue for *Some more old folks at home* was not Ramsay! He had always been under the impression, he said, that the Manx people were first cousins to the Cornish – and this was the greatest compliment he could pay them. Their language was akin to Cornish, both being branches of the old Celtic. The Celtic peoples, he contended, were more excitable than the English, and for that reason Wesleyanism – which had a great deal of fervour about it – spread and increased in their midst. In particular he described how John Wesley had repeatedly visited Cornwall, setting it ablaze from end to end with religious rapture. The Celt, Mark Guy felt, was nearer the unseen, and religion in some form was a part of his nature. The Nonconformist pulpit in particular had been largely supplied by Celtic preachers, who outnumbered those from the whole of England. The stories that he went on to tell were, reported the *Isle of Man Examiner*, appreciated to the full by the large audience who understood the strong affinity between the Cornish dialect and the Manx idiom. The collection of £20 10s taken during the evening meant that, in total, the sum raised in connection with the Sunday school anniversary amounted to over £85.[16] What is more, of the £200 that was collected over a number of weeks in April and May in connection with Methodism in Douglas, about £130 was contributed at the services taken by the Rev. M. G. Pearse. In the estimation of the Rev. T. Rippon who had made the arrangements, his visit to the island had been a great success. 'Of all [the] preachers we have heard,' he concluded, 'Mr Pearse comes nearest the highest model, in that 'he speaks unto the multitude in parables; and without a parable speaks he not unto them'. 'The common people heard him gladly.'[17]

Chapter 14

'Please walk in. Doors closed for dust.'[1]

South Africa 1896

In his classic study of the Cornish miner which was first published in 1927, the historian A. K. Hamilton Jenkin articulated for a wider public what the Cornish people had known for many years – that a special relationship existed between Cornwall and South Africa. 'The name 'South Africa',' he wrote, 'is cut deep in the heart of mining Cornwall, not so much engraved with an instrument of steel as jagged and ghastly with the malignant quartz that hid the gold and filled the lungs of the Cornish pioneers.'[2] As the late Richard Dawe showed in his extensive research into the subject, the colony became more important to Cornwall than any other part of the world where Cornishmen could be found, although it probably attracted no more than 10,000 settlers altogether.[3] *The Cornish Post and Mining News* explained the symbiotic relationship thus:

> When the button is pressed in Africa, the bell rings in Cornwall... a change in thought and action in South Africa affects the little Western county which has contributed so much of the labour and enterprise to... the land of gold and diamonds.[4]

A writer in *The Cornubian & Redruth Times* described Cornwall as 'living on South Africa'[5] and in his *Highways and Byways in Devon and Cornwall*, Arthur H. Norway wrote graphically of the human cost involved, of

Cornwall's population being 'drained off from Camborne or Redruth to toil for foreign taskmasters at Johannesburg or Kimberley… their bodies… sweating in the heat of an African mine'.[6] Every Friday morning from 1890 to 1900 the up-train from West Cornwall included special cars labelled 'Southampton', the embarkation port for South Africa.[7] During 1895, for instance, no less than 2,086 Cornishmen left, the highest number in one week being a total of 127 for that ending 8 November. In that month alone, 226 left Cornwall for the Transvaal.[8] Of particular interest to Mark Guy Pearse would have been the fact that a gain of 1,122 members in the Transvaal and Swaziland Wesleyan District during that same year was paralleled by a loss of nearly 600 members in the West Cornwall District.[9] A decade or so later C. Lewis Hind witnessed the scenes one Friday morning at Camborne and Redruth stations where the long train on which he was leaving Cornwall was boarded by Cornish miners bound for Southampton, and remarked, 'Johannesburg is but a suburb of Cornwall'.[10]

At the end of a third tour to tell people about the work of the West London Mission in fighting the poverty and misery prevalent in the capital of Britain's empire, Mark Guy Pearse himself hinted at this special relationship in the context of what is now increasingly known as the Cornish Diaspora. In the last of a series of articles that he contributed to the *Methodist Times* while on tour, he wrote:

> No sunnier memories live with us or can ever live in this world than those of our visit to South Africa.[11]

Three months earlier, on Saturday 28 March 1896, with the weather forecast predicting that the squally south-westerly winds would greatly increase, he must have wondered what kind of reception awaited him, given that the abortive Jameson Raid, in which Britain had again attempted to annex the Transvaal, was but three months old. Accompanied by his wife and daughter Maud whose travelling expenses, like his own, he paid for himself, he was seen off at Waterloo by the Price Hugheses, the Tindalls, the Sisters and other friends. At Southampton a rough, cold journey 'by tender' brought them downriver from the quay to their home for the next three weeks, the 3,000-ton *Harlech Castle* – 'floating palace or gloomy prison, as wind and weather might decide'. Completed in June 1894 as an extra steamer for the Castle Fleet, she had the previous month carried from Durban to

'A jolly round-faced, oldish "boy"', one of the sketches of Mark Guy Pearse in Moonshine*, 25 October 1890*

Southampton the troops who had taken part in the ill-fated Jameson Raid.[12] Already something of an old hand where travelling was concerned, Mark Guy was prepared to rough it a little, having chosen the *Harlech Castle* because she was an intermediate ship, taking only second-class passengers. In the event he found everything first-class. On board he was part of what he called 'a floating village' made up of all nationalities, including Polish and Russian Jews, Norwegians, Swedes, Dutchmen and Germans, all intent on seeking their fortunes at the Cape or going further afield to Madagascar and Mauritius. There were, too, almost certainly other Cornish men and women on board, given the numbers at that time still leaving the western land. After a night of discomfort, many passengers understandably failed to put in an appearance at breakfast on a stormy Sunday morning. 'So few were serviceable', as Mark Guy so colourfully put it, that the day passed without a service. Not wishing to impugn the dignity of the West London Mission, he and Mrs Pearse duly breakfasted! Once described by an old friend as 'a genius in the art of companionship',[13] he lost no time, in spite of the weather, in making friends. By Wednesday the *Harlech Castle* was off the coast of Africa and conditions had very definitely changed for the better, with the result that he could finish his first letter under the shadow of the awning and rejoice in the beauty of the sky and sea and in the deliciously soft and balmy air.

Their first scheduled stop was at Las Palmas on the Canary Islands on 3 April (Good Friday) when they stepped out on deck at daybreak to find the ship 'invaded by a set of dusky natives… with canaries in cages, parrots that scold profusely, Florida water, oranges, citrons, figs, pineapples, huge bunches of bananas, tobacco, and cigars ranging from two-and-sixpence a box'. The oranges – picked fresh from the gardens on the islands – were delicious and according to one fellow traveller, Mark Guy bought two hundred to distribute to those on board, along with cigars. Deeply impressed by the minister's actions and philosophy, this Scotsman left us with the following generous appraisal:

> We have with us the Rev. Mark Guy Pearse. He is a jolly, round-faced, oldish "Boy", with such a stock of goodness. Thoroughly English [*sic*], which at first inclined Scotch me to keep off a bit. But such a heart. He *spends* himself on others. He is a living exponent of his own words to me, "I am the more convinced the longer I live that love is the only orthodoxy, and selfishness the only heterodoxy." Right dear man. I utterly agree with you.

> What a gulf is fixed between his life and the idiocy of self-pleasing of many lives... He is ever making sketches in ink to hand about or to ornament some book. He goes amongst the people in the steerage talking kindly to everyone. He has been foremost in promoting games for the delectation of idlers. God bless the man. He is a *man*. The true ring of manhood is about him.[14]

That Mark Guy was fascinated not only by the attractions of Las Palmas and the other places he visited, but also by travel itself and the opportunities it afforded for observation and discussion, is evident from the sheer detail of his articles or 'letters' home. That dated 'Good Friday' included an account of a typical day on-board the *Harlech Castle*, with passengers being awoken by a bell at 8 o'clock to enable them to get themselves ready for a more than substantial breakfast at 8.30am. Generally speaking, the time between 10 am and 10 pm was spent on deck, with ship-quoits and other games affording a chance of exercise. At midday the captain and chief officer took observations on the bridge prior to announcing the only news of the day – the longitude and latitude, the twenty-four hours' runs and their distance from home (the ship covered nearly 300 miles each day). With lunch at 1 o'clock, wines and spirits of all sorts could be consumed by those willing to pay for them, although at the Pearses' table nothing but water was served. Mark Guy, who had been a teetotaller for nearly twenty years, made the following apposite and pithy observation:

> They who live on the water, like those on land, live best with nothing stronger. That which avails to drive our ship on the seas day and night can fit a man for any work surely.

A spell of quiet in deckchairs followed, with afternoon tea in the saloon at 4 o'clock and dinner – 'a somewhat elaborate proceeding' – at 6. For Mark Guy, the pleasantest part of such a day was dusk. Fanned by the north-east wind, he would sit up on deck where there was scarcely a throb of the engine to disturb the peace and quiet. The only sound was 'the seething past... of the waters, broken into phosphorescent crests and curves', until, that is, there was a cry for someone to 'spin a yarn'. Whereupon Mark Guy told the story of fellow-Cornishman John Couch Adams'[15] discovery of the planet Neptune, dramatised with imagined dialogue between the scientist and Mr Tremaine, a farmer friend with whom he was accustomed to spend an evening when in

Cornwall. Easter Day was celebrated with gusto, a choir composed of upwards of twenty voices under an old choirboy from St Paul's and accompanied by the ship's doctor leading the morning service which, because of the heat, was held in the ship's stern. In the afternoon Dr Thompson of the United Presbyterian Church gave the company an account of his work as a medical missionary. The day's celebrations closed with 'Hymns Ancient and Modern, Scotch Psalms, Moody and Sankey's' ringing out in turn. Although Easter Monday follows hard on the heels of Easter Sunday, a great gap often separates them, as on board the *Harlech Castle* where services gave way to 'the great event of every voyage', the ship's sports. 'How thoroughly English it is!' wrote Mark Guy. 'The Italians sit playing cards all day, now and then with sudden eruptions flaming forth like their own Vesuvius, mostly ending in smoke. The spectacled Germans sit holding their books close to their eyes. But those Englishmen have given their sports to the world, cricket, and football, and tennis.' There were all sorts of competitions, including high jump, long jump, tug of war, sack races, 'cock-fighting' without cockerels, ladies' potato race, thread-the-needle race and egg-and-spoon race. The crowning event, though, and the one that required the whole length of the ship, was the obstacle race. While conceding that, in itself, it was absurd to see three hundred people in all positions of discomfort, panting and perspiring in a tropical sun hour after hour, shouting, clapping, and madly excited as to which of three men could jump highest or which team pull most stoutly, Mark Guy admired the 'manly virtues' – energy, endurance, pluck and coolness – of which such behaviour was indicative. Though quintessentially Cornish when with his compatriots, he was nevertheless enough of a product of his time and class to feel that all this was 'the stuff that gave to our English race its place in the world' – and no secondary place would do for 'the world's best colonists'! In the evening Mrs Pearse had the honour of distributing the prizes, many of which were won by some of Jameson's troopers who were returning to South Africa. Indeed, one of the judges was Capt. Murray who had fought at Doornkop, near Krugersdorp. A concert rounded off what for some had been an energetic Easter Monday. Two weeks later the *Harlech Castle* reached the Cape, casting anchor in Table Bay on the night of Sunday 19 April, and the record of Mark Guy's stay aboard came to a close. 'I never had so pleasant a journey,' he wrote, 'and cannot speak too gratefully of the courtesy and kindness of Captain Warden and the officers, and of the comforts of our ship.'

The first thing that Mark Guy saw from their anchorage in Table Bay on the Monday morning was convicts at work excavating an area of some seventy-five acres for docks. The excavated stone was being used to extend the long breakwater built in the 1860s to protect the port from the frequent storms which resulted in the loss of both ships and life.[16] The steamer slowly making for the pier afforded fine views of the town which itself had a foreign look – 'the houses white and flat-roofed, with large verandahs, each standing in its own patch of greenery'. There was a strange mingling of home and abroad. 'A back-ground of familiar advertisements first meets the eye,' he continued, 'and in front of it a group of Kaffirs[17] are squatting on a pile of drain pipes – Kaffirs indeed! Had we not been familiar with them from our youth up – mostly a fine black figure in undress with assegai and shield, hunting the hippopotamus, or rushing wildly at their foe. And there they sat in cast-off English clothes of divers colours – the mystic letters GNR adorning the collar of one coat – so, alas, do our illusions vanish. Here is a row of hansom cabs painted white, and each with a name inscribed. "Little Maud" holds out her charms. "Dr Jim" appeals to others. "Justice" is a touching pledge of honesty, and "Try me" comes as a coaxing whisper. The drivers are mostly Malays, some of them with straw hats that rise to a point, and with a knob at the top like the crown of a pagoda'. A colourful scene indeed – brought alive by Mark Guy's vivid prose. There to meet and greet them as they leaned over the ship's side was their host Mr Attwell, 'an old Taunton boy', the Rev. A. H. Hodges and Mr Garland, the circuit steward. There, too, was Mark Guy's old friend the Rev. William Flint[18] whom he had known at Weston-super-Mare. He it was who, with foresight, had mapped out for the guest preacher his route all the way up-country to Johannesburg, written to all the circuits on the itinerary and generally made all the arrangements. There was also a telegram of greetings from the Superintendent, the Rev. C. Pettman, explaining that he was in Durban attending the Conference.[19] Having said a hasty goodbye to the many friends they had made on board the *Harlech Castle* and passed through customs, they made for 'Twist Niet', the house of their hosts. 'The hospitality of the colonies always leaves me embarrassed and ashamed,' Mark Guy wrote. 'The reception of the visitor to our busy and crowded London must often be a painful contrast.' He experienced what he described as 'a strange reversal of the seasons', for there, in South Africa, it was winter. The weather, though, was that of a delicious August day; the flora, extraordinary and unfamiliar. Things in general struck him as being quite up to date, with the electricity supply, for instance, stretching for miles into the suburbs.[20] A very fine walk through an avenue of oak trees brought them into the town centre, the features of which impressed him as much as those of Rio, Sydney or Hobart:

> The streets… and the shops are all England at its best and much brighter than its brightest – no smoke stains its buildings, no fog has begrimed its statues. What strikes one most of all is the luxury and leisure on every side – not the luxury of the West-end, of carriages and liveried servants, of great houses and the clubs, but a middle-class luxury, as if everybody had a share in the pleasure and leisure of life. There is no hurry, no eagerness, no rush; the shops are shut at six o'clock, except on one day of the week, when they close at two. There are ten days in the year when they close altogether as holidays. I have seen no beggars, no ragged children; I have seen no sign of poverty, and since I left England I have not heard a barrel-organ. That alone is enough to tempt one to settle here.

His first service in Cape Town was on the day of their arrival, Monday 20 April, when he preached in the Metropolitan Church, 'a very handsome Gothic structure – one of the finest buildings in the town'. The round of services and lectures during the week was varied by a breakfast to which the Rev. W. Flint had invited local ministers so that they could hear their guest give an account of what he considered to be the most notable events in British religious life and of the general movements of the day. This working breakfast resulted in an invitation to Mark Guy to meet the workers of the churches at a social gathering. The following Monday, therefore, a large number of Christians from different mission organisations met in the Metropolitan Hall before proceeding to the Wesleyan Church where he gave them an account of the work of the West London Mission, describing to his audience the conditions of London and some of the methods used to meet the inhabitants' needs. Such meetings – he must have conducted scores during his tours of the colonies and former colonies – never failed to impress upon the preacher and lecturer the scale of the work facing the Mission:

> One must come away so far to see what London means. Darwin tells us that the Spanish settlers in Patagonia had an impression that England was the somewhat obscure tract of country called

> London. There is a sense in which this is true… To me here in this colony it certainly is a fact that amazes and frightens one – that in all this great continent of South Africa, occupying an area as large as thirteen Great Britains, there should be fewer souls than are crowded into London.

In the Wesleyan Church the day before, instead of preaching the sermon he had intended to use, on impulse he chose the story of the Prodigal Son as his theme, beginning in a way he had never done before:

> It was the first of May. The young man was twenty-one this day. The birds were singing, the sun was shining, the young man could at last throw off the restraints of home.

As he continued, he noticed a young man in the gallery who was visibly affected by what he heard, to the extent that tears ran down his face. Haggard, ravaged by drink and dissipation and generally down at heel, he came to the preacher afterwards and explained the reasons for his distress. Born on the first of May, he had run away from home on his twenty-first birthday and since then had sunk deeper and deeper. 'I knew you in the old country,' he explained. 'You often stayed at my father's house, and I often sat on your knee.' The young man was converted that night, and began to live a changed life. Twelve months later, when preaching in Camborne, Mark Guy was approached by the young man's father who, unable to speak, handed him some letters he had received from his son – the first he had heard of him for years. The letters told of the service in Cape Town and of his conversion there, and bore witness to his changed character.[21] One of Mark Guy's maxims was 'Preach the obvious and make it plain'.[22] As far as this young Cornishman was concerned, he most certainly achieved his aim on that Sunday evening in April 1896. One has the feeling that he would willingly have spent more time in Cape Town, so impressed was he by its very fine buildings, its streets, its shops, its people and, most especially, by the beauty of its surroundings.

On Tuesday 28 April, though, at 4 o'clock in the afternoon, he, his wife Jeanie and their daughter left on the first stage of an 800-mile rail journey that would take them north-east up through the mountain ranges of the Karoo to De Aar and then south-east down to Grahamstown. It took them three hours to cover the thirty-eight miles to Wellington, 'not the rate of speed,' commented Mark Guy, 'that would satisfy us in England in these days of racing trains'. However, allowance had to be made for the fact that the line rises steadily on leaving Cape Town until, at the end of four hundred miles, it is four thousand feet above sea level. And three hours in a train was preferable to twenty-four in a bullock wagon! Many years previously Mark Guy had lived, as a boy, among the Moravians at Zeist, near Utrecht and 'worshipped God amidst the sweet simplicities of those quiet and devout people'. He considered himself to be in debt to the Dutch, therefore, and was particularly anxious to visit Wellington where the South African Convention – an annual gathering of various religious groups – was being held. In advance of his attendance, the services and meetings he had conducted in Cape Town were very favourably reported in the pages of *De Kerkbode*, the journal of the Dutch Reformed Church. His *Old Folks at Home* was particularly well-received, especially the way in which he played the parts of the different characters.[23] His books, too, preceded him, having already achieved a wide circulation in South Africa, especially among the Dutch-speaking population. Many of them had been translated by the Rev. Andrew Murray,[24] the moderator of the Dutch Reformed Church whose ministers at the Convention therefore extended to the visiting preacher 'the hearty greeting of an old friend' and 'a right brotherly welcome'. The religious census of 1894 had shown that 189,375 people in the Cape Colony belonged to the Dutch Reformed Church and that, of these, 148,565 were white. The breakdown for the other leading denominations was as follows: Anglicans 87,480, of whom 37,463 were white; Wesleyans 132,087, of whom 21,718 were white; Congregationalists 34,140, of whom 3,482 were white; Presbyterians 12,752, of whom 7,000 were white. The influence of the Dutch Reformed Church and its moderator in both education and evangelical work was, therefore, considerable. Indeed, Mark Guy likened Wellington to Northfield, of which it reminded him, and Andrew Murray, who had made it 'a vast scholastic centre', to Dwight Moody. The town, which was crowded with those attending the convention, he described as 'a quaint old Dutch town, the wide streets lined with trees, giving a very pleasant shade. Everything is Dutch – the names, the speech, the look of things.' Having given an address immediately after his arrival on the Tuesday evening, he returned as the Murrays' guest. As well as addressing the convention again on the Wednesday evening and making a very deep impression, that afternoon he had the novel experience of preaching to the Boers in the Dutch

Church, with Minister De Beer interpreting sentence by sentence.[25] 'It was less embarrassing than I feared,' he wrote, 'and to those who understood both languages, as many did, it must have given the Word a double force and a time to get it further into the mind.' In the atmosphere of friendliness and goodwill that he experienced in Wellington, Mark Guy found it difficult to believe in any bitter antagonism between Dutch and English, although when he ventured to ask someone further north about it, the reply was unequivocal:

> 'Well,' he laughed…, 'you shall judge for yourself how much the Dutch love us.' In the team of oxen is one that is close against the wagon, and on the side handiest for the whip. Here they put the most mischievous and ill-disposed ox, and for him the favourite name is *Englander*. There is a crack of the huge whip and an angry guttural yell '*Loup, Englander*'.

The Pearses should have left Wellington at eleven o'clock that Wednesday night, but the northbound train was so crowded that delays ensued. Fortunately, a saloon had been reserved for them. As the train travelled through the vast Karoo wilderness, much of it now the Karoo National Park, Mark Guy found himself comparing the landscape with the English countryside in spring. Situated three to four thousand feet above sea level, it seemed to him to be an endless expanse of stones and stunted bushes, broken occasionally by flat-topped or conical-shaped sandstone hills. Here and there a green line of mimosa trees marked the river beds, which were mostly dry. There was scarcely a sign of life. 'Occasionally a coloured boy startles you at the side of the railway,' he wrote, 'and behind him, you see a flock of sheep and goats. Sometimes a group of ostriches breaks the monotony.' Day and night they journeyed on and on over the vast plain, aware of 'the great stretch of sunny sky, the dry and buoyant air, the still, starry, dewless night, the measureless solitude, the weird desolateness…' and realising that it had a charm of its own. At long last they reached Beaufort West where their host, Mr Gathercole, had arranged for them to break their journey for twenty-four hours and for Mark Guy to conduct a service. Once again the hearty welcome they received and the hospitality they enjoyed led the visiting preacher to eulogise those he found such pleasure in visiting. A 'pretty little town' which was becoming known as one of the finest health resorts in the world for consumption, on account of its wonderfully dry and fine air, Beaufort West, like much of the Karoo, suffered

REV. MARK GUY PEARSE

WILL PREACH IN

COMMEMORATION CHURCH,

ON SUNDAY NEXT, MAY 3,

AND

Lecture in the Town Hall, on Monday, at 7.30,

Subject:—"OLD FOLKS AT HOME."

Chairman, SIR JACOB BARRY.

AND ON WEDNESDAY,

Subject to be announced later.—Chairman, HENRY WOOD, Esq.

Admission, 1s. Reserved Seats, 1s. 6d.

Plan at H. J. Sole's, Church-square.

Notice in the Grahamstown Journal, *2 May 1896*

from lack of rain. Indeed, it had rained but twice, apparently, during the year that Mr Gathercole had spent there and the river on which it is situated was at the time often dry for three years at a stretch. Another problem, which no one seemed to take very seriously, was the sheer number of scorpions, tarantulas and snakes. The next day they were off again, travelling now at nearly five thousand feet above sea level, mostly through the same vast stretch of scrubby bush and flat-topped mountains. The nights were bitterly cold and changing trains – probably at De Aar – was a thoroughly unpleasant experience. As they turned south-east, heading down to the coast for Grahamstown, Mark Guy thought he recognised a face at one of the stations. It turned out to be an old friend with whom he had studied many years before, when Thomas Vasey was proposing them for the ministry. A former president of the South African Conference and now governor of the boys' school in Grahamstown that Mark Guy visited briefly, Mr Chubb was on his way home from the Conference. As the train glided among the hills skirting the banks of the Fish River, the two men stood side by side at the back of the corridor carriage and Chubb spoke at length about the flora and fauna of his adopted country and about the native races which inhabited it. They obviously discussed, too, what Pearse obliquely called 'graver matters of which everybody talks'. Declining once again to express an overt opinion concerning the Jameson raid, he nevertheless noted that everybody considered it a terrible mistake; furthermore, everybody thought that Rhodes had 'rendered services to South Africa which have earned for him a great claim upon the gratitude of England and that the Chartered Company[26] – under rigid control, it may be – should yet have the opportunity of completing the work they have begun'. Generally speaking, though, there was, in his opinion, more heated discussion at home in Britain than in South Africa itself.

At Grahamstown, which marked the end of the Pearses' 800-mile journey from Cape Town, they were met at the station by their host, Henry Wood. The arrangements for Mark Guy's services during the five-day visit were made by Mr Pendlebury, the first being in the Commemoration Church on Sunday 3 May, the day after his arrival. The preacher's fame, as we have already seen, had preceded him and *The Grahamstown Journal* warned its readers that, as all seats for the evening service were to be free from 6.45 pm onwards, seatholders wishing to secure their own pews should arrive before that time, as it could be impossible to reserve them later. The next day he lectured in the Town Hall (the Shaw Hall) on *Old Folks at Home*. He lectured again on the Wednesday before conducting a final meeting on the Thursday in the Commemoration Church where he spoke to a large audience about the work of the West London Mission.[27] With the spire of the cathedral of St Michael and St George rising at the centre and with the wide streets stretching either side of it, Grahamstown struck Mark Guy as essentially English, although the long spans of oxen, the numerous coloured people, the cloudless sky overhead and the eucalyptus trees lining the sidewalks all reminded him that it was still South Africa. During what he called 'that incessant round of hospitality', he was delighted to meet up with 'those whose names I had heard in my childhood when the crowded missionary meeting supplied the stuff of which my dreams were made' – a Mr Impey, William Holden,[28] an ancestor of William Shaw who was instrumental in establishing the Christian Church in the settlement and beyond, and the Ayliffs.[29] A Mrs Roland, in particular, regaled him with stories of the town's weekly slave market at which she had bought for three pounds an old female slave in order to give her her liberty. As friends old and new gathered at the station to see them off, the

West Country phrase that came to mind was 'You're cruel kind'! During the journey over the hills and through the bush to Port Elizabeth, they caught glimpses of baboons, elephants, kudus – a species of antelope – and wildebeest. If huge snakes, spiders and scorpions seemed to pose little threat, the same could not be said of mosquitos. 'No reverence makes them spare my bald head,' lamented Mark Guy, 'and great bumps of benevolence rise up mocking at phrenology. My wife has risen so disfigured that I have declared she was not herself at all.'

Described at that time as 'the Liverpool of South Africa', Port Elizabeth seemed to Mark Guy to be more of a bay than a harbour, looking too open for safe anchorage.[30] Nevertheless, the presence of large ships, steamers and a crowd of smaller craft indicated that business was thriving. 'It is the only place I have seen in South Africa where people are really in a hurry,' he wrote. They were greeted by another group of friends, foremost among whom were the ministers, Mr Wynne, Mr J.W. Thompson, Mr Davies and others, and their hosts Mr and Mrs Edgar Walton,[31] whom he had known many years previously in Highbury. After a hurried meal, they were taken to a social evening in the schoolroom where, once the introductions were over, Mark Guy had an hour in which to tell the company about his work in the West London Mission. The Sunday morning service was held in a handsome new church, while that night he preached in the Drill Hall 'with orchestral accompaniment, as if it were St James's'. By nature – and of necessity – gregarious, he enjoyed his conversations with Edgar Walton, editor of the *Port Elizabeth Herald*, Joseph Whiteside,[32] 'another old friend… [from] Liverpool Road and Clifton and elsewhere', and Wakefield Thompson, 'an ardent lover of nature' with whom he discussed the wildlife of the bush, especially the devastation caused by the locust.

Breaking the next stage of the tour – the 360-mile journey to Kimberley – at what was known as the Railway Camp at Noupoort, in order 'to give them an evening', they left again at 12.30 am and arrived at noon the next day at the town which is still synonymous with diamonds. Cornishmen were lured to the area very early on by the prospect of riches, although they were often brought down to earth by the conditions that prevailed. Indeed, two Camborne men writing home the very year of Mark Guy's visit described digging for diamonds as 'nothing but a lottery' where for every man making a few pounds, there were twenty who lost more. For them life was anything but easy, with the heat, the dust storms, the floods in the rainy season and the plagues of locust and rinderpest all taking their toll.[33] Like his fellow Cambornians, Mark Guy had mixed feelings about Kimberley, describing it as 'a place to dream about, until you get there'. 'Diamonds suggest the fairies,' he continued, 'everything that is flashing and splendid.' In fact, much of the town he did find to be well-drained, well-paved and brilliant with electric light, boasting a park and cricket ground, and with pleasant gardens surrounding the houses. There was, too, a good water supply. All of this was a far cry from the insanitary conditions in which an estimated 50,000 miners had lived and worked some twenty-five years previously. However, the surroundings he found to be 'by no means beautiful' and very dusty. The diamond mines were 'shut away within enclosures of sheet iron, and the only view you have from the road is tram-wagons running noiselessly along, guided by an overhead wire, and troops of convicts, in grey suits covered with the broad arrow, knocking to pieces the blue shale after it has been dried in the sun'. In the centre, dominating everything, was the compound where the natives who worked in the mines lived. 'These 'compounds',' he wrote, 'consist of walls of corrugated iron, shutting in a square of many acres. Here lived the natives, gathered from all the tribes of Africa – Kaffirs, Basutos, Zulus, Bechuanas, Matabele, Fingoes, Shangaans, Makalakas etc. They engage themselves for a service of four months, which is generally renewed. The arrangements made for them are admirable. Firewood and fresh water are provided by the Company. There is a swimming-bath, a hospital well-appointed. There are stores where they can purchase all they need'. One very great advantage of the compound system, as far as Mark Guy was concerned, was that no alcohol could be obtained inside. In addition, the illicit trade in diamonds which had once cost the company dear was virtually stopped under the system, because the men were constantly searched and, before being discharged, kept for two or three days in strict seclusion.

One Sunday during his stay he visited the largest of the eight compounds on the diamond fields, where the workers or 'buoys', as they were called, numbered two thousand. His address to the two hundred or so present was translated by a Mr Morris into Kaffir, and by a native minister into Tswana. In all, there were present at the gathering men from no less than thirteen different peoples, of whom nine understood the Xhosa (Kaffir) dialect and the rest, the Tswana. While the congregation was singing hymns and kneeling in prayer, the beat of a tom-tom could be heard outside and the colourful spectacle which greeted them at the end of the service was described at length by the visiting preacher:

> It [the compound] represented almost all South Africa in miniature. Here were some lordly Kaffirs, huge figures of bronze shining in the sun, with skins of the wild cat wrapped around their loins, constituting the full dress. Here were others strutting like Romans in the toga, the gaily-coloured blanket falling in folds about the figure adding almost a cubit to the stature. Others indulged a taste for European dress. From beneath a militia jacket of great antiquity stretched a pair of lean brown legs. Another, entirely regardless of expense, was arrayed in a 'blazer' jacket, with the lower limbs enwrapped in cricketing trousers. There were groups in all sorts of picturesque attitudes. Some crouched about the big iron pot cooking 'mealies' over the wooden fire, while some cooked meat in the ashes. Others gathered over a feast, where fingers skilfully did for knives and forks. Here another group was engaged in a game which Livingstone found everywhere in Central Africa. It is played with little stones placed in little holes in the ground, the point of which I failed to see. Here were solitary squatters smoking hemp which seemed chiefly to set up a furious coughing.

The contrast between the basic lifestyle of the indigenous tribes and the scramble for the wealth of others in which they were employed prompted Mark Guy to write at some length about the injustices of the law relating to the finding of diamonds. Once again he declined initially to express an opinion on South African politics, claiming that those at home could get truer information on such matters from the daily papers. If he printed what he heard, it would be 'a curious conglomerate of contradictions'. In his opinion, though, whatever the feelings between the English and the Boers, the misfortune of South Africa was that the politician was also the financier, and politics were used to advance his own financial ventures. A prime example was the law whereby a rough diamond found on the bank of a river or on the side of a mountain – far away from anyone's claim – had to be handed over to the government, with an explanation of how it had been obtained. Failure to do so could result in the finder being sentenced to five years' penal servitude. 'Of anything else proof must be adduced that it was stolen, but of the diamond proof must be adduced that it was come by honestly, or you are at once a prisoner, and there is no alternative but five years as a convict,' commented Mark Guy. His host, the Rev. James Thompson, had found the parsonage rather too small for his family and had obtained a government permit to dig up the soil of the garden, knowing it to be debris from the diamond mines. The dozen coloured men employed on the task found diamonds which, when labour and materials (water) were paid for, had been valued at more than three hundred pounds. Not one, however, could be kept; each had to be duly registered, weighed and valued. Such a system, argued Mark Guy, bred a climate of suspicion and mistrust. Indeed, there were numerous instances of rough diamonds being planted on people by their enemies in order to incriminate them. 'By all means let the proprietors of the diamond mines make their own regulations *within their own property*,' he argued, 'but there is something horrible in a whole colony being subject to such a law for the benefit of these monopolists.' One has the distinct impression that he was glad to leave Kimberley, if the following comment is anything to go by:

> Diamonds have made this place, and they rule it with a tyranny that runs through everything. You have a sense of being suspected and watched at every turn. A secret service fund, amounting to thousands of pounds, is spent annually in guarding the diamonds, and the spies must do something for their pay.

As one example of the changes that civilisation was bringing about amongst the native population, Mark Guy described a Kaffir wedding to which his wife and daughter were invited. Weighed down by the effort to appear natural amid surroundings that were utterly alien to them, the bride and groom, decked out in Western clothes, remained impassive throughout what should have been a joyful occasion. Sacrificing comfort to appearances and doing something you don't like but pretend to like was, to his way of thinking, 'a contemptible slavery'. He recalled a few years later how he had seen Kaffirs walk to church under a blazing sun 'in top-hat and high collar and uncomfortable English costume and tight boots' and sit through a heated service trying to look as if they were enjoying it. 'It was the beginning of civilisation!' he concluded. 'I rejoiced for their sakes that Sunday came only once a week.'[34]

The next stage of their journey took the Pearses south-east to Bloemfontein which, though only a small village, had in 1854 become the capital of the newly-created Orange Free State.[35] There to greet them were Mr and Mrs Scott whom Mark Guy had first met at Newport some fifteen years earlier, and their hosts, the Sowdens, who had been friends of his at Liskeard[36] and who consequently extended to them 'a right-warm-hearted Cornish welcome'. Here the Uitlanders[37] were granted a voice in the affairs of the city and the fact that his host was the mayor prompted Mark Guy to suggest that Bloemfontein's well-lit streets and general air of well-being might well convince the Boers of the Transvaal that it was a good thing to give the citizens a share in running the city. Time and space meant that, once again, he felt that he could not do justice in these letters home to the kindness shown by scores of friends which made it 'a place to linger over in one's dream'.

It must have been with some trepidation that the Pearses approached the next stage of their South African tour which involved crossing the Vaal River into the Africaner heartland of the Transvaal. The Jameson fiasco had left the Boers bitter and very suspicious of the British, as Mark Guy was to find out! Finding himself willy-nilly in the political arena, he found it difficult, as a visitor, to discriminate between the prejudices or preferences of some and the clearer perceptions of others. He heard conflicting opinions of the Boer. For some, he was 'the Puritan of today – God-fearing, narrow, bigoted, brave; not scrupulously clean, diligently reading his Bible, especially the Old Testament, and content to be ignorant of any kind of literature, apt to regard himself as the elect of God, and regarding other people as mostly left to the uncovenanted mercies'. According to others, he was 'ready to resort to any means of spoiling the Amalekite, meaning the Uitlander; if necessary or advantageous, ready to promise anything but fulfilling nothing'. Mark Guy was at pains to stress that if Englishmen entered the Transvaal they should be content to come subject to the conditions laid down by the authorities and should use only constitutional methods to secure what they wanted. In short, the Jameson raid was a blunder and a crime and could not in any way be justified. However, he felt obliged to admit that he came out of the Transvaal with very different feelings from those with which he entered it. Though 'not a Jingo by any means', he tried honestly to see things as they were and faithfully to describe what he saw:

> We had crossed the Vaal River, the boundary of the State, at four o'clock in the morning, and were delayed until seven for the convenience of the Custom House officers. The door of our compartment was thrust open, and a gruff voice roared at us 'Get up!' Then the doors at the ends of our corridor were

> locked. A portmanteau was seized and thrust out of the window. Other articles in the carriages were examined on the spot. All new articles of apparel were suspiciously scrutinised, and three shillings were demanded for some unworn linen. I must say that neither in the Cape Colony nor in Orange Free State, nor in Natal, is the personal luggage of railway passengers examined at all. The contrast made this ordeal the more exasperating. We had then to turn out into the frosty air and go to the shed in which our larger trunks were examined. A suspicion of revolvers haunted every official, and we were all regarded as raiders in disguise. Here and there men reluctantly left behind them some little belonging rather than pay the absurd charge that was made upon it. To speak Dutch was to have the mystic sign put at once upon everything. To be English meant an irritating snub. Now a man may be a good Christian, and yet to be delayed for hours, to be ordered out into the cold, to creep forth breakfastless for this kind of ordeal, to stand waiting until it shall please some lordly underling to snap at you, and then to turn your wife's petticoats inside out in search of revolvers – all this does not tend to provoke one's brotherly love. This was our introduction to the Transvaal.

Long before they reached Johannesburg, they began to pass through stretches of mining country that reminded him of Cornwall and made him wish that he could send some of this new land's prosperity to 'the dear old country'. At long last, dreaming of gold, they reached Johannesburg, only to be blinded, choked and buried with dust. There to meet them at the crowded railway station were Mr Hudson, whom Mark Guy had last seen at Finsbury Park, and his colleagues, the Goodwins. Driving through the busy streets, they noticed that the names of the shops were familiar, well-known English firms having set up in business. 'The whole place is English,' wrote Mark Guy, although 'Cornish' would have been a more accurate description. To the south-east of the city and just a few miles from its centre is the industrial district of Alberton where a criss-cross of Cornish streets in New Redruth still bears witness to the Cornish influence. As Paul Burton points out, you can walk and drive along Bodmin, Truro, Camelford, Launceston, Camborne, Penzance, Chasewater, Helston and Porthpean, and visit Trelawny Park.[38]

Soon after the discovery of gold on the Rand, it was necessary to dig deep for it, and along with the stamp batteries and crushing mills came the skilled hard-rock men, most of them Cornish. With unskilled labour provided by the ordinary native, it was the skilled miner, the blacksmith and the carpenter who were in great demand. The managers of many of the mines were also Cornishmen. Indeed, in an interview in the *Cornish Post and Mining News* in 1896 William Hosken estimated that there were 7,000 Cornishmen employed in the Witwatersrandt gold mines, with still a demand for rock drill men who were 'sure of at least 20% more wages [than in Cornwall] and constant employment'.[39] *The Cornishman*'s correspondent F. J. Tiddy conveyed something of the status enjoyed by the Cornish miner in Johannesburg when he wrote that 'a Cousin Jack sheds a lot of his clothes and perhaps more of his accent, in the land where his wages multiply by ten. At home his clothes and his tongue stunk of the Bal. Here he is not a miner after he leaves work. He lives well, dresses well, enjoys himself well and invests in shares… Our Cousin Jacks from the Transvaal are at home, the greatest living and promenading authorities on Boers, Capitalists, Native Questions, Managers' methods of mine working, Financial wastages, the value of shares in this property or in that.'[40] Inevitably, though, there were risks to run and a high price to pay, and for many of those leaving Cornwall for South Africa, an early death from fever, smallpox or miners' phthisis was waiting. The dangers attached to living in Johannesburg were spelled out in one contemporary report which described it as 'unpaved, undrained and jerry built… a city of death…'[41] Indeed, at a meeting of the Sanitary Board in September 1896, the year of the Pearses' visit, the medical officer reported that the Johannesburg's death rate was the highest of any civilised town in the world.[42] A few months later, commenting on the sheer number of deaths it had to report, the *Cornish Post and Mining News* contrasted the death rate of 50 per 1,000 with that of Truro which was only 14 per 1,000.[43] The frequent reports in the press of the deaths of Cornishmen abroad, however, did not in any way stop them from leaving their native land to seek employment and better prospects overseas. In addition to the thousands of miners who made the journey were fellow-Cornishmen who realised the commercial potential of an army of miners needing food, water, clothing and equipment.[44]

However, up to the time of Mark Guy Pearse's visit and beyond, the deep distrust with which the English-speaking Uitlanders – and the blacks – were regarded by the Boers, the Transvaal government and especially by the president, Paul Kruger, meant that they had little say in the running of the city which their energy, enterprise and capital helped develop and sustain. 'There is,' he wrote, 'what is called a Sanitary Board, of which certain members are elected by the people, but the Government keeps a majority and makes it but a mocking semblance of power.' The great source of mischief, he maintained, was that the Government had made itself powerless by selling, for large sums of money, a series of 'concessions' or bribes which made it safe for the concessionaire to defy the law and dangerous for anyone else to interfere with him. And so, although, in theory, the Boer laws were quite Puritan in their severity, they were not enforced. A prime example was the sale of drink to the native population which, though forbidden by law, still happened to such an extent that an estimated 25% of them were unfit for work each day through drunkenness. In order to try and combat this state of affairs, some of Johannesburg's mine managers had appointed a detective to watch the numerous canteens. On one Sunday morning alone, he found one hundred bottles of Cape brandy and discovered that, in one case at least, gold amalgam stolen from the mine had been exchanged for drink. When, however, these facts were laid before the relevant Government official, the detective was himself prosecuted and heavily punished on the grounds that he had stolen liquor from the natives! 'Is it any wonder that Englishmen are made indignant by things like these?' asked Mark Guy. 'They are permitted to invest their capital, to build splendid and costly buildings with which they have already adorned Johannesburg. Are they to have no right to protect themselves against abuses of this sort?' A prime example of Government maladministration or inertia was that the streets of this wealthy city were completely unlit and Mark Guy walked in total darkness to the church where he was to preach. There was in place, it seems, a whole hierarchy of 'concessions' ranging from large ones offered by the Government to small ones at the lower end of the scale. All those operating the system not only saw no harm in such gain, but considered it as a right. Everybody he met had some story to tell of such abuse of power. A lady who had driven to church to hear Mark Guy preach told him how her Kaffir coachman was wrongly arrested on the return journey for reckless driving and 'run in' until a sum of money was paid for his release. As they returned they saw a policeman confront a coloured driver, accusing him of being on the wrong side of the street. Certainly nobody else thought so, and it was amidst the angry protests of all those present that the policeman leapt into the trap and drove off to the police station.

'There were three such cases that I chanced to hear of on that one day,' continued Mark Guy. 'I might say a very great deal more that I heard of the outrageous conduct of the police and their dealings with the natives. I saw enough myself to stir my blood to a fever of indignation that I felt it difficult to control.' With a return visit part of their schedule, the Pearses left the dust and the whirl of Johannesburg for the well-watered suburbs of Pretoria.

Mark Guy and his family were met at the station of what is now South Africa's administrative capital by Mr Scholefield Morris and were soon very much at home with their hosts Mr and Mrs E. T. Bourke and their three daughters. They found Pretoria on that Saturday morning in May 1896 buzzing with excitement because many of those imprisoned for their involvement in the abortive uprising five months earlier had just been released. Among those who were still in prison was George Farrar who was still a boy when Mark Guy had known him some twenty-five years earlier in Bedford and was now one of the foremost men in South Africa.[45] Obtaining a pass without difficulty, Pearse visited Farrar, his brother Percy and Colonel Rhodes in prison. 'It was curious to see the bevy of lightly-dressed ladies within these precincts, come to visit those whose fate had been followed with such eager and thrilling interest all over the world,' he wrote. Having talked together of old times and old friends, the two parted company, with Mark Guy expressing the hope that he would see him again in Johannesburg. In fact, he was there to witness the tumultuous welcome that Farrar and Lionel Phillips[46] received on their arrival in the city when 'amidst the hurrahing of an immense crowd they were hoisted on to the shoulders of some eager friends, and borne with a kind of trembling triumph to the carriage… [Later] I saw my friend clinging to a couple of bare heads, whilst again he was shouldered and borne in triumph to his office.'

Whilst in Pretoria, Mark Guy felt duty-bound to visit President Kruger in order to convey to him his gratitude for having shown clemency to the prisoners.[47] As the President was busy with a prolonged sitting of the Executive, Mark Guy talked for half-an-hour with Mrs Kruger who assured him that her husband would see him at seven in the morning – the only time that he was free. 'Whatever may be the influences that surround and the corruptions that are inseparable from the concessions,' he wrote after the meeting, 'I believe he is a man who seeks thoroughly to do his duty in the fear of God, and I came away feeling that his wife was a grand old mother in Israel that would have made at home as fine an old Methodist as one could wish to see.' Mark Guy's purpose in touring South Africa was to raise the profile of and money for the West London Mission, and the proceeds of his lectures and services were, after sharing, as arranged with the local churches, devoted to this object. Having not, as yet, received any large subscriptions, he was delighted when the Bourkes, his hosts in Pretoria, generously donated £100 plus another £25 to be used for the work amongst the children at home.

On his return, his week-long schedule in Johannesburg was a very busy one. His first lecture, *How I came to sign the pledge*, was delivered on the evening of Saturday 6 June in President Street Chapel where a large audience listened 'with rapt attention'. The following afternoon he preached to a packed congregation at 'the native church' which was under the care of the Rev. George Rowe. Two interpreters were needed to translate his address into Xhosa and Sechuana, the dialects that were understood by the thirteen or so different tribes in attendance. That evening he returned to President Street Chapel to preach to a congregation of 700, of whom 600 were men and 500 under forty years of age. 'Here are Cornishmen by the hundred,' wrote the preacher. 'Tre, Pol and Pen are everywhere. Not a parish "down west" but had its representative. Dear, old familiar names met me on every side, and familiar places at home sprang up before me as I shook hands with one and another – from St Just to Morwenstow, and from Newquay to Polruan, every parish had its representative.' Writing to the *Cornish Telegraph*, Mr H. Perrow reported that those gathered together 'had the appearance of a Cornish congregation in a Cornish Methodist chapel. The singing, by Cornish voices, to the old tunes used at home, could not be mistaken. Mr Pearse seemed to enjoy the service equally with his congregation.'[48] It is perhaps not surprising that the Cousin Jacks and Jennies turned out in such numbers, for it was less than a year since a meeting had been held at the Goldfields Hotel with a view to forming a Cornish Association for the Rand.[49] On the Monday Mark Guy gave an account of his work at the West London Mission and afterwards a Cornish tea meeting was organised in his honour. The following day Fordsburg Wesleyan Chapel was the venue for a lecture on *More Old Folks* attended by a large crowd who, Mr Perrow informed those back home, would gladly have paid twice or even three times the amount charged for admission rather than miss such a treat. 'I thoroughly enjoyed the homely Cornish brogue which delighted his large audience,' he wrote.

'Some were ready to spring from their seats in ecstacy.' On Wednesday afternoon a Bible reading was held in Bree Street Presbyterian Chapel, while in the evening Mark Guy conducted a full-length service in the Congregational Chapel. Finally, on the Thursday a Bible reading took place in the Dutch Reformed Chapel in the afternoon before he preached his final sermon in the Presbyterian Chapel. 'Such a week's services and lectures will long live in the memory and hearts of all Cornishmen in Johannesburg,' concluded Mr Perrow.[50]

Mark Guy, too, seems to have been smitten with Johannesburg, though not for any superficial reason. Had he been twenty years younger, he would have liked 'nothing better under the sun so much as to plunge into the midst of that great and growing city, with its hosts of men – and mostly young men'. His colleague Mr Hudson estimated that of the white population, not less than two-thirds were of Methodist association. In the circumstances, thought the Rev. M. G. Pearse, the Conference could do nothing better than to send out one of its foremost and successful missioners, together with two or three young men whom he might choose to go with him. 'Nowhere could such a man find such another sphere; nowhere could such an expenditure reap so speedy and rich a harvest'. In short, it was the place above all others where, if he could, he would settle for the rest of his life's work.

A series of delays meant that the Pearses did not arrive at Heidelberg, about thirty miles from Johannesburg, until half-past seven on the Friday. Having hastily snatched some refreshment, Mark Guy was guided by a lamp to the church where his congregation had already gathered. Arriving in the dark and leaving again just three and a half hours later meant that he saw nothing of the town itself! Sleeping arrangements in the railway carriages were fairly basic – pull-out shelves with pillows and rugs obtainable from the conductor – and led Mark Guy to doubt that he had ever slept in a train! At daybreak the next morning they found themselves over the Vaal River and once more under the British flag in the colony of Natal, the smallest of South Africa's provinces. A derailment on the line ahead meant that breakfast had to be provided for the passengers at Charlestown, over 5,000 feet above sea level, a situation which led Mark Guy gratefully to pay tribute to the first-rate – often al fresco – catering arrangements on these marathon journeys. 'For a very reasonable rate at some little wayside station, sometimes without another house in sight,' he wrote, 'you step out to find a table spread in the wilderness. For breakfast porridge is always a first course, and all over the country I have found this admirable institution.' The descent from Charlestown made this railway journey 'one of unceasing beauty'. At times, though, it became too steep for curves, and the engine had to zigzag by being uncoupled and reversed. Their route took them near the battlefields of Laing's Nek and Majuba Hill, the sites of British defeats in the first Anglo-Boer War, and the coal mining town of Sheffield. They reached their destination, the Natal capital, Pietermaritzburg, at nine o'clock that Saturday evening, their ears, as Mark Guy put it, 'dinned with the long, long whirr of wheels' and their heads 'shaky with the switchback gradients and swinging curves'.

The name of Natal's capital celebrates the two Voortrekker leaders who led the early settlers against the attacks of the Zulus – Pieter Retief and Gert Maritz.[51] Commenting that the name had a sound 'somewhat unpleasantly Dutch for English ears', Mark Guy was nonetheless thankful that the city had not retained its Kaffir name 'Umgungunhlov' [Mgundgundlovu], which was perpetuated on the borough seal! As he walked through the streets to the spacious and beautiful Town Hall for his service, he found himself contrasting the peace and quiet of that June Sunday with the bitter conflicts between Boer and Zulu, British and Zulu and British and Boer that had plagued the area until relatively recently. He may have recalled, too, that it was here that fellow-Cornishman John William Colenso, first bishop of Natal, had died thirteen years earlier.

Once again 'colonial warm-heartedness' was much in evidence as twenty to thirty friends gathered at the open window of the Pearses' saloon carriage to see them off. The railway to Durban took them for the most part along a line of hills that gave them splendid views of what was going on around them. Looking up from his official handbook, Mark Guy could see that the plain which stretched before him was 'dotted by the Zulu kraals, rounded huts like great bee-hives, with a hole for the door just corresponding to the entrance of the old fashioned beehive. Here are hundreds of "raw natives", as they are called, in their picturesque dress and undress…' From the heights the train descended into a subtropical region where acres of banana trees were interspersed with fields of pines and where, at the stations, coolie women stood with baskets of fruit. After a very brief stopover at Durban, with only sufficient time to hurry to the house of Mr Nuttall, the ex-President of the South African Conference, they caught the train for Verulam, some twenty miles to the north. Passing through great sugar cane plantations, tobacco fields and tracts of land where arrowroot was cultivated, they stopped at Mount Edgcumbe. In contrast to the beauty of the estate at the mouth of the Tamar, here a huge sugar factory producing four thousand tons annually dominated the skyline. Another crop making a name for itself was Natal tea. Mr Hulett, the proprietor of the Kearsney Estate which produced four thousand pounds a year, was good enough to give Mr Pearse eight chests of tea each containing fifty pounds, for the benefit of the poor at the West London Mission. Their reception committee at Verulam consisted of the minister, a Mr Jenkin, whose trial sermon Mark Guy had heard at Launceston years before, and their host Mr T. W. Garland. The morning after his service there, the visiting preacher was taken on horseback by a Mr Armstrong, a fluent Zulu speaker, to the kraal of the chief Umgwa. Seeing the cattle ranging over a great expanse of pasture, shut in by high mountains and deep valleys, led Mark Guy to contrast what he described as 'the happy condition of this heathen chief and his people' with the plight of those in the slums and alleys back home:

> The kraal consisted of a score of huts within an enclosure, at the opening of which the headmen of the tribe, each with a wooden ring about his head, sat waiting for the coming of their chief. The wives were at work grinding corn or polishing the bottom of the hut with cow-dung until it shone. Everything and everybody was clean, and everybody was happy.

Mark Guy was introduced to the chief, a man of very fine stature with a blanket around his shoulders and a wildcat skin around his loins, as a great 'umfundisi' – a minister – from London. The size of London was described as consisting of 'kraals one on the other six and eight high, and side by side as thick as they could stand, reaching so far that one could walk every way for six or eight hours before getting outside them'. Although conversation was difficult where thought processes were so different, Mark Guy asked that the company be told that Her Majesty the Queen of England would be glad to know that the chief Umgwa and his wives were well. 'The statement was received with simple seriousness,' he wrote. 'To them no sovereign was greater than their chief.' The news that their guest had only one wife to the chief's twenty-five produced 'a wail of distress for that unknown sister of theirs… Only one wife, to till the fields and gather the mealies and reap the corn and carry the loads of firewood on her poor old head and light the fires and boil the pot and polish the floor of the kraal! I was indeed a man to be pitied. Henceforth I fear I was nothing and nobody in their eyes.'

For the Pearses no week was more enjoyable than the last full week in June which they spent in Durban with their hosts, the Povalls. Mark Guy thought that the town itself had 'every advantage of position' and that this had been made the most of. 'A gentle slope is covered with the houses and grounds of the well-to-do,' he wrote, 'and everybody seems well-to-do in Durban. The town, with its broad streets and many fine buildings, reaches to a deep-blue estuary extending some three miles inland. Here are the busy wharves and shipping. The other side rises the wooded bluff, crowned by a lighthouse. There is the Bar, on which the surf breaks perpetually, dredged to keep an entrance…' Climate-wise, Durban in winter was 'simply the very perfection of an ideal English summer; day after day a sky of cloudless blue, and a blaze of sunshine. It is delicious simply to live'. In this, the garden of South Africa, there was an abundance of oranges, 'nartches', bananas, pineapples and guavas. The day that he discovered 'the Avocarda pear' was a memorable one:

> I am not sure of the spelling – but the fruit itself is something which leaves you wondering what heaven is like… If another Paradise is to be lost by the temptation of a fruit I am persuaded that the fruit will be the Avocarda pear.

Another novelty for Mark Guy, was the Papaw, 'a tree whose leaves may well be used for the healing of the nations. There is prepared from it a drug which has the power of dissolving animal tissues, and which is said to cure warts and membranous growth of diphtheria'. Meat wrapped in its leaves certainly became tender, but stories of tough old cocks renewing their youth and becoming as tender as chickens just by roosting in its branches and of a bullock's heart hung in its shade being found in tears needed to be taken with a pinch of salt! He thought one experiment, though, would be well worth trying – namely binding all future annual reports of the West London Mission in the leaves of the *Papaw* tree!!

After two months of extensive travel through the heartlands of South Africa, the prospect of a short run by steamer from Durban along the coast to East London must have seemed like a welcome change to the Pearses. First, though, they had to get aboard the steamer anchored in the bay beyond the bar. Did they have any inkling as to the unorthodox boarding procedure that awaited them there? I hope not! Often shipping a 'green sea' as it snaked its way out, the tender was eventually made fast to the ocean steamer, 'now lifted to the level, and now sunk in a great hollow of the sea. The ordinary gangway is worse than useless – the "companion" ladder would avail nothing. From up on high somewhere a rope is slung from off the ship with a huge round basket, a tower in wicker-work; and this is lowered to the tender. The door is opened, and some five or six passengers get into the cavity and are made fast; then they are lifted with laborious creaking into mid-heaven and lowered until finally they are dumped down on the deck of the steamer. One comes out of the basket as if it were a parcel by post, and is inclined to demand a receipt.' Their passage out on the afternoon of Saturday 27 June was exceptionally smooth, and the numerous friends who saw them off assured them that they would certainly be in East London the next day in time for the service which Mark Guy was to take. Although they did reach the mouth of the Buffalo River the next morning and could see the town clearly in the sunlight, between it and them was the bar buried in surf, and along the coast broke great columns of spray. Today East London's surf beach rivals Sydney's famous Bondi Beach. In the past, though, such conditions were a considerable hindrance to navigation, many shipwrecked Dutch and British sailors having been stranded on the shores near East London at one time or another. No less than a score of ships spent that Sunday 'in alternately rolling towards each other until their decks seemed to stand perpendicular, and then rolling away, until only the hull was visible'. What made the delay so galling for Mark Guy was that overhead there was a clear blue sky! What is more, a service on board in such conditions was out of the question. The knowledge that the previous steamer had waited for three days and nights did nothing to improve morale! In the morning, though, the signal informed them that the bar was passable and soon they were steaming up the smooth water of the Buffalo River to a warm welcome from the minister and their hosts. That missed Sunday service was the only failure of the entire tour, which owed its success largely to the skill and care with which Mark Guy's good friend and colleague William Flint of Cape Town had made the arrangements.

Their next destination, King William's Town, was described by Mark Guy as 'a pleasant place shut in by wooded hills on the banks of the Buffalo River'. Once again, he was impressed by the kindness shown to them by their hosts, Mr and Mrs Duckles, and by the 'admirable programme of services' arranged for him by the Revs. Cotton and Robb. By way of light relief they were driven – 'No words of mine could convey any conception of a ride in a Cape cart,' wrote Mark Guy – through a series of native kraals to the edge of the upland forests in the neighbourhood of King William's Town. It was in consultation with Mr J. Peacock that Mark Guy's proposal to visit South Africa had first taken definite shape and a seventy-mile journey north to Queenstown for a four or five day stay reunited the Pearses with their friends there.

The town of Cradock had been allocated a slot in Mark Guy's gruelling schedule and 'a dreary journey of a day and a night' brought the Pearses to this former military outpost on the banks of the Great Fish River at 10 o'clock on the morning of Wednesday 15 July. The Rev. J. E. Parsonson and his committee made the most of the limited time available and at 11.30 am the guest preacher gave a Bible reading in the Dutch Young Men's Christian Association, choosing as his text the 23rd psalm. In the afternoon a reception, complete with light refreshments, was held in the Wesleyan Schoolroom, and in the evening he gave his lecture on *Old Folks at Home* in the Town Hall where the large audience was 'kept in merriment the whole time'. The next day the mayor, Mr A. E. Austin, presided at an afternoon meeting where Mark Guy gave an account of the West London Mission. Although the attendance was not large, the collection – for the Mission – was very good.[52] That evening the Pearses left Cradock and, after two days and nights crossing the Karoo desert, were back in Cape Town at Twist Niet, the home of their friends the Attwells. Among the parting gifts that the Pearses took with them on board the Royal Mail steamer *Dunottar Castle* on 22 July was a large iced cake for the workers at Cleveland Hall from Miss Robbins of Cape Town, who had been a voluntary worker with the Mission before coming out to South Africa. Among the decorations on the cake was a representation of the Mission's badge.[53]

Mark Guy Pearse's tour of South Africa was a resounding success. On a purely financial level, a total of £1,424 was raised for the work of the West London Mission, the only deductions being £15 duty on the chests of tea and their delivery, and the sums spent on telegrams and postage by those involved in arranging his itinerary. In addition, 'goodly sums' were raised for various local purposes in many of the towns that he visited. Mark Guy himself must have acquired a fuller understanding of the nature and possibilities of the work of the Methodist Church in South Africa. Indeed, in his last letter to the *Methodist Times* he expressed his amazement at the extent of the Mission work already being done, given that the Church's English membership was 5,543, while their native membership stood at 36,212, a figure which almost equalled that of the Foreign Missions back home. His one regret was that many small towns and mission stations that had requested his services, had of necessity to be left out of the itinerary. Gratifying though the raising of so much money undoubtedly must have been, it was not, from his hosts' point of view, the chief result of his tour. Anticipated, as it had been, with 'feelings of high expectation' which had been 'abundantly realised', the visit had acted as a major stimulus to clergy and laymen alike. 'In numberless instances,' continued the *Methodist Churchman*, 'the spiritual life of our people, and of the members of other churches has been quickened. To many the Gospel has come to have a new meaning, of which they had scarcely dreamed before, and in many cases the ministers of the different churches have received blessings which they have now the joy of communicating to others.'[54]

Chapter 15

'Just a friendly visit on my own responsibility'[1]

India 1906–1907

Although Mark Guy Pearse returned from his North American tour in August 1904 to official retirement from both the Mission and from circuit work, any changes in his lifestyle would have been relatively insignificant, at least over the next few years. 'We saw little of him at the Mission,' wrote the Rev. George Parkinson who was his colleague there in the early 1900s, 'for he was out all over the country raising funds for the work…'[2] His public profile was such that he could never really retire and any distinction between leisure and work continued to be blurred, although the pressure eased somewhat. Early one spring, for example, he went up to Yorkshire for a week's fishing holiday at a moorland village not far from Whitby. The villagers quickly discovered his presence amongst them and the Wesleyan Society was asked to invite him to preach and lecture. This he agreed to do, although he had not intended to do either. The day fixed for the service and lecture was wintry in the extreme but, nevertheless, many church and chapel folk came considerable distances from very scattered houses and farms to pack into the village chapel, and the stewards felt obliged to provide tea in the schoolroom for them.[3] He continued to be a favourite with the children and just before Christmas 1904, he joined Dr Gregory, the principal of the Children's Home and Orphanage, on the platform of Queen's Hall, Langham Place for the Home's Annual Christmas Festival. After four days of practically continuous fog, the capital was still shrouded in darkness on 22 December. The day before, Queen Alexandra had been forced to postpone her visit to Sandringham, the Chancellor of the Exchequer had had to walk to Euston because no cabman would undertake to drive him and clubmen were offering 2/- to those willing to take them across Piccadilly. In short, conditions were enough to cast a shadow over the activities at the Children's Home. However, on the day the Queen's Hall was virtually full and 'a genial chairman, a cheery speaker, and a bright-faced company of children facing the audience [were] determined to do their best to dispel the gloom'. Following the children's rendition of 'Ring out the old, ring in the new', Mark Guy set the tone for his address when he quipped that although he was old, they had not rung him out! He went on to express his delight at seeing the children's cheerful faces, especially when he thought of what their lives might have been like without the Children's Home. Having expressed his thanks to Dr Gregory for his care of the boys and girls and taken the opportunity to honour the name of Dr Stephenson, the home's founder, he dwelt at some length on what he saw as the three main strands of the Forward Movement, namely temperance work, the Sisterhood and social work. They needed to show people how best to live while down here, as well as the way to heaven. He would like every father and mother, he said, to put a shilling into their children's stockings on behalf of the Children's Home, and for the children themselves to join the Young Leaguers' Union. As it took £16 to keep a child for a year, it would be worthwhile if every family would undertake to keep one child. In response to a vote of thanks, he said that the girls did not know what they were being saved from. Just the other day, he had heard about a dreadful society when a woman had come to one of the Mission's Sisters and said, 'Ugh! He knocked his wife about shameful, he did, and she was my daughter; but I am going to be level with him, Yes, I am. I'm going to that there Society for the Prevention of Women and Children'.[4]

Having preached at Stoke Newington on Christmas Day, Mark Guy began what was to be another busy year with a lecture in the Metropolitan Tabernacle in aid of South-West London Mission funds on 6 January, when he chose as his subject 'Counsels for the New Year'.[5] Two weeks later he was in Newcastle for the anniversary of the city's Wesleyan Mission, preaching at Jesmond Church on the morning of Sunday 22 January and at Westgate Hall in the afternoon. On the Monday he gave an inspiring address in which he praised the work of the missions in bringing a new spirit into Methodism. The Salvation

Army, he maintained, had been brought into existence to provoke the Methodists to jealousy, and the missions were helping them to do something heroic for Christianity. Had the churches' current involvement in social work been started some years previously, he argued, secularism would not have been alive to the extent it currently was.[6] Towards the end of the month he appears to have spent some time in Nottingham.[7]

Although his published output in book form inevitably decreased in the later years of his life – nothing appeared between *Christ's Cure for Care* and *West Country Songs* in 1902 and a collection of short stories entitled *The Pretty Ways o' Providence* in 1906 – Mark Guy was still writing and often corresponded with the Rev. J. A. Sharp who, as Connexional Book Steward from 1911 onwards, did his utmost to present the works of Methodist scholars to the public in the most attractive form. Mark Guy's close friend and colleague, the Rev. Egerton R. Young, was due to arrive in England towards the end of February 1905 for a lecture tour lasting some months[8] and it is highly likely that Mark Guy was able to repay much of the kindness shown to him by the Youngs, both father and son, when he toured Canada in 1887 and 1903–4. Indeed, it is possible that he accompanied Young on his return journey for, just after he preached and lectured at Hindhead and Grayshott on the Hampshire-Surrey border on 24 May, he announced that he was leaving England shortly and would be 'beyond the reach of letters' until October.[9] In the event, the Pearses toured North America until the end of October, leaving New York by the *Oceanic* on Wednesday 1 November.[10] One of his first tasks on reaching home was to write an appreciation of another friend and colleague, Thomas Champness, whose retirement two years earlier had proved to be shortlived.[11] A similar pattern, combining support for home missions and foreign travel, followed in 1906 when his engagements included a new series of midday services at the Sheffield Mission in Norfolk St Chapel on Tuesdays[12] and preaching – and lecturing on 'Christian Socialism' – at Oakley Place Chapel on behalf of the South London Mission on Friday 30 March.[13]

In contrasting the respective characters of her father and his close friend Mark Guy Pearse, Emmeline Pethick-Lawrence stressed how the one was a passionate believer in justice and freedom in the political sense, while the other believed in one power only, the power of love. Though a firm advocate of Christian Socialism, Mark Guy was not in any sense a political animal. Indeed, in the words of the woman who was all but a daughter to him, 'political life with its conflicts and insecurities and cruelties was utterly alien to him. Of the rules of that game he knew nothing'. Conflict in any shape or form was to be avoided in favour of peace and love.[14] It must have been with some anxiety, then, that he watched the growing militancy of the Pethick-Lawrences. Following the arrest and imprisonment of Christabel Pankhurst and Annie Kenney in October 1905, Emmeline began to take an interest in the suffrage movement. On 23 October the following year, shortly after joining the Women's Social and Political Union, she was herself arrested while trying to make a speech in the lobby of the House of Commons. Charged with 'using threatening and abusive words and behaviour with intent to provoke a breach of the peace', she and nine other women were ordered to keep the peace for six months or go to prison for two. On that and subsequent occasions they all chose prison.[15] Although, like many others, not opposed to the principle of women's political equality, Mark Guy Pearse regarded militancy with extreme distaste and very much regretted Emmeline's association with it. 'He showed great forbearance,' she later recalled, 'but when our behaviour grew from bad to worse, he wrote me a letter to tell me that our friendship could no longer continue. I threw it into the fire. I made no appeal against his decision.' In the solitude of a prison cell, though, the memory of their deep relationship would help sustain her, as did the memory of the songs that he had written for her.[16]

Towards the end of 1906 he embarked on what was to be his last foreign tour, barring one or two holidays. As he made clear at the time, his two month visit to northern India and what in now Pakistan was essentially a personal one, undertaken specifically to visit his eldest daughter, Maud, who had gone there as a missionary. For all that, Mark Guy conducted services or delivered lectures to the English-speaking community whenever he had the opportunity. Prior to leaving, he preached a farewell sermon on the evening of Sunday 21 November to a packed congregation at Amhurst Park Church in the north London circuit of Stoke Newington.[17] The Pearses arrived in Bombay one day towards the end of December and left for Lucknow the following afternoon in order to be with Maud for Christmas. In five sparkling letters to the *Methodist Recorder* Mark Guy recorded his detailed impressions of India and of some of the difficulties facing the missionaries of the Wesleyan Methodist Church there.[18] For the hospitality of their Bombay hosts, Mr and Mrs Ryder Smith, and for the welcome they received everywhere, he was full of praise. 'A royal welcome; a most refreshing meal, and then

Emmeline Pethick-Lawrence (©Museum of London)

a Christian bed' went some way towards compensating for the shortcomings of the ship's berths where they slept 'under a kind of Coercion Act – sleep you must and shall, but with all imaginable discomfort'. His impressions of what is now India's most westernised city are necessarily brief, though colourful and informative:

> It is to me a glare of blue sky; a blaze of sunshine; a fierce heat which they call their midwinter; many stately buildings in Oriental styles; shaggy banyan trees; streets with carriages and tram-cars, and the ubiquitous motor with its familiar "toot". Then the native bazaar with its narrow streets; a mass of people gay with turbans of every imaginable hue, and robes of every colour ending in a brave show of mahogany legs – except when some English lady or gentleman came in the universal "topee", and dressed from head to foot in white.
>
> Here it is in the native bazaar that the tides meet, the old and the new, the East and the West. Here are the little shops open to the street where the master sits cross-legged, or works at his calling, willing, and even anxious to spend half and hour in coming down from the "asking price" to the "taking price" – which may be less than half the amount named at first. All about the shops besides the oriental names are the notices of "Alarming sacrifice", "Sale now on", "English style, English make, all English". Over the door of fluttering finery stretched the notice, "As worn by Queen Alexandra". A list of stationery at the door included, "Objection lessons". And through the crowd the drivers of the lumbering carts drawn by a pair of white oxen urged their way with shouts, and the carrion crow, the scavenger of India, hops along looking at you with a wicked eye as if to say, "I was here before you; why should I get out of your way?"

On the day after their arrival Mr Ryder Smith helped them find a native servant for the duration of their visit, someone who would see to their luggage throughout the journey, interpret for them, make their beds and provide them with information about their stopping places and with refreshments. 'There they stood,' wrote Mark Guy, 'a row of them, producing their "chits", or testimonials – which sometimes said more than the owner dreamed of – as, for instance, that which ran, 'This man is most capable – indeed, I believe he is capable of anything.' It was proudly folded and treasured as a recommendation in excelsis.' Twenty years later he recalled how, while in Bombay [Mumbai] – either before Christmas or, as seems more likely, on the return journey – he found

Selina Budge whom he had known in Camborne in the 1840s and '50s, working as 'Mother May' in 'the sailor's Bethel'. The two enjoyed a good chinwag, with another Cambornian – class leader and local preacher Anthony Cock – their main topic of conversation.[19]

At Jhansi, towards the end of their 850-mile rail journey to Lucknow, the Pearses met the Methodist chaplain, the Rev. John Shenton, who joined them for lunch. They spent Christmas at Sultanpur with Mr and Dr Harrison of the Church Mission Society who had arranged for Maud to join them. With Mr Harrison Mark Guy visited Faizabad where the Mission House stood in a large compound, the central compartment of which housed the tomb of a Muslim princess.[20] Sleeping in an adjoining room, he confessed to being disturbed by nothing more sinister than the hum of bloodthirsty mosquitos. The sacredness of life among the Hindus seemed to endow birds and beasts with a confidence unheard of in the West. Of all the creatures which, especially when the nearby River Gumti overflowed its banks, infested the Mission House at Faizabad, monkeys were the most destructive. One had found its way into the church through a broken window and devoured the greater part of the Book of Revelation! They swarmed everywhere, making the most of the sanctity in which they were held. As he drove from the station, Mark Guy noticed outside the houses a lattice-work which served as protection against 'the impudent intrusion of the monkeys'. As he and Mr Harrison sat under the heavy, projecting walls of the tomb at sunset, vultures came to roost in a lofty palm on one side of the gardens, while huge buzzards found their home in another. From the grassy margins of the river came the bark of foxes and the cry of jackals. Later in the evening they dined with the Gregorys at the Wesleyan Mission. For Mark Guy the main interest of Faizabad was its connection with Padri Elliott, whose loss he described as being 'deplored' at home and throughout northern India.[21] The next day they visited Ajodhya, some three miles to the east, to see the iron pulpit from which the well-known and respected missionary had preached to the hundreds and thousands of pilgrims who, on the occasion of the fairs, even then poured into the small town on the River Ghaghara reputed to be the birthplace of Rama. Mark Guy found it 'filled with temples, monkeys, and fakirs', the latter, holy men belonging to different orders who spent years subjecting themselves to rigid discipline before becoming fully qualified. 'As I stood on the high roof of the monkey temple, surrounded by scores of grinning monkeys,' observed Mark Guy, 'I saw three of the holy men, stretched in the blaze of sunshine, playing cards; whilst another, amidst a group of listeners, played on a little American organ with one finger, and without any pretence of a tune.' Here and there he came upon a fakir stretched upon a bed of spikes that looked terribly cruel, although he was assured that it was not as bad as it looked, pieces of wood being used as supports and as protection. 'As we drove back through the native bazaar,' he continued, 'I noticed frequently the sacred bull, strutting along with a leisurely pride, taking what he pleased from the vegetable stall, and condescending to accept the sweetmeats that were held out to him. And monkeys everywhere.'

At Agra, the capital of all India under the Moghuls, he preached in the Havelock Memorial Chapel, a Baptist Mission under the care of Mr De Russet. The Amir was visiting the city at the time and Mark Guy was obviously impressed by the opulence of his tent, 'an amazing thing of costly splendour – silver pillars, that had been lent by a neighbouring Raja; silver hangings of daintiest colour and richest fabric; carpets of great value'. With camps everywhere, it seemed as if all India had emptied itself into Agra. He was impressed, too, by Agra Fort and, of course, by the Taj Mahal, which he visited twice, the second time by the light of the full moon, when it seemed to him indeed 'a poem in stone, a dream in marble'. 'As I sat on the roof [of Agra Fort],' he continued, 'and looked out over the river in the sunset, the rosy tints lending a new charm to the Taj, I saw the flames rising from the bier of some Hindu, whose ashes were afterwards to be cast into the sacred stream. On the other side of the Fort was the railway station. Below me thronged natives in the bazaar. Beyond lay the miles of British camps. The contrast was striking.'

A day at Kanpur brought to mind memories of the atrocities committed during the Indian Mutiny or First War of Independence as recalled by a dying soldier whom Mark Guy was visiting. He himself visited the memorials which at that time stood over the site of the terrible Bibighat Well in the centre of the city, where Brigadier-General Havelock discovered the still-warm remains of the massacred women and children. Although independence was still forty years in the future, the Liberal Party's electoral victory of 1906 marked the dawn of a new era of reforms. Reflecting on the British presence in India, Mark Guy – himself a man of strong Liberal convictions – saw it not in forts, palaces and tombs, but 'in roads and railways; in truth, for an Englishman's word is gospel to the native; in justice; in security to life and property'. Whereas other conquerors had come to slay or enslave, the British, he maintained, had, for all their faults, developed the country and given the natives the safe possession of it.[22] Travelling north-west from Agra to Lahore and Rawalpindi in what is now Pakistan, he saw what was formerly a wilderness transformed by means of irrigation into fields of wheat and cotton, producing two, and sometimes even three crops a year. Similarly, he saw the condition of the native 'transformed from abject poverty to one of happiness and wealth'.

Allahabad, at the confluence of the Ganges and Yamuna rivers, is one of the great pilgrimage destinations of India and comes alive during its melas or religious fairs. Mark Guy had the good fortune to witness the first day of one of these great festivals, Makar-Sankranti or Pongal, which now seems to be confined to Kamataka, Andhra Pradesh and the east of India. In January 1907, the trains were crowded to overflowing, with thousands of pilgrims in trucks, packed as closely as they could squat. The roads were thick with men, women and even children, thronging to the banks of the river. From the huge battlements of Akbar's Fort, Mark Guy surveyed the scene:

> Away, as far as the eye could reach, stretched an enormous crowd – hundreds of thousands – the men with shaven heads, bare of clothing except a loin cloth; the women in their long, graceful dresses of red or yellow or white. In the midst of them the English chief constable sat mounted, a native attendant behind him, and divided the crowd, those who pushed and shouted towards the stream, and those who came dripping back from it. It was a strange illustration of British authority. An outstretched hand with silent control guided the hosts. But for that protection many must have been trodden to death, for the bank of the river, sodden by the bathers and churned by the tread of the million feet, was a mass of slippery mud. In the water stood the men and women, each dipping three times beneath its surface. And here were others with baskets of flowers, yellow marigold and white jessamine, which the pilgrims bought and cast as an offering to the river. Here and there in the crowd was led a heifer, and I watched many come and hold the tip of its tail, saying a prayer and then handing some money to the attendant Brahmin. The roar of the host as they pushed their way, those seeking to reach the stream and those returning from it, was as the roar of the sea, vast and incessant.

As far as Hindus are concerned, the holiest city in all India is Varansi or

Benares which, for Mark Guy, was in itself worth coming from England to see. Indeed, he declared that of all the cities that he had visited, the two that had impressed him most were Damascus and Benares which, he felt, was in some respects the most wonderful city in the world. With Mr Trevellick Cape he took a boat along the Ganges, passing the long flights of stone steps or 'ghats' down which thousands of pilgrims and residents still come for their daily ritual ablutions. Above the sloping heights rose the towers of the temples – temples on whose walls, in some cases at least, were engraved what he described as 'almost every conceivable form of filthy abomination'. The flames of the funeral pyre crackled and blazed where the dead were being burned, and there lay untended three dead bodies in the blazing sun, waiting, he supposed, for the astrological hour when it would be most auspicious for them to be consumed. Benares may have looked beautiful from the river, but as they landed and came up to its narrow street, where not more than two could walk abreast, the stench was sickening. And in a deep tank, reached by some thirty steps, and but a few yards in extent, an incessant crowd of men and women were dipping into the filthy water. 'It is called the 'Well of Salvation',' wrote Mark Guy. 'Why by such toil and discomfort any should add to the ensured salvation of all that live in Benares is perplexing. Here every particle of ground is held to be holy, and the very air is hallowed. He who dies within the sacred radius, which stretches ten miles around the city, whether Hindu or European, is assured of entrance into celestial bliss. And yet there are at least two thousand temples, and thousands of smaller shrines, each with its immodest symbols. Here is the temple of the divinity who makes small-pox his special care; and in another temple they seek the god of the stomach ache. It is calculated that the whole number of gods scattered throughout the city numbers at least half a million.' They found it refreshing to drive from the crowded and ill-smelling streets of Benares to another sacred spot some six miles away at Sarnath – the quiet grove where, in the sixth century BC, Siddhartha Gautama, who came to be known as the Buddha, gave his first sermon. There was no crowd here – indeed, there was no one except a man to show and explain the results of recent excavations. 'It was with the deepest impressiveness,' wrote Mark Guy, 'that this place appealed to me… I breathed another air – the air as of a heaven undefiled. I felt the hush of the place in my soul as I stood in the shade of its trees amid the singing of the birds.' Reflecting on the story of Buddha and the immense influence that he had exerted upon mankind, Mark

Guy found himself wondering whether it was 'too much to expect… too much to pray, that some man shall rise up proclaiming the truth as it is in Jesus to win a victory as swift and infinitely more blessed in the India of to-day, and indeed throughout the Eastern nations where Buddhism prevails'.

The District Synod had assembled at Benares, meeting in the Rev. T. Cape's study, where the Chairman, a Mr Gregory, sat with three ministers on each side of him – seven in all, in a district with more than 55,000,000 souls! Indeed, at every station Mark Guy found himself repeatedly humbled and ashamed as he thought of the ease and advantages of the work at home compared with the difficulties and disadvantages encountered by his colleagues in India. At home Sunday might be largely a day of pleasure, but there was certainly a Sunday atmosphere, 'a tide that sets towards rest and worship', as he put it. In India, though, there was no Sunday, no day of rest. To the masses, it was a day of toil, much like any other. Whereas at home it might be easy to neglect Sunday observance, in India it was hard to know that it was Sunday. For eight months out of twelve, too, the climate made work difficult. From 10 o'clock in the morning till four in the afternoon, the heat made moving from the house a chore. Soldiers were not permitted to march to church, but the minister had to be at the barracks by 7.30 am to conduct a service for them. Then he had to be back at the English Church for worship at 8.30, holding it later than that being out of the question. Sunday school, too, had to be adapted, in much the same way, to the requirements of the climate, and all the year round, the children had to be fetched in carriages and taken home again. The lectures that Mark Guy gave in Calcutta, even early in the year, began at 9.15 pm. With temperatures over 100 degrees in the shade, sometimes 105 degrees, the humidity in this part of India made conditions even more unbearable. At such times there was a further disadvantage in the form of the heavy fans that were suspended from the roof of a church – an irritating diversion, hiding alternately the congregation and the preacher, and setting up a breeze that was apt to send notes and notices flying all over the place, unless they were secured by means of lead weights. Another unsettling problem for those charged with ministering to the spiritual needs of English-speaking people was 'the season for the hills' which lasted from March to November and saw many of those employed in government migrating to Simla or Darjeeling, the business of government transferring with them. And in almost every case among the English, there was the periodical furlough, long or short, but not less than six months in duration, which meant that the church congregations were constantly changing. Two other problems not found in Church work back home were the organ, which had to be tuned every week or climatic conditions would make it useless on Sundays, and servants whose service was rigidly limited by caste. In India each would only do his own work; it was useless to argue – it was their traditional way of doing things, and tradition left no choice and knew no change. During his visit Mark Guy took a keen interest in the work of the chaplains to Methodist soldiers, particularly in what is now Pakistan, and made a plea for a better understanding of their work by those at home.

The Pearses spent a delightful week in Calcutta in the company of the Chairman of the Wesleyan Methodist District, the Rev. G. W. Olver, and the minister of the English congregation, the Rev. J. Stainer Wilkinson. Preaching in the church on Sunday, Mark Guy noticed with interest a brass tablet on the wall which read:

> In loving memory of John Remfry, a faithful member of the Wesleyan Methodist Church. It was mainly through his influence that a Wesleyan Mission was established in Bengal. In the building of this sanctuary he took an initiatory and active part; and was uniformly the generous friend of ministers of all denominations. Born in Truro, Cornwall, June 16, 1804. Died at Clapham, London, Dec 27, 1884.

Thoughts of Truro gave rise in turn to memories of another Cornishman who had distinguished himself as a missionary in India, translating the New Testament into Hindi and Hindustani, and the Book of Common Prayer into Hindustani. 'To me,' wrote Mark Guy, 'there was no spot in India so sacred as that Pagoda, where Henry Martyn suffered, and studied, and prayed.' Although what remained after much of it had been destroyed in a cyclone had generally suffered from neglect, Lord Curzon had had it repaired and furnished with a marble tablet recording its associations with 'one of the most devoted saints and heroic souls that ever lived'. 'The Revival of Missionary enthusiasm at home,' concluded Mark Guy, 'could find no better fuel than a brief and popular life of Henry Martyn.' He also visited the college high on a bank overlooking the River Hooghly that William Carey established in 1819 and where he, Joshua Marshman and William Ward not only worked at translating the scriptures into so many Indian languages and into Chinese, but also set up their own printing press. Serampore College later became Asia's first modern university.[23]

He finished his last letter to the *Methodist Recorder* as he sat on the veranda of the Scottish Mission House at Ajmer, looking out over 'the flat-roofed white houses clustering about the great brown fort of Akbar, with temples, Hindu and Jain, and above all, the mosque of Kwaja, who in the thirteenth century wrought here his many miracles, and whose shrine is said to rank in sanctity as next to that of Mecca itself'.[24] Lack of space prevented him from writing further of the forts, palaces, temples and ruins that adorned the hills and valleys in the vicinity of Jaipur. Instead, he concluded by sharing some of the more abiding images of India that jostled for pride of place in his memory as they prepared for their homeward journey:

> India is, above all, the land of religion, where all the nation is seeking God, but ignorant ever, as one has well said, of the God who is seeking them. My mind is stored with imperishable pictures of the crowded bazaar, a blaze of colour, made more vivid by the fierce sunlight – crowds of men with turbans and robes of every hue; and women with the red shawl flung over their head and shoulders; and everywhere men and women alike, with their bare, brown legs. Here go the lumbering carts with huge wheels, drawn by the patient, cross-coloured oxen or black buffaloes. Here stalks the ungainly camel with a towering load, flinging out its soft feet, and swaying on its way. Here the elephant passes, gaily caparisoned, a mountain of flesh moving in stately massiveness, as docile as he is huge. In a bullock cart sit a family group, as many and as closely packed as perplexed the lady of the nursery rhymes who lived in a shoe.[25]

Chapter 16

'The Ministry of Nature.'

On his return from India, Mark Guy resumed the way of life into which he had settled into on his retirement, remaining both physically and mentally active well into his 80s. He travelled about all the time, combining preaching and lecturing with leisure pursuits such as walking, sketching and fishing. 'I have not a *Monday* free for the year,' he wrote on 23 February, 1912 in response to a request for him to lecture. 'I could give you *Thursday March 21st*... A Bit of Bread, Christian Socialism: Stories of need in West London, Some Old Folks at Home, West Country Sketches, What's the matter with most of us. Choose what you prefer. My fee is... five guineas...'[1] *What's the matter with most of us* seems to have been a favourite of his at this time and he used it on at least two occasions when he visited Cornwall towards the end of September the following year. He received a warm welcome from a large congregation at Helston Wesley on the morning of the 28th when he based his sermon on the words, 'The Lord is my Shepherd; I shall not want'. In the evening he reminded his congregation of the need to be vigilant during the week when the Devil was most active and urged them to take Christ into their ship and make Him captain. The following day he was at Falmouth Wesley for the continuation of their harvest thanksgiving celebrations. Having been the venue for an expository address in the afternoon and a well-attended public tea, the chapel was full for the evening lecture during which he judged covetousness and worry to be at the root of most people's problems, arguing that both were sins because they made things the master of man. The remedy he advocated was the adoption of the Gospel of Jesus Christ – not merely as a creed or belief, but as a 'power that made man the master of things'.[2]

Taking 1907 as a representative year, we can get some idea of the breadth of his activities which, as ever, centred very firmly on his Christian faith. At the end of March he spent a week or two fishing, with no little success, from the Drumnadrochit Hotel on the shore of Loch Ness. On 30 Saturday, for instance, he landed an 11lb salmon, while two days later a twenty-six-pounder fell to his rod. Of this or a similar success that year he wrote home:

> Don't be frightened when a great big salmon of twenty-four pounds comes walking in on Tuesday morning. I caught him to-day, and did want you to see him in his glory. The scars are *seal bites* of former days... Set him out on the table and look at his depth: then at the great hooked jaw – that is for fighting! It took about twenty-five minutes to land him. Well, 'a tight line to you,' as Jamie the gillie says, when he takes his wee drappie o' whuskey.[3]

Of course, there were engagements to be honoured even during holidays such as this and the previous evening he was one of a number of guests who had joined the Rev. Alex Mackay on the stage of the new public hall at Glenurquhart for the annual social meeting of the local United Free Church.[4] On 18 July he was in London for the first full day of the 164th annual Conference and posed for the camera with the Rev. Alfred Vine who had been a close friend since they had shared lodgings in Brixton Hill over forty years earlier. It was at this conference that he ceased to be a member of the Legal Hundred.[5] August saw the publication of his thirty-seventh book, *Bridgetstow*, and two months later its publisher, Robert Culley, issued the first of a series of illuminated texts, printed in three colours on stout bevelled and gilt-edged cards. Of the first four titles, which were marketed as being 'amongst the novelties of the season', three – *My Daily Walk*, *My Daily Prayer* and *He Restoreth my Soul* – were by Mark Guy Pearse.[6] Towards the beginning of the month he travelled up to the Welsh Marches both to preach and lecture on 'Hugh Latimer' at Oswestry's English Wesleyan Church.[7] October, too, saw the death of another dear friend of long standing, Edward Pethybridge of Launceston, whose great act of kindness in lending the Pearses Lake Cottage, Bude, in 1876 – at what was a difficult time for them – was never forgotten. Although he was unable to attend what was one of the largest funerals ever seen in Launceston, Mark Guy wrote to the family to express his regrets.[8] As we have already seen, the Pearses' connection with the West London Mission was a lifelong one and they both continued to support it whenever they could.

Once the children had left home and settled elsewhere, the Pearses moved to a flat at 29, Buckingham Mansions, West End Lane, West Hampstead and, as long as she enjoyed good health, Jeannie often accompanied her husband on his preaching expeditions. On a bright, sunny afternoon at the end of May 1909, she returned to her home town to attend the stone-laying ceremony for Dunstable's new Wesleyan Methodist Chapel – the second, like its predecessor, having fallen victim to fire – and to lay a stone on behalf of the Sunday school that she had attended as a child.[9] She maintained her interest in the varied work of the Mission and during the last few months of 1913 organised a sale of work at home in order to help raise further funds for the Rescue Committee. On Thursday 18 December she and Mark Guy were both present at a Christmas dinner at Katherine House to which all the Sisters of the Mission were invited. Noticeably tired at the time, she was taken ill a few days later. Her condition worsened as the month of January went by and in spite of being nursed by their eldest daughter Maud, she died in the early hours of Wednesday 4 February, 1914, a couple of months short of her seventy-third birthday. Following her burial at Hampstead Cemetery three days later, Hugh Price Hughes' widow Katherine wrote movingly of the colleague she described as 'one of that little band of faithful souls who... fought its [the West London Mission's] early battles and shared in its triumphs'. The declaration of war exactly six months later would have compounded Mark Guy's distress although, on a purely personal level, this would have been tempered by the news that the suffragettes had abandoned their militant stance. A reunion between Emmeline Pethick-Lawrence and her 'Daddy' took place early in 1915. 'Once more I could sit on the cushion at his feet with my cigarette,' she recalled, 'while he in his old armchair smoked his cigar. Once more it was a delight to be together. There was now no need for speech, we had reached a point of silent understanding. We never spoke of the years during which we had been separated. He was too frail at that time to be agitated. Only once a sentence fell from him with a sigh. "I have found my little one again; the political person never belonged to me."'[10]

A firm advocate of 'fair Nature' as a comforter, Daniel Quorm had a special place among the rocks on his native coast – a place to which he went on innumerable occasions when he wanted, as he said, 'to get right away alone with the Lord for *something particular*'.[11] Like his most celebrated fictional creation, Mark Guy Pearse, too, felt the constant need to get away from the hurly-burly of city life, the need as he put it in *Bridgetstow* 'to come into contact with nature to put us into the true possession of ourselves'.[12] He described in some detail in a number of articles and occasional pieces such as *The Gamekeeper*, the benefits of such withdrawal:

> According to a happy custom of mine when I can find the opportunity, I had wandered away into the country for meditation and for communion. It is good for one's soul to gain the greater stretch of heaven, the quiet of the woods, the ministry of nature in tree and flower, in bird and many a wee beastie. There nothing jars. The sounds are as a sweet silence. The place becomes a sanctuary where it is easy to wait patiently for the Lord.[13]

'If we would do much for God we must be much with God,' he wrote elsewhere. 'The root must grow hidden and silent if the tree is to put forth its branches and yield much fruit. In the life of all the mighty men of God you shall find these hiding-places, where they may wait upon God and renew their strength.'[14] Hugh Price Hughes's favourite retreat had been the Swiss Alps. In Mark Guy's case, holidays – when walking, sketching, reading and fishing were essential ingredients – were often taken in Wales in the 1890s. In her biography of her father, Frances Pearse recalled how, having on one occasion left his camel-hair paintbrush at home, he went to the village shop at Dolwyddelan to buy a new one and was offered a large hairbrush, with the assurance that it was made of the very best camel's-hair! At Betws-y-coed he and his son would fish by night in the Beaver Pool for sewin, a salmon trout native to Welsh rivers. The Rev. S. Shrimpton recalled fishing with him at Milford Haven in the early 1890s when he was editing the *Preacher's Magazine* with the Rev. A. E.Gregory. On one occasion they called at a nearby cottage for lunch and Mark Guy asked their host whether she would like him to send her a little book. She agreed, on condition that it wouldn't hurt her religion! The two ministers rose considerably in her estimation when she realised that they were friends and colleagues of Charles Spurgeon whose portrait had pride of place in her home.[15] In 'The Song of the Oyster Shell' – one of many occasional pieces published by the *Methodist Recorder* during his fifty years as a regular contributor – Pearse described how, during the course of a holiday in the Channel Islands, he joined some local fishermen for a day at sea. Becalmed at noon, the crew lay down to doze or smoke their pipes, while he whiled away the time 'reading Geikie on Geology'.[16] The analogy between the fisherman pursuing his calling or indulging his fancy and the preacher, like Daniel Quorm, fishing or 'gropin' for souls' struck a strong personal chord with the Rev. M. G. Pearse and permeates his writing. 'Men have to be caught,' he insisted one Sunday morning in St James's Hall. '… If we would have fish… we must catch them. It is no use our standing in dignified attitude on the river-bank and in the greatness of our authority as Pope, or Priest, or Minister, commanding men to come into our net. Jesus Christ has promised to make His disciples *fishers* of men, and that means *that they must be caught*.'[17] Whether collectively, or as real-life or fictionalised individuals, fishermen are portrayed with respect and affection, being always associated in his mind with Peter, James and John. 'Yesterday I went alone down the valley of the Tamar,' he wrote home one spring, 'with a rod and a sermon, just like the apostles of old.'[18] Indeed, the Cornish fisherman came to assume a quasi-mythical status, particularly, as we shall see, during Mark Guy's later years.

In the meantime, Scotland became the favoured destination for his holidays during the first decade of the twentieth century and his fishing exploits there would, as his daughter and biographer pointed out, fill a volume. Whatever the setting – Cornish stream or coastal waters, mountain tarn in Ireland, or Scottish loch or burn – and weather permitting, he usually wore an old grey flannel suit, red tie, and cap on these expeditions. This 'worldly gear', as he called it, was sometimes the source of some confusion and amusement, as on the occasion when he was greeted by a grave-looking Scottish divine:

> 'Pray, sir, are ye not the Reverend Mark Guy Pearse?'
> 'I am,' I said, with all the cheeriness that a holiday puts into a tired Londoner.
> 'Ye are na what I pictured ye when I read your buiks,' said he.
> 'I am very sorry,' I stammered.
> 'Ah, but when I read your books I pictured ye as long and theen and sanctimonious-looking!'

On another occasion, when preaching in Glasgow, he had a very different experience – being mistaken for the Archbishop of Westminster![19] As we have already seen in the account of his Canadian visits, adverse weather conditions were no deterrent and he was over seventy when he sent home the following account of one fishing trip:

> I laughed yesterday more than once at the thought of your seeing us. What would you have said? And we called it pleasure! It was an awful day of bitter cold and wild snowstorms. Four or five inches of snow in the boat, and a wind that drove the flakes into your eyes and tickled your nose and almost blinded you. It lay thick on cap and wrap. A nice dry snow would not have mattered, but it half melted, and then changed its mind and froze into a coat of mail. I had a series of coats and wraps, but nothing could keep out the damp cold – my hands were mottled blue and red. We got a salmon of some nine pounds. We got back sopping: drenched. Coats and capes were soaked. I flung off these things and away to a hot bath, and *was none the worse*.[20]

Although salmon-fishing provided him with his greatest triumphs, more often than not trout was the quarry and Thomas Bainbridge, his close friend and an ardent supporter of the Mission, his companion. 'Fishing with Bainbridge in Skye was the crown,' he wrote after one adventure. 'He had put up a shanty on the lake, and there, with a couple of gillies, we lived, putting thick layers of the *Scotsman* over the windows to make it dark enough to sleep. Our beds were on the floor. We averaged 100 trout apiece a day; we put back all under two pounds, as we were away on the moors far from any crofter and could not send them away.'[21] A similarly remote location provided the setting for 'What a sea trout did', an autobiographical piece in which Mark Guy explores a theme that was very close to his heart – the minister as shepherd to his flock. Its opening pages provide us, too, with an excellent account of an expedition that he and Jimmy the gillie made to a mountain loch to which few ever ventured because of its remoteness.[22] In 1908 he scored what his daughter Frances called 'his last and greatest triumph'. 'How shall I begin to tell you of my glory!' he wrote. 'The village rings with the fame of it. Jamie and I were drifting before an east wind. I fish with three rods, one on each side of the boat and a short thick one in the middle. Suddenly the middle reel rang out the signal of a fish, and I took the rod and let the fish run. Then began an awful fight, the monster very scientific, never wasting an ounce of his strength by a leap or a plunge, but boring down, down in the depths. When I could wind in I felt I had something tremendous, and then down he rushed again – I taking every advantage he gave and he steadily bending the little rod until I feared it would snap. I was on my knees, an attitude I always take so as to get well round the stern. My knees ached and my arms too; my thumbs are still conscious of the winding and the strain. Nearly an hour the fight lasted, and then he came on top of the water and we saw his great length. A dash with the gaff, and then, with both hands and all his might, Jamie lifted the great fish into the boat. He is the biggest ever brought into the hotel; the record hitherto was thirty-one pounds. My fish was thirty-seven pound – length forty-six inches... It is to be blazed abroad in the papers.'[23]

While repudiating the view of one famous old Cornish fisherman that fish were 'so contrary as women', Mark Guy understood the truth behind it and, like many an angler, often experienced their contrariness. When he was holidaying in Ireland, on one occasion the fish were 'sulky' and not to be tempted by any fly that he could offer them. With no companion to turn to, he described how he sat on a mossy rock and ate his lunch in the hope that they would be in a better mood later. 'My sketch-book afforded me a further entertainment for half-an-hour...' he continued.[24] His skill in using pencil, pen and ink or brush and ink to produce the little lightning or thumbnail sketches with which he often illustrated letters, envelopes, postcards and books was appreciated and recorded by numerous friends and acquaintances, as well as by his family. H. M. Cresswell Payne described how 'with a swift line or two made by a soft black pencil, Mark Guy would use the top of his thumb – rubbing the pencil marks into a charming soft drawing' and was of the opinion that he could have been a successful artist. The Rev. T. W. Slater picked out as his favourite a 'thumb-nail water-colour sketch of a Cornish boy and a brown-sailed fisherman's boat' which graced one of the shelfful of books that bore the Rev. M. G. Pearse's name.[25] One of his standard sketches depicting 'an evening sky, a calm lake with reflections of trees and a lone bird flying low over the waters'[26] adorns the front end-paper of my copy of *The Gentleness of Jesus and other sermons*, together with the inscription 'Drawn by The Rev. Mark Guy Pearce [*sic*] after lecturing in Town Hall. 17 Nov 1904'. Another writer, recalling his childhood in the Mevagissey area at the turn of the century, described how the famous Cornish preacher kept his right thumbnail sharpened specially for the purpose of executing his legendary sketches and how he would mix ink and water in a saucer before proceeding to produce 'in a few seconds the most marvellously delicate landscapes and cloud effects'.[27] 'Give him a sheet of paper and drop a big blob of ink on it,' advised Dr F. L. Wiseman who, as a young man, was a member of Mark Guy's congregation at Launceston in the late 1870s. 'Watch him now,' he continued, 'as his finger smears the ink over the paper and by and by brings out of the chaos a lovely landscape of hill and plain, sea and sky, and then with six strokes of the pen makes "fowl to fly in the heaven".'[28] Yet another writer remembered how members of the congregation would often come up to him at the end of a service and ask him to do a little picture for them. As these only took him three minutes, he rarely refused. Taking any odd piece of paper, sometimes the order of service, he would scrape lead from a pencil on to it. Then with his thumb he would work the lead into clouds, seascapes, and cliffs, and put in a seagull or two with a couple of strokes. The result was a pleasant little sketch worth three or four pounds.[29]

Mark Guy himself discussed his ability to dash off a landscape or seascape in anything from one to five minutes in the interview he gave to Arthur Lawrence for Quiller-Couch's *Cornish Magazine* and recommended blue black as opposed to Indian ink. 'The skin-mark of the finger is used to get a softened distance,' wrote Arthur Lawrence, 'the skin-mark of the thumb for the middle-distance, whilst the soft part of the closed hand is used to give the feathery heather effect in the foreground.'[30] Dr Rattenbury, who was Superintendent of the West London Mission from 1907 to 1925, first met Mark Guy at a house where he was staying and later recalled the pleasure that his artistic talent gave in the numerous homes that he visited. On one such occasion, the guests had assembled, but there was no sign of Mark Guy who, after a prolonged search, was eventually found in another room with a group of children. Having used his pen to make big blots on the cards and sheets of note paper laid out on a table, with the aid of the stump of the penholder and his thumb, he was turning the blots into seascapes – 'bits of the Cornish coast, and sea and cliffs, and always birds, to the great entertainment of boys and girls and the young minister'.[31] Another family that had good cause to praise his considerable talents was that of the Rev. William Lewis of Sydenham who knew Mark Guy when he was stationed at Brixton Hill in 1865. His daughter recalled that when her little brother, of whom Mark Guy was very fond, died in 1871, he wrote a booklet about him, entitled *Isaac Watkin Lewis – A Life for the Little Ones*. Subsequently, the Lewises moved to Croydon and when he came to

Addiscombe to lecture, he showed Miss Lewis's invalid sister Jennie how to sketch with ink and brush – an art in which she later became very accomplished.[32] Long before the picture postcard became popular, Mark Guy's own method of illustrating his envelopes and cards became known to British postmasters and postmistresses. Indeed, during his years in Bristol the Post Office always knew when he was on holiday by the beautiful little sketches on the postcards sent by him to his friends from wherever he was staying. They were greatly admired by the sorting staff who would pass them around the office for all to see.[33] The fact that most of the surviving examples I have seen were never franked, though, suggests that wherever he travelled, he took a small store of postcards with him and drew for the sheer pleasure that it gave him. On his death in 1930, a close relative remembered how, on one of his fishing holidays in north Cornwall, Mark Guy put his artistic skills to novel use. This relation was an inside passenger on the Launceston coach when it stopped a few miles outside Camelford. A farm boy appeared at the door with a basket of trout and asked for 'Mr Pearse'. On learning that there was, indeed, a Mr Pearse on board, the boy looked at him contemptuously before producing a sheet of notepaper showing a sketch of a fine old gentleman with mutton chop whiskers. 'That gentleman is on the box seat,' the relative informed him and the basket of trout was duly delivered. Some years later Mark Guy recalled how he had arranged for the fish to be delivered to his father on the coach and that, on his return, the lad had told him that a young man inside 'zed his name was Pearse, the liard'![34]

Mark Guy Pearse, then, sketched in and autographed his books with abandon throughout his life and there are almost certainly many of his fine miniatures hidden away in houses the length and breadth of the land. Although the reviewer of *Bridgetstow* for the *Methodist Recorder* expressed his pleasure at seeing 'the eight fine pictures from the author's or perhaps some related hand',[35] with one exception there is no evidence that Mark Guy was ever tempted to illustrate his own books, preferring instead to leave that task either to his daughter Frances or to Charles Tresidder. The exception is, appropriately enough, the fine watercolour that accompanies 'Cornwall', the opening poem of *West Country Songs*.

Chapter 17

'Mark Guy! Cornubia's son…'

Cornwall seems to weave a spell around its sons and daughters that never loses its power.[1] Certainly, Mark Guy Pearse's passion for his homeland was a lifelong one – 'a love that grows with the years' is how he himself described it at the turn of the twentieth century.[2] And for one close friend, the Cornish setting added something mystical to his life and work – something which that friend felt unable to describe and which he had never encountered elsewhere.[3] As for so many Cornish men and women, the very fact of exile was in itself a spur to this passion. At twenty-one he wrote to his sister as follows concerning a visit to Switzerland:

> Still nothing beats dear old Cornwall. I mean to get about the dear lanes and the sublime cliffs, and the 'same sounding sea' till I am full of its grand spirit. The solitude, its unlikeness to anything else, its calm great rocks, its great expanse of sea and singing waves – they all have a beauty that Devonshire is too tame to equal, Derbyshire too small to touch, and Switzerland too common ever to come near in my mind… First among treats I put the granite tors and black cliffs of Cornwall.[4]

And talking with journalist Arthur Lawrence in his London home some thirty-six years later, he confirmed that the Cornish landscape – especially 'the grand coast between Portreath and Gwithian' – still meant so much to him that he sometimes thought that, if he were dying and could get a breath of the Atlantic blast and hear the thunder of the breakers on the rocks, he would live again.[5] He continued to sing Cornwall's praises all his life in his numerous stories and in his lectures – particularly *Some*

Old Folks at Home – with the same sentiments sometimes finding expression almost verbatim in both:

> 'You Cornishmen think a great deal of your county,' said my old friend Mr Smith, as we talked of many circuits and many matters.
>
> 'Little wonder that we do – where is there one to match it?' was my modest reply.[6]

> No-one thinks so much of his country as a Cornishman. People are born elsewhere, but they don't seem to make half so much fuss about it as Cornishmen.[7]

There is a subtle distinction between his use of the word 'county' in the opening lines of 'A Cornish Ghost Story' and that of 'country' in the version of the lecture *Some Old Folks at Home* that he delivered to a captive, Cornish audience in Gawler, South Australia, in March 1891. Although he spent most of his life beyond the Tamar, Mark Guy was aware of the impact that the arrival of the railway, the collapse of tin and copper mining and the advent of tourism was having on his homeland. He was undoubtedly aware, too, of the reawakening of interest in the Celtic countries and their cultures. An annual 'Cornish Dinner' was re-established in London in 1886, the year he accepted Hugh Price Hughes's invitation to join him in the West London Mission, and the idea of forming an association of Cornishmen in the capital was first given serious consideration in the late 1890s.[8] As we have seen, there were flourishing Cornish associations in Australasia and South Africa.

Although he rarely discussed party politics, Mark Guy Pearse was, like his erstwhile mentor Andrew Hingston and his superintendent at the West London Mission, Hugh Price Hughes, strongly supportive of Liberalism in general and of Gladstone in particular. Indeed, in the 1880s, concerned about the candidature for a certain Cornish constituency of a wealthy Conservative who, unusually, was also a Methodist, he contributed, albeit anonymously, a dialect piece to the *Western Daily Mercury* entitled 'The Two-headed Calf'.[9] He was very well aware of Cornwall's rightful place in a burgeoning 'Celtic' community and his novels, stories and lectures are full of expressions of 'solidarity' and 'difference'. For instance, although, as his name suggests, Jeremiah Gribble was as Cornish as the next man, his birthplace was 'some forty miles away in the eastern part of the county – an unknown region which the neighbours spoke of rather contemptuously as 'up the country', or occasionally as "up in England"'.[10] In 'The Smuggler', which admittedly is set some time in the past, Jerry Lanyon, whose Celtic blood is 'easily set on a blaze', has little time for John Wesley's tract 'A Word to a Smuggler'. 'Le've Mr Wesley 'bide home 'long with his own folks that he do understand,' he fumes, '– he's nothing but a foreigner, after all said and done, and we aren't.'[11] In *Bridgetstow*, which is set in 'the hundred yards or so of soil which links the western county to England', Mark Guy, as narrator, sits opposite the ageing Mary Melhuish and ponders on '[t]he Celtic nature with its imagination and spiritual impressiveness' lying 'more open to the mysteries of the unseen than the more practical and prosaic Saxon'.[12] Before Celtic audiences or those of Cornish descent, he was forthright in asserting that 'Cornishmen were not English, they thought themselves a little better than the English, they were Celts, fervid, excitable, full of poetry, humorous, and when they liked, stubborn'.[13] Addressing an audience at Douglas on the Isle of Man, he was reported as saying that the Manx and Cornish alike looked down on the English![14] Of course he toned down the rhetoric in publications that were destined for more general consumption, adopting a rather pessimistic – some would say realistic – stance, although Cornwall's inherent 'difference' was never an issue on which he compromised. 'The characteristics of Cornwall and the Cornish are rapidly passing away,' he wrote in the preface to *West Country Songs*. 'The Celt, in England at any rate, is doomed to be absorbed by the Saxon.'[15] Twenty-four years later, in one of his last works, he expressed himself in much the same way, lamenting that Cornwall was 'rapidly losing all that marked it off from England', though refusing – at least on paper – to deplore the fact that it had become 'the playground of hundreds in summer and the health-resort of scores in winter'.[16] For all his rhetoric, though, I suspect that Mark Guy would have baulked at any nationalist agenda. He would undoubtedly have empathised with the stance taken by Cornwall's first Grand Bard, Henry Jenner, who in his New Year message to the Cornish people on behalf of the Old Cornwall Societies and the Cornish Gorsedd at the beginning of 1933, recommended that they should recognise their little motherland as a Celtic nation and be loyal to it 'without prejudice to your loyalty to King and Empire'.[17]

Although his main aim in all his writing was 'to show forth the beauty of holiness and to lead men to the Saviour',[18] he also sought to entertain, using to great effect what the Rev. T. Slater called his 'loyal love for everybody and everything Cornish'.[19] Slater's use of the phrase 'every-

Port Isaac Bay from Pine Haven, May 1882, sketch by Mark Guy Pearse (Courtesy of Mrs A. Milne)

body and everything' is perceptive, for the strong sense of Cornish 'difference' that permeates Mark Guy's writing extends way beyond a setting that he uses so effectively, for instance, in early books such as *Daniel Quorm and his religious notions* and *Simon Jasper*. For it encompasses the ordinary fishermen, miners, local preachers and wrestlers – converted and reformed, of course! – whose home it was and, particularly in his later writing, culminates in short but nonetheless apposite examinations of Cornwall's history, culture and language and their place in a wider Celtic context. The scenery of Cornwall became a template for his imagery, and whether or not they explore the Cornish way of life, his stories, lectures and sermons are peppered with introductions such as 'It was away in a remote parish of Cornwall',[20] 'Away in a little fishing village in the farthest corner of Cornwall…',[21] 'I was staying at a little village on the Cornish coast…'[22] and 'Some time since I was driving across the Cornish moors…'[23] In the short story 'Christmas Eve in the "Vivid"', the rain is even described as coming down with 'a Cornish "one-and-all"-ness about it that was unmistakable'![24]

As Slater so rightly claimed, the two volumes of *Daniel Quorm…* probably constitute the most perfect expression of his love for Cornwall and its people, set as they are in his home territory of Camborne-Redruth. In none of his other writings is there such a complete evocation of a landscape and the characters that inhabit it, taking in Market Day, Peter's fair-day and the soup-kitchen at 'Redburn', Carn Brea and Beacon Hill, 'the muddy-red river, going deep and silent to the solemn sea', the big folks fishing up at Carwinnin', the beach at Portreath and pilchards being landed at what was for him the cradle of Cornish Methodism, namely St Ives. Although it would win no prizes for its external appearance or for its austere seats and fittings, the chapel at Penwinnin in which Dan'el worships exudes homeliness and heart. 'Good reader,' exhorts Mark Guy Pearse, 'do not despise these little whitewashed chapels which dot the bleak hill-sides of Cornwall, or cluster in the villages. Ugly and old-fashioned though they be, yet they are hallowed places…' Although the West Cornish Methodists were an excitable and sometimes noisy people, they had some real religion to make a noise about and it was only fair to ask, 'Where again can we find such a host of devout, praying, godly men as amongst these Cornish miners, born and bred amidst noisy services?'[25] I think that it was this portrayal of 'real religion', of simple chapels and ordinary people that accounted for the enormous popularity which *Daniel Quorm* enjoyed from the 1870s onwards. For, as the Wesleyan historian A. W. Harrison put it, from the middle years of the nineteenth century Wesleyan Methodism entered its mahogany age – an age when chapels acquired 'mahogany pulpits and the preachers found their way to the mahogany tables of wealthy laymen'.[26] *Daniel Quorm*, in which the dangers of being '"churched" into stiffness and coldness and formality' are spelled out, was a powerful antidote. 'Better a hundred times that little place at Penwinnin,' wrote Mark Guy, 'if people feel *at home* in it, than the most perfect Gothic structure, if they should sit uncomfortably subdued by a style of things to which they are all unused.'[27]

Although he was brought up in a middle-class household and, as a boy, attended a chapel the exterior of which was described on its completion in 1828 as 'extremely chaste and beautiful' and 'remarkably unique and elegant' inside,[28] he came into daily contact with the ordinary folk who constituted the population of Camborne and the surrounding area. Then and later he mixed with miners, fishermen, farm-workers and local preachers, and it was among these 'men of fine simple honesty, of stalwart bearing… [and] of wonderful piety'[29] that he always felt happiest. 'The world is mostly dependent,' he wrote in one of his numerous collections of sermons and parables, 'not upon its geniuses its splendid scholars, its famous leaders, but upon the simple, quiet, earnest men who keep their eyes open, who are observant and thoughtful, and who carry in them a heart, not a mere digestive apparatus, but a heart eager to help.'[30] Those who have left us with portraits of this great preacher and lecturer always emphasised, too, his dislike of formality which often found expression in his own spontaneous behaviour and in that of his characters, and underlined the extent to which he was at home among humble folk, able to speak their dialect and possessing 'the master-key to unlock their hearts'.[31] His daughter records, for instance, how he would sometimes be sought when ministers had gathered for a ceremonious farewell at some railway station, only to be found at the end of the platform, entertaining a group of porters. And Emmeline Pethick-Lawrence recalled that while, as a lecturer, he enjoyed the response he evoked from an audience, he hated being lionised afterwards and would often offend people by hiding from them and escaping to the seashore [at Weston-super-Mare] or to the woods instead of presenting himself at the tea-table to which he had been invited.[32] 'If I had put on the parson,' he once said, 'I might have been President of the Conference or a Doctor of Divinity. Thank God I am neither'. In spite of his education, he could turn on the broad Cornish that he heard each and every day as a boy in Camborne. Having on one occasion lectured on *Some Old Folks at Home*, he responded to a vote of thanks by explaining that he was able to reproduce the Cornish dialect so faithfully because he had been a Cornish *minor* for the first twenty-one years of his life! Much to his amusement, the local newspaper reported that 'the reverend gentleman with praiseworthy candour… confessed that he might well know the dialect, since he himself had worked in the Cornish mines until he was twenty-one'![33]

This popularity with ordinary people was not, of course, confined to his fellow countrymen; his ministry among the downtrodden of Bristol, London and elsewhere was, as we have already seen, highly successful. But it was at home in Cornwall where he 'belonged' that such popularity found its fullest expression, as on the occasion when Mark Guy and a friend walked one hot summer afternoon along the Cornish cliffs for several miles. Coming at last to a little village where a tea meeting was in progress, they entered the chapel and joined in. Although he was not wearing his clerical clothes, Mark Guy was recognised by some of the leaders, one of whom approached him and said in an anxious whisper:

*'No cliffs like those that guard the western shore', sketch by Mark Guy Pearse for 'Cornwall' (*West Country Songs*)*

> 'Be you the Rev. Mark Guy Pearse?' 'Yes, I be,' he answered. 'I thought as how you was. Now you do see, we want to raise a little money, and a thought have struck us. Now do 'ee just come out quiet-like, and say nothing to nobody, and then we will put 'ee in the vestry, and we will go into the chapel and say: 'The Rev. Mark Guy Pearse, author of 'Dan'l Quorm', is in the vestry, and can be see'd, at threepence each, the proceeds to go for the good of the cause!'[34]

In his essay 'Early Methodism in Cornwall', Pearse explored the reasons for the warm welcome that the movement received in a land inhabited largely by fishermen and miners. 'Both exposed to the hourly perils of "the deep",' he wrote, 'their employment developed a character rugged, independent, and intense... How the calling and occupation affect the character appears even amidst the more equalising influences of today; – wherever the miner and fisherman give place to the agricultural labourer there the hold of Methodism is notably less.'[35] The Cornish, he maintained in one of his lectures, were like their Celtic brothers the Welsh, the Scots and the Irish, 'dramatic, emotional, imaginative, fervid, intense, good lovers and good haters, inflammable, out and out one side or the other'.[36] In another set-piece lecture, *Some Characteristics of West Cornwall*, he elaborated on how he saw the Cornish temperament:

> Of average height, but of rather more than average courage, toughness, and endurance; with a quickness of perception and a love of adventure developed by their occupation; a temperament emotional, impulsive, and yet capable of a faithful devotedness; of the stuff that makes good lovers and good haters; strong in their preferences and in their prejudices; sensitive, and somewhat suspicious of strangers; stubborn if opposed, and if threatened dreadfully pig-headed, yet quick to respond to the first approach of tenderness and generosity. Loving companionship, the Cornishman is a poor bachelor, and lives almost all the world over in communities, making the interest of his set completely his own, and cheerfully sharing their hardships. Take them altogether, they are men with good heads well set on broad shoulders, men with backbones in them – vertebrate creatures – not mere jelly-fish, taking the shape of any hand that squeezes them; and with hearts in them – not mere digestive apparatus, as Carlyle would say.[37]

He had many friends among the ordinary people who were as dear to him as Cornwall herself, and by sitting with them and talking and listening to them, he acquired at first hand a huge fund of tales that he was able to use in fine sketches such as 'The Cornish fisherman', 'The Cornish miner', 'The Old Town Crier', 'The Old Sexton', 'Dick Croggan's Redemption' and 'How I get my stories'. Into the latter piece he managed, by literary sleight of hand, to weave several portraits of himself on the occasion when, accompanied by a friend, he preached in 'the pop-shop', a little ginger beer and lemonade shed where refreshments were served to tourists visiting the fishing village:

> … When we got home, we found supper was set in the best parlour. 'But,' said Mr Pearse, 'not a bit of it; we are not going to have supper up here all by ourselves, we are coming down to the kitchen to have supper with you.' And down we went and had *fish* and *'tats*. And when we were all seated round the fire, you know, and Mr Pearse had a child on each knee, and three or four of the fisher-lads about us, and he began to tell stories, and they began to tell stories; and he went on telling stories, and they went on telling stories, and so they didn't know *him from them*.[38]

In both sketches such as these and in his longer works, fictional characters sit with ease alongside real life ones. There are converted wrestlers such as Dick Curnow and Abraham Bastard, blacksmiths – Tom Melhuish and John Tregenoweth – local preachers such as Daniel Quorm, Joe Smitham and Billy Bray, and miners – for example, Frankey Vivian, Peter Roberts and Martin Dell. In view of Mark Guy's background, it is perhaps rather curious that in his writings on Cornwall, mining and miners play second fiddle to fishing and fishermen. However, as we have already seen, the analogy between the fisherman and the preacher was so central to his philosophy of life that it is hardly surprising that those who followed the shoals off the Cornish coast were looked up to with something approaching reverence. He was, too, a firm believer in the power of nature to stir the depths of the soul. Taking the phrase 'Stormy wind fulfilling his word' from Psalm 148 as his inspiration, he recalled in one of his Homely Talks going out with a fisherman one August evening for a night on the open sea. As they drifted out of the harbour with the tide, he was struck by the beauty of the scene – the sun setting behind them in a blaze of gold and crimson, with the little town under its canopy of blue smoke lying beneath the wooded hills. The brown sails of the fishing boats and the rigging of the larger ships were perfectly reflected in the glassy water which was so still that not a ripple broke the surface. At about one in the morning, though, a breeze sprang up and by the time they had left land far behind them, it was blowing a gale. There was nothing for it but to run before the wind to the nearest harbour some fifty miles away. 'On we flew over tremendous seas,' wrote Mark Guy, 'with now and then unpleasant tokens of what our fate might be. About eight next morning the little harbour hove in sight; there were the piers, with just a winding narrow channel between them, and on them a crowd that watched us eagerly, with shouts and signals. Onward we swept, past the waves that tumbled and broke on the rocks to right and left of us; and then, in a moment, that blessed calm! We breathed again in safety, and gave God thanks.' What had on innumerable occasions in the past seemed a hopelessly dull and dreary place – a muddy harbour on an unromantic coast peopled by uninteresting individuals – was transformed that day into a haven – a place of beauty and perfection. In fulfilling God's word, the stormy winds had revealed the little port's worth.[39]

One of his earliest converts was a Polperro fisherman who attended a service that he took as a local preacher while staying with Dr Hingston at Liskeard, and the deep affinity and affection that he felt with and for Cornish fishermen increased with the years. He often went out with them in the drift boats where, with 'the sou'-wester tied down round his ears, and the collars of the oilskin turned up to his eyes, and nothing showing but the tip of his nose… *they* didn't know *him from them*'![40] After one expedition in 1911, his daughter Maud took a photograph of him holding two pollack of 25lbs each that he had caught off the Longships, with the rest laid out beside him on the grass, the smallest being 15lbs in weight. He described with relish how they 'had shifted the ballast three times and then with a heavy sea on, dared not take any more on board. Left the monsters rolling after the *mackerel*, while the flocks of gannet and big herring-gulls pounced down on those that flew on the surface – to escape from the pollack.'[41] Writing in 1963, H. C. Lanyon recalled how once, when the famous preacher was staying with them at the turn of the century, his father had taken him down to Mevagissey. As the two men walked along the quay, the fishermen stared and nudged one another as the striking figure of Mark Guy Pearse with his long, flowing, black cape and his long white hair, passed by. Mr Lanyon, who was not without a certain sense of humour, went over to them and the following conversation ensued:

> 'Who do you think I've got with me this morning?'
> 'Tidn't Asquith, I s'pose?
> 'No, not Asquith.'
> 'Lloyd George then?'
> 'No, not Lloyd George.'
> Who is it then?'
> 'Why, it's the Reverend Mark Guy Pearse.'
> 'I'll tell 'ee, Mr Lanyon,' said the eldest, 'we didn't know who he was but we knowed he was somebody.'[42]

Mark Guy was no doubt tickled pink!

Mevagissey over on the south coast of Cornwall was, of course, the birthplace of Moses Dunn,[43] the Bible Christian fisherman and sea pilot whose friendship he valued so highly. Moses, who always reminded him of Jesus and who, in his letters to the Rev. M. G. Pearse, signed himself 'your Rough Brother', is immortalised in a number of his lectures and stories, namely *How I get my stories*, *Some Old Folks at Home*, *The Ship Where Christ Was Captain*, *The 'Moses Dunn'* and *The Cornish Fisherman* where their first meeting is described as follows:

> Some time ago I was strolling along by the southern coast of the county, when I chanced upon a little village where everything was picturesque and beautiful, only that the air was somewhat tainted by an ancient and fish-like smell. It was the home of the mackerel and pilchard fishermen. Lying in the little harbour were a dozen fishing boats – fine, well-built crafts, fitted to stand any seas. Amongst them was one the name of which at once attracted me – *The Sir Wilfred*. In England that name is enough to indicate a staunch teetotaller, and in this case it was a sign, too, that the owner was prepared to nail his colours to the mast in sight of his little world – a world somewhat given to spending idle hours at the public-house. Curious to see the owner of such a craft, I put my hands to my mouth and shouted, '*The Sir Wilfred* ahoy!' Presently out of the forecastle came a furry cap, and then a furry face, and finally a stalwart fisherman in blue jersey and a pair of big water-boots.
>
> 'Ay, ay, sir,' said he, looking at me as I stood on the quay, and evidently wondering what I wanted of him.
>
> 'May I come aboard your boat?' I asked.
>
> 'Certainly,' said he, speaking with a little catch in his voice, scarcely amounting to a stammer. At once he slipped into his little boat and came to fetch me.
>
> I began to try and read the character of the man, but there was not much at first to betray the genius that lay within. I climbed on board, and went down with him into the cabin.
>
> The first thing I picked up was the *Alliance News*, the organ of the temperance societies in England.
>
> 'You take this, do you?'
>
> 'Every week, sir,' was the reply.
>
> Beside it lay a book, and picking it up, I was surprised to find a copy of *Rutherford's Letters*.
>
> 'Do you read this?' my voice having in it a hint of surprise.
>
> 'I do that! I always keep that book handy.'

'You must get deep down to enjoy that,' I said.

There the face brightened, the smile spread over his face and lit up his eyes. 'I do enjoy it; and no mistake. I come down, and get a little bit of that in my mind, and 'tis wonderful how it do set your heart a-talking with the Lord Jesus Christ.'

Instinctively I held out my hand to him, and we were friends. Here was a man well worth the knowing.

'I should like to have a sail with you,' I said; and soon we were well outside the little harbour and flying along over that deep blue Cornish sea.[44]

Moses Dunn, whom Mark Guy accompanied on numerous fishing expeditions, always had an eye for anyone in trouble, it seems, whether it was a little maid crying her eyes out in Plymouth or an old woman struggling home alone with a 'flasket' of washing. One story that is central to both *How I get my stories* and the poem 'The "Moses Dunn"' concerns the time when Moses and his companions were fishing for herring up north and had their nets cut to shreds by a drunken local. Moses's belated response – saving the same man's boat when he sees it dragging its anchors in Sunderland Harbour two days later – puzzles the ruffian who enquires,

'What do 'ee call yourself, Moses Dunn? –
    I tell 'ee I never knew
That there was living upon the earth
    A man that could do like you.'
'Call myself? Well – a Christian I s'pose.'
    'I don't think much of they,'
Says the chap, 'but I'd be a Christian myself
    If I could be one your way.

'Here, Moses Dunn,' and his voice it choked,
    'Will 'ee please to shake hands with me?
You've saved my boat, but I'll tell 'ee what
    You've a-broke my heart,' says he.
And now a kinder and better man
    I don't think the world could show
Than the drunken fellow that cut the nets
    That day two years ago.[45]

As long as he could get about, Mark Guy was always talking to his fisherman friends, and later on they were still very much in his thoughts, especially in rough weather. Just six weeks before his death he wrote to Alfred Jackson, at whose house in Porthgwarra in the parish of St Levan he had often stayed: 'It always does me good to hear from you and to hear of your big catch of pollack and bream and mackerel'.[46] Another of his haunts was the 'Shamrock' fishermen's shelter or lodge on the wharf at St Ives, of which he was made an honorary member after a talk he once gave to thirty or forty of them and where two framed photographs of him used to hang. 'The fishermen spoke very affectionately of him, and I know they will mourn his loss,' wrote Mrs R. J. Eland, recalling a visit that she and her husband had made to St Ives in September 1929.[47]

Mark Guy Pearse continued to write long after the strain of public service became too heavy for him to bear. Indeed, as the *Methodist Recorder* pointed out in its glowing review of *Bridgetstow*, he showed 'no falling off in that Celtic quickness of perception, warmth of feeling, breadth of sympathetic comprehension and appreciation, both of nature and of human life and character, and richness of poetic fancy and imagination which, together with his kindly humour and pervasive piety have long since made him familiar as a preacher and a writer far beyond the limits of his land and church'.[48] First published in the *Wesleyan Methodist Magazine* as 'Bridgetstow: some chronicles of a Cornish Parish' and dedicated to the Rev. Arthur E. Gregory and Mrs Gregory of the West London Mission's Children's Home and Orphanage, *Bridgetstow* is, to my mind, one of his best and most complete works. Characters such as Farmer Gregory, the postman and preacher James Cobbledick and Bedey and Betsey Chugg are worthy of a place in the author's Cornish gallery alongside Daniel Quorm and Simon Jasper. With some exceptions, there were noticeably fewer overtly religious works published after his 'retirement' and a correspondingly greater number of Cornish stories, with the 1923 collection entitled *The Orthodox Devil* consisting of a mixture of the two. 'I am... always so grateful to anyone who will find me a subject for a new story,' Mark Guy confided to a certain Rev. Parkinson[49] that same year, while two years later he expressed the wish that he could make someone his legatee in order 'to let the stories live that crowd my mind whenever I think of the old home'.[50] After *The Prophet's Raven* (1908), which centres on the altruism of Miss Zelia Tremenheere, nearly all his 'Cornish' books – notably *A Village Down West* (1924) and *The Ship where Christ was Captain* (1926) – consisted of reissues in collected form of pieces that had first appeared in the *Methodist Recorder* and other journals and newspapers. Early in 1927 he revealed to Connie Tilley that he was thinking of acquiring a cheap, secondhand typewriter. Two months later he wrote again:

> I am thankful to say that I have gone through the winter so far very well and can manage to walk four or five miles a day. And can keep at work with my pen. The recent articles [?] in the Recorder ['A bullet for a present' and 'The Gamekeeper'] have been typed – much to the comfort of the editor and printer.[51]

One can but sympathise with Mark Guy's editors, for his handwriting, which had never been particularly good, had by this time degenerated into a barely legible scrawl.

In his later years he spent a lot of time, too, reading history and delving into odd corners that took his fancy, especially Elizabethan England. Inspired no doubt by the months that he spent in his homeland each year, he began to consult Cornish records and stories of early Methodism, often writing to the Methodist Publishing House to request the loan of old magazines and books that might help him in his research. He also turned for help to his son-in-law George Unwin who was Professor of Economic History at the University of Manchester.[52] In studies of Henry Trengrouse, the Helston-born inventor of the rocket-and-line apparatus for saving the shipwrecked, and Joshua Cristall, the Camborne-born artist, and articles about Cornish folklore and places as far apart as Tintagel and Newlyn,[53] we get a glimpse of that 'mental buoyancy' witnessed by the Rev. Isaac Shimmin who came to Penzance as Superintendent Minister in 1926, the year that Mark Guy started to spend a few months every summer at 'Up-Along', his daughter's little cottage in Newlyn. 'He loved his work,' wrote Shimmin. 'On one occasion he said to me, "I have now four articles on the stocks, and I must get them off as soon as possible".' He would stroll along the promenade between the fishing village and Penzance, or sit reading in one of the shelters that look out over Mount's Bay. Best of all he loved a chin-wag! 'One morning I shall never forget,' continued Shimmin. 'The sun was shining on the bay, on our right were the houses and harbour of Newlyn, and away on our left St Michael's Mount rose like a rocky fortress out of the water. We had a quiet seat, where we could talk undisturbed. I have never heard anything like that stream of reminiscences – his travels and adventures in many lands, amusing incidents he had seen, and strange people he had met. It was like a continuous film of arresting and living pictures.'[54]

Frances Pearse recorded how her father began to build up this fund of images in his younger days by making a point of taking what he called 'mental photographs'. He would look long and hard at the scene and then, withdrawing his gaze, would try to see it with his inner eye, repeating the process until he had mastered every detail. Subsequently, memory and imagination combined to keep the picture permanently alive.[55] Like Mephibosheth Tucker, whose love of the phrase 'momentous incomprehensibility' results in him lying in bed repeating it to himself until he can feel the words 'rollin' like the breakers down 'pon the sands, one over the other, and roarin' like God's thunders',[56] Mark Guy Pearse had a passion for words – a passion that served him well as a lecturer and writer. Few have captured so accurately the Cornish dialect, much of which is derived from the Cornish language itself and which for him was 'a charm as of our mother tongue, into which I find myself drifting as soon as I have crossed the Tamar. I sometimes shock their new proprieties when they greet me. "Well, sir, we are glad to see you. I hope you are better". "Iss, my dear, iss, thank 'ee. I reckon I'm so well as I do belong for to be". Then comes that pretty Cornish interrogative "Please", and in a moment there is a recognition of the phrase – and we are at home. I have met with it all over the world where the Cornish miners are. A word of the dear old dialect, and instantly I am no more a distinguished stranger, but one of them.'[57] Dialect and local colour abound in his Cornish stories. Those attending a Christmas gathering in 'The Prophet's Raven', for instance, hand each other 'the delicious Cornish buns that we call "nubbies" or a slice of saffron cake'[58] while at an interdenominational parish festival near Bridgetstow, they tuck into "splits", covered with the delicious clotted cream, a tracery of treacle on top of it – a luxury known in the West as "thunder and lightning"'. 'I ben't tiddivated up for no company,' laments Mary Melhuish in the same volume on learning that she has a visitor. 'It ben't company, mawther,' Mark Guy reassures her; ''tis a *friend*.'[59] The latter-day Chaucer trying to get some shut-eye in Jan Trigg's coach, the 'Vivid', feels little sympathy for the spoiled boy who cries out, 'I been an' gone an' clunked my nicey without chowin' ov un!'[60] And one would have to search high and low to find a better Cornish yarn than that of the prolonged courtship of Petter Polkinghorne and Martha Ann Tregaskis in 'Terrible Expensive'![61]

Delving into the history and meaning of words involved researching the old language. Although it is generally accepted that Cornish died out as a means of communication in about 1800, it lived on into the nineteenth and twentieth centuries in a number of ways, enabling Henry Jenner, Robert Morton Nance and other Cornish patriots to initiate and oversee its revival.[62] Firstly, it survived in hundreds of dialect words; secondly, in thousands of place-names; and thirdly, in many traditional fragments such as versions of the numerals that fishermen in St Ives' and Mount's Bays used well into the twentieth century, as Mark Guy himself discovered.[63] We have already seen the extent to which his knowledge of his Cornish heritage came out in his lectures and writing. In a tale of early Methodism entitled 'The Smuggler', for instance, the fishermen of the little seaside parish of 'St Glewyas' are described as being able to speak enough of the old tongue to disguise their words when they wanted to.[64] Although there is no evidence to suggest that he went to meetings of either the London Cornish Association or the Old Cornwall societies themselves, he was well aware of their existence and contributed to their publications. Indeed, on being asked in 1899 if he ever attended the Cornish dinner in the capital, he replied:

> I am glad you have mentioned that, because I so much regret that I have been unable to do so, not from any lack of interest in and regard for that delightful occasion, but because the dinners are held on Saturday nights, and it is impossible for me to make Saturday anything else than a day of preparation for my work on the Sunday. Indeed, Saturday night is the only one I can keep free from the many services and engagements held during the week, and I am compelled to keep it for this special purpose of preparation for Sunday. I merely mention this by way of very sincere regret for my non-attendance at the Cornish dinner.[65]

Had he been younger, he might very well have joined the Cornish language classes that Trelawny Roberts and R. St V. Allin-Collins were conducting in London in the 1920s. Certainly, the old Cornish language was for him in his later years 'an inexhaustible mine', as his daughter put it, with the result that his copy of the Rev. John Bannister's *Glossary of Cornish Names* was in constant use as he endeavoured to track down the source of local names and expressions. On fishing expeditions he would undoubtedly have learned a great deal from local fishermen, although the shoe was sometimes on the other foot, as on the occasion in 1922 when he was fishing below Port Isaac. Asking the boatman the name of a big rock they were passing, he was told that it was called 'Many mother-s'. '"Many-mothers"!' I said. 'Why, it is good old Cornish. Your great-grandfather could have told you what it meant. I think I know what happened there. A ship was wrecked, and the sailors climbed up the side of it and were saved... it is maen-y-morun,[66] the rock of the sailor.' While at Newlyn he was delighted to hear that children at schools in the Camborne area were being taught local history at the express wish of Cornwall Education Committee. He had a hundred cards printed in gold lettering, bearing the Cornish motto 'Meor Ras Ma Dew' [Meor Ras Dhe Dhew – Thanks be to God] and distributed them on special occasions such as when he gave a talk to thirty or forty fishermen at St Ives. What is either a reproduction or a retouched original still hangs in the 'Shamrock' shelter on the harbour front; others could be found framed in schools and private houses.[67] It is on record, too, that he learned to say the Lord's Prayer in Cornish.[68]

In later life he was tempted to give up his London home and do what he had fully intended doing back in 1886 – namely, return to the land of his birth. He may well have given some thought to this on the death of his wife in 1913, and Frances' move to Cornwall following the death of her husband in January 1925 certainly presented another golden opportunity. But he knew he would miss the daily visits of his eldest son, Guy, and his wife who lived near his West Hampstead flat, and therefore chose the best of both worlds, using his London flat as his base for most of the year and travelling down to Cornwall in order to preach and lecture – and, towards the very end of his life, just to be there – in the spring or late summer. Naturally enough he gravitated towards west Cornwall, although Newquay was a favourite destination alongside Camborne, Penzance and Newlyn. On Sunday 26 September 1920, he preached to large congregations at the resort's Wesleyan Church and the following evening lectured on 'West Country Sketches', once again in aid of the Trust funds.[69] The following week he was at Camborne Wesley[70] lecturing on a subject that was, as he put it in his opening sentence, 'in everybody's mouth' – 'A Bit of Bread'! It is largely thanks to the Rev. T. W. Slater that we have eyewitness accounts of the sermons and lectures with which Mark Guy inspired and entertained his Cornish congregations and audiences in the last years of his life. Writing in one of the many pieces about his fellow Methodist that he contributed to the *Cornish Guardian* and the *Newquay Express*, Slater recalled hearing Mark Guy speak on a Tuesday afternoon in the 1890s in the Wesleyan Central

Shamrock Lodge, St Ives (Courtesy of the St Ives Museum)

Mission Hall, Oldham Street, Manchester. 'That sermon ['A Bit of Bread'] is as well known as the preacher himself,' he continued. '... Who is there, that is accustomed to hearing sermons and lectures, that has not heard this? And where is there a Wesleyan Church in the Duchy that has not been filled to the doors with an expectant crowd, listening to a dramatic presentation of the 23rd Psalm in the afternoon, and to the lecture in the evening...' When that same harvest lecture was delivered in the Queen's Mission Hall, Hull, the audience applauded at such length and so loudly when the lecturer sat down, that he was forced to give an encore, leading Slater to ask, 'I wonder if any one of them [Mark Guy's critics], or for that matter, all the lot put together, could produce a lecture on "A bit of Bread" or on a bit of anything else, that would thrill a thousand people to the point of their demanding "an encore"?'[71]

Between 12 and 27 October 1924, there was a series of reopening services at Camborne Wesley following renovation work that involved the installation of a new heating system. In addition, the entire chapel premises were repainted, the pews revarnished and the front of the galleries faced with mahogany panels. On Sunday 26th every available space was filled by those wishing to hear the Rev. M. G. Pearse's sermons. On the Monday evening, just as many crowded in to hear him lecture on 'Stories of the West London Mission'. His close friend

Charles Tyack was on hand to welcome him to his spiritual home and spoke for everyone present when he said how delighted they were to see him in such good health. For an hour Mark Guy kept his audience spellbound with a mixture of facts and anecdotes, and when only slight applause greeted his tribute to Hugh Price Hughes, he exclaimed, 'Do not be afraid to clap your hands... You are awfully respectable down here, but I am glad to see you are waking up.' He recalled how, when he started his ministry, he used to speak to a respectable congregation like they were and preach on his chosen text, but later he gave up preaching and took to talking, choosing no particular text, but waiting instead for an inspiration. 'Do you know what an inspiration is?' he enquired of his audience. Laughter greeted his reply: 'When a terrier seizes a rat and shakes it all over, that is an inspiration to the rat.'[72]

Further east, his wicked sense of humour was much in evidence when he visited the little hamlet of Lerryn, near Lostwithiel, to take a special service. Of course, both the congregation and a much-augmented choir had practiced hard for the great day. The first hymn was announced and sung with great gusto, as were the second and subsequent choices. Then came the anthem. A terrific effort was made to ensure its success and, no doubt pleased with its performance, the choir waited for the visiting preacher's verdict. Having begun his address with the customary remarks about how pleased he was to be with them, Mark Guy said, 'My dear friends at Lerryn, it is said that when we go yonder, we shall sing more sweetly and more loudly. Sweeter you *may* sing, but *louder* you never can.'[73] At Penzance, too, his visits were always looked forward to with great pleasure and large congregations flocked to Chapel Street to hear his unorthodox, often hard-hitting sermons. A measure of how much religion an individual had in him, he argued on one occasion, was how he felt towards the people outside the church door. Creeds, theology and feeling happy – 'hallelujah raptures on Sunday evenings' – were of no use if people failed to pay their debts on Monday mornings.[74]

Although he preached what proved to be his last sermon on 21 November 1926, to a large congregation in Newlyn Wesleyan Church,[75] it is to Newquay exactly a year earlier that we must return for an eyewitness account of the occasion when he took his own favourite portion of Scripture – the 23rd Psalm – as his text. The Rev. T. W. Slater often enjoyed Mark Guy's company both 'up-country' in his native North and in Cornwall, and considered that to hear him at his best or to spend an hour at home with him was 'to see an exhibition and demonstration of [genius] and to feel the impact of a personality endowed with the highest gifts and beautified with the finest graces'.[76] Since arriving in Newquay in about 1912 he had heard no end of preachers, from 'home-grown' to 'specially imported... big Bishops, Presidents of Conference, Chairmen of Congregational and Baptist Unions, not to mention the smaller fry, such as wandering evangelists and what the old lady called "depredations" from various societies'. There was not one among them, though, who could for an instant be compared 'for general acceptance and universal favouritism' with Mark Guy Pearse – not one who was such a draw, not one who had been so often and worn so well and given such general satisfaction. He did not maintain that Mark Guy was the greatest preacher that Newquay had known, or the most learned or the one who could 'weave the finest oratorical spells and sweep the audience off its feet with the grandeur of his thoughts, the glamour of his fancy and the irrepressible presentation of his facts'. Every time he came to Newquay, though, the people rallied round him in great crowds and, Sunday or weekday, listened spellbound to his sermons or lectures, nodding their heads in approval. Slater described how good, old-fashioned souls found it hard to stifle their amens and hallelujahs. The difference between the wonderful, powerful preachers who had ministered to Newquay on special occasions and Mark Guy Pearse was best summed up, he thought, by one of their townswomen when she said, 'We do like them, but we love 'e'. It seems that in 1925 he spent several months in Newquay convalescing after a long period of illness. The Rev. Frank Edwards, who was Superintendent minister at the time, with great difficulty persuaded him to preach once more in the Wesleyan Church on the evening of Sunday 29 November. A few days previously, the Rev. T. Slater had gone to see him in the house in Tower Road where he was staying. Although he was far from well, 'his face,' he recalled, 'shone with the light that never was on land or sea, and his voice was touched with the deepest emotion as he recounted happy memories, spoke of the lure of Cornwall, and anticipated his return, if only for one more sermon, to the pulpit'. On the Sunday night the church was filled from end to end by one of the biggest crowds ever seen within its walls. When the time came, Mark Guy rose to his feet and 'like the master of assemblies that he was, held the vast crowd for 45 minutes as in the hollow of his hand', showing that at eighty-three 'he still knew how to practise the gentle art of the oratorical spell-binder'. Those present would never forget the wonderful singing of favourite hymns and the venerable appearance of the preacher who reminded Slater of an old Hebrew prophet. The very best part of the service, though, was the sermon, which he described as 'a masterpiece, a bit of the best of even such a prince among preachers'. 'He was evidently quite at home and perfectly happy,' he remembered. 'Floods of memory seemed to be flowing over him, and the urge of great emotions made him at times speak like a man possessed by some spirit other than his own. Tears and smiles played on his beautiful face, and there were points in his discourse when he even chuckled with delight at the blessedness of the things it was his privilege to preach… It was the last verse of that Psalm [the 23rd] that seemed to captivate his mind and kindle his imagination – the word of the Shepherd Psalmist that picture his triumphant trust, 'surely goodness and mercy shall follow me all the days of my life'; and his all-conquering spirit of hope, with its infinite outlook, and at last, 'Dwell in the house of the Lord for ever'. The way in which he connected the words with some old Cornish saint he once knew down west, Camborne way, and even pictured his own approaching earthly end, was so rapturous, so triumphantly death-defying, that many were evidently carried away with ecstacy and some, unable to keep silent, vented their happy feelings with exclamations of praise in the good old-fashioned Methodist way'.[77]

Frances was not the only one of the Pearses' children to establish a presence in Cornwall. In the mid 1920s their younger son Warwick Guy was appointed Diocesan Missioner and whenever he preached – at Blisland Parish Church towards the end of September 1926, for instance, or at St Austell two months later[78] – he would pay his father flying visits at Newlyn. That year marked the four hundredth anniversary of Tyndale's translation of the New Testament into English and Mark Guy helped celebrate what he regarded as one of the seminal events in English history by contributing an article to the *London Quarterly Review*. Although he was plagued by illness throughout much of the final decade of his life, he managed to retain his great sense of humour. When the editor considered it necessary to cut out some sentences of his piece on Tyndale, for instance, he wrote in characteristic fashion:

> There was a method of martyrdom by which poor victims were crushed to death between boards. Are the covers of your Review going to subject me to such a cruel fate? Pity and spare.[79]

Back in Newlyn special services were conducted at the Wesleyan

Church on 9 October 1927 in order to celebrate Paul Feast. On the Monday evening Mark Guy was one of the large congregation which enjoyed a programme of anthems, solos and choruses performed by the choir, and during the service gave what was to be his last address.[80]

He continued to be mentally alert and interested in books and writing, and in 1928 oversaw the publication of his last book, *'He Must Reign' and other Bible studies* which he dedicated to Charles Ensor Walters 'in happy memory of years in the West London Mission'. That spring he wrote to John Telford to enquire whether or not he could find an account of Dean Stanley's address on the occasion of the unveiling of the tablet to John and Charles Wesley in Westminster Abbey. He remembered that the Dean had been visibly moved on that day in 1876, having just lost his wife, and had concluded his address with part of Charles Wesley's hymn 'Come, O Thou Traveller unknown':

> My company before is gone,
> And I am left alone with Thee;
> With Thee all night I mean to stay,
> And wrestle till the break of day.

Like Pearse, Stanley insisted that the essence of Christianity lay not in doctrines, dogmas and institutions, but in a Christian character. As his biographers pointed out, one cannot help feeling that Mark Guy had his own dear Jeanie in mind when making this request.[81]

One day that summer the Rev. Isaac Shimmin and his wife climbed the steep Newlyn hill to 'Up-Along' in order to invite Frances and her father to tea. He later recalled that when the eighty-six year old preacher arrived, he realised that he had forgotten to send a postcard on some business matter and at once sat down to write it. His reply to his host's enquiry as to the whereabouts of his spectacles – 'I never wear spectacles, when I am an old man I may need them' – surely sums up his indomitable spirit. Having finished the text, he proceeded to dash off on another card one of his little sketches.[82] A delicate seascape that survives from that very year shows that he sometimes sent them to friends or colleagues – in this instance, the Rev. J. Henry Cartwright – out of gratitude. 'Your letter is too kind,' he wrote on 11 February. 'I feel that I must say thank you somehow. Herewith a little sketch of mine to do it for me.'[83] Another, dated 10 March, depicts a bleak, wintry landscape; on the reverse is the following rhyme:

Oh, Oh, Oh
It's dreadful you know:
Day after day
The frost and the snow:
Dig, dig, dig
But it's all no go:
Never a worm
For a poor old crow:
Blow, blow, blow
South wind blow:
Pity the sorrows
Of a poor old crow.[84]

He was often physically weak and weary as a result of the long, painful periods of illness that he experienced towards the end of his life, but, as this rhyme shows, his spirits never flagged and his optimism invariably shone through. When his health first began to fail, he told a friend that he had had a bit of a breakdown but was better and kept pegging away. 'Like a bicycle,' he wrote, '*I keep up by going on*… The present is stormy at times with thunder, but bright intervals. So I will sing in the intervals and groan in the storm. No man ever had more to be thankful for, and I carry a song in my soul and sing in the sunny intervals, as I have said.'[85] 'Thank God I can laugh yet,' he told a Newquay congregation towards the end of 1925 and a week later he concluded a letter to a colleague in Camborne with the following up-beat advice:

> Well, be of good cheer – these times are a hundredfold better than mine. The world is getting better every day – kindlier, more brotherly, more helpful.[86]

Although no one was more adept at evoking former times in Cornwall for the benefit of a captive audience, in reality he had no sympathy for those who were always bewailing 'the good old times'. On the contrary, the 'good new times, thank God, are a great deal better,' he wrote towards the end of the nineteenth century; 'and they are going to be a great deal better still. I am always very sorry for those poor folks who get that sort of crick in the neck which keeps them looking backward like Lot's wife'.[87] He considered it a sin to be gloomy and downhearted and would often admonish his audience or congregation with an aphorism or 'Pearseism' such as, 'I hate to hear these lackadaisical souls sighing about 'the world'. Whose world is it? Why, God's world, and we ought to rejoice in it'.[88] Perhaps the most succinct expression of his natural optimism is to be found in 'A Homely Counsel on Care' which he claimed to have learnt from 'an old [Cornish] mother' knitting busily outside her cottage door. It begins: 'Don't you trouble trouble/Till trouble troubles you./Don't you look for trouble;/Let trouble look for you.' and ends: 'Then don't you trouble trouble/Till trouble troubles you:/You'll only double trouble,/And trouble others too.[89]

The reawakening of the Cornish people to a sense of their nationhood and their cultural and linguistic difference that had begun towards the end of the nineteenth century, gathered momentum in the first two decades of the twentieth, with the inaugural Cornish Gorsedd taking place at Boscawen-Un stone circle near St Buryan on Friday 21 September 1928. Although Mark Guy Pearse was one of those deemed worthy of the 'honour of a Bardic Degree',[90] it was felt that the initiation ceremony would be too much for the octogenarian, and the Grand Bard, Henry Jenner, announced that the title 'Pyscajor a Dus' (Fisher of Men) would be conferred on him 'by commission'.[91]

Down in Cornwall when his last illness began, he would be helped to the garden next door which belonged to his dear friends, the Ridges.[92] There he would sit for hours, absorbed in the beauty of the sea and sky as the tide ebbed and flowed, and the fishermen came and went in the harbour below. He loved to gather visitors around him, sometimes telling them stories, sometimes drawing on his wonderful memory for information about natural history and sometimes producing sketches. He would argue that the study of birds and flowers should be compulsory for prospective clerics, followed by a spell in the police, studying men and women! In June 1929 he journeyed to London to see a specialist, hoping that, after a simple operation, he might be able to return to his beloved Cornwall within the space of two or three weeks. In the event, his health deteriorated still further to the extent that he could not go out or walk at all except with extreme difficulty. Restricted to what one family friend remembered as 'his hospitable flat in West End Lane',[93] he adapted his life to take account of his changed circumstances, finding pleasure in simple things such as the sun and breeze in the leafy poplar outside his window or the flowers that friends were always sending. He maintained his interest in public affairs and in books, writing in July to Edward Pethybridge, the son of his former fishing companion, in order to recommend the autobiography of Richard Burdon, 1st Viscount Haldane, which had been published that year. He developed a passion for romantic adventure stories in a period setting and 'tales of derring-do', with Jeffery Farnol's novels being particular favourites. He may, too, have enjoyed the Rev. W. Gregory Harris's *Trengwith*, the story of a ministerial year in a Cornish Methodist circuit, which was published in 1928. His illness ebbed and flowed. When unable to write, he would sit in bed composing poetry and reciting it to those around him. 'I was sometimes inclined to shirk my visits to him when I realised I could do so little to help him,' wrote his doctor after his death, 'but I was always compensated by his cheery welcome and often by humorous anecdotes. His patience and gratitude for any help one could give him were wonderful. I don't think any one could have known him long without feeling a profound and affectionate regard for him.'[94]

Some time during the course of 1929 he sent Robert Morton Nance, editor of *Old Cornwall*, what may well have been his last piece of writing, a short study of the inventor and fellow-Cambornian, Richard Trevithick. When this was duly published in the Summer 1930 issue, Nance paid its author a fine tribute. 'It is characteristic,' he wrote in a short introduction, 'that in it [this article] he should be championing another great Cornishman, for no one can have done more than he in giving the world at large a favourable idea of Cornish character: not only by his own example, but by his interpretations of Cornish life as a writer and lecturer. By his visits to almost every town in England he rendered unique service to the Cornish cause, for wherever he went he left the 'exiles' more devoted than ever to the land of their origin, and more determined to maintain their own Cornish individuality.'[95] Although his increasing weakness inevitably made him dependent on those around him, he was, like Frankey Vivian, the dying miner in *Daniel Quorm* in whom 'the old light and joy shone out more radiant than ever'.[96] He had absolutely no fear of death. Preaching once on the text, 'And He took clay and anointed his eyes,' he said:

> That is what Death does with us. Many people are afraid of the doctor, and the more clever the doctor, the more apt to be rough and quick. Old Dr Death is a wonderful doctor. He wraps us up in clay and heals us. We go in at the back door of the doctor's house and come out at the front. We go in blind, and come out gazing on golden streets and heavenly mansions; we go in deaf, and we come out with ears unstopped, and hearing softest celes-

> tial sounds; we go in mute, and we come out with tongues unloosed to join in angelic songs; we go in halt [lame], out of breath, decrepit, and we come out strong, to 'run up with joy the shining way'.[97]

When, in November, news came that he was sinking, his former colleague and friend, the Rev. C. Ensor Walters, wrote him a letter expressing the London Mission Committee's love, although he had grave doubts as to whether its recipient could read it. However, Mark Guy rallied and wrote in reply and in a strong, firm hand, one of the most beautiful and cheerful letters that his friend had ever received from him.[98] Towards the very end he sent for Ira Goldhawk, the then Superintendent of the West London Mission, in order to give him directions for the service that he wished to be held at Kingsway Hall, the Mission's headquarters, on the day of his funeral. 'I found him very weak and in much pain,' wrote Goldhawk, 'but nothing could suppress the gaiety of this radiant Christian. We talked together, we laughed together, and we prayed together. What an hour it was!' In order to emphasise his conviction that he was going, as he put it at the end of the letter that he left for his eldest son, 'not into the gloom, but into the dawn', he made it amply clear that there should be 'no mourning, no grief, no gloom, no "Dead March"'. Instead, they were to start the service with the Doxology ('Praise God from whom all blessings flow'), letting the organ stops out and asking those present 'to thunder it out when they sing it in triumph'.[99] On 19 December the *Methodist Recorder* reported that his condition was thought to be very serious and that only someone with his amazing vitality and courage could have endured for so long the suffering that had afflicted him. Later that same week he rallied somewhat, but when it went to press on Christmas Eve, the *Recorder* carried the news that his condition was 'not so reassuring' and that he was thought to be very weak.[100] In fact, the grand old man of Cornish Methodism saw the year out before dying at home on the afternoon of Wednesday 1 January 1930, two days short of his eighty-eighth birthday.

Three days later, in keeping with his dying wish that none of the usual signs of mourning should be displayed, a spirit of rejoicing and celebration pervaded his memorial service at Kingsway Hall. While the congregation was assembling, the organist played pieces that included Handel's 'I know that my Redeemer liveth'. Joining Ira Goldhawk on the platform were other Mission ministers and workers, together with the Revs. F. L. Wiseman and W. Hodson Smith, the Rt Hon. David Lloyd George MP and fellow Liberal politician, Dr James Macnamara. A large number of ministers and laymen representing both London and the provinces joined family and relatives in the body of the hall. After a hearty rendition of the Doxology, the service continued with Charles Wesley's affirmation of faith and regeneration, 'And can it be that I should gain'. Other hymns included 'This, this is the God we adore', 'Nearer, my God, to Thee' and John Mason Neale's celebration of the resurrection, 'The foe behind, the deep before', sung, as Pearse had specified, to 'Barnicott'. The psalm was his favourite, the 23rd. A junior colleague of the man he came to call his 'beloved master', his successor as chaplain of St Luke's House and Hughes' successor at the Mission itself, the Rev. Ensor Walters chose, in his brief address, to concentrate on Mark Guy's cheerfulness and confidence in God. Although he spoke, too, of his preaching, of his partnership with Hugh Price Hughes and of his gilts as an artist and writer, it was Mark Guy the friend and compassionate supporter of the underprivileged and the poor that he remembered with particular love and wonder. Katherine Price Hughes paid tribute to what he had done for the Mission – especially the Sisterhood. Indeed, the only wreath placed in front of the platform was one in the form of the badge of the Mission, consisting of a Maltese cross made of violets, with a circle of snowdrops in the centre, and bearing the letters WLM and the anchor of Hope, also in snowdrops, on its four flanges. There were other flowers in abundance, although at Mark Guy's request, they were not taken to the cemetery but distributed afterwards among the poor. After the Benediction, Kingsway Hall resounded to the strains of Handel's mighty 'Hallelujah Chorus'. A simple service at Golders Green Crematorium followed.[101]

Camborne paid tribute to its illustrious son on the Sunday morning when the Rev. H. Granville Morley conducted a memorial service at Wesley Chapel, the source of what he called 'the deepest and most powerful influences in the life of the Rev. Mark Guy Pearse'. He, too, stressed that they were gathered together not to mourn, but to thank God for a wonderful life and said that one of his earliest memories was of listening to the deceased in the old Cherry Street Chapel, Birmingham. On that occasion he had gone to please his father; later, though, he went to please himself.[102] Another Methodist clergyman who, as a boy, had fallen under the spell of Mark Guy Pearse's personality, was the Rev. Gregory Harris who, as we have seen, spent his summers with his uncle at Morwenstow. All too aware that Cornwall had suffered a good deal – as she still does – from writers who had noted and exploited her oddities, but had missed what he called 'her deeper aspects of thought and character, especially such as are concerned with Religion',[103] Harris was ideally placed to pay tribute to Mark Guy's unique qualities as a Cornish preacher, lecturer and writer, and did so in this fine poem that appeared in the local press the week after his death:

MARK GUY! Cornubia's son, who, through long years
  Bore the rich chalice of a radiant heart,
Though thou art gone there is no need for tears,
  For thou hast said thy say, and played thy part.

Right gallantly, in days when came the call
  To preach the Word amidst the city's din,
Thou did'st respond, desiring above all
  To break the chains that bound the slaves of sin.

Like a clear clarion rose thy golden voice
  Above the clamour of life's social stress,
Speaking of holy things in language choice,
  Wooing men's hearts to God's great loveliness.

But not for cities was thy spirit made,
  Though thou did'st in them nobly toil a space;
The country's spell was strongly on thee laid,
  A spell transmitted through an ancient race.

Thy native county, rugged and remote,
  Claimed all the best thy heart and mind could give;
Thou in her charms did'st find an antidote,
  And midst her magic thou did'st truly live!

Her haunted cairns, her solitary moors,
  Her granite cliffs, her amethystine seas,
Her gaunt, grim mine-stacks, and her echoing shores –
  All these did thy romantic spirit please.

And thou did'st love the simple words and ways
    Of fisher-folk, and such as did attend
The way-side chapels – there to pray and praise –
    And with them thou did'st oft thy spirit blend.

Poet and artist – ever swift to see
    Pathos and humour whence so e'er they came;
Wizard, who, in thy prime, right cheerily
    Did exorcise life's demons, dull and tame!

Mark Guy! Thy memory ever will abide
    As one God-gifted in unusual ways;
Thy soul has gone out on the ebbing tide,
    Its glow will cheer us still in future days.[104]

Chapter 18

'An' mind not to forget the windows…'

The Rev. Mark Guy Pearse's unique gift as a preacher and lecturer was acknowledged and enjoyed by people from all walks of life. From the day that, as a sixteen or seventeen year old, he preached his first sermon in the little Cornish chapel at Couch's Mill to his final pulpit appearance at Newlyn almost seventy years later, he 'breathed the spirit of love and comfort, and cheered and gladdened tens of thousands', as the Rev. Ira Goldhawk put it at his memorial service.[1] Certainly old age never dimmed his vision or quenched his passion for souls, and for the Rev. Joseph Johns he was as fresh at 83 as at 38, 'full of zeal and full of love'.[2] Perhaps there was no preacher of the period whose services were more eagerly sought; certainly few, if any, drew larger congregations. For the editor of the *Methodist Recorder* at the time of his death he was 'perhaps the one minister amongst us with the authentic mark of genius'[3] – a view supported by the Rev. Joseph Johns,[4] the Rev. C. Ensor Walters[5] and his friend and champion, the Rev. T. W. Slater for whom he was quite simply 'a Cornish religious genius'.[6] Walters recalled how, during the years of his superintendency of the West London Mission, he preached on one occasion at Carrs Lane Chapel, Birmingham and in the vestry after the service had a memorable conversation with Dr J. H. Jowett. When preaching and preachers came up, he asked his fellow minister who, in his opinion, was the greatest living preacher. Without hesitation Dr Jowett volunteered two names – one of them, a prominent Congregationalist, the other, Mark Guy Pearse whom he considered was not only always interesting, but also always instructive.[7] And the great Baptist minister Charles Spurgeon wished that he could have nominated him as his successor at the Tabernacle. Mark Guy was in many ways a pioneer who turned his back on contentment and personal salvation as a creed, advocating instead Christian socialism centred firmly on the belief that the only way to save one's soul was to give oneself away in love. The substance of this and of his preaching generally is enshrined in the forty-six or so books that he published during his lifetime. In *Jesus Christ and the People* he spelled out his message thus:

> The most helpful and most blessed thing in all the world [is] a simple loving heart that just gives itself its all to God: that waits not for any organisation or orders, but yields its whole being to the impulses of love and gives itself away in doing good. The best thing, the only thoroughly good thing, that we can do for the great world, is to fill our own little world with love. This is the sorest need of the world, which neither Parliament nor Councils, nor School Boards, nor stately Churches can meet: *Brotherly Love*. Not patronage is mostly wanted: nor even pity only: nor simple gifts, but the true love that can keep nothing back: the love that claims and consecrates its all to God and charity.[8]

Although he was successful and happy, both in his calling and in his personal life, he was still unworldly enough to believe that doing good and being good mattered more than anything else. A fellow traveller on one of his voyages overseas witnessed at first hand the extent to which he spent himself on others – a living exponent, as he saw it, of his own words, 'I am the more convinced the longer I live that love is the only orthodoxy, and selfishness the only heterodoxy'.[9] A life that was self-centred and self-contained with no root in God and no fruit for man was 'the bramble life' and those who served 'King Bramble' exchanged usefulness for show and position.[10]

While his message was essentially a simple one, the method he used to deliver it was not. Taking both his social charm and his artistic temperament into the pulpit or onto the lecture platform with him, he developed a style of preaching and lecturing that entranced all kinds of people. Indeed, he had what the *Methodist Recorder* called 'the artist's perception of truth… saw everything in a picture, expressed what he saw as a poet, developed it as a dramatist, and presented it with the abandon and grace and convincing power of a consummate actor'.[11] He certainly put all his soul into his preaching and lecturing, using the power of eye and voice, coupled with humour and pathos, to hold huge crowds.

Reporting on sermons that he preached at Penzance when well into his eighties, one local newspaper underlined how inadequate the written word was to convey a sense of the 'wonderful dramatic powers' of such 'a born humorist and mimic'.[12] This was a view echoed by the editor of the *Cornish Guardian* who considered that Mark Guy was perhaps the most difficult preacher that he ever remembered hearing for a reporter properly to represent afterwards in his newspaper. 'You could only appreciate "Mark Guy" by seeing him and hearing him,' he concluded.[13] For its part, *The Times* felt that in exposition, illustration and description he had command of powers that belonged to 'a born dramatic artist',[14] while for his friend and colleague W. J. Dawson, he was 'an unconscious actor of the first order' and unique as a storyteller.[15] Fellow Cornish bard Henry Cresswell Payne described him as 'an actor-lecturer' who could have been famous on the stage,[16] and the Rev. Granville Morley, Camborne's superintendent minister at the time of his death, dubbed him the Henry Irving of churchgoers.[17]

The pictorial style of preaching with which he held thousands spellbound in chapels and halls at home and abroad was explored by its exponent in the second series of *Daniel Quorm and His Religious Notions*. As he cobbles away in his workshop one Monday morning, Dan'el reveals to young Cap'n Joe his firmly held notions about preaching:

> 'An' mind not to forget the windows. Be sure o' that. Every sermon ought to be builded like the Lord told Noah to build the ark – *a window shalt thou make in the ark*.'
>
> 'Windows, Dan'el!' said Cap'n Joe, looking up perplexed. 'What are they?'
>
> Dan'el turned from his work and pointed to the little window, crowded as it was with tools and scraps of leather and odds and ends. 'Why, for to let the light in through, to be sure, Cap'n. An' not only for to let light in – a skylight would do that well enough. See how nice it is to *look out through*... That's what windows are for, in houses an' sermons too, Cap'n Joe.'
>
> 'You mean illustrations, Dan'el?'
>
> 'O' course I do! An' a sermon without them is like a house without windows. Everybody must ha' noticed how the Blessed Jesus kept tellin' the people about the lost sheep, or the prodigal son, or the faithless steward, or the ten virgins. An' how He kept saying, 'The kingdom o' heaven is like' this an' like that. Folks will always prick up their ears so soon as ever the Preacher do begin with his *likes*...'[18]

There are numerous accounts of the way in which Mark Guy Pearse used his dramatic expression and his pictorial imagination to inject life into his sermons, thereby holding the attention of his congregation or audience from beginning to end. In a letter received after his death, one worshipper remembered wonderful sermons such as that on Peter's denial – sermons whereby he lived 'in the minds and hearts of thousands who sat spellbound before the wonders of the pictures that he drew'.[19] Thomas Champness saw him preach at the very beginning of his long ministry in a Leeds theatre where the picturesque service had what he described as 'all that bizarre look that seems to harmonise with Pearse's style'. He was at home on the stage, possessing 'enough of the Bohemian… to make you feel that he could preach as well to a company of sailors or gypsies as to the respectable sinners who frequent our churches'.[20] Dr J. Ernest Rattenbury recalled how, in his sermons at St James's Hall, he had an eye for the hidden beauties of the Scriptures. 'One cannot think of him as a preacher,' he enthused, 'without calling to mind his terse sentences and witty sayings; his invective and his tender comfort. He sometimes put a sermon into an unexpected accent; or a dramatic gesture told a story without words. He was always the artist. He saw, and made his audience see. I remember scenes he depicted so graphically that the figures in them stand out in my memory with the distinctness of statues. I recall, for instance, his description of the ladies of Egypt crying in time of famine for bread. Their dress, features, gestures, intonations, were superbly imagined and pictured with the consummate skill of a great dramatic artist.'[21] We have already seen, too, how, like the children around him, the Rev. Samuel Keeble sat entranced by Mark Guy's anniversary address at City Road in the 1870s. On this and countless other occasions, the magic of both his voice and his facial expressions brought what were essentially simple events to life. Indeed, when he lectured, his chairman would sometimes leave the stage and sit among the audience in order to see the speaker's face. 'One of the most astonishing things about him,' wrote one well-known journalist, 'is his voice. It is clear, sonorous, ringing, jocund. There are no cracks, no rough edges, no jars. His voice is the man… One seems to see the plunging sound as it leaps from his lips into the air, roundly sonorous, smoothly deep. With such a voice Chaucer might have smote the rafters at the Tabard Inn; with such a voice rare Ben Jonson might have trolled a chorus at the Mermaid Tavern. And what a face he has! First it beams with good humour, then grows serious and clouds gather sullenly and bitterly; the storm breaks violently with crash after crash of thunder; it ceases suddenly, the sun bursts from behind a cloud, and the birds begin to sing again...'[22]

Although there were few preachers more rhetorical than Mark Guy Pearse, he eschewed the use of rhetoric for its own sake, rejecting what W. J. Dawson, in his perceptive analysis of the preacher's character and style, called 'the elaborate and ornamented style of preaching... the old pompous, swelling, unnatural diction of the pulpit'. Instead, naturalness and vitality were qualities that Mark Guy brought to the pulpit, together with the ability to be 'simple without being commonplace... real, and yet imaginative; plain, and yet poetic; direct and cogent, and yet nobly rhetorical'.[23] Only too aware, himself, of the dangers of sacrificing content to style, on the death of Thomas Champness in October 1905 he recalled a conversation he had had with Dwight Moody at Northfield eighteen years previously. 'The first time you came to England,' he wrote, 'our Church was affected with the ugliest *ism* that could befall a people. Ritualism may be empty. Intellectualism may be cold. Rheumatism may be painful. But the ugliest *ism* in the world is *Pretty-ism* – when it does not matter so much what you say as how you say it. Pretty little sentences with all their points polished off, rounded till they went gliding from the memory as fast as they fell. And nothing stuck. Thomas Champness could not do that sort of thing – could not attempt it. So he went down amongst "the men in the smockfrock" and there did noble work.'[24] No more could Mark Guy Pearse 'do that sort of thing'! As W. J. Dawson pointed out, he hated preaching that tried to be great. He hated the sort of sermon that was constructed more with a view to displaying the preacher's powers than to reaching the hearts of his congregation. He hated the sort of approach that put preparation of the sermon before preparation of the preacher. What he called 'pretty-ism', though, was not the only thing he disliked in a preacher. Pulpit dullness was to be avoided at all costs. In *Daniel Quorm* the author has Dan'el compare class-meetings to awls and needles – 'they'll go so long as ever you can keep 'em bright; but when they get dull they'll rust, and then it be hard work'. Never were they meant to be rounds of vague little sermons; still less were they for preaching the very same little sermons, week after week, until everyone knew them by heart. What Dan'el must and would have was '*heart-talk* – real, fresh, living heart-talk'. In exactly the same way, a sermon had to come 'out of a man's own heart, wrapt up in his own flesh an' blood, an' breathin' with the man's own life'. If it did not, then all that remained would be 'bones; dead bones; nothing but bones. Put together all in order, I dare say, but bones only… for all that. No naturalness about 'em – I do mean no life an' no realness, but a sort of a ghostly thing that you can see through. All varnished an' shinin', may be, but dead bones still.'[25]

On one occasion overwork meant that Mark Guy was in the unusual position of being in the congregation where he picked up some hints on preaching that he thought he might use. In a letter to his wife he described the four sermons he had heard as 'very thoughtful, very good – but with no grip, no force'. There was nothing in them, he felt, that 'punched the heads of those who thought themselves good, and made the bad feel that they ought to, and might, be better'.[26] 'Punching' the heads of the congregation could, and sometimes did, cause offence, as in Sydney in May 1891 and at Ramsey on the Isle of Man two years later. The fact that he put all his soul into his preaching and lecturing meant that as well as for the occasional, ill-timed outburst, he was criticised for the impatience he sometimes showed towards late-comers, those who left during a service or lecture, fussy stewards and others who disturbed the pictures in his mind and shattered the spell he was trying to weave. The Rev. C. Ensor Walters remembered being with him in a crowded chapel in the Midlands and the consternation that prevailed when, in the course of the service, he said, 'Will that man with the 'creaky' boots sit down?' 'That man' was both aisle steward and circuit steward! On another occasion he was taking an evening service in a Cornish chapel when a member of the congregation seated in the gallery tried to slip out quietly. With his concentration broken by the noise of the poor person's squeaky shoes, the preacher spoke out:

> Well, goodnight brother if you are going. Next time you come, bring your slippers with you!

As his biographers stressed, this sensitiveness was not the result of a lack of sympathy with busy or simple people, but was something physical – the helplessness of an artist when someone stepped between him and his canvas.[27] On such occasions, though, his abiding sense of humour and his compassion for humanity always helped defuse the situation and he would invariably apologise. Those well-to-do women who were in the habit of arriving late at a fashionable West End church where he used to preach, simply to draw attention to themselves, were a notable exception. One Sunday morning, it seems, several of them entered the church during the first prayer. At its conclusion, before announcing the second hymn, Mark Guy gravely remarked, 'I wish you would not look up when late-comers enter. Every allowance must be made for them, they are only the maids, and have to finish the housework before coming to church.'[28] He contrasted the 'simple times' enjoyed by Adam and Eve with the temptations of his – and our own – material world in a wonderfully tongue-in-cheek poem entitled 'The world's first washing Jan viii: 0001':

How happy were those simple times!
No smuts defiled the sunny climes
    When our dear Mother Eve,
Set up the line against the sky,
And left two fig leaves out to dry,
    Which she feared not to leave.

No mangling needed to be done,
Of starching, ironing, there was none,
    No lacing, hook or eye.
When this sufficed to meet their needs
Adam in peace could smoke his weed,
    While Eve eats pumpkin pie!

Ah, if those blessed days had stayed
No drapers shops had been arrayed
    No tempting store of goods.
When change of clothing they required
Each singly in the shade retired
    And found them in the woods.

No head with vanity had turned,
No spiteful soul with envy burned
    At sight of other's clothes!
Then husbands had been spared the ills
Of having those tremendous bills
    In which the money goes!

Monday March 18: 1918.[29]

During his visit to Ontario in the autumn of 1903, one local newspaper saw 'unconventionality [breathing] from every accent and gesture'[30] and for numerous colleagues and friends, it was his individualism and personality that singled him out. Too original and daring to be cast in any mould, Mark Guy copied no model, either in or outside the pulpit. He refused to 'put on the parson', as he called it and for Luke Wiseman, anyone less like the traditional divine – 'the erudite, dry, didactic theologian, slightly aloof and superior' – could hardly be imagined.[31] Such originality, though, resulted in conflicts and pressures. Although he spent the greater part of his life in cities – notably London – they were, as we have seen, far from being his natural habitat, and the need to escape to the country – especially to Cornwall, his ancestral home – was deep-seated and sometimes urgent. He needed also to escape the demands of Church administration, officialdom or routines when these impinged on his belief in homeliness, simplicity and brotherliness as ways to salvation. He always resisted the tendency to localise God, seeing that 'under the baldest names and simplest forms there lurk the essence of High Churchism: the tendency to limit the Real Presence to churches, to services, to sacraments'.[32] In the words of James Cobbledick, this was tantamount to trying to 'shut up the sun in your own li'll cucumber-frame'.[33] One of the Sisters remembered that if people or committees or meetings bored him, he became 'an imp of mischief' and Katherine Price Hughes recounted how, as he sat on the platform beside her one day listening to a learned, but somewhat verbose cleric 'proving' Christianity, he whispered, 'If he goes on another five minutes I shall become an atheist!'[34] And we have already seen how in Toronto in 1903, he persuaded his friend and tour organiser E. Ryerson Young to flee the clamouring crowds so that they could swap fishing anecdotes in the comfort of their hotel room. Like Dan'el Quorm, Mark Guy was never happier than when savouring the delights of a pasty under a Cornish hedge![35] The Rev. C. Ensor Walters could never remember seeing his 'beloved master' at either a Committee or Quarterly meeting, and although he was a member of the Legal Hundred for many years, his visits to Conference were rare and brief.[36] He never aspired to high office in the Methodist Church; indeed, he confessed to having 'a shrinking from prominence and publicity' and a marked preference for 'a quiet and half-hidden ministry'.[37]

In the event, of course, he lived nearly all of his life in the public eye. In one area, at least, there was no conflict and that was his supreme belief in the rightness of what he did to reinterpret Christianity as a religion that held the secret of a great joy. His rule of life was, '*Start the day with a clear view of Jesus Christ*'. Thereafter, he counselled, 'Be like the fisherman who is busied in the cabin about a score of things that must be seen to – but every now and then the head is thrust out; the helm is trimmed a little; he lifts his eyes to the sky and sees to the wind; he searches the sea for any approaching craft; and then down again to work, singing a cheery song.'[38] As the instructions he gave for his memorial service showed, in death as in life, Mark Guy Pearse – *Pysajor a Dus* – called on people to be brave, to rejoice and to keep well out to sea. The only thing that helped nobody was a dead calm. Rather, the Christian's prayer should be that of another old Cornishman:

> O Lord, send us out to sea – out in the deep water. Here we are in so close upon the rocks that the first bit of a breeze with the devil and we are all knocked to pieces. Lord, send us out to sea – out in the deep water, where we shall have room enough to get a glorious victory.[39]

Notes

Introduction

1. Arthur Lawrence (1899) 'The Rev. Mark Guy Pearse' in A. T. Quiller-Couch (ed), *The Cornish Magazine*, vol. 2, Truro: Pollard, pp. 244-245.
2. Unless otherwise specified, this genealogical information is from the Church of Jesus Christ of Latter-Day Saints' FamilySearch Internet Genealogy Service, http://www.familysearch.org. Note, though, that William Pearse (1766–1842), Mark Guy's great uncle, is on record as saying, "Our parents were Dissenters, natives of Hatherleigh, in Devonshire…" See [Rev. Francis Truscott] (1816), 'Some Futher Account of Mr T. Pearse of Camelford' in *The Methodist Magazine*, July 1816, p. 481.
3. [Rev. Francis Truscott] (1816), 'Some Account of the late Mr Thomas Pearse, of Camelford, Cornwall' in *The Methodist Magazine*, May 1816, p. 323.
4. Ibid, May 1816, pp. 321-331 and 401-410, and July 1816, pp. 481-493.
5. William P. Burgess (1854) '[Robert Pearse]' in *Wesleyan Methodist Magazine*, p. 570.
6. Thomas Shaw (1993) 'Tamarside Methodism' in *Journal of the Cornish Methodist Historical Association*, vol. 8, no. 3, p. 78.
7. Burgess (1854), op. cit., pp. 570-572.
8. Monica Winstanley (1978) *High Tide at Port Isaac: the Life and Times of Warwick Richard Guy 1821–1905*, Padstow: Lodenek Press, p. 8; Lawrence (1899), p. 244.
9. Mrs George Unwin and John Telford (1930) *Mark Guy Pearse, Preacher, Author, Artist*, London: Epworth Press/J. Alfred Sharp, p. 14.

Chapter 1 *Camborne 1842–1857*

1. Mrs George Unwin and John Telford (1930) *Mark Guy Pearse, Preacher, Author, Artist*, London: Epworth Press/J. Alfred Sharp, p. 42.
2. F. E. Halliday (1975) *A History of Cornwall*, London: Duckworth, pp. 281-283.
3. *Pigot's National Commercial Directory of England and the whole of South Wales* (1830), cited in Janet Thomas (1987) *The Wheels Went Around: the story of Camborne town*, Redruth: Truran, p.15.
4. R. Lanyon (1841) 'Statistics of Camborne' in *9th Annual Report of the Royal Cornwall Poytechnic Society*, cited in Thomas (1987), pp. 42-43.
5. *West Briton,* August 1849, cited in Thomas (1987), p. 43.
6. Information supplied by Professor Charles Thomas, Robert Hall's great grandson. The shop is variously described in trade directories and in the population censuses of 1851 and 1861 as being in Commercial Square, Basset Road, Fore Street and Market Place. In April 1841, the Pearses were living here with their 4-year-old daughter Ellen and Sarah Whitehair, a 20-year-old servant. Ellen became a Sunday School teacher at Camborne Wesley and in the late 1860s moved with her father to London. Shortly afterwards she married Henry Burton. She dies at Blundellsands, Merseyside on 3 July 1901. See *Methodist Recorder* 11 July 1901.
7. Baptisms solemnised in the Wesleyan Methodist Chapels in the Camborne Circuit, Cornwall Record Office, MR/CB/607, no. 215.
8. Unwin and Telford (1930), op. cit., p. 42.
9. Arthur Lawrence (1899) 'The Rev. Mark

Guy Pearse' in A. T. Quiller-Couch (ed), *The Cornish Magazine*, vol. 2, Truro: Pollard, p. 246.

10. Cited in Thomas (1987), p. 35. See also Halliday (1975), op. cit., Lawrence (1899), op. cit., and D. B. Barton (1967), *The History of Tin Mining and Smelting in Cornwall*, Truro: Bradford Barton.
11. Rev. R. Corlett Cowell (1903) 'The Conference Town' in *Wesleyan Methodist Magazine*, vol. 126, p. 510.
12. T. R. Harris (1974), *Dolcoath: Queen of Cornish Mines*, Trevithick Society, p. 61.
13. Barton (1967), op. cit., p. 111.
14. Albert Bluett (1898) 'The Great Dolcoath' in A. T. Quiller-Couch (ed), *The Cornish Magazine*, vol. 1, Truro: Pollard, pp. 168-181.
15. Harris (1974), op. cit., pp. 53-54.
16. See J. F. Odgers [195-] *Camborne Trustee Savings Bank 1860–1954*, Camborne: [J. F Odgers], p. 10.
17. Dr H. Miles Brown (1947) *Methodism and the Church of England in Cornwall, 1738–1838*, typescript, County Library, cited in J. F. Odgers [1959] *Early Methodism in Camborne: Wesley Chapel, 1828–1958*, Camborne: [J. F. Odgers], p. 14.
18. John C. C. Probert (1989) 'Redruth Methodist Businessmen: an Assessment' in *Gain, Save, Give*, Cornish Methodist Historical Association Occasional Publication 20, p. 62.
19. Odgers (1959), op. cit., p. 18.
20. T. R. Harris (1963) *Samuel Dunn, reformer, 1798–1882*, Redruth: Cornish Methodist Historical Association, p. 11.
21. Odgers (1959), op. cit., pp. 18-22.
22. Unwin and Telford (1930), op. cit., p. 14.
23. Camborne Wesley Class leaders [and stewards] attendance register 1835–1855, Cornwall Record Office, MR/CB 151.
24. Camborne Wesleyan Institute Minute Book 1857– ,Cornwall Record Office, MR/CB 149.
25. Odgers (1959), op. cit., pp. 96-97.
26. Ibid, p. 51.
27. Mark Guy Pearse (1892) *Sermons for Children*, London: Charles Kelly, p. 31.
28. Baptisms solemnized… MR/CB/607. Born on 3 December 1843 'Maggie Dewsnail', as he affectionately addressed her in his letters, later married the Rev. James Pratt. One child of this union became, early last century, headmistress of Camborne Grammar School and was remembered affectionately by Anne Treneer in *Cornish Years*.
29. Odgers (1959), op. cit., p.38.
30. Samuel Coley (1868) *The Life of Thomas Collins*, London: Hamilton, Adams & Co., p. 288.
31. Odgers (1959), op. cit., p.38.
32. Unwin and Telford (1930), p. 33. "Grammar-sow" is Cornish dialect for a wood-louse.
33. Having first appeared in *The City Road Magazine*, *Daniel Quorm and his religious notions* was published in book form by the Wesleyan Conference Office in December, 1874. It ran into many editions and a second series bearing the same title was published in 1875.
34. 'Truth', 'Mark Guy Pearse's Publications', *Methodist Recorder* 14 August 1885.
35. Mark Guy Pearse (1876) *Daniel Quorm and his religious notions*, London: Wesleyan Conference Office, p. 30.
36. Information supplied by Professor Charles Thomas.
37. Odgers (1959), op. cit., p. 134.
38. Pearse (1876), op. cit., pp. 32-33.
39. Ibid, pp. 86-87.
40. Mark Guy Pearse [1880] *My Old Friend John*. First published as a tract c. 1873 and reprinted in *Short Stories and other papers*, 5th thousand, [n.d.] London: Wesleyan Conference Office, p. 151.
41. Muriel Sara (1974) *More about Cornwall and My Cornish Friends*, Hayle: [Muriel Sara], p. 48.
42. Formed by the collapse of a large cave which was said to have been used by a Camborne smuggler to store contraband in, Ralph's Cupboard is situated out on the North Cliffs, less than a mile west of Portreath.
43. Pearse (1892), op. cit., pp. 1-12.
44. Ibid, pp. 146-147. The incident also found its way, in an expanded form, into 'Little Breeches and what he did at Christmas' which first appeared in the Christmas Number of the *Methodist Recorder*, vol. 14, 1874.
45. Mark Guy Pearse [1893] *The Gospel for the Day*, London: Kelly, pp. 51-52.
46. A Protestant denomination founded in

the eighteenth century, the Moravian Church traces its origins to the Unitas Fratrum of the fifteenth century Hussite movement in Bohemia and Moravia. John Wesley came to know the Moravians en route to Georgia in 1735–36, and on his return home two years later, both he and his brother Charles affiliated with them. As the congregations of the Church of England began to close their doors to him, John Wesley went to religious societies, trying to inject new spiritual vigour into them, particularly by introducing "bands" similar to those of the Moravians. The two movements worked together until 1740, after which they went their separate ways. See *Encyclopaedia Britannica*.

47. Pearse (1892), op. cit., pp. 155-156.
48. Mark Guy Pearse [1885] *Some Aspects of the Blessed Life*, London: T. Woolmer, pp. 163-164.
49. Born in Swannington, Leicestershire in November 1840, Dr Burton was well known as a Bible scholar, although his reputation rests on his poems and hymns which were published in *Wayside Songs of the Inner and the Outer Life* (1886) and *The Songs of the Highway* (1924). He died at West Kirby, Cheshire in April, 1930.
50. 'The Rev. Mark Guy Pearse' (1895) in *C[ornish] M[ethodist] C[hurch] R[ecord]*, December, cutting in the Shaw Methodist Collection, Courtney Library, Truro.
51. Mark Guy Pearse (1884) 'Portland St. Chapel' in *Wesleyan Methodist Magazine*, p. 658.
52. Eliza A. Wood (1902) *Memorials of James Wood, LL.D., J.P.*, London: Kelly, pp. 28-31, 216. The Rev. T. B. Stephenson (1839–) was relieved from circuit work in 1873 so that he could devote his energies to the Children's Home which he had founded. He was elected President of the Wesleyan Conference in 1891.

Chapter 2 *Liskeard 1857–1861*

1. See Kate Muir, *Arms and the woman: a review of famous Scottish trials*, London: Sinclair-Stevenson, 1992.
2. Mrs George Unwin and John Telford (1930) *Mark Guy Pearse, Preacher, Author, Artist*, London: Epworth Press/J. Alfred Sharp, p. 22.
3. The Rev. M. G. Pearse was obviously confusing two journeys home in these memories, for, even allowing for climate changes, he would surely not have been delayed by snow at the end of June/beginning of July.
4. Warwick Guy Pearse, Chairman of the Board of Guardians, died at Camelford House on October 26th, 1861, aged 53. See *Royal Cornwall Gazette*, 2 November 1861.
5. Andrew Hingston's paternal grandmother was Elizabeth Pearse.
6. Unwin and Telford (1930), op. cit., pp. 23-24.
7. Ibid, p. 24.
8. Viv Twornicki and John Rapson (1996), 'Blazing inferno marked the end of Liskeard's first Methodist Church' in *Cornish Times*, June.
9. Paul Bolitho (1967) *Methodism in the Liskeard Circuit 1751–1967*, [Liskeard]: [Paul Bolitho], pp. 21-23. 'Death of Mr Andrew Hingston' in *Cornish Times*, 23 October 1897. See also Lawrence Maker (1935) *Cob and Moorstone: the curious history of some Cornish Methodist churches*, London: Epworth Press, pp. 27-31.
10. 'The late Mr Andrew Hingston of Liskeard. Impressive funeral service – address by Rev. Mark Guy Pearse' in *Cornish Times*, 30 October 1897.
11. Unwin and Telford (1930), op. cit., pp. 91-92. 'Whispers and Echoes: Memories of 'Mark Guy'...' in *Cornish Guardian*, 9 January 1930. An article in the *Cornish Methodist Church Record*, December 1895, suggests that his preaching debut occurred even earlier, while he was at Wesley College, Sheffield, where, under the influence of Dr Waddy, he was converted: "...a Yorkshire village congregation witnessed his maiden pulpit effort. No authentic report of the service has been preserved, but Mr Pearse has always been alive to the value of proportion, whilst his artistic sense of the fitness of things is innate in his nature, and we are not surprised to be told that, not possessing a coat of his own sufficiently clerical and dignified, he borrowed for the occasion a suitable

garment from a more fortunate schoolfellow.' Cutting in the Shaw Methodist Collection, Courtney Library, Truro.

12. Unwin and Telford (1930), op. cit., pp. 128-129.
13. Ibid, p. 25.
14. Bolitho (1967), op. cit., p. 24.
15. Unwin and Telford (1930), op. cit., p. 25. *Cornish Times*, 8 October 1920.
16. In *General Booth's vision and other addresses*, Louisville: Pickett Publishing Co., 1860, source Firstsearch WorldCat, accession no. 7608875. The early date, however, is suspect, given that Billy Bray did not die until 1868.
17. Arthur Lawrence (1899) 'The Rev. Mark Guy Pearse' in A. T. Quiller-Couch (ed), *The Cornish Magazine*, vol. 2, Truro: Pollard, p. 244.
18. 1861 Census.
19. *Cornish Times*, January 1859.
20. *Cornish Times*, 30 October 1897.

Chapter 3 *St Bartholomew's Hospital and Didsbury College 1861–1863*

1. St Bartholomew's Hospital Archives and Museum, ms. 1/2, p. 61.
2. Ibid, ms. 51.
3. Ibid, *Student's Handbook* 1861–62, p. 8.
4. Ibid, ms. 61/1, p. 9.
5. Like many of the Rev. M. G. Pearse's stories, 'Old Rosie; a story for the children' was first published as a tract in the 1870s before finding its way into book form – in this case in *Short Stories and other papers*, London: Wesleyan Conference Office, [1877]. This extract is from a more vigorous version entitled simply 'Old Rosie' which appeared in *The Spectator and Methodist Chronicle*, Melbourne, 29 May 1891.
6. Mrs George Unwin and John Telford (1930) *Mark Guy Pearse, Preacher, Author, Artist*, London: Epworth Press/J. Alfred Sharp, p. 30.
7. Arthur Lawrence (1899) 'The Rev. Mark Guy Pearse' in A. T. Quiller-Couch (ed), *The Cornish Magazine*, vol. 2, Truro: Pollard, p. 246.
8. Unwin and Telford (1930), op. cit., pp. 19-20.
9. Pearse (1891), op. cit.
10. Mark Guy Pearse (1926) *The Ship Where Christ Was Captain*, London: Epworth, p. 42.
11. F. W. Bourne (1892) *The King's Son*, new and revised edition, London: Bible Christian Book Room, pp. 145-146. Cyril Davey (1955) *The Methodist Story*, London: Epworth, pp. 81-82.
12. Report in the *Methodist Recorder*, 16 February 1883, on a meeting of between six hundred and eight hundred Wesleyan Methodist young men at Victoria Chapel, Bristol on 2 February.
13. 'The Rev. Mark Guy Pearse' (1895) in *C[ornish] M[ethodist] C[hurch] R[ecord]*, December, cutting in the Shaw Methodist Collection, Courtney Library, Truro.
14. Unwin and Telford (1930), op. cit., p. 26.
15. Ibid, p. 27.
16. *Methodist Recorder*, 10 July 1862.
17. J. F. Odgers [1959] *Early Methodism in Camborne: Wesley Chapel 1828–1958*, Camborne: [J. F. Odgers], p. 127.
18. *Methodist Recorder* 5 August 1862.
19. Mark Guy Pearse (1876) *Daniel Quorm and his religious notions*, London: Wesleyan Conference Office, p. 110.
20. Before her marriage, Mary Hingston was a Dingley from Sherborne, Dorset.
21. Unwin and Telford (1930), op. cit., pp. 180-182.
22. Lincoln-born Dr John Hannah (1792–1867) entered the Wesleyan ministry in 1814 and was elected President of the Conference in 1842 and again in 1851. That same year he became divinity tutor at the recently-opened Didsbury College, remaining there until his death.
23. Unwin and Telford (1930), op. cit., p. 30.
24. Ibid, p. 29.
25. *Methodist Recorder*, 9 January 1863.
26. *Methodist Recorder*, 30 January 1863.
27. Unwin and Telford (1930), op. cit., p. 29.
28. *Methodist Recorder*, 3 April 1863.
29. *Methodist Recorder*, 21 August 1863.

Chapter 4 *Leeds and London 1863–1867*

1. *Manx Wesleyan Methodist Church Record*, vol. 1, April 1893, p. 39.
2. Information supplied by D. Colin Dews of the Yorkshire Branch of the Wesley Historical Society.
3. *Methodist Recorder*, 13 October 1863.
4. Mrs George Unwin and John Telford (1930) *Mark Guy Pearse, Preacher, Author, Artist*, London: Epworth Press/J. Alfred Sharp, p. 34.
5. D. Colin Dews.
6. *Methodist Recorder*, 21 December 1883.
7. Unwin and Telford (1930), op. cit., p. 34.
8. Lambeth Archives Methodist Records, Introductory notes to lists IV/55 and IV/186.
9. Edward Bickersteth (1786–1850) was an English evangelical clergyman who compiled over 700 hymns which were published in his *Christian Psalmody* (1833).
10. Unwin and Telford (1930), op. cit., pp. 36-37.
11. William Morley Punshon (1824–1881) devoted much time and energy to the mission cause.
12. Unwin and Telford (1930), op. cit., p. 37.
13. Ibid, p. 39.
14. Ibid.
15. Ibid, pp. 74-75.
16. Ibid, p. 75.
17. Ibid, p. 71.
18. Ibid, p. 72.
19. Straw plaiting had developed as a cottage industry, along with lace-making, during the sixteenth century. In the eighteenth, people began to move into the town from surrounding villages to work in small factories, and by the nineteenth century almost every woman and girl in Dunstable was employed either in straw plaiting or lace work. The Dunstable Straw Bonnet became well-known in the capital and in many other parts of the country and when, largely as a result of the Napoleonic Wars, Italian 'Leghorn' straw ceased to be readily available, London manufacturers of straw goods began to open branches in the town. By 1869, there were at least five large factories and twelve small plaiting workshops with a total estimated workforce of 1,300. After the railway line between Luton and London opened in 1858, however, the Dunstable straw-hat trade began to decline, with businesses gradually moving to be closer to Luton's main-line station. The J. J. & G. Cooper hat and bonnet factory, however, survived until at least 1877, though it had closed by 1885. See Nigel C. Benson, *Dunstable in Detail*, Dunstable: The Book Castle, 1986.
20. Colin Bourne (ed) (1993) *The Dunstable Methodist Circuit: one hundred and fifty years of witness, 1843–1993*, Dunstable: Dunstable Methodist Circuit.
21. Unwin and Telford (1930), op. cit., p. 72.
22. Ibid, p. 74.
23. *West Briton*, 7 September 1866.
24. Letter dated 18 June 1867 in the Methodist Archive and Research Centre, Manchester.
25. Unwin and Telford (1930), op. cit., p. 76.
26. 'The Rev. Mark Guy Pearse' (1895) in *C[ornish] M[ethodist] C[hurch] R[ecord]*, December, cutting in the Shaw Methodist Collection, Courtney Library, Truro.
27. Mark Guy Pearse (1902) *A Bit of Shamrock*, London: Horace Marshall & Son, p. 31.
28. Unwin and Telford (1930), op. cit., pp. 40-41.
29. Ibid, p. 78.
30. Ibid, pp. 79-80.
31. Ibid, p. 83.
32. *The Times*, 2 January 1930.
33. Unwin and Telford (1930), op. cit., p. 83.
34. Ibid, pp. 83-84.
35. Emmeline Pethick-Lawrence (1938) *My part in a changing world*, London: Gollancz, pp. 100-101.
36. Katherine H. Price Hughes (1914) 'Death of Mrs Mark Guy Pearse' in *Methodist Recorder*, 12 February.
37. Unwin and Telford (1930), op. cit., pp. 84-85.
38. J. Johnson and A. Greutzner (comps.) (1976) *Dictionary of British Artists 1880–1940*, Woodbridge: Antique Collectors' Club.
39. Rev. T. W. Slater (1930) 'A Cornish Religious Genius' in *Cornish Guardian*, 24 April. The frontispiece of *The Ship Where*

Christ Was Captain (1926) consists of a portrait of the author 'taken in his Daughter's Studio at St Ives'.

40. Unwin and Telford (1930), op. cit., p. 236.
41. Ibid, pp. 86 and 176. W. McG. Eagar (1953) *Making Men: the History of Boys' Clubs and Related Movements in Great Britain*, London: University of London Press, pp. 228-229.
42. Letter to *The British Weekly*, dated 10 January 1930.

Chapter 5 *Ipswich and Bedford 1867–1872*

1. Mark Guy Pearse (1879) *Mister Horn and His Friends*, revised and enlarged edition, London: Wesleyan Conference Office, p. 23.
2. *Suffolk Chronicle*, 25 August 1888.
3. Mrs George Unwin and John Telford (1930) *Mark Guy Pearse, Preacher, Author, Artist*, London: Epworth Press/J. Alfred Sharp, p. 112.
4. Ipswich Wesleyan Methodist Circuit Baptism Register 1867–1871, FK1/18049/28. The entry is incomplete.
5. 'Presentation to the Rev. M. G. Pearse', undated cutting, probably from the *Suffolk Chronicle*, [July?] 1869, supplied by Elizabeth Watthews, Circuit Archivist, Ipswich.
6. 'Whispers and Echoes: Memories of 'Mark Guy'…', in *Cornish Guardian*, 9 January 1930.
7. *Suffolk Chronicle* (1869), op. cit.
8. Ibid.
9. Information kindly provided by Sheila Hardy of Tattingstone.
10. Rev. T. N. Ritson (ed) [1910] *The Story of a Century: the history of Wesleyan Methodism in the Ipswich Circuit*, p. 145.
11. Unwin and Telford (1930), op. cit., p. 40.
12. Pearse (1879), op. cit., p. 2.
13. Morley Adams (1908) 'Mister Horn and His Friends in Real Life', in *Methodist Recorder*, 30 April, p. 351.
14. Pearse (1879), op. cit., p. 3.
15. Ritson [1910], op. cit., p. 145.
16. Pearse (1879), op. cit., pp. 66-67.
17. *Suffolk Chronicle*, 9 September 1876.
18. Pearse (1879), op. cit., pp. 61-62.
19. *Suffolk Chronicle* (1869), op. cit.
20. *Methodist Recorder*, 6 August 1869.
21. 1871 Census.
22. Unwin and Telford (1930), op. cit., p. 41.
23. 'The Rev. Mark Guy Pearse' (1895), in *C[ornish] M[ethodist] C[hurch] R[ecord]*, December, cutting in the Shaw Methodist Collection, Courtney Library, Truro.
24. Mark Guy Pearse [1887] *Praise: meditations on the one hundred and third psalm*, London: Woolmer, pp. 33-36.
25. Born at Kelvedon, Essex, Charles Haddon Spurgeon (1834–1892) became pastor of the New Park Street Chapel, London in 1854. Thirty-three years later he withdrew from the Baptist Union. As well as sermons, he wrote *John Ploughman's Talk* (1869) and numerous other works. The Metropolitan Tabernacle, seating 6,000, was opened at Newington on 18 March 1861 and destroyed by fire in April, 1898.
26. Unwin and Telford (1930), op. cit., pp. 41-42. Frederick Howard was a leading local manufacturer who, in partnership with his brother James, built the Britannia Iron Works at Bedford in 1857.
27. Ibid, pp. 154-155.
28. C. H. Spurgeon (1900) *Autobiography; compiled from his diary, letters, and records, by his wife, and his private secretary*, Vol. IV, London: Passmore & Alabaster, pp. 162-163.
29. Joyce Godber (1969) *History of Bedfordshire, 1066–1888*, Bedford: Bedfordshire County Council, p. 505.
30. From a review cited in the *Methodist Recorder*, 25 October 1872.
31. The reviews from *The Buffalo Christian Advocate* and *The Christian Miscellany* were cited in Mark Guy Pearse (1877) *John Tregenoweth: his mark*, 2nd edition revised, New York: Nelson & Phillips.
32. Unwin and Telford (1930), op. cit., p. 174.
33. Ibid, p. 42.
34. Emmeline Pethick-Lawrence (1938) *My part in a changing world*, London: Gollancz, pp. 110-111.

Chapter 6 *Highbury and Westminster 1872–1876*

1. See Roy Porter (1994), *London: a social history*, London: H. Hamilton, and Guy R. Williams (1975), *London in the country: the growth of Suburbia*, London: H. Hamilton.
2. M. V. Hughes (1977), *A London child of the 1870s*, Bath: Chivers Press, pp. 78-79. This, the first in her 'London Family' trilogy, was first published in 1934.
3. Ibid., pp. 120-122.
4. *The Methodist Recorder* 12 September 1873 announced the birth of Mark Guy Pearse, jnr., at this address.
5. 'The Rev. Mark Guy Pearse', *C[ornish] M[ethodist] C[hurch] R[ecord]* December 1895; newspaper cutting in the Shaw Methodist Collection, Courtney Library, Truro.
6. *Methodist Recorder,* 30 October 1862.
7. Ibid. 10 January 1873.
8. Ibid. 7 November 1873. Broad Churchism was an Anglican faction hoping the Church would embrace all sorts of persuasions, from Methodism to Christian Socialism. High Churchism sympathised with the Oxford Movement, sought to relocate the Church of England within the Catholic Church and, in some cases, adopted rituals that outraged Christians opposed to Rome.
9. *Methodist Recorder* 12 May 1874.
10. Mark Guy Pearse (1892), *Sermons for Children*, London: Charles Kelly, pp. v-vii.
11. *Methodist Recorder* 10 December 1875.
12. Ibid. 7 January 1876.
13. Ibid. 3 March 1876. *The Sword and Trowel* had been produced monthly by Charles Spurgeon since 1865.
14. See Peter Hunt (1994), *An Introduction to Children's Literature*, Oxford: Oxford University Press; Humphrey Carpenter and Mari Prichard (1984), *Oxford Companion to Children's Literature*, Oxford: Oxford University Press.
15. Pearse (1892), op. cit., p. vi.
16. Ibid. pp. 125-6.
17. See Isaac Foot (1946), *Michael Verran of Callington and Thomas Carlyle*, London: Epworth Press. For another version of the story, see Mark Guy Pearse (1926), 'Thomas Carlyle and a Methodist Hero' in *The Ship Where Christ Was Captain*, London: Epworth Press/Sharp, pp. 132-142.
18. Keeble contributed articles for labourers to Hugh Price Hughes's *Methodist Times* for many years and in 1900 started the short-lived *Methodist Weekly* to advocate both a socialist and pacifist stance. See Christopher Oldstone-Moore (1999), *Hugh Price Hughes, Founder of a New Methodism, Conscience of a New Nonconformity*, Cardiff: University of Wales Press, pp. 313 and 333.
19. Mrs George Unwin and John Telford (1930), *Mark Guy Pearse, Preacher, Author, Artist*, London: Epworth Press/Sharp, pp. 44-5.
20. *Methodist Recorder,* 30 January 1874.
21. Ibid. 22 May 1874.
22. Ibid. 6 November 1874.
23. Ibid. 19 December 1873.
24. Ibid. 22 January 1875.
25. Ibid. 27 November 1874.
26. Jose Harris (1994), *Private lives, public spirit: Britain 1870–1914*, London: Penguin Books, pp. 157-162.
27. *Methodist Recorder,* 16 October 1874.
28. See Gillian Wagner (1979), *Barnardo*, London: Weidenfeld & Nicholson; Norman Wymer (1962), *Dr Barnardo*, London: Longmans.
29. *Methodist Recorder,* 11 December 1874.
30. Ibid. 25 October 1872.
31. William Kent (1938), *The Testament of a Victorian Youth: an autobiography*, London: Heath Cranton, p. 207.
32. *Methodist Recorder,* 28 August 1874.
33. See James F. Findlay (1969), *Dwight L. Moody: American Evangelist, 1837–1899*, Chicago: University of Chicago; J. C. Pollock (1963), *Moody without Sankey*, London: Hodder & Stoughton.
34. *Methodist Recorder,* 26 February 1875.
35. Hughes (1977), op. cit., p. 122.
36. *Methodist Recorder,* 28 May 1875.
37. *Spectator & Methodist Chronicle* [Melbourne], 1 May 1891.
38. Rev. Samuel Wesley (1887), *Memorials of Elizabeth Ann Wesley, 'The Soldiers Friend'*, 2nd edition, London: Woolmer, pp. 77-79. See also Mark Guy Pearse (1927), 'A Bullet for a Present' in *Methodist Recorder,* 6 January.

39. Unwin and Telford (1930), op. cit., pp. 67-68.
40. *Methodist Recorder,* 11 December 1874.
41. Ibid. 9 January 1930.
42. *West Briton,* 9 January 1930.
43. Currently in the possession of Margaret Walton, the Rev. Mark Guy Pearse's great, great niece.
44. Arthur Christopher Thynn (1832–1908) was appointed rector of Kilkampton in 1859 and later became Canon and Treasurer of Truro Cathedral.
45. The patient – a Mr Whalley – was probably the Gloucester merchant and banker James Whalley; his daughter was a Mrs Foote.
46. H. Hawken (1893), 'Wreckers and Methodists' [review of H. D. Lowry's first collection of stories], in *Wesleyan Methodist Magazine*, vol. 116, p. 923.
47. Rev. T. W. Slater (1927), 'Great Cornishman's fine record', in *Cornish Guardian,* 21 January.
48. Rev. T. W. Slater (1930), 'Mark Guy Pearse: An appreciation', in *Cornish Guardian* 9 January.
49. Arthur Lawrence (1899), 'The Rev. Mark Guy Pearse', in A. T. Quiller-Couch (ed), *The Cornish Magazine* vol. 2, Truro: Pollard, p. 245.
50. See [Mrs B. Hocking], 'A Cornish Artist-Engraver', in *Old Cornwall* vol. 2, no. 9, Summer, 1935, pp. 11-12.
51. *Methodist Recorder,* 9 July 1875.
52. Ibid.
53. Ibid. 17 August 1875.
54. *C[ornish] M[ethodist] C[hurch] R[ecord]*, op. cit., (1895)
55. Mark Guy Pearse [1886], *Some Aspects of the Blessed Life*, seventh thousand, London: T. Woolmer, pp. 228-9.
56. *Methodist Recorder,* 22 October 1875.
57. Ibid. 26 November 1875.
58. Ibid. 8 October 1875.
59. Ibid. 5 November 1875.
60. Ibid. 25 February 1876.
61. Ibid. 15 October 1875.
62. Ibid. 11 February 1876.
63. Ibid. 19 November 1875.
64. Rev. C. Ensor Walters, 'A Personal Tribute', newspaper cutting in the Shaw Methodist Collection, Courtney Library, Truro.
65. Unwin and Telford (1930), op. cit., pp. 77-78.
66. Mark Guy Pearse (1898), *The God of our pleasures*, 2nd edition, London: Nisbet, pp. v-vi.
67. Mark Guy Pearse (1906), *The Pretty Ways of Providence*, London: Horace Marshall & Son, pp. 203-4.
68. Unwin & Telford (1930), op. cit., p. 50.
69. Ibid. p. 138.
70. Lawrence (1899), op. cit., p. 247.
71. Ibid.
72. E. Ryerson Young (1930), 'Mark Guy Pearse in Canada – a Canadian's reminiscences', in *Methodist Magazine*, May 1930. Thomas Hudson Bainbridge (1842–1912) was born into a devout Methodist household, the second son of the founder of the famous Newcastle department store. He entered the family concern in 1859 and, with the early death of his brother Cuthbert in 1873, the conduct of the business fell to him and a younger brother, George. He took control of the firm in 1892, a year before Mark Guy Pearse dedicated *The Gospel for the Day* to him.
73. Unwin and Telford (1930), op. cit., pp. 78-79.
74. *Methodist Recorder,* 12 September 1873; General Register Index of Births, Marriages and Deaths in England & Wales 1837–1950.
75. *Methodist Recorder,* 26 May 1876.
76. Ibid. 27 October 1887.
77. Ibid. 25 July and 4 August 1876.
78. Ibid. 11 August 1876.

Chapter 7 *Bude, 1876–1877*

1. From its peak in 1856, Cornish copper mining had declined rapidly, the richer and more extensive deposits of Chile, South Australia, Michigan and, later, Montana making it impossible for the longer-worked Cornish mines to survive in the fiercely competitive world market. Dolcoath, in which Mark Guy Pearse senior held a large number of shares, was worked out for copper quite early on, but had successfully made the transition to tin. However, after a boom in the early 1870s, tin prices were, by 1873, falling and the following year forty-seven Cornish mines closed. 1875 proved to be

marginally worse, with a further forty-eight being abandoned, and in 1876 another thirty-seven closed. See John Rowe (1953) *Cornwall in the age of the Industrial Revolution*, Liverpool: Liverpool University Press, p. 323, and Philip Payton (1996) *Cornwall*, Fowey: Alexander Associates, pp. 231-232.

2. Mrs George Unwin and John Telford (1930) *Mark Guy Pearse, Preacher, Author, Artist*, London: Epworth Press/J. Alfred Sharp, p. 50.
3. Ibid, p. 51.
4. Ibid.
5. Ibid, p. 52.
6. Arthur Lawrence (1899) 'The Rev. Mark Guy Pearse' in A. T. Quiller-Couch (ed), *The Cornish Magazine* Vol. 2, Truro: Pollard, p. 246.
7. Unwin and Telford (1930), op. cit., p. 53.
8. Ibid, p. 81.
9. [Mark Guy Pearse] (1879) 'Bass-fishing at Bude' in *The Boy's Own Paper*, London: Religious Tract Society, p. 212.
10. Ibid.
11. Clive Carter (1978) *Cornish Shipwrecks: the north coast*, London: Pan, p. 10.
12. Unwin and Telford (1930), op. cit., pp. 54-55.
13. *Methodist Recorder*, 9 March 1877.
14. 'The Rev. Mark Guy Pearse', *C[ornish] M[ethodist] C[hurch] R[ecord]* December 1895; newspaper cutting in the Shaw Methodist Collection, Courtney Library, Truro.
15. 'Mark Guy Pearse Memories' in *Methodist Recorder*, 16 January 1930.
16. Unwin and Telford (1930), op. cit., p. 55.
17. George Herbert Schofield (1922) *The History of Methodism in Stratton and Bude*, Bude: [G. H. Schofield], pp. 21-22.
18. *C[ornish] M[ethodist] C[hurch] R[ecord]* (1895), op. cit.
19. *Cornish and Devon Post*, Launceston, 3 August 1878. This material formed the basis for 'Early Methodism in Cornwall' which was published in *The Sunday Magazine*, 1880, pp. 24-30, 260-264 and 415-420.

Chapter 8 *Launceston 1877–1880*

1. M. Guy Pearse (n. d.), 'It was all through the Foot and Mouth Disease', in *The Man Who Spoiled the Music and other stories*, London: Epworth, p. 134.
2. Mrs George Unwin and John Telford (1930) *Mark Guy Pearse, Preacher, Author, Artist*, London: Epworth Press/J. Alfred Sharp, p. 141.
3. *Cornish & Devon Post,* 10 January 1891.
4. H. Spencer Toy [1964], *The Methodist Church at Launceston*, Launceston.
5. *East Cornwall Times,* 29 September 1877.
6. *Cornish & Devon Post,* 16 February 1878.
7. Ibid. 23 March 1878.
8. Dr F. L. Wiseman (1942), 'Mark Guy Pearse: some centenary reminiscences', in *Methodist Recorder,* 11 June.
9. *Cornish & Devon Post,* 4 January 1879.
10. Ibid. 10 January 1880.
11. Ibid. 25 May 1878.
12. Ibid. 8 June 1878.
13. Ibid. 20 July 1878.
14. Ibid. 20 December 1878.
15. Ibid. 14 June 1879.
16. Ibid. 23 August 1879.
17. Ibid. 12 June 1880.
18. Ibid. 18 May 1878.
19. Ibid. 14 and 28 February 1880.
20. Ibid. 21 February 1880.
21. Ibid. 26 July 1879.
22. Ibid. 19 July 1879.
23. Ibid. 26 July 1879.
24. Ibid. 23 November 1878.
25. Ibid. 19 July 1879.
26. Ibid. 29 March and 1 November 1879; 20 March 1880.
27. Ibid. 31 May 1879.
28. Herbert W. Bolitho (1947), *Truly Rural: lights and shadows on the history of North Hill Circuit (Cornwall) of the Methodist Church 1743–1946*, p. 40; Index of Cornish Biography, Murdoch House Adult Education Centre, Redruth.
29. Thomas Shaw (1967), *A History of Cornish Methodism*, Truro: D. Bradford Barton, pp. 114-5.
30. *Cornish & Devon Post,* 1 June 1878.
31. Ibid. 22 March 1879.
32. Unwin and Telford (1930), op. cit., p. 185.
33. *Cornish & Devon Post*, 20 July 1878.
34. Ibid. 21 June and 5 July 1879.
35. Sidney O. Dixon (1969), *The Road to Unity in Cornish Methodism*, Cornish Methodist Historical Association

Occasional Publication 15, pp. 8-10.
36. *Spectator and Methodist Chronicle* [Melbourne], 27 March 1891.
37. Mark Guy Pearse (1908), *The Prophet's Raven*, New York: Eaton & Mains, p. 4.
38. *Cornish & Devon Post,* 12 July 1879.
39. Ibid. 29 March 1879.
40. Ibid. 18 May 1878.
41. Unwin and Telford (1930), op. cit., p. 56.
42. Ibid. p. 184.
43. *West Briton,* 10 October 1910; Index of Cornish Biography.
44. Although the Wesleyans helped found Dunheved College, it was not, like Truro, an official Methodist School. Information per John Probert.
45. *Cornish & Devon Post,* 21 September 1878 and 2 August 1879. He continued to be a Director after leaving Launceston in 1880 and was still one in November 1924.
46. Ibid. 20 December 1879.
47. 'Whispers & Echoes: Memories of 'Mark Guy'...', *Cornish Guardian,* 9 January 1930.
48. *Cornish & Devon Post,* 18 October 1879.
49. Unwin and Telford (1930), op. cit., p. 187.
50. Ibid. p. 59.
51. *Launceston Examiner,* 1 June 1891.
52. *Cornish & Devon Post,* 27 April 1878.
53. Mark Guy Pearse (1926), *The Ship Where Christ was Captain*, London: Epworth, p. 16.
54. Henry D. Rack (1983), 'Wesleyan Methodism 1849–1902' in *A History of the Methodist Church in Great Britain*, vol. 3, London: Epworth Press.
55. For more information concerning the Teetotal Methodists in Cornwall, see Shaw (1967), op. cit., and Dr Oliver Beckerlegge [1960–1], *Free Methodism in Cornwall*, Truro: Cornish Methodist Historical Association Occasional Publication 2.
56. Shaw (1967), op. cit., pp. 80-81. Although the Band of Hope movement had had its beginnings in Leeds in 1847, it was not until thirty years later that Conference officially adopted the temperance cause and established official guidelines for both these and adult temperance societies.
57. W. J. Townsend, H. B. Workman and George Eayrs (eds.) (1909), *A New History of Methodism* vol. 1, London, p. 529.
58. Unwin and Telford (1930), op. cit., p. 60.
59. *New Zealand Methodist,* 25 July 1891.
60. *West Briton,* 20 December 1888. *The Methodist Temperance Magazine*, which was founded by Garrett in 1868, was from 1884 edited by Hugh Price Hughes. Garrett later became President of the Wesleyan Methodist Conference.
61. In Pearse, [n. d.], op. cit., p. 97.
62. Mark Guy Pearse (1877), *John Tregenoweth: his mark*, New York: Nelson & Phillips, p. 32.
63. Mark Guy Pearse(1882), *Simon Jasper*, London: Woolmer, p. 40.
64. Unwin and Telford (1930), op. cit., pp. 184-5.
65. Ibid. p. 140.
66. Letters to the author from Margaret Rawling of Leamington Spa.
67. Pearse (1882), op. cit., pp. 2-4.
68. Ibid. p. 8.
69. Ibid., pp. 14-15. 'Simon Jasper' – together with 'Frankey Vivian' and 'Daniel Quorm' – was arranged, too, as a service of sacred song by John Burnham; see *Methodist Recorder,* 31 October 1884.
70. *Methodist Recorder* 31 July 1885.
71. Ibid. 17 July 1885.
72. Ibid. 31 July 1885. In *Hard Times*, Dickens made Thomas Gradgrind put so much faith in facts and statistics that he suppresses the imaginative sides of his children's natures.
73. Ibid. 7 August 1885.
74. Ibid. 14 August 1885.
75. '90 Years ago November 24, 1883', *Cornish & Devon Post,* 24 November 1973.
76. *Cornish & Devon Post,* 5 June 1886.
77. All were subsequently reprinted in *Cornish Stories* in 1883.
78. *Cornish & Devon Post,* 21 December 1878; Mark Guy Pearse (1883), *Cornish Stories*, fourteenth thousand, London: Kelly, pp. 141-175.
79. Lawrence (1899), op. cit., p. 245.
80. *Cornish & Devon Post,* 12 October 1878.
81. Ibid. 8 November 1879.
82. Ibid. 20 March 1880.
83. *Western Morning News,* [6] May 1961.
84. W. Gregory Harris (1923), *West Country Volk*, London: John Lane/The Bodley Head, p. 49.
85. *West Briton,* 9 January 1930.

86. *Cornish & Devon Post,* 31 July 1880.
87. Pearse, (1882), op. cit., pp. 98 and 101.
88. Ibid. p. 158.

Chapter 9 *Bristol 1880–1886*

1. For further information see C. M. MacInnes and W. F. Whittard (eds.) (1955) *Bristol and its adjoining counties,* Bristol: British Association for the Advancement of Science, Local Executive Committee; Brian S. Smith and Elizabeth Ralph (1972) *A History of Bristol and Gloucestershire*, Beaconsfield: Darwen Finlayson.
2. *Methodist Recorder* 7 October 1881.
3. Ibid. 11 November 1881. In MacInnes and Whittard (1955) a figure of 15,363 or 14% is quoted for all the Methodist denominations, although in this source school children are not included.
4. Henry J. Spear and J. W. Arrowsmith (eds.) (1884) *Arrowsmith's Dictionary of Bristol*, Bristol: Arrowsmith, p. 269.
5. 'Victoria Methodist Church, Bristol – past, present and future' in *Victoria Methodist Church*, Bristol, www.compulink.co.uk/~victoria.htm, accessed 13 October 2005.
6. On the night of the 1881 Census, the household also included Mary Elizabeth Palmer, a 23-year-old cook-cum-servant from South Petherwin, and Emma Fletcher, a 20-year-old housemaid from Houghton Regis, Bedfordshire. Having joined the family as a 17-year-old, Miss Palmer became a greatly loved and trusted member of the household, moving with them from circuit to circuit until her retirement in 1927. See Mrs George Unwin and John Telford (1930) *Mark Guy Pearse, Preacher, Author, Artist*, London: Epworth Press/J. Alfred Sharp, p. 87.
7. *Methodist Recorder*, 19 October 1883.
8. From figures given at annual meetings reported in the *Methodist Recorder*, 2 June 1882 and 22 May 1885.
9. *Methodist Recorder*, 29 April 1881.
10. *West Briton,* 25 and 28 July 1881; *Methodist Recorder*, 29 July 1881.
11. *Methodist Recorder*, 13 October 1882.
12. Ibid. 20 January 1882.
13. Unwin and Telford (1930), op. cit., pp. 81-82.
14. Emmeline Pethick-Lawrence (1938) *My part in a changing world*, London: Gollancz, pp. 99-102.
15. Letter to Connie Ries, née Tilley, dated 1 February 1927, in the author's collection.
16. *Methodist Recorder*, 7 October 1881.
17. Unwin and Telford (1930), op. cit., p. 201.
18. See Derek R. Williams (1987) 'Methodism in Treswithian, 1743–1977' in *Old Cornwall*, vol. x, no. 4, Spring, p. 194.
19. Rev. C. Ensor Walters, 'A Personal Tribute', newspaper cutting in the Shaw Methodist Collection, Courtney Library, Truro.
20. Unwin and Telford (1930), op. cit., p. 187.
21. Thomas Shaw (1967), *A History of Cornish Methodism*, Truro: D. Bradford Barton, p. 120.
22. As a member of the London Mission Committee and a social purity activist, it was the Rev. R. W. Allen who would later suggest to Hugh Price Hughes that the wealthy West End would be an appropriate target for evangelism. See Christopher Oldstone-Moore (1999), *Hugh Price Hughes, Founder of a New Methodism, Conscience of a New Nonconformity*, Cardiff: University of Wales Press, pp. 153-154.
23. *Methodist Recorder*, 18 November 1881.
24. *West Briton*, 27 and 31 October, 3 and 10 November 1881; *Methodist Recorder*, 4 and 18 November 1881.
25. *Methodist Recorder*, 16 February 1883.
26. Mark Guy Pearse (1898) 'The New Weapon' in Mark Guy Pearse and Arthur E. Gregory (eds.) *The Preacher's Magazine*, vol. ix, London: Kelly, p. 57.
27. Mark Guy Pearse (1893) *The Gospel for the Day*, London: Kelly, p. 113.
28. Mark Guy Pearse (1889) *Short Talks for the Times*, London: Kelly, p. 50.
29. Mark Guy Pearse [1901] *The Christianity of Jesus Christ: Is It Ours?* Cincinnati: Jennings and Pye, pp. 121-122. See also Unwin and Telford (1930), op. cit., pp. 92-93.
30. *Methodist Recorder*, 19 October 1883.
31. Unwin and Telford (1930), op. cit., pp. 57-59.

32. Ibid, p. 59.
33. *Methodism in 1879. Impressions of the Wesleyan Church and its Ministers. A Review suggested by the Thanksgiving Fund*, London: Haughton & Co., p. 52.
34. *Methodist Recorder*, 5 May 1882.
35. Ibid, 12 November 1880.
36. Ibid, 2 November 1883.
37. Unwin and Telford (1930), op. cit., p. 110.
38. *Methodist Recorder*, 14 December 1883. One first-hand account of the impact of *Thoughts on Holiness* is to be found in Unwin and Telford (1930), pp. 108-109. Another was published under the heading 'Far Reaching Influence' in the *Cornish and Devon Post*, 24 April 1886.
39. *Victoria Methodist Church*, Bristol, op. cit. Mark Guy Pearse contributed an article entitled 'Portland Street Chapel, Bristol' to the *Wesleyan Methodist Magazine*, July and September 1884. See also A. J. Lambert (1929) *The Chapel on the Hill*, Bristol: St Stephen's Press.
40. *Methodist Recorder*, 5 January 1883.
41. Ibid, 19 October 1883; Spear and Arrowsmith (1884), op. cit., pp. 137-138.
42. *Methodist Recorder*, 7 September and 9 October 1883.
43. Ibid, 5 October 1883.
44. Ibid, 19 October 1883.
45. Ibid, 18 April 1884. This was one of a series of revival missions that Hughes, together with Thomas Cook, conducted in 1883 and 1884.
46. Ibid, 27 March 1885.
47. Ibid, 12 March 1886.
48. Ibid, 28 May 1886.
49. Spear and Arrowsmith (1884), op. cit., p. 274. The Church of England Temperance Society was founded in 1862 as the first church-affiliated temperance organisation.
50. *Methodist Recorder*, 3 March 1882.
51. *Cornish Times*, 29 August 1885, reproducing a sketch which had appeared in that week's *Christian Age*.
52. *Methodist Recorder*, 28 March 1884.
53. Ibid, 19 October and 21 December 1883.
54. Ibid, 19 December 1884.
55. Ibid, 22 May 1885.
56. Mark Guy Pearse [n.d.], *The Man Who Spoiled the Music and other stories*, London: Epworth Press, p. 42.
57. *Methodist Recorder*, 25 and 29 July 1884.
58. The Rev. Charles Kelly (1833–1911) was President of Conference, 1889–1890, President of the National Council of Evangelical Free Churches, 1900–1901 and Connexional Book Steward for over 20 years in the 1890s and early 1900s.
59. *Methodist Recorder*, 4 August 1885. Kingswood was originally founded by John Wesley in Bristol.
60. Ibid, 31 July 1885.
61. Muriel Sara (1974) *More about Cornwall and My Cornish Friends*, Hayle: [Muriel Sara], pp. 47-48. The story 'Becky Murgatroyd speaks her mind' first appeared in the *Methodist Recorder* before being collected for publication in *The Orthodox Devil*.
62. *Methodist Recorder*, 26 September 1884 and 11 September 1885; G. C. Boase (1890) *Collectanea Cornubiensis*, Truro: Netherton and Worth, p. 691.
63. Helen G. McKenny (1978) *A City Road Diary: the record of three years in Victorian London*, Bognor Regis: World Methodist Historical Society Publications, p. 6.
64. *Methodist Recorder*, 2 October 1885.
65. *Cornish Times*, 3 October 1885.
66. Mark Guy Pearse [1907] *Bridgetstow*, London: Culley, p. 13.
67. See Thomas Shaw (comp.) (1991) *A Methodist Guide to Cornwall*, Methodist Publishing House, pp. 8-9; Shaw (1967), op. cit., pp. 26 and 110; Thomas Shaw (1953) *Methodism in Bridgerule 1800–1953*, Bridgerule: Thomas Shaw, pp. 21-26. Of course, in this as in his other works of 'fiction', Mark Guy Pearse mixes settings, events and personalities to suit his purpose.
68. Pearse [1907], op. cit., pp. 130-131.
69. W. Gregory Harris (1931) ' "Parson Hawker" of Morwenstow' in *Old Cornwall*, vol. ii, no. 1, Summer, p. 19; Thomas Shaw, handwritten note in Shaw Collection, Courtney Library, Truro.
70. Cited in C. E. Byles (1905) *The Life and Letters of R. S. Hawker*, London: J. Lane/Bodley Head, p. 156.
71. Pearse [1907], op. cit., pp. 29-30.
72. Byles (1905), op. cit., p. 155.
73. Pearse [1907], op. cit., p. 55.
74. Ibid, p. 67.

75. Unwin and Telford (1930), op. cit., p. 139.
76. *Methodist Recorder*, 16 April 1886; *Cornish and Devon Post*, 8, 15 and 29 May 1886.
77. R. M. Heard [1985] *Methodism in Kilkampton*, p. 18.
78. W. Gregory Harris (1923) *West-Country Volk: sketches in prose and verse...*, London: J. Lane/Bodley Head, p. 49.
79. Unwin and Telford (1930), op. cit., pp. 186-187.
80. *Methodist Recorder*, 4 April 1884.
81. Lambert (1929), op. cit., p. 100.
82. Unwin and Telford (1930), op. cit., p. 64.
83. *Methodist Recorder*, 1 January 1886.
84. *Methodist Times*, 19 March 1885, cited in K. S. Inglis (1963) *Churches and the Working Classes in Victorian England*, London: Routledge and Kegan Paul, p. 70.
85. Malcolm Pearce and Geoffrey Stewart (1992) *British Political History 1867–1990*, London: Routledge, p. 50.
86. *Methodist Recorder*, 12 and 19 February 1886.
87. J. A Robinson (ed.) (1902) *Hugh P. Hughes as We Knew Him*, London: Horace Marshall, pp. 27-28.

Chapter 10 *The West London Mission 1886–1903*

1. Philip S. Bagwell's excellent *Outcast London – a Christian Response; The West London Mission of the Methodist Church 1887–1987*, London: Epworth Press, 1987, forms the basis for much of the background to this chapter.
2. J. Gregory Mantle (1901) *Hugh Price Hughes*, London: Partridge, pp. 99-100.
3. Ibid, pp. 96-97.
4. Ibid, p. 97. For a definitive study of the man whom David Lloyd George described as 'the greatest spiritual force my race has produced for a generation', see Christopher Oldstone-Moore (1999) *Hugh Price Hughes, Founder of a New Methodism, Conscience of a New Nonconformity*, Cardiff: University Of Wales Press.
5. Mantle (1901), op. cit., p. 21.
6. *Methodist Times*, 12 March 1885, cited in Bagwell (1987), p. 8. During his years as superintendent of the West London Mission and leader of the Forward Movement, Hughes would fight hard for the extension of pastoral appointments.
7. Katherine Price Hughes (1945) *The Story of my Life*, London: Epworth Press, p, 64, cited in Bagwell (1987), p. 10.
8. Bagwell (1987), op. cit., p. 7. Oldstone-Moore (1999), op. cit., pp. 123-126.
9. Mantle (1901), p. 83.
10. *Methodist Times*, 19 March 1885, cited in Bagwell (1987), p. 143. See also Oldstone-Moore (1999), pp. 135-181, for the beginnings and development of The Forward Movement.
11. *Methodist Times*, 30 July 1885, cited in Bagwell (1987), p. 8.
12. Minutes of Conference, July 1885, p. 228, cited in Bagwell (1987), p. 9.
13. *Methodist Recorder*, 19 February 1886.
14. J. Armitage Robinson (ed.) (1902) *Hugh Price Hughes as We Knew Him*, London: Horace Marshall, pp. 24-26. J. Ernest Clapham was chairman of the London Mission Committee.
15. This was quite possibly at Oxford on 13 September, 1883.
16. Robinson (1902), op. cit., pp. 27-28.
17. *Spectator and Methodist Chronicle*, Melbourne, 10 April 1891.
18. Methodist Archives and Research Centre, Manchester.
19. Dorothea Price Hughes (1904) *The Life of Hugh Price Hughes*, London: Hodder and Stoughton, p. 198.
20. Robinson (1902), op. cit., p. 28.
21. Mantle (1901), op. cit., p. 110.
22. Mrs George Unwin and John Telford (1930) *Mark Guy Pearse, Preacher, Author, Artist*, London: Epworth Press/J. Alfred Sharp, p. 147.
23. *Methodist Recorder*, 7 August 1886.
24. The Rev. M. G. Pearse's sermons were a regular feature of the *Methodist Times* after 1887.
25. *Methodist Recorder*, 7 August 1886.
26. Ibid, 24 September 1886.
27. *Newcastle Daily Chronicle*, 3 November 1886.
28. Ibid, 4 November 1886.
29. *Birmingham Daily Post*, 19 January 1887.
30. *Methodist Recorder*, 17 March 1887.
31. *Manchester Guardian*, 16 March 1887.

32. *Methodist Recorder*, 31 March 1887.
33. West Central Mission, *First Annual Report*, 1888, p. 2, cited in Bagwell (1987), p. 15.
34. Helen G. McKenny (1978) *A City Road Diary: the record of three years in Victorian London*, Bognor Regis: World Methodist Historical Society Publications, p. 76.
35. *Methodist Recorder*, 27 October 1887.
36. Ibid.
37. Ibid.
38. This was how Hugh Price Hughes described the service that he saw as being directed at those who, though already converted, were seeking saintliness and were attracted by the 'peculiar lucidity and sweetness with which Mr Pearse expounds the Scriptural doctrine of holiness'. Hugh Price Hughes, in West Central Mission, *First Annual Report*, 1888, pp. 4-5, cited in Oldstone-Moore (1999), p. 166.
39. Mark Guy Pearse [1893] *Naaman the Syrian*, London: Kelly, pp. vii-viii.
40. Charles Booth (1902) *Life and Labour of the People of London*, vol. 2, London: Macmillan, p. 195, cited in Bagwell (1987), p. 17.
41. West Central Mission (1888), p. 5, cited in Bagwell (1987), p.17.
42. Emmeline Pethick-Lawrence (1938) *My part in a changing world*, London: Gollancz, p. 104; William H. Lax (1937) *Lax, his Book: The Autobiography of Lax of Poplar*, London: Epworth, p. 167.
43. Unwin and Telford (1930), op. cit., p. 150.
44. *Methodist Recorder*, 3 November 1887.
45. Bagwell (1987), op. cit., p. 22.
46. Mantle (1901), op. cit., p. 116.
47. *Tasmanian Mail*, Hobart, 13 June 1891.
48. Mark Guy Pearse (1889) *Short Talks for the Times*, London: Kelly, p. 47.
49. *Spectator and Methodist Chronicle*, Melbourne, 8 May 1891.
50. *Methodist Recorder*, 27 October 1887.
51. Mark Guy Pearse [1891] *Jesus Christ and the People*, London: Kelly, p. 216.
52. Mark Guy Pearse (1903) *The Gentleness of Jesus and other sermons*, new edition, London: Horace Marshall, pp. 38 and 118.
53. Unwin and Telford (1930), op. cit., p. 151.
54. *Methodist Recorder*, 27 October 1887.
55. Mark Guy Pearse [1901] *The Christianity of Jesus Christ: Is It Ours?* Cincinnati: Jennings and Pye, p. 54.
56. *Methodist Recorder*, 3 November 1887.
57. *Wesleyan Methodist Magazine*, November 1887, pp. 871-872.
58. Mantle (1901), op. cit., p. 154.
59. The Rev. Mark Guy Pearse', *C[ornish] M[ethodist] C[hurch] R[ecord]* December 1895; newspaper cutting in the Shaw Methodist Collection, Courtney Library, Truro.
60. Hughes (1904), op. cit., p. 199.
61. Silas K. Hocking (1923) *My Book of Memory*, London: Cassell, p. 191.
62. Rev. C. Ensor Walters, 'A Personal Tribute', newspaper cutting in the Shaw Methodist Collection, Courtney Library, Truro.
63. *West Briton*, 4 March 1937.
64. Mantle (1901), op. cit., p. 157.
65. Walters, op. cit.
66. Unwin and Telford (1930), op. cit., p. 147.
67. Ibid, p. 153.
68. Walters, op. cit.
69. Lax (1937), op. cit., p. 167.
70. Robinson (1902), op. cit., pp. 28-29.
71. Ibid, p. 24.
72. Ibid. p. 26.
73. Ibid, pp. 29-30.
74. Bagwell (1987), op. cit., p. 15.
75. *Times* 2 January 1930. In fact, his support for them did not cease when he officially left the Mission in 1903. In the financial statement which he presented at its nineteenth annual meeting three years later, Mr J. Bamford Slack revealed that the Rev. Mark Guy Pearse had contributed £600 to the Sisterhood. See *Methodist Recorder*, 17 May 1906.
76. Mantle (1901), op. cit., p. 135.
77. Bagwell (1987), op. cit., p. 44.
78. Pearse [1891], op. cit., pp. 19-20.
79. Pearse [1901], op. cit., p. 120.
80. Bagwell (1987), op. cit., p. 29. For a comprehensive overview of the Sisters' work, see chapter 4.
81. *Spectator and Methodist Chronicle*, 8 May 1891.
82. *Tasmanian Mail*, 13 June 1891.
83. West London Mission (1890), *Annual Report*, p. 7, cited in Bagwell (1987), p. 25.
84. Pearse [1891], op. cit., p. 21.

85. Mark Guy Pearse (1891) *Elijah, the Man of God*, London: Kelly, pp. 72-73.
86. W. McG. Eagar (1953) *Making Men: the History of Boys' Clubs and Related Movements in Great Britain*, London: University of London Press, pp. 228-229; Unwin and Telford (1930), op. cit., p. 176.
87. Vera Brittain (1963) *Pethick-Lawrence, A portrait*, London: Allen and Unwin, p. 27.
88. Pethick-Lawrence (1938), op. cit., pp. 104-107.
89. Unwin and Telford (1930), op. cit., p. 162; *Spectator and Methodist Chronicle*, 11 April 1891.
90. *Spectator and Methodist Chronicle*, 8 May 1891.
91. Ibid.
92. Bagwell (1987), op. cit., p. 32.
93. Unwin and Telford (1930), op. cit., p. 167.
94. Arthur Lawrence (1899) 'The Rev. Mark Guy Pearse' in A. T. Quiller-Couch (ed), *The Cornish Magazine*, vol. 2, Truro: Pollard, pp. 250-251.
95. Unwin and Telford (1930), op. cit., pp. 168-169. Mark Guy Pearse regularly drew such seascapes on the front endpapers of the books that he sold at lectures or in appreciation for the hospitality he enjoyed in innumerable Methodist homes.
96. Mark Guy Pearse [1899] *What the Flowers Did*, London: Horace Marshall, pp. 11-13.
97. An Oxford merchant and a member of Hugh Price Hughes's congregation whom he had persuaded to become a local preacher, Nix accompanied him to Brixton in 1884 and became a full-time lay revivalist. See Oldstone-Moore (1899).
98. Pearse [1899], op. cit., p. 20.
99. Unwin and Telford (1930), op. cit., p. 152. It was at the annual meeting of the YMCA in April 1883 that Hughes first 'argue[d] for Christian Audacity on the part of the Christian young men who heard him, because Christians were the greatest revolutionaries in the world... It was the Christian's business to turn the world upside down because it was wrong side up...' See *Methodist Recorder*, 1 May 1883.
100. See Doreen Yarwood (1983) *Science and the home*, London: Batsford, p. 150.
101. *Tasmanian Mail*, 13 June 1891.
102. West Central Mission (1888), op. cit., pp. 10-12, cited in Bagwell (1987), p. 18.
103. Robinson (1902), op. cit., pp. 24-25.
104. Letter from 11, Bedford Place, dated 1 October 1894, in the author's collection.
105. *Royal Cornwall Gazette*, 17 September 1886. According to John Probert, though, the 1885 Camborne Plan suggests otherwise. See J. C. C. Probert (1978) *The Worship and Devotion of Cornish Methodism*, Redruth: John C. C. Probert, p. 86.
106. *West Briton*, 7 September 1899.
107. *Methodist Recorder*, 22 August 1889.
108. Notebook in the possession of Mark Guy Pearse's great, great niece, Margaret Walton, who provided the transcription.
109. Unwin and Telford (1930), op. cit., pp. 15-16.
110. *Isle of Wight County Press*, 17 August 1889. *Royal Cornwall Gazette*, 22 August 1889.
111. Robinson (1902), op. cit., p. 31.
112. John Kent (1978) *Holding the Fort: studies in Victorian Revivalism*, London: Epworth, pp.302-303. See also Oldstone-Moore (1999), pp. 183-202.
113. Sir Henry S. Lunn (1918) *Chapters from my life*, London: Cassell, pp. 86-87 and 101.
114. Oldstone-Moore (1999), op. cit., p. 220.
115. *Methodist Recorder*, 8 June 1893. Sir Henry Simpson Lunn (1859–1939) pursued the interest in travel that the organisation of these conferences kindled in him and in 1909 founded the travel company which still bears his name.
116. Pethick-Lawrence (1938), op. cit., p. 102.
117. Mark Guy Pearse [1896] 'To South Africa and Back IX' in *The Methodist Churchman*, p. 196.
118. Oldstone-Moore (1999), op. cit., pp. 311-313.
119. Philip Payton [1992] *The Making of Modern Cornwall*, Redruth: Truran, p. 153.
120. Stephen Koss (ed.) (1973) *The Pro-Boers*, Chicago and London: University of Chicago Press, pp. 67-68 and 81; G. W. Daniels (1926) *George Unwin: a memorial lecture*, Manchester: Manchester University Press; Payton [1992], op. cit., p. 153. Pethick-Lawrence (1938), op. cit., pp. 121-122. Oldstone-Moore (1999), op. cit., p. 313.

121. *Methodist Recorder*, 18 July 1901.
122. Ibid, 25 July 1901.
123. Ibid, 18 July 1901.
124. Ibid, 12 September 1901.
125. Hughes (1904), op. cit., p. 641.
126. *Methodist Recorder*, 10 October and 14 November 1901.
127. Ibid, 27 November 1902. Robinson (1902), op. cit., p. 30.
128. *Methodist Recorder*, 20 November 1902.
129. Ibid, 27 November 1902. Robinson (1902), op. cit., pp. 30-31.
130. Both in Unwin and Telford (1930) and in the *Wesleyan Methodist Magazine* vol. 126, 1903, the Rev. John Telford states that Mark Guy was planning to visit the West Indies, but North America was his eventual destination in 1903.
131. E. W. Walters (1937) *Ensor Walters and the London he loves*, London: Epworth, p. 51.
132. *Methodist Recorder*, 21 May 1903.
133. Muriel Sara (1974) *More about Cornwall and My Cornish Friends*, Hayle: [Muriel Sara], p. 49.
134. Unwin and Telford (1930), op. cit., p. 161.
135. Ibid, pp. 161-162.
136. Mark Guy Pearse (1898) 'London: A Sermon for Citizen Sunday' in Pearse and Gregory (eds.), *The Preacher's Magazine*, p. 490.
137. *West Briton*, 7 September 1899.
138. *Cornish Post and Mining News*, 1 November 1924.
139. Unwin and Telford (1930), op. cit., p. 173.
140. W. J. Dawson (1891 and 1892) 'Mark Guy Pearse' in The Young Man, pp. 402-404 and *The Bible Christian Magazine*, pp. 455-458.
141. Unwin and Telford (1930), op. cit., pp. 155-156.

Chapter 11 *North America 1887 and 1903–1904*

1. John Rowe (1974) *The Hard-Rock Men: Cornish Immigrants and the North American Mining Frontier*, Liverpool: Liverpool University Press, p. 17.
2. A. C. Todd (1967) *The Cornish Miner in America*, Truro: Bradford Barton, pp. 24-25.
3. Cited in *The Spectator and Methodist Chronicle*, Melbourne, 27 March 1891.
4. See James F. Findlay (1969) *Dwight L. Moody: American Evangelist 1837–1899*, Chicago: University of Chicago, and J. C. Pollock (1963) *Moody without Sankey*, London: Hodder and Stoughton.
5. Mrs George Unwin and John Telford (1930) *Mark Guy Pearse, Preacher, Author, Artist*, London: Epworth Press/J. Alfred Sharp, pp. 206-207.
6. Egerton Ryerson Young (1890) *By Canoe and Dog-Train among the Cree and Salteaux Indians... with an introduction by Mark Guy Pearse*, London: Kelly, pp. 1-2.
7. E. Ryerson Young (1930) 'Mark Guy Pearse in Canada: a Canadian's reminiscences' in *Methodist Magazine*, May, pp. 286-289. The story of the rogue wolf later found its way into Pearse's short story 'Dick Brimacombe's Wedding' which is set in the backwoods of Canada in the 1840s. It was published in *The Pretty Ways of Providence and other stories*, London: Horace Marshall, [1906].
8. Young (1930), op. cit., p. 286.
9. Ibid, p. 288.
10. Unwin and Telford (1930), op. cit., p. 191.
11. Mark Guy Pearse [1891] *Jesus Christ and the people*, London: Kelly, p. 130.
12. *Christian Guardian*, Toronto, cited in *The Methodist Recorder*, 26 May 1887. The Methodist Church of Canada was formed in 1874 by the amalgamation of the Union of the Wesleyan Methodist Church of Canada, the New Connexion Methodist Church and the Wesleyan Methodist Church of Eastern British America. Nine years later it joined the Methodist Episcopal Church of Canada and the Primitive Methodist and Bible Christian Churches of Canada to form The Methodist Church.
13. Unwin and Telford (1930), op. cit., p. 207.
14. Ibid.
15. Ibid, p. 209.
16. W. J. Dawson (1891 and 1892) 'Mark Guy Pearse' in *The Young Man*, pp. 402-404 and *The Bible Christian Magazine*, August, pp. 455-458.
17. Unwin and Telford (1930), op. cit., p. 209.

18. J. Wilbur Chapman (1900) *The Life and Work of D. L. Moody*, Philadelphia: Winston, online edition, www.biblebelievers.com/moody/, accessed 23 October 2005.
19. Unwin and Telford (1930), op. cit., p. 210.
20. Ibid, p. 211.
21. Mark Guy Pearse, 'Old Apollos' in Mark Guy Pearse (1906), *The Pretty Ways o' Providence, and other stories*, London: H. Marshall, p. 165.
22. *The Gazette*, Montreal, 13 June 1887.
23. Unwin and Telford (1930), op. cit., pp. 211-212.
24. *Christian Guardian*, Toronto, 29 June 1887, cited in *The Methodist Recorder*, 21 July 1887.
25. Unwin and Telford (1930), op. cit., pp. 171-172.
26. For full reports of his services, see the *London Advertizer*, Ontario, 10 and 12 October 1903 and the *London Free Press*, 12 October 1903.
27. Young (1930), op. cit., p. 287.
28. Unwin and Telford (1930), op. cit., pp. 219 and 171.
29. *San Francisco Chronicle*, 18 January 1904.
30. *The Institute Tie* [Journal of the Moody Bible Institute], May 1904, pp. 304-305.
31. Unwin and Telford (1930), op. cit., p. 221.
32. Ibid, p. 219.
33. *New York Times*, 18 April 1904.
34. *Methodist Recorder*, 9 June 1904.
35. Ibid, 23 June 1904.

Chapter 12 *Australia and New Zealand 1891*

1. Mark Guy Pearse (1882) *Daniel Quorm and his religious notions*, 2nd series, London: Woolmer, pp. 42-43.
2. *Cornish & Devon Post and East Cornwall Times*, 10 January 1891.
3. *Methodist Recorder*, 15 January 1891.
4. Ibid 15, 22 and 29 January 1891.
5. *Spectator & Methodist Chronicle*, Melbourne 20 February 1891. Mrs George Unwin and John Telford (1930) *Mark Guy Pearse, Preacher, Author, Artist*, London: Epworth Press/J. Alfred Sharp, p. 212.
6. Philip J. Payton (1984) *The Cornish Miner in Australia (Cousin Jack Down Under)*, Redruth: Truran, pp. 52 and 69. As Payton points out, in much the same way that Methodism provided both emotional fulfillment and practical help for the Cornish back home, so the success and strength of religious non-conformity, particularly Methodism, in early South Australia was in no small measure a result of the extensive migration from Cornwall.
7. The Rev. G. E. Rowe became the first President of the Western Australian Methodist Conference and was described as a man who could tell a Cornish story exceptionally well. Indeed, Frances Pearse records that when on one occasion her father was suddenly unwell and unable to keep an engagement, Rowe himself went and delivered the lecture without the aid of notes. See Payton (1984), p. 185 and Unwin and Telford (1930), p. 213.
8. *The Bunyip*, Gawler 6 March 1891. From small beginnings as a blacksmith and wheelwright in 1848, James Martin from Stithians developed his engineering foundry to the point where, at his death in 1899, it had a workforce of 700 constructing some of the largest mine engines ever built in Australia.
9. Mark Guy Pearse (1896) 'To South Africa and back IV' in *Methodist Churchman*, Capetown, p. 86.
10. Unwin and Telford (1930), op. cit., p. 213.
11. *South Australian Register*, Adelaide 14 March 1891.
12. *Spectator and Methodist Chronicle*, Melbourne, 27 March 1891
13. Edward Ward (1891) 'Mark Guy Pearse and Sunday-Schools' in *Christian Weekly* and *Methodist Journal*, 20 March 1891.
14. Henry Ward Beecher (1813–87) was an American Congregationalist preacher who took a firm stand on temperance and slavery and made repeated lecture tours of Europe and Britain.
15. *South Australian Register*, 16 March 1891
16. *Spectator and Methodist Chronicle*, 27 March 1891.
17. Devon-born legislator and merchant, Sir John Colton (1823–1902), arrived in Adelaide with his parents and four

brothers in 1839. After an apprenticeship in the saddlery trade, he rose to prominent positions as a businessman and politician. See *Australian Dictionary of Biography*, vol. 3, Melbourne: Melbourne University Press, 1969, p. 444.

18. Ward (1891) op. cit.; *Spectator* and *Methodist Chronicle*, 27 March 1891; Rob Linn (1991) *Malvern Uniting Church: a centenary history*, Blackwood, South Australia: Historical Consultants, pp. 5-6. See also Arnold D. Hunt (1985) *This side of Heaven: a history of Methodism in South Australia*, Adelaide: Lutheran Publishing House.
19. *Royal Cornwall Gazette*, 19 March 1891.
20. *South Australian Register*, 17 and 18 March 1891.
21. Ibid 18 March 1891.
22. *Royal Cornwall Gazette*, 14 May 1891.
23. *The Bunyip*, 27 March 1891.
24. Transcript by Rob Linn of Blackwood, South Australia, of a cutting that he judges to be from the South *Australian Advertizer*, 1 January 1930.
25. Mylor-born James Penn Boucaut (1831–1916) emigrated to South Australia with his parents in 1846. After working as a stockman, he turned to the law and in 1861 was elected to the Adelaide Parliament. In the early 1870s he emerged as clear leader of the liberal opposition groups. He was eventually elected Premier, and knighted in 1898. See *Australian Dictionary of Biography* (1969), pp. 69-70.
26. *Royal Cornwall Gazette*, 28 May 1891. Born at Botatham, near Launceston, John Langdon Parsons (1837–1903) was brought up as an Anglican, but was converted to the Baptist cause and subsequently trained as a minister. Arriving in South Australia in 1863, he became President of the South Australian Baptist Union six years later. See *Australian Dictionary of Biography*, vol. 11, 1989, p. 148.
27. *Royal Cornwall Gazette, 28 May 1891.*
28. *Ibid.*
29. Mark Guy Pearse (1902) *West Country Songs*, London: Marshall, pp. viii, 60-64.
30. *Royal Cornwall Gazette*, 28 May 1891.
31. *Spectator and Methodist Chronicle*, 10 April 1891.
32. Ibid.
33. Ibid.
34. Ibid.
35. Mark Guy Pearse (1893) *The Gospel for the Day*, London: Kelly, pp. 33-34.
36. Unwin and Telford (1930), op. cit., p. 214.
37. *Spectator and Methodist Chronicle*, 24 April 1891.
38. Ruth Hopkins (1984) 'Bendigo – The Cornwall of Victoria' in *An Baner Kernewek/The Cornish Banner*, 35, February, pp. 11-14. Founded as a sheep run in 1840, its official name was Sandhurst until 1891 when it was formally changed to honour a local prizefighter who compared his prowess to that of the Nottingham-born pugilist, William Thompson, who was known as 'Bendigo'. See *Encyclopaedia Britannica*, 15th edition, 1994.
39. *Spectator and Methodist Chronicle*, 1 May 1891.
40. Ibid. 8 May 1891.
41. Ibid. 22 May 1891.
42. Unwin and Telford (1930), op. cit., p. 214.
43. *Spectator and Methodist Chronicle*, 5 June 1891.
44. Ibid. 24 April 1891.
45. Unwin and Telford (1930), op. cit., pp. 214-215.
46. Hugh Finlay et al (1994) *Australia – a Lonely Planet travel survival kit*, 7th edition, Hawthorn: Lonely Planet, p. 645.Launceston-born Philip King (1758–1808) entered the navy and in 1787 became a Lieutenant to Capt. Phillips when he sailed with the conflict fleet to Botany Bay. King surveyed the coast and, as a result, the colony moved to Port Jackson. In 1880 he was appointed Governor of New South Wales. See I. D. Spreadbury (1972) *Famous men and women of Cornish birth*, Mevagissey: Kingston, p. 39.
47. *Launceston Examiner*, 1 June 1891.
48. Ibid. 1, 2 and 4 June 1891.
49. Ibid. 4 June 1891.
50. This is the true story of Michael Verran which is told in Mark Guy Pearse (1892) *Sermons for Children*, London: Kelly, pp. 125-126 and explored more fully in Mark Guy Pearse (1926) *The Ship Where Christ*

was Captain, London: Epworth Press, pp. 132-142.

51. *North-West Post*, Devonport, 4 June 1891.
52. Mark Guy Pearse (1891) 'The Cornish Fisherman' in *Spectator and Methodist Chronicle*, 12 June 1891.
53. It was published as 'A Local Preacher's Sermon' in Pearse (1926), pp. 77-88.
54. *North West Post*, 4 June 1891.
55. *Tasmanian Mail*, 13 June 1891.
56. Unwin and Telford (1930), op. cit., p. 215.
57. Arthur Lawrence (1899) 'The Rev. Mark Guy Pearce' in A. T. Quiller-Couch (ed), *The Cornish Magazine*, vol. 2, Truro: Pollard, pp. 246.
58. Letter to the author, 18 October 1996.
59. *New Zealand Methodist*, 20 June 1891. Although in his *History of Methodism in New Zealand*, vol. 2, Wellington, 1900, p. 471, the Rev. William Morley wrote of "the three months of his [Mark Guy Pearse's] visit", the itinerary published in the *New Zealand Methodist* on 20 June lists engagements between 26 June and 21 July inclusive.
60. *New Zealand Methodist*, 20 June 1891; William Morley, 'The Rev. Mark Guy Pearse in New Zealand' in *Methodist Recorder*, 10 September 1891.
61. Tony Wheeler et al (1994) *New Zealand: a travel survival kit*, 7th edition, Hawthorn: Lonely Planet, p. 610.
62. *New Zealand Methodist*, 11 July 1891.
63. Although Cornish as a means of communication is said to have all but died out by 1800, there were a few speakers whose knowledge of it lived on into the latter half of the nineteenth century. According to Michael Trotter (1987) 'Settlements, Sites and Structures around Ship Cove' in Glynn Barrett (ed) *Queen Charlotte Sound: The Tradition and European Records 1820*, Cornish explorers in New Zealand were still using words of their native tongue in the 18th century. Cited in James Belish (1996) *Making Peoples: a history of New Zealanders...*, London: Allen Lane/Penguin Press, p. 14.
64. *New Zealand Methodist*, 11 and 18 July 1891.
65. Ibid. 11 July 1891.
66. Ibid. 20 June and 18 July 1891.
67. Ibid. 8 August 1891; *New Zealand Mail*, 24 July 1891.
68. The letter was reprinted in the *New Zealand Methodist*,8 August 1891.
69. *New Zealand Mail*, 24 July 1891; *New Zealand Methodist*, 8 August 1891.
70. *New Zealand Methodist*, 8 August 1891.
71. Ibid. 25 July and 8 August 1891.

Chapter 13 *The Isle of Man 1893*

1. Rev. C. Ensor Walters, 'A Personal Tribute', newspaper cutting in the Shaw Methodist Collection, Courtney Library, Truro.
2. *Ramsey Weekly News*, 3 May 1893.
3. *Manx Wesleyan Methodist Church Record*, June 1893.
4. *Isle of Man Examiner*, 29 April 1893.
5. *Manx Sun*, 29 April 1893; *Isle of Man Examiner*, 29 April 1893. The island was granted "home rule during pleasure" in a United Kingdom Government Act of May, 1866. Its status was further defined in the report of the Royal Commission on the Isle of Man Constitution (14 March 1959) which stated that "the Isle of Man is not part of the U.K.", but "the power of the Imperial Parliament (Westminster) to legislate for the Isle of Man is supreme". See Peter Berresford Ellis (1985) *The Celtic Revolution*, Talybont: Y Lolfa, p. 149. Manx women were given the vote in 1881.
6. *Manx Sun*, 29 April 1893.
7. *Isle of Man Examiner*, 29 April 1893; J. F. Odgers [1959] *Early Methodism in Camborne: Wesley Chapel, 1828–1958*, Camborne: [J. F. Odgers], p. 137.
8. The Budge family's connections with the Methodist cause in Camborne and nearby Treswithian go back well into the eighteenth century. James Budge senior, a friend and contemporary of George Smith, contributed £300 to the building of the first chapel in Camborne, while his sons (?) James and Peter were, in 1828, among the trustees of a new chapel for which Peter had laid the foundation stone the previous year. See Odgers [1959], op. cit. The drapery store of J. H. and C. Budge was acquired by Hugh Rice in 1902, the resulting department store and adjoining business serving the town for ninety years.

9. Edward Burgess was appointed Class Leader in 1856, along with Mark Guy Pearse senior. See Odgers [1959], p. 65.
10. Letter dated 8 December 1925, in the possession of Professor Charles Thomas (ms. CAM33).
11. *Isle of Man Examiner*, 29 April 1893; *Manx Wesleyan Methodist Church Record*, June 1893.
12. *Ramsey Weekly News*, 3 May 1893.
13. W. J. Dawson (1891 and 1892) 'Mark Guy Pearse' in *The Young Man*, pp. 402-404 and *The Bible Christian Magazine*, August, pp. 455-458.
14. *Manx Wesleyan Methodist Church Record*, June 1893, p. 70.
15. Ibid p. 71; *Isle of Man Examiner*, 6 May 1893.
16. *Isle of Man Examiner*, 6 May 1893.
17. *Manx Wesleyan Methodist Church Record*, June 1893, pp. 64 and 70.

Chapter 14 *South Africa 1896*

1. Mark Guy Pearse (1896), 'To South Africa and back XI – "Johannesburg Dust"', in *The Methodist Churchman*, Cape Town, p. 230.
2. A. K. Hamilton Jenkin (1962) *The Cornish Miner*, 3rd edition, London: Allen and Unwin, p. 330.
3. Richard D. Dawe (1986) *The Role and Influence of the Cornish in South Africa 1886–1925*, unpublished MA thesis, Middlesex Polytechnic, p. 3. The late Richard Dawe, whose research I have drawn on to set the scene for Mark Guy Pearse's visit to South Africa, later expanded his findings in *Cornish Pioneers in South Africa*, St Austell: Cornish Hillside Publications, 1998.
4. *Cornish Post and Mining News*, 20 December 1906.
5. *Cornubian and Redruth Times*, 31 January 1902.
6. Arthur H. Norway (1898) *Highways and Byeways in Devon and Cornwall*, London: Macmillan, p. 317.
7. Harry Pascoe (1924) 'The Adventurous Cornish Miner' in *The Cornishman*, 9 January.
8. *Cornish Post and Mining News*, 9 January and 29 October 1896.
9. *The Cornubian*, May 1896, cited in John C. C. Probert (1971) *The Sociology of Cornish Methodism to the present day*, Redruth: Cornish Methodist Historical Association Occasional Publication 17, p. 64.
10. C. Lewis Hind (1943) *Days in Cornwall*, 6th edition, London: Methuen, pp. 351-352.
11. Mark Guy Pearse (1896) 'To South Africa and back XIV', in *The Methodist Churchman*, Cape Town, p. 278. The fourteen articles or "letters", which were all reprinted in the newly-published *Methodist Churchman*, provide us with a first-hand account of his three-month tour. Unless specified otherwise, all the information and quotations in this chapter are from them.
12. Duncan Haws (1990) *Merchant fleets 18: Union-Castle Line*, Hereford: TCL Publications, pp. 84-85.
13. Mrs George Unwin and John Telford (1930) *Mark Guy Pearse, Preacher, Author, Artist*, London: Epworth Press/J. Alfred Sharp, p. 205.
14. Ibid p. 206.
15. Born in the parish of Laneast, near Launceston, John Couch Adams (1819–1892) was honoured by the Astronomical Society in 1848 as the joint-discoverer – with Leverrier – of Neptune.
16. Richard Everist and Jon Murray (1993) *South Africa... a travel survival kit*, Hawthorn: Lonely Planet, p. 319.
17. The Xhosa (formerly Kaffir or Kafir) are a cluster of related tribes now living primarily in Eastern Cape province and forming part of the southern Nguni group of Bantu-speaking peoples.
18. Having studied for the Wesleyan ministry and served the cause in England, the Rev. William Flint (1855–1943) went to South Africa in 1889. He wrote extensively on education and edited the conference newspaper, *The Methodist Churchman*, from its appearance on 6 August 1896. See Eric Rosenthal (comp) (1966) *The Southern African Dictionary of National Biography*, London: Warne, p. 125.
19. Born in Whitstable, Kent, the Rev. Charles Pettman (1851–1935) qualified for the Wesleyan ministry and came to the Cape in 1876 to become the first minister of his denomination in East London. See

Rosenthal (1966), p. 289.

20. This was almost certainly a recent, ongoing development for, soon after Mark Guy's departure, *The Methodist Churchman* reported that the Dutch Wesleyan Church in Buitenkant Street, central Cape Town, was 'fitted up with electric light… in the presence of an immense crowd of people' on Sunday 30 August, 1896.
21. Unwin and Telford (1930), op. cit., p. 218.
22. Dr F. L. Wiseman (1942), 'Mark Guy Pearse: some centenary reminiscences', in *Methodist Recorder* 11 June.
23. *De Kerkbode* [Journal of the Dutch Reformed Church], 23 April 1896.
24. Dr Andrew Murray, junior, (1828–1917) was born in Graaff-Reinet where his father was prominent in the Dutch Reformed Church. He was six times elected Moderator of the Church. See Rosenthal (1966), p. 264.
25. *De Kerkbode*, 7 May 1896.
26. Cecil Rhodes secured the charter for the British South Africa Company, whose territory was later to be known as Rhodesia, in 1889 and was its managing director until 1896. Dr Jameson was its administrator. See Trewhella Cameron (ed) (1986) *An Illustrated History of South Africa*, Johannesburg: Ball, pp. 189 and 191.
27. *Grahamstown Journal*, 23 April and 2 and 9 May 1896.
28. The Rev. William C. Holden (1829–1897) was a Methodist missionary who worked among the Basuto prior to establishing the first Wesleyan church in Durban. He wrote numerous books, among them a history of Methodism in South Africa. See Rosenthal (1966), p. 173.
29. The Rev. John Ayliff (1797–1862) was a pioneer missionary who accompanied the 1820 British settlers in John Wilson's party. His work for the Methodist Church included translating portions of the New Testament into Xhosa and producing a vocabulary of the Kaffir language. These Ayliffs were presumably his descendents. See Rosenthal (1966), p. 11.
30. In point of fact, six years later, on 31 August 1902, nineteen ships in the bay broke anchorage in a strong southwest gale and were driven onto the rocks. Today South Africa's fifth largest city has a secure, deep-water harbour.
31. Born in Ceylon and educated in Northampton, Sir Edgar H. Walton (1856–1947) reached the Cape Colony in 1879 and joined the staff of the Eastern Province Herald in Port Elizabeth. Ten years later he became its proprietor and editor and converted it into a daily newspaper. He later entered politics. See Rosenthal (1966), p. 406.
32. Having entered the Wesleyan ministry in 1859, Nottinghamshire-born Joseph Whiteside (1838–1921) settled in the Eastern Cape Province twenty years later. On his retirement in 1898, he became widely known for his school histories and geographies of South Africa and for his history of the country's Wesleyan Methodist Church. See Rosenthal (1966), p. 415.
33. *Cornish Post and Mining News*, 14 November 1896, cited in Dawe (1986), p. 11.
34. Mark Guy Pearse (1900) *The Bramble King and other Old Testament Parables*, London: Kelly, p. 35.
35. Everist and Murray (1993), op. cit., p. 218.
36. A stained glass window of Christ the Good Shepherd commemorating S. J. P. Sowden who died at Bloemfontein, where he had been mayor, in 1898, can be found in Liskeard Wesley Chapel. See Thomas Shaw (comp.) (1991) *A Methodist Guide to Cornwall*, Methodist Publishing House, p. 25.
37. Uitlander, an Afrikaans word meaning 'outlander' or 'foreigner', was used to describe any British or other non-Afrikaner immigrants in the Transvaal in the 1880s and 1890s.
38. Paul Burton (1995) 'Redruth Reincarnated' in *Cornish World* 5, Redruth: Cornish World, p. 27.
39. *Cornish Post and Mining News*, 19 September 1896.
40. *Cornishman*, 9 June 1899, cited in Dawe (1986), p. 24.
41. *Cornish Post and Mining News*, 12 March 1892, cited in Dawe (1986), pp. 16-17.

42. *Cornishman*, 10 September 1896, cited in Dawe (1986), p. 17.
43. *Cornish Post and Mining News*, 17 December 1896, cited in Dawe (1986), p. 18.
44. See Richard Dawe and Paul Burton (1995) 'Johannesburg is but a suburb of Cornwall', in *Cornish World* 6, Redruth: Cornish World, pp. 28-29.
45. Sir George Herbert Farrar (1859–1914) was born in Cambridge and educated at Bedford, where the family engineering firm of Farrar & Co. was based. With his brother Sydney he played a leading role in opening up the eastern side of the gold fields and in 1893 established the East Rand Proprietary Mines which eventually became one of the largest in the world. See Rosenthal (1966), p. 120. Howard, Farrar & Co. were the Transvaal representatives of Holman Brothers of Camborne. George Farrar was also Katherine Price Hughes's cousin.
46. The London-born mining magnate Sir Lionel Phillips (1855–1936) moved to the Rand in 1889. Sentenced to death after the 1896 raid, he turned to constitutional politics in the opening decades of the 20th century. See Rosenthal (1966), p. 291.
47. Some of the ringleaders were condemned to death, but their sentences were later commuted by the President to fines of £25,000 each which were met by Cecil Rhodes. See Cameron (1986), p. 191 and Geoffrey Wheatcroft (1985) *The Randlords*, London: Weidenfeld and Nicholson, p. 184.
48. *Royal Cornwall Gazette*, 16 July 1896.
49. It was this association that presented Redruth-born Fanny Moody, 'The Cornish Nightingale', with a diamond tiara bearing the Cornish coat of arms picked out in fifteen huge diamonds and the motto 'One and All' in silver and jewels on the occasion of her final concert in Johannesburg in 1897.
50. *Royal Cornwall Gazette*, 16 July 1896.
51. Everist and Murray (1993), op. cit., p. 283.
52. 'Penman' (1896), 'Cradock Notes: Visit of the Rev. Mark Guy Pearse', in *Methodist Churchman*, Cape Town, p. 10.
53. *Methodist Churchman*, 1896, p. 3.
54. 'The Visit of the Rev. Mark Guy Pearse', in *Methodist Churchman*, 1896, pp. 21-22.

Chapter 15 *India 1906–1907*

1. Mrs George Unwin and John Telford (1930) *Mark Guy Pearse, Preacher, Author, Artist*, London: Epworth Press/J. Alfred Sharp, p. 222.
2. George A Parkinson (1930), 'From Eight to Sixteen. "Mark Guy"', in *Methodist Recorder*, 16 January.
3. Unwin and Telford (1930), op. cit., p. 99.
4. *Methodist Recorder*, 29 December 1904.
5. Ibid.
6. *Methodist Recorder*, 19 and 26 January 1905.
7. Postcard to the Rev. J. A Sharpe, postmarked 28 January, in the Methodist Archive and Research Centre, Manchester.
8. *Methodist Recorder*, 29 December 1904.
9. Ibid. 4 and 25 May 1905.
10. Ibid. 2 November 1905.
11. Mark Guy Pearse (1905) 'Thomas Champness. Some Reminiscences', in *Methodist Recorder* 16 November. *Short Talks for the Times* (1889) had been dedicated 'to my friend Thomas Champness in admiration alike of the man and his work…'.
12. *Methodist Recorder*, 4 January 1906.
13. Ibid. 22 March 1906.
14. Emmeline Pethick-Lawrence (1938) *My part in a changing world*, London: Gollancz, pp. 102 and 111.
15. See David Mitchell (1977) *Queen Christabel: a biography of Christabel Pankhurst*, London: Macdonald and Jane's; Roger Fulford (1976) *Votes for Women*, London: White Lion; Diane Atkinson (1996) *The Suffragettes in pictures*, London: Sutton. Emmeline Pethick-Lawrence (1867–1954) served as WSPU treasurer between 1906 and 1912 before being expelled because of her growing reservations about the organisation's shop window smashing campaign and a proposed arson campaign. During the First World War she was a prominent member of the Women's International League for Peace and in the 1918 General Election stood as a Pacifist Party candidate. In the 1920s and 1930s she worked for the Women's International League, becoming its president in 1926.

16. Pethick-Lawrence (1938), op. cit., p. 108.
17. *Royal Cornwall Gazette*, 29 November 1906; *Methodist Recorder*, 18 November 1906.
18. The letters appeared under the heading 'Mark Guy Pearse in India' in the issues of 24 January, 7 February and 7, 14 and 21 March 1907, with that of 28 February carrying an omission of a page from the second letter under the headline 'Mark Guy Pearse among mutiny memories'. All the information and quotations in this chapter are from them, unless otherwise specified.
19. Letter from the Rev. M. G. Pearse to the Rev. Albert Brockbank, Camborne dated 8 December 1925, now in the possession of Professor Charles Thomas (ms. CAM 33).
20. Probably that of Bahu Begum, the widow of Shuja-ud-Daula, the ruler of the Kingdom of Avadh, 1756–75.
21. The Rev. J. A Elliott died in December 1905.
22. This had been very much the view of fellow-Liberal Hugh Price Hughes who had argued that '[our] tenure in India would cease tomorrow if it rested only or mainly on the sword. It reposes really upon the justice of our rule, the influence of our missionaries.' See Hugh Price Hughes (1890) *The Philanthropy of God*, New York: Funk and Wagnalls, p. 19, cited in Christopher Oldstone-Moore (1999) *Hugh Price Hughes, Founder of a New Methodism, Conscience of a New Nonconformity*, Cardiff: University of Wales Press, p. 180.
23. David Abram et al (1994) *India: the Rough Guide*, London: Rough Guides, p. 1112.
24. The small brick tomb in which the Sufi, Khwaja Muin-ud-din Chisti, founder of the Chistiya Order, was buried in 1236, is today engulfed by a large marble complex known as the Dargah.
25. *Methodist Recorder*, 21 March 1907. The Pearses reached home on the evening of Tuesday 12 March.

Chapter 16 *'The Ministry of Nature'*

1. Letter in the Wesley Historical Society Library, Oxford.
2. *West Briton*, 2 October 1913.
3. Mrs George Unwin and John Telford (1930) *Mark Guy Pearse, Preacher, Author, Artist*, London: Epworth Press/J. Alfred Sharp, pp. 193-194.
4. *Inverness Courier*, 2 and 5 April 1907; *Methodist Recorder*, 18 April 1907.
5. *Methodist Recorder*, 25 July and 1 August 1907.
6. Ibid., 17 October 1907.
7. *Oswestry and Border Counties Advertizer*, 2 and 16 October 1907
8. *Cornish and Devon Post*, 12 October 1907.
9. Colin Bourne (ed.) (1993), *The Dunstable Methodist Circuit: one hundred and fifty years of witness, 1843–1993*, Dunstable: Dunstable Methodist Circuit, p. 48.
10. Emmeline Pethick-Lawrence (1938) *My part in a changing world,* London: Gollancz, pp. 110-111.
11. Mark Guy Pearse (1882) *Daniel Quorm and his religious notions*, second series, London: Woolmer, pp. 50-53.
12. Mark Guy Pearse (1907) *Bridgetstow*, London: Culley, p. 67.
13. Mark Guy Pearse (1927), 'The Gamekeeper', in *Methodist Recorder*, 13 January.
14. Mark Guy Pearse (1891), *Elijah, the Man of God*, London: Kelly, p. 16.
15. Unwin and Telford (1930), op. cit., pp. 195-196.
16. Mark Guy Pearse (1923), 'The Song of the Oyster Shell', in *The Orthodox Devil*, London: Jenkins, p. 146. Geikie was either the Scottish geologist Sir Archibald Geikie (1835–1924) or his brother James (1839–1915) who was also a geologist.
17. 'The West Central Pulpit LXVI – Fishers of Men by the Rev. Mark Guy Pearse', one of a number of cuttings from the *Methodist Recorder* and the *Methodist Times* contained in a scrapbook in the Wesley Historical Society Library, Westminster College, Oxford. For a slightly different version, see also Mark Guy Pearse (1928), 'A Command and a Promise' in *He Must Reign and other Bible Stories*, London: Epworth Press, p. 78.
18. Unwin and Telford (1930), op. cit., p. 192.
19. Ibid., pp. 192-193.
20. Ibid., p. 194.

21. Ibid., p. 193.
22. Mark Guy Pearse (1923), 'What a sea trout did', in *The Orthodox Devil*, op. cit.
23. Unwin and Telford (1930), op. cit., pp. 194-195.
24. Mark Guy Pearse (1902), *A Bit of Shamrock*, London: Marshall & Son, p. 9.
25. Rev. T. W. Slater (1925), 'Newquay's Favourite Preacher', in *Newquay Express*, 4 December.
26. H. M. Cresswell Payne, letter to the *Western Morning News*, dated 5 September 1961.
27. H. C. Lanyon (1963), 'Some Memories of Methodism in Cornwall', in *Methodist Magazine*, March, p. 107.
28. Dr F. L. Wiseman (1942), 'Mark Guy Pearse: some centenary reminiscences', in *Methodist Recorder*, 11 June.
29. 'Whispers and Echoes...', in *Cornish Guardian*, 9 January 1930.
30. Arthur Lawrence (1899) 'The Rev. Mark Guy Pearce' in A. T. Quiller-Couch (ed), *The Cornish Magazine*, vol. 2, Truro: Pollard, p. 248.
31. Unwin and Telford (1930), op. cit., pp. 183-184.
32. Letter from Mrs R. J. Eland, in *Methodist Recorder*, 9 January 1930.
33. Unwin and Telford (1930), op. cit., p. 179; A. J. Lambert (1930), *The Chapel on the Hill*, Bristol: St Stephen's Press, p. 103. The latter contains a delightful little watercolour sketch of a Cornish coastal scene executed by Mark Guy on a postcard in 1928.
34. Letter dated 10 June [1930], unidentified newspaper cutting in the Shaw Methodist Collection, Courtney Library, Truro. A slightly different version of this story appears in Unwin and Telford (1930), p. 186.
35. *Methodist Recorder*, 3 October 1907. The illustrations do, in fact, bear Charles Tresidder's monogram.

Chapter 17 *Mark Guy! Cornubia's Son*

1. Mrs George Unwin and John Telford (1930) *Mark Guy Pearse, Preacher, Author, Artist*, London: Epworth Press/J. Alfred Sharp, p. 127.
2. Mark Guy Pearse (1902) *West Country Songs*, London: Marshall, p. vii.
3. Rev. T. W. Slater (1930a), 'A Cornish Religious Genius', in *Cornish Guardian*, 24 April.
4. Unwin and Telford (1930), op. cit., p. 127.
5. Arthur Lawrence (1899) 'The Rev. Mark Guy Pearse' in A. T. Quiller-Couch (ed), *The Cornish Magazine*, vol. 2, Truro: Pollard, p. 246.
6. Mark Guy Pearse [n.d.] 'A Cornish Ghost Story', in *Cornish Stories*, fourteenth thousand, London: Kelly, p. 121. The story was first published in *The Holly Bush* in 1876.
7. Mark Guy Pearse (1891), 'Some Old Folks at Home', lecture given in Gawler Wesleyan Church on 24 March 1891 and reported in *The Bunyip*, 27 March.
8. See R[ichard] B[owden]-D[an] (1994), 'The History of the London Cornish', in *London Cornish Association Circular* 23, September 1994, pp. 13-19.
9. Unwin and Telford (1930), op. cit., pp. 188-190.
10. Mark Guy Pearse (1882) *Daniel Quorm and his religious notions*, second series, London: Woolmer, p. 117.
11. Mark Guy Pearse (1906) *The Pretty Ways o' Providence and other stories*, London` : Marshall, pp. 73 and 77.
12. Mark Guy Pearse (1907) *Bridgetstow*, London: Culley, pp. 212 and 18.
13. *New Zealand Methodist*, 11 July 1891.
14. *Isle of Man Examiner*, 6 May 1893.
15. Pearse(1902), op. cit., p. vii.
16. Mark Guy Pearse (1926) *The Ship Where Christ was Captain,* London: Epworth Press, pp. 9-10.
17. *Western Morning News*, 31 December 1932.
18. *Spectator and Methodist Chronicle*, Melbourne, 1 May 1891.
19. Rev. T.W. Slater (1927), 'Great Cornishman's fine Record', in *Cornish Guardian*, 21 January.
20. Mark Guy Pearse (1908) *The Prophet's Raven*, N. York: Eaton and Mains, p. 1.
21. Mark Guy Pearse (1924) *A Village Down West*, London: Epworth Press, p. 125.
22. Mark Guy Pearse [1891] *Jesus Christ and the People,* London: Kelly, p. 201.
23. Mark Guy Pearse [c.1885] *Some Aspects of*

the Blessed Life, London: Woolmer, p. 217.
24. Pearse [n.d.], op. cit., p. 141.
25. Pearse (1882), op. cit., pp. 94-97.
26. A. W. Harrison et al (1932) *The Methodist Church*, London: Methodist Publishing House, pp. 68 and 72, cited in K. S. Inglis (1963) *Churches and the working classes in Victorian England*, London: Routledge and Kegan Paul, p. 85.
27. Pearse (1882), op. cit., p. 95.
28. J. F. Odgers [1959] *Early Methodism in Camborne: Wesley Chapel, 1828–1958,* Camborne: [J. F. Odgers], p. 17.
29. W. J. Dawson (1891 and 1892) 'Mark Guy Pearse' in *The Young Man*, p. 402 and *The Bible Christian Magazine*, p. 455.
30. Mark Guy Pearse (1900) *The Bramble King and other Old Testament Parables*, London: Kelly, p. 87.
31. *Times* 2 January 1930.
32. Emmeline Pethick-Lawrence (1938) *My part in a changing world*, London: Gollancz, p. 99.
33. Unwin and Telford (1930), op. cit., pp. 205 and 132.
34. Dawson (1891 and 1892), op. cit., pp. 404 and 458. In his *My Book of Memory*, pp. 120-121, Silas K. Hocking gives a slightly different version of events and has Mark Guy refuse to agree to the stewards' plan.
35. Mark Guy Pearse (1880), 'Early Methodism in Cornwall' (First Paper), in *Sunday Magazine,* January, p. 24.
36. *Bunyip*, Gawler, 27 March 1891.
37. Unwin and Telford (1930), op. cit., p. 137.
38. Rev. Mark Guy Pearse (1891a), 'How I Get My Stories', in *Spectator & Methodist Chronicle*, Melbourne, 19 June.
39. Mark Guy Pearse [c.1880] *Homely Talks*, twenty-fifth thousand, London: Kelly, pp. 209-210.
40. Pearse (1891a), op. cit.
41. Unwin and Telford (1930), op. cit., p. 142.
42. H. C. Lanyon (1963), 'Some Memories of Methodism in Cornwall', in *Methodist Magazine*, March.
43. See 'J' (1926), 'Mr Moses Dunn', in *United Methodist*, 21 October, p. 485.
44. Mark Guy Pearse (1891b), 'The Cornish Fisherman', in *Spectator & Methodist Chronicle*, 12 June.
45. Pearse (1891a), op. cit; Pearse (1902), op. cit., pp. 101-102.
46. Unwin and Telford (1930), op. cit., pp. 234-235.
47. *Methodist Recorder*, 9 January 1930; Unwin and Telford (1930), p. 200.
48. *Methodist Recorder*, 3 October 1907.
49. Letter dated 8 January 1923, in Wesley Historical Society Library, Oxford.
50. Letter to the Rev. Albert Brockbank, Camborne, dated 8 December, now in the possession of Professor Charles Thomas, ms. CAM 33.
51. Letter to Connie Ries, née Tilley, dated 2 April 1927, currently in the author's collection; information supplied by Diane Smith, Connie Ries' niece.
52. Unwin and Telford (1930), op. cit., pp. 227-228. Born at Stockport in 1870, Unwin was, from the late 1890s to 1907, private secretary to the Cornish Liberal Unionist MP, Leonard Courtney. He married Mark Guy Pearse's eldest daughter Frances in 1902. Eight years later he was elected to the first chair of Economic History to be established in the country.
53. Mark Guy Pearse, (1914), 'A wreck that saved lives', in *Wesleyan Methodist Magazine*, February; Mark Guy Pearse (1927)'A Famous Artist from Camborne', in *Cornishman*, 23 February and *Cornish Post & Mining News*, 26 February; 'Mark Guy Pearse tells of some charms that cured', unidentified newspaper cutting in the Shaw Methodist Collection, Courtney Library, Truro; Mark Guy Pearse (1926a), 'A true story of Tintagel', in *Old Cornwall* 4, October, pp. 3-7; Mark Guy Pearse (1929), 'An Old-World Corner of Cornwall: some stories of Newlyn and Mousehole', unidentified newspaper cutting dated 2 January, in the Shaw Collection, Courtney Library, Truro.
54. Isaac Shimmin (1930), 'Mark Guy Pearse in Cornwall', in *Methodist Recorder*, 23 January.
55. Unwin and Telford (1930), op. cit., pp. 127-128.
56. Mark Guy Pearse (1928), 'The Prayers of the Congregation', in *Tre Pol and Pen: The Cornish Annual* 1928, London: Dodsworth, pp. 8-12.
57. Pearse (1926), op. cit., p. 10.

58. Pearse (1908), op. cit., p. 124.
59. Pearse (1907), op. cit., pp. 229 and 17.
60. Pearse [n.d.], op. cit., p. 147. The boy had swallowed his sweet without chewing it.
61. Pearse (1906), op. cit., pp. 139-162.
62. See P. Berresford Ellis (1974), *The Cornish Language and its Literature*, London: Routledge & Kegan Paul; A. S. D. Smith, revised E. G.Retallack Hooper (1969), *The Story of the Cornish Language*, Camborne: An Lef Kernewek; P. A. S. Pool (1975), *The Death of Cornish (1600–1800)*, Penzance: [P. A. S. Pool].
63. Pool (1975), op. cit., p. 29; Unwin and Telford (1930), op. cit., p. 200.
64. Pearse (1906), op. cit., p. 77.
65. Lawrence (1899), op. cit., p. 247.
66. 'Men an voror' in Unified Cornish.
67. Unwin and Telford (1930), op. cit., pp. 199-200.
68. Robert Morton Nance (1925), 'Breton and Cornish', in *Old Cornwall* 2, October, p. 37.
69. *Newquay Express*, 1 October 1920.
70. *West Briton*, 7 October 1920.
71. *Cornish Guardian*, 15 October 1926.
72. Odgers [1959], op. cit., p. 35; *West Briton*, 30 October 1924; *Cornish Post & Mining News*, 25 October and 1 November 1924.
73. Story told to Donald Hosking of Newquay by his father.
74. 'Rev. Mark Guy Pearse in Penzance', in *Cornish Evening [Tidings]*, undated newspaper cutting in the Shaw Collection, Courtney Library, Truro.
75. *Cornishman*, 24 November 1926.
76. Slater (1930a), op. cit. See also Rev. T. W. Slater (1925), Newquay's Favourite Preacher', in *Newquay Express*, 4 December; Rev. T. W. Slater (1930), 'Mark Guy Pearse: An appreciation', in *Cornish Guardian* 9 January; and 'Mark Guy', an undated newspaper account of Slater's lecture to Newquay Old Cornwall Society, in Cornish Methodist Historical Association Library, Cornish Studies Library, Redruth.
77. Slater (1930), op. cit.
78. *Cornish Guardian*, 17 September and 10 December 1926.
79. Unwin and Telford (1930), op. cit., p. 229.
80. *Cornishman*, 12 October 1927.
81. Unwin and Telford (1930), op. cit., pp. 231-232. I am indebted to Gordon Booth for identifying the source of these lines.
82. Postcard in the author's collection.
83. Postcard in the possession of Margaret Burton, a descendant of Mark Guy Pearse.
84. Shimmin (1930), op. cit.
85. Unwin and Telford (1930), op. cit., p. 229.
86. Pearse to Brockbank 8 December 1925, op. cit.
87. Mark Guy Pearse (1898), 'New Weapon', in Mark Guy Pearse and Arthur E. Gregory (eds.), *The Preacher's Magazine*, vol. ix, London: Kelly, p. 55.
88. *London Free Press*, Ontario, 12 October 1903.
89. Pearse (1902), op. cit., pp. 117-121; Mark Guy Pearse (1914), *Christ's Cure for Care*, London: Kelly, pp. 79-80.
90. *Cornish Gorsedd Minute Book*, p. 33.
91. The Cornish Gorsedd at Boscawen-Un Stone Circle, Near St Buryan (September 21st, 1928), Penzance: 'The Cornishman' Group, p. 13. This was probably done *in absentia* at Carn Brea in 1929.
92. Their inscribed copies of *The Gospel for the Day* and *The Christianity of Jesus Christ: Is It Ours?* were for sale in a Falmouth bookshop in 1999.
93. Janet M. C. Gray, letter dated 10 January 1930, to the editor of *The British Weekly*.
94. Unwin and Telford (1930), op. cit., pp. 238-239.
95. Mark Guy Pearse (1930), 'The First Locomotive', in *Old Cornwall*, no. 11, Summer, p. 1.
96. Pearse (1882), op. cit., p. 1.
97. Unwin and Telford (1930), op. cit., pp. 103-104.
98. *Methodist Recorder*, 9 January 1930.
99. Unwin and Telford (1930), op. cit., pp. 239-240.
100. *Methodist Recorder*, 19 and 24 December 1929.
101. Unwin and Telford (1930), op. cit., pp. 241-242; *Methodist Recorder*, 9 January 1930; *West Briton*, 9 January 1930; *Cornish Post & Mining News*, 11 January 1930.
102. *West Briton*, 9 January 1930.
103. W. Gregory Harris (1928), *Trengwith: a chronicle of clerical and social life in West Cornwall*, London: J. Lane/Bodley Head, p. xv.

104. W. Gregory Harris (1930), 'Mark Guy Pearse (In Memoriam)', in *Cornish Guardian*, 9 January and *Methodist Magazine*, March, p. 139.

Chapter 18 *'An'mind not to forget the windows...'*

1. *Cornish Post and Mining News*, 11 January 1930.
2. *Methodist Recorder*, 9 January 1930.
3. Ibid.
4. Ibid.
5. Rev. C. Ensor Walters, [n.d.], 'A Personal tribute' unidentified newspaper cutting in the Shaw Collection, Courtney Library, Truro.
6. Rev. T. W. Slater (1930), 'Mark Guy Pearse: An appreciation', in *Cornish Guardian*, 9 January.
7. Rev. C. Ensor Walters, (1930), '[An] Appreciation', in *Methodist Recorder*, 9 January 1930; Walters, [n.d.], op. cit.
8. Mark Guy Pearse [1891], *Jesus Christ and the People*, London: Kelly, pp. 251-252.
9. Mrs George Unwin and John Telford (1930) *Mark Guy Pearse, Preacher, Author, Artist*, London: Epworth Press/J. Alfred Sharp, p. 206.
10. Mark Guy Pearse (1900) *The Bramble King and other Old Testament Parables*, London: Kelly, p. 34.
11. *Methodist Recorder*, 9 January 1930.
12. 'Rev. Mark Guy Pearse in Penzance', in *Cornish Evening [Tidings]*, undated newspaper cutting in the Shaw Collection, Courtney Library, Truro.
13. 'Whispers and Echoes...', in *Cornish Guardian*, 9 January 1930.
14. *Times*, 2 January 1930.
15. W. J. Dawson (1891 and 1892) 'Mark Guy Pearse' in *The Young Man*, p. 404 and *The Bible Christian Magazine*, p. 457.
16. H. M. Cresswell Payne (1961), letter to Western Morning News dated 5 September, newspaper cutting in the Shaw Collection, Courtney Library, Truro.
17. *West Briton*, 9 January 1930.
18. Mark Guy Pearse (1882) *Daniel Quorm and his religious notions*, second series, London: Woolmer, p. 89.
19. Unwin and Telford (1930), op. cit., p. 92.
20. Ibid., pp. 35-36.
21. Ibid., p. 149.
22. Ibid., pp. 45-46.
23. Dawson (1891 and 1892), op. cit., pp. 404 and 457.
24. Mark Guy Pearse (1905), 'Thomas Champness: 'Some Reminiscences by Mark Guy Pearse'', in *Methodist Recorder*, 16 November.
25. Mark Guy Pearse (1876), *Daniel Quorm and his religious notions*, London: Wesleyan Conference Office, p. 104; Pearse (1882), op. cit., pp. 55-56 and 83-84.
26. Unwin and Telford (1930), op. cit., pp. 95-96.
27. Ibid., pp. 97-98; Walters, [n.d.], op. cit.; story told to Donald Hosking of Newquay by his father.
28. 'Whispers and Echoes...', op. cit.
29. Manuscript poem in the possession of Margaret Burton.
30. *London Free Press*, Ontario, 12 October 1903.
31. Dr F. L. Wiseman (1942), 'Mark Guy Pearse: some centenary reminiscences', in *Methodist Recorder*, 11 June.
32. Mark Guy Pearse (1898), *The God of our pleasures*, 2nd edition, London: Nisbet, p. ix.
33. Mark Guy Pearse (1907), *Bridgetstow*, London: Culley, p. 161.
34. Unwin and Telford (1930), op. cit., p. 111.
35. Ibid., p. 142; Pearse (1876), op. cit., p. 123.
36. *Methodist Recorder*, 9 January 1930.
37. J. Armitage Robinson (ed.) (1902) *Hugh Price Hughes as We Knew Him*, London: Horace Marshall, pp. 27-28.
38. Mark Guy Pearse (1889), *Short talks for the times*, London: Kelly, pp. 146-147.
39. Mark Guy Pearse [c.1880], *Homely Talks*, twenty-fifth thousand, London: Kelly, p. 212.

Bibliography of the writings of Mark Guy Pearse

Whilst, to my knowledge, this bibliography lists Mark Guy Pearse's entire output in book form, it does not pretend to be complete as far as his tracts and other writings are concerned. Pearse wrote for such a plethora of periodicals and newspapers – 'blazing an exciting and well-established trail of pulp Methodism across these islands,'[1] is how Alan M. Kent puts it – that a complete listing of articles and sermons would be a truly formidable task. Similarly, there may well be other chapters from his books, which were issued by the Wesleyan Conference Office as tracts. Many of his books went into numerous editions; only the earliest, English printing is listed here, with undated titles heading the lists in each section.

The bibliography has been compiled using the COPAC Union Catalogue (http://copac.ac.uk), the Library of Congress Online Catalog (http://catalog.loc.gov), FirstSearch's WorldCat, Boase and Courtney's *Bibliotheca Cornubiensis*, Boase's *Collectanea Cornubiensis*, the stock of The Courtney Library, Truro, and announcements and adverts in the *Methodist Recorder* and in Pearse's own books.

1. Alan M. Kent (2002) *Pulp Methodism: The Lives & Literature of Silas, Joseph & Salome Hocking, Three Cornish Novelists*, St Austell: Cornish Hillside Publications, p. 129.

Books

Mister Horn and his Friends or Givers and Giving. London: Hamilton, Adams and Co.; Manchester: Tubbs and Brook, 1872. First published in installments in *The Methodist Messenger*. Numerous revised and enlarged editions.

John Tregenoweth: his mark [A tale]/[A story of Western Cornwall]. London: Wesleyan Conference Office, 25 February 1873. Numerous editions and reprints and published as a Service of Song.

Daniel Quorm and his religious notions. London: Wesleyan Conference Office, 21 December 1874. First published in installments in *The City Road Magazine*, iv. Numerous editions.

Daniel Quorm and his religious notions, second series. London: [Wesleyan Conference Office], 1875. Numerous editions.

Sermons for Children. London: Wesleyan Conference Office, November/December, 1875. Numerous editions.

Good Will; a collection of Christmas Stories. London: Wesleyan Conference Office, 1877. Numerous editions.

The child Jesus: readings and texts of holy scripture. With songs and music by G. S. Rowe, M. G. Pearse… and others. London: Hodder and Stoughton, 1877. However, it was advertised by the Wesleyan Methodist Sunday School Union as *The child Jesus. A Gift and Prize Book containing the cartoons*… in *Methodist Recorder*, 10 December 1875.

Short Stories and other papers. London: Wesleyan Conference Office, [1877]. Numerous editions.

Rob Rat. A story of barge life. London: Wesleyan Conference Office, 1878.

Homely Talks. London: Wesleyan Conference Office, c. November, 1880. First published in installments, as 'Homely talks to those at home', in the *Wesleyan Methodist Magazine*, 100, 1877. Numerous editions.

John Tregenoweth: his mark. Rob Rat: a story of barge life. The old miller and his mill [combined volume]. London: Kelly, [c.1881].

Simon Jasper. London: T. Woolmer, November 1882. First published in installments in the *Wesleyan Methodist Magazine*. Numerous editions.

Isaac Watkin Lewis: a life for the little ones. London: T. Woolmer, [1882].

Cornish stories. London: T. Woolmer, December 1883. Numerous editions.

Thoughts on Holiness. London: T. Woolmer, 1884. Numerous editions.

Some aspects of the Blessed Life. London: T. Woolmer, c. September 1885. Some of the pieces were first published in *The Quiver*, others in *The Sunday Magazine*.

The Christianity of Jesus Christ. Is it ours? London: T. Woolmer, [c.1885].

The Christian's secret of holiness. Boston: Ira Bradley & Co., 1886. American edition of *Thoughts on Holiness*?

Mrs W. E. Boardman, *Life and Labours of the Rev. W. E. Boardman… with a preface by the Rev. Mark Guy Pearse*, London: Bemrose & Sons, 1886.

Praise. Meditations in the one hundred and third Psalm. London: T. Woolmer, [1887]. First published in installments in the *Wesleyan Methodist Magazine* throughout 1886. Numerous editions.

Short Talks for the Times [on religious subjects]. London: C. H. Kelly, 1889.

The Big Wheel of the Church and some hints on working it. London: T. Woolmer, [1889]. Numerous editions.

Egerton Ryerson Young, *By Canoe and Dog-Train among the Cree and Salteaux Indians…with an introduction by Mark Guy Pearse*. London: C. H. Kelly, 1890. Numerous editions.

The Preacher's Magazine: for ministers, lay-preachers, teachers and Bible students. [vols. 1-12]. *Editors: Mark Guy Pearse and Arthur E. Gregory*. London: C. H. Kelly, 1890–1901. Mark Guy Pearse wrote for most of the monthly issues, contributing 10 sermons to vol. 9 (1898), for example.

Elijah, the man of God. London: C. H. Kelly, 1891. First published in *The Preacher's Magazine*, vol. 1, 1890.

Jesus Christ and the People. London: C. H. Kelly, [1891].

Mrs W. E. Boardman, *How to maintain life without worry… with an introduction by Mark Guy Pearse*. London: Marshall & Bros., [1891].

The Man who Spoiled the Music and other stories. London: C. H. Kelly, 1892.

The Gospel for the day. London: C. H. Kelly, [1893]. First published in *The Preacher's Magazine*, vol. 2, 1891.

Naaman, the Syrian: and other sermons. London: C. H. Kelly, [1893].

Moses: his life and its lessons. London: C. H. Kelly, 1894. First published in *The Preacher's Magazine*, vol. 4, 1893.

Gold and Incense. A West-country story. London: H. Marshall & Son, [1895].

In the Banqueting House. A series of sacramental meditations. London: C. H. Kelly, 1896.

Temperance by Mark Guy Pearse and others. Chicago: Bible Institute Colportage Association, 1896.

"Come break your fast." A daily meditation. London: S. W. Partridge, 1897.

Parables and pictures. London: C. H. Kelly, 1897.

The gentleness of Jesus, and other sermons. London: H. Marshall, 1898.

The God of our pleasures. London: J. Nisbet, 1898.

The story of a Roman soldier. London: H. Marshall, 1899.

His mother's portrait, and other stories. London: H. Marshall, [1899].

What the flowers did. London: H. Marshall, [1899].

The Bramble King and other Old Testament parables. London: C. H. Kelly, 1900.

A Service for the Sick in Home and Hospital. London: H. Marshall, 1901.

A Bit of Shamrock. London: H. Marshall, 1902. Reprinted in *The Pretty Ways o' Providence and other stories*, 1906.

Christ's Cure for Care. London: Hodder & Stoughton, 1902.

West Country Songs. London: H. Marshall, 1902.

J. Armitage Robinson, W. Robertson Nicoll, Lady Henry Somerset, Mark Guy Pearse et al. *Hugh Price Hughes As We knew Him*, London: H. Marshall, 1902.

The Pretty Ways o' Providence, and other stories. London: H. Marshall, 1906. Several editions.

Bridgetstow. London: R. Culley, September 1907. First published in *The Wesleyan Methodist Magazine*, 1907.

The Prophet's Raven. London: R. Culley, [1908].

Wounds of the world; short stories by Mark Guy Pearse, W. Scott King, and other members of the Wesleyan Methodist Union for Social Service. London: J. Ouseley, 1912.

Prayers for sailors and soldiers on active service. London and Oxford, 1915.

The Orthodox Devil. London: H. Jenkins, 1923 [1922].

A Village Down West. London: Epworth, 1924.

The Ship where Christ was Captain. Stories of Cornish Methodism. London: Epworth, 1926.

'He Must Reign' and other Bible stories. London: Epworth, 1928.

Tracts

It was all through the Foot and Mouth Disease. London: C. H. Kelly, n.d.

A soft answer. [Wesleyan tract 1009], [London], n.d.

The Victory of Trust. n.d. In the Handley mss, 1862–1908, correspondence and papers of the Jesse Handley family of Oak Springs, Brown County, Illinois. Mss Dept, Lilly Library, Indiana University. [www.indiana.edu/~liblilly/lilly/mss/html/handley.html]

The Story of Billy Bray. London: Wesleyan Conference Office, [tract 1025], [1870?]. Although this piece is recorded as having first appeared in 1860 in a book of Sermons entitled *General Booth's vision and other addresses*, Louisville: Pickett Pub. Co., the early date is suspicious, given that Billy Bray did not die until 1868. Further editions, including an envelope one for enclosing in letters. Reprinted in *Short Stories and other papers*, [1877].

Can I be saved? London: Wesleyan Conference Office, [tract 1120], [1870?]. Further editions, including an envelope one. Reprinted in *Short Stories and other papers*, [1877].

A Homily of Mister Horn's. London: Wesleyan Conference Office, [1870?]. From *Mister Horn and his Friends...*, 1872.

My old friend John. London: Wesleyan Conference Office, [tract 1003], c. February 1873. Also issued as an envelope edition and reprinted in *Short Stories and other papers*, [1877].

A Good Old Prescription. A cure for care. London: Wesleyan Conference Office, [tract 1008], c. February 1873. Also issued as an envelope edition and reprinted in *Short Stories...* [1877].

Getting saved; a tract for those who are seeking Christ. London: Wesleyan Conference Office, [tract 1015], c. June 1873. Also issued as an envelope edition and reprinted in *Short Stories...* [1877].

A question for everybody, can I be saved? London: Wesleyan Conference Office, c. July, 1874.

What the Lark sang to Robert Morley. London: Wesleyan Conference Office, [tract 1011], 1874. Also issued as an envelope edition and reprinted in *Short Stories...*, [1877].

The Old Clock. London: Wesleyan Conference Office, 1877. From *Daniel Quorm and his religious notions*, 1874.

How Bill Smith got right. London: Wesleyan Conference Office, [1880]. From *Mister Horn and his Friends*, 1872.

'I have redeemed thee.' London: Wesleyan Conference Office, [1880]. From *Sermons for Children*, 1875.

Old Rosie: a story for the children. London: Wesleyan Conference Office, [1880]. From *Short Stories and other papers*, [1877].

The Terrible Red Dwarf [A religious story]. London: Wesleyan Conference Office, [1880]. From *Short Stories and other papers*, [1877].

Where is the Bible? London: Wesleyan Conference Office, [1880]. Reprinted in *The Man who Spoiled the Music*, 1892.

Advice to Beginners. London: Chas H. Kelly, [c. 1880]. From *Daniel Quorm*, second series,1875.

Inside the breakwater. London: Wesleyan Conference Office, c. May 1881

One-Sided Religion. London: Wesleyan Conference Office, c. May 1881. From *Homely Talks…*, 1880. Reissued as one of *The Blessed Life* Series, [1885].

The earnest evangelist and successful class leader: Memoir of William Thompson… London: Wesleyan Conference Office, 1881.

Simon Jasper's conversion. [London], c. July 1883.

Bob. A true story. [London], c. July 1883. Reprinted in *The Sunday Magazine*, January 1885 and in *The Man Who Spoiled the Music*, 1892.

[Three Services of Song]: Daniel Quorm, Frankey Vivian, Simon Jasper. London: Wesleyan Conference Office, c. October 1884.

Strike while the Iron's Hot. [London], 1885. [Advertised in the *Methodist Recorder*, 22 May.]

Hast thou here any besides? Or, Salvation in every house: A New Years's address to parents. London: T. Woolmer, 1885

The Blessed Life Series. London: T. Woolmer, [1885] 1. *The Homeliness of Jesus*. 2. *A Prayer for cleansing*. From *Homely Talks*, 1880. Also issued by the Religious Tract Society as one of a series of tracts entitled *Light from the Cross*. 3. *One-sided religion*. From *Homely Talks*, 1880. 4. *The Starting Point*. From *Thoughts on Holiness*, 1884. 5. *Ye are the salt of the Earth*. From *Thoughts on Holiness*, 1884. 6. *Defeat and victory*. From *Thoughts on Holiness*, 1884. 7. *Christ's Love to the Church*. From *Thoughts on Holiness*, 1884. 8. *The Blood that speaketh*. 9. *Communion*. Reprinted in *Some Aspects of the Blessed Life*, 1886. 10. *My Lord and my God*. Reprinted in *Some Aspects of the Blessed Life*, 1886. 11. *Consecrated and transformed*. Reprinted in *Some Aspects of the Blessed Life*, 1886. 12. *Behind him – Before him*. Reprinted in *Some Aspects of the Blessed Life*, 1886. 13. *Love*. Reprinted in *Some Aspects of the Blessed Life*, 1886. 14. *Rest*. Reprinted in *Some Aspects of the Blessed Life*, 1886. 15. *All his Benefits*. 16. *The song of Forgiveness*. 17. *The Pitiful Father*. 18. *His Kingdom Ruleth Over All*.

It won't sink. [London], c. April 1886. Reprinted in *The Man Who Spoiled the Music*, 1892.

A gift for you. London: C. H. Kelly, [1890]. Reprinted in *The Man Who Spoiled the Music*, 1892.

The God that answereth by fire. London: C. H. Kelly, [1890]. Reprinted in *Elijah, the Man of God*, 1891.

Is not this the Blood of Men? London: C. H. Kelly, c. November 1897.

How Mr Rhodda broke the spell. New York, Boston: T. Y. Crowell & Co., [1899].

Go Forward! London: R. Culley, 1900.

My Daily Walk. [Illuminated text]. London: R. Culley, [October] 1907.

My Daily Prayer. [Illuminated text]. London: R. Culley, [October] 1907.

He Restoreth my Soul. [Illuminated text]. London: R. Culley, [October] 1907.

The Cornish postman and his l'll angel. London, [1908]. From *Bridgetstow*, 1907... adapted as a Service of Song by Arthur Wallington.

Henry H. Fuller, *Sleep, my little one, sleep: song* and *Beloved one, sleep on: song*, Minnesota: H. Fuller, 1916. Scores for voice and piano adapted from Mark Guy Pearse's 'A Cradle Song' and 'A Requiem' from *West Country Songs*, 1902.

Frank W. Boreham, *Penny Booklets by F. W. Boreham and Mark Guy Pearse*, London: Epworth, [1926–1928]. 6. *A Gift for You*.

William H. Buckley, *I kneel to pray*, Philadelphia: T. Presser, 1940. Score for voice and piano adapted from an unidentified Mark Guy Pearse title.

Articles, sermons and other writings

'Harry's pint, or threepence a day'. In: *The British Workman*, January 1872, pp. 99-100. Reprinted in *Short Stories and other papers*, [1877] and issued as a temperance tract in [1880].

'How Squire Geoffrey warmed himself and got an appetite for his Christmas dinner'. In: *The Methodist Recorder*, vol. xii, Christmas number, 1872, pp. 8-9. Reprinted in *Good Will: a collection of Christmas stories*, 1877.

'The Love of the Spirit' [sermon]. In: *The Methodist Pulpit*, January, 1873.

'The Living Sacrifice' [sermon]. In: *The Methodist Pulpit*, March, 1873.

'Farmer Oldways law-suit and how it ended'. In: *The Methodist Recorder*, vol. xiii, Christmas number, 1873, pp. 3-4. Reprinted in *Good Will…*, 1877.

'Show us a sign, a true story for the times'. In: *City Road Magazine*, iii, 1873, pp. 118-121. Reprinted in *Cornish Stories*, 1883.

'A singular character, Richard Hampton'. In: *The Methodist Family*, v, 1874, pp. 136-139. Issued as Wesleyan tract 1057 and reprinted in *Short Stories…*, [1877].

'Little Breeches and what he did at Christmas. A story for the young folks'. In: *The Methodist Recorder*, vol. xiv, Christmas number, 1874, pp. 6-7. Reprinted in *Good Will…*, 1877.

'Matt Stubb's dream, or, Christmas Eve at the Blue Boar.' In: *The Methodist*, vol. i, Christmas Supplement, 1874, pp. 1-4. Reprinted in *Good Will…*, 1877 and published in book form by Woolmer, Hayman Bros. and Lilly, London, 1881.

'King's Garden: a sermon for children.' In: *Wesleyan Sunday School Magazine*, no. i [new and enlarged format], January 1875. Reprinted in *Sermons for Children*, 1876.

'A Good Old Man.' In: *The Methodist Family*, vi, 1875, pp. 75-78. Issued as Wesleyan tract 1075 [1880] and reprinted in *Short Stories…*, [1877].

'A Cornish ghost story.' In: *The Holly Bough*, 1876. Reprinted in *Cornish Stories*, 1883.

'The barges of Great Britain.' In: *Wesleyan Methodist Magazine*, c, 1877, pp. 115-119.

'The little red dwarf.' In: *Our boys and girls* [Wesleyan Methodist Sunday School Union Magazine], January-February, 1877.

'Mr and Mrs Rogers. A Christmas story in 7 chapters.' In: *The Methodist Recorder*, [vol. xvii], Christmas number, 1877, pp. 5-7. Issued as a tract, 'Mr and Mrs Rogers of Tregleave', 1894 and reprinted in *Cornish Stories*, 1883.

'Christmas Eve in 'The Vivid'.' In: *The Cornish & Devon Post*, beginning 21 December 1878. First published in *The Holly Bough* and reprinted in *Cornish Stories*, 1883.

'How they got the chapel at St Piran's. An old story modified and adapted.' In: *The Methodist Recorder*, [vol. xviii], Christmas number, 1878, pp. 9-11. Reprinted in *Cornish Stories*, 1883.

'Bass fishing at Bude.' In: *Boys' Own Paper*, 1879.

'Dick's adventure.' In: *Boys' Own Paper*, 1879.

'The two brothers: the story of a lie.' In: *Boys' Own Paper*, vol. 1, nos. 3 and 4, 1 and 8 February, 1879, pp. 43 and 53. Also issued as a tract.

'Dick Curnow's conversion.' In: *The Methodist Recorder*, Christmas number, 1879. Reprinted in *Cornish Stories*, 1883, as 'Uncle Dick Curnow's conversion'.

'Early Methodism in Cornwall.' In: *Sunday Magazine*, January, April and June, 1880, pp. 24-30, 260-264 and 415-420. The second paper was devoted to Parson Thomson of St Gennys who was also the subject of 'The First Cornish Methodist(s)' in the *Wesleyan Methodist Magazine* (1881) and *The Cornish Magazine* (1899), and of *'The Ship Where Christ was Captain'* (1926).

'The old miller and his mill.' In: *Our boys and girls* [Wesleyan Methodist Sunday School Union Magazine], 1880. Issued as a tract and reprinted in *John Tregenoweth: his mark. Rob Rat...* [c. 1881].

'The First Cornish Methodist' [George Thomson of St Gennys]. In: *Wesleyan Methodist Magazine*, January and February 1881.

'Some modern theories tried by an old experiment.' In: *Wesleyan Methodist Magazine*, January 1884, pp. 7-11.

'How to use the Bible.' In: *The Quiver*, May 1884, pp. 385-386, 493-494.

'My dream.' In: *The Sunday Magazine*, July 1884, pp. 421-423.

'History of Portland Street Chapel, Bristol.' In: *Wesleyan Methodist Magazine*, July and September 1884, pp. 518-525 etc.

'Aspects of holiness.' In: *The Sunday Magazine*, September

1884, pp. 605-607 etc. From *Thoughts on Holiness*, 1884.

'Behind him – Before him.' In: *The Quiver*, October 1884, pp. 729-732. Reissued as one of *The Blessed Life* Series, [1885] and reprinted in *Some Aspects of the Blessed Life*, 1886.

'The man who spoiled the music.' In: *The Sunday Magazine*, January 1885. Issued as a tract in May 1885, as "a service of song" for Sunday School choirs in June 1886 and reprinted in *The Man who Spoiled the Music and other stories*, 1892.

'What will he make of it.' In: *The British Workman*, January 1885.

'Sunday Readings in the Psalms.' In: *The Quiver*, 1885.

'What a Friend we have in Jesus.' A sermon [on Matt. xi. 19. The Gift of God's Love. A sermon [on John iii. 16]. Preached in the Metropolitan Tabernacle, London… Dec. 18th, 1887 and Dec. 23rd, 1888. London, [1888–1889]. *The People's Pulpit*, nos. 7 and 21.

'Dick Croggan's redemption: a story in three chapters.' In: *The Spectator and Methodist Chronicle*, Melbourne, 15 May 1891. Also issued as a tract c. 1905.

'Old Rosie.' In: *The Spectator and Methodist Chronicle*, Melbourne, 29 May 1891.

'The Cornish Fisherman.' In: *The Spectator and Methodist Chronicle*, Melbourne, 12 June 1891.

'How I Get my Stories.' In: *The Spectator and Methodist Chronicle*, Melbourne, 19 June 1891.

'Anthony Cock.' In: *The Spectator and Methodist Chronicle[?]* [1891]

'Moses Dunn.' In: *The Spectator and Methodist Chronicle[?]* [1891]

'How I became a teetotaller.' In: *The Spectator and Methodist Chronicle[?]* [1891]

'Strength and Beauty.' In: *Home Messenger*'s Plain Talk With The People column, November 1893.

'Christmas in the Home.' In: *The Young Man and the Young Woman*, Christmas 1893.

'To South Africa and Back' I-XIV. In: *The Methodist Churchman*, Cape Town, beginning 6 August 1896. First published in *The Methodist Times*, London.

'The First Cornish Methodists.' In: *The Cornish Magazine*, vol. 2, 1899.

'Love's Little Humours.' In: *The Quiver*, 1903, pp. 384-389.

'Thomas Champness: Some Reminiscences by Mark Guy Pearse.' In: *The Methodist Recorder*, 16 November 1905.

'What God Gives.' [verse]. In: *The Wesleyan Methodist Magazine*, April 1906.

'Thomas Coryat: a forgotten pilgrim.' In: *London Quarterly Review*, January 1908.

'The Miner in Foreign Parts: Australia and Klondyke.' [Poems from *West Country Songs*, 1902]. In: *Cornwall beyond the Seas*, [souvenir produced for the Cornwall Missionary Exhibition held in Camborne, 10-18 June] 1909.

'Gems from the Antique.' Unidentified cutting, dated 1909, in the Courtney Library, Truro.

'A wreck that saved lives.' [The story of Henry Trengrouse]. In: *The Wesleyan Methodist Magazine*, February 1914.

'A Village Down West. Mark Guy Pearse tells of the passing of Peter Tregwin.' In: *The Methodist Recorder*, 6 February 1919.

'Mark Guy Pearse on *Shadow and Sun*, Mr Francis Horner's story of the Children's Home.' In: *The Methodist Recorder*, 6 November 1919.

'A true story of Tintagel.' In: *Old Cornwall*, No. 4, October 1926.

'A bullet for a present.' In: *The Methodist Recorder*, 6 January 1927.

'The Gamekeeper.' In: *The Methodist Recorder*, 13 January 1927.

'A famous artist from Camborne.' [Joshua Cristall]. In: *The Cornishman*, 23 February 1927 and *The Cornish Post and Mining News*, 26 February 1927.

'An Adventure into the unknown.' [Review of two books by the Rev. James Butterworth]. In: *The Cornishman*, 20 April 1927 and *The Cornish Post and Mining News*, 23 April 1927.

'The Prayers of the Congregation.' In: *Tre Pol and Pen – Cornish Annual*, 1928.

'An Old-world Corner of Cornwall; some stories of Newlyn and Mousehole.' Unidentified cutting, dated 2 January 1929, in the Courtney Library, Truro.

'The First Locomotive.' [Short piece about Richard Trevithick]. In: *Old Cornwall*, No. 11, Summer 1930.

'He Giveth His Beloved Sleep.' In: *The Methodist Magazine*, October 1930.

'Brave trust in God be thine Always…' In: [*Camborne*] *Wesley Journal*, No. 10, November 1945.

Index